# SOCIAL
# REGISTER
# 2006

# THE SOCIALIST REGISTER

Founded in 1964

EDITORS:
LEO PANITCH
COLIN LEYS

FOUNDING EDITORS
RALPH MILIBAND (1924-1994)
JOHN SAVILLE

Visit our website at:

http://www.socialistregister.com
for a detailed list of all our issues, order forms and an online selection of
past prefaces and essays, and to find out how to join our listserv.

..

# SOCIALIST REGISTER 2 0 0 6

## TELLING THE TRUTH

Edited by LEO PANITCH and COLIN LEYS

THE MERLIN PRESS, LONDON
MONTHLY REVIEW PRESS, NEW YORK
FERNWOOD PUBLISHING, HALIFAX

First published in 2005
by The Merlin Press Ltd.
99 WALLIS ROAD
London E9 5LN

www.merlinpress.co.uk

British Library Cataloguing in Publication Data is available from the British
Library

Library and Archives Canada Cataloguing in Publication
Socialist register 2006 : telling the truth / edited by Leo Panitch and Colin Leys.
Includes bibliographical references and index.
ISBN 1-55266-176-8
1. Intellectual life. 2. Intellectual freedom. I.-Leys, Colin, 1931- II.-Panitch, Leo,
1945-

P95.8.S62 2004    001.1    C2005-904285-0

ISSN. 0081-0606

Published in the UK by The Merlin Press
0850365600  Paperback
0850365597  Hardback

Published in the USA by Monthly Review Press
1583671374  Paperback

Published in Canada by Fernwood Publishing
1552661768  Paperback

Printed in the UK by MPG Books Ltd., Bodmin, Cornwall

# CONTENTS

Preface                                                                          vii

Colin Leys                    The cynical state                                    1

Atilio A. Boron               The truth about capitalist democracy               28

Doug Henwood                  The 'business community'                           59

Frances Fox Piven &           The truth about welfare reform                     78
Barbara Ehrenreich

Loïc Wacquant                 The 'scholarly myths' of the new
                              law and order doxa                                 93

Robert W. McChesney           Telling the truth at a moment of truth:
                              US news media and the invasion and
                              occupation of Iraq                                116

David Miller                  Propaganda-managed democracy:
                              the UK and the lessons of Iraq                    134

Ben Fine &                    Correcting Stiglitz: from information
Elisa Van Waeyenberge         to power in the world of development              146

Sanjay G. Reddy               Counting the poor: the truth about
                              world poverty statistics                          169

Michael Kustow                Playing with the truth: the politics of
                              theatre                                           179

John Sanbonmatsu              Postmodernism and the corruption
                              of the academic intelligentsia                    196

G. M. Tamás                   Telling the truth about class                     228

Terry Eagleton                On telling the truth                              269

# CONTRIBUTORS

ATILIO A. BORON is Executive Secretary of CLACSO, the Latin American Council of Social Sciences, and teaches political theory at the University of Buenos Aires.

TERRY EAGLETON is professor of cultural theory in the Department of English and American Studies at the University of Manchester.

BARBARA EHRENREICH is a political essayist and commentator and the author of the best-selling book, *Nickel and Dimed*.

BEN FINE teaches economics at the School of Oriental and African Studies, London.

DOUG HENWOOD is the editor of *Left Business Observer*, which he founded in 1986, and the author of *Wall Street* and *After the New Economy*.

MICHAEL KUSTOW is a writer and producer of film, theatre and television, and a Visiting Fellow at Royal Holloway University in London.

COLIN LEYS is co-editor of the *Socialist Register*.

ROBERT W. McCHESNEY is a professor in the Institute of Communications Research at the University of Illinois at Urbana-Champaign.

DAVID MILLER teaches sociology at the University of Strathclyde, Glasgow, and is co-editor of *Spinwatch*.

FRANCES FOX PIVEN teaches political science and sociology at the Graduate School of the City University of New York.

SANJAY G. REDDY teaches economics at Barnard College, Columbia University.

JOHN SANBONMATSU teaches philosophy and politics at Worcester Polytechnic Institute in Massachusetts.

G. M. TAMÁS, a former member of Hungary's parliament and currently deputy chair of ATTAC Hungary, has recently taught philosophy at Yale and the New School.

ELISE VAN WAEYENBERGE is a doctoral student at the School of Oriental and African Studies, London.

LOÏC WACQUANT teaches in the Department of Sociology, University of California-Berkeley.

# PREFACE

A generalized pathology of chronic mendacity seems to be a structural condition of global capitalism at the beginning of the 21$^{st}$ century. Previous volumes of the *Socialist Register* have analyzed the imbrication of national states and economies in the American neoliberal imperial order, and the stresses this generates within them, as well as between them. What has become increasingly clear is that it is not just falling in line with the increasingly crude, militarized geopolitics of the imperium that threatens the legitimacy of governments that join 'coalitions of the willing'. Equally profound, and perhaps ultimately more serious, problems of legitimacy are created by the relentless pressure of the market forces unleashed by global neoliberalism, and the ecological degradation and social dislocation they are generating. These legitimacy problems are reflected in the unprecedented levels of secrecy, obfuscation, dissembling and downright lying that now characterize public life.

The declaration of a 'war on terror' has aggravated this situation by allowing governments to take new powers to conceal what they are up to. In the USA, the number of official documents classified as secret rose from under 6 million a year in 1996 to nearly 16 million in 2004, while the number of pages declassified each year fell by more than 80 per cent. Basic information is now routinely called 'sensitive' and withheld from the public, while measures like the USA Patriot Act place citizens under comprehensive state surveillance, covering everything from their travel to the books they borrow from the library (readers beware!). Armed policing is becoming commonplace, people are arrested and detained indefinitely without trial or even being told what they are suspected of.

The egregious lies told in Washington and London in connection with the invasion of Iraq are only a conspicuous case of a more general problem. Honesty and plain speaking by politicians has become exceptional, and there is abundant evidence of the shameful complicity of the journalistic profession. The empty motivational language and sales-pitch mentality of corporate culture increasingly pervade all areas of life. Less widely recognized, but in the long run no less important, is the growing subordination of scientific research to commercial ends. The deliberate abdication of a significant segment of the academic intelligentsia from the vocation of telling the truth makes matters worse. Indifference to truth in the academy soon resurfaces directly in public life. For example, 'narratives' have been a favourite concept among the staffers working for New Labour – Blair's director of communications even appointed a 'Head of Story Development'. And after living through the era of George W. Bush will post-structuralists and postmodernists still claim that any 'narrative' is as true as any other?

But the degeneration of public discourse is neither unchallengeable nor irreversible, even if the structural condition that underlies it could only be removed by a thoroughgoing democratic revolution. For the present the important thing is to help make the problem and its causes as visible as possible. In the middle of the Vietnam war Robert Lowell could see that it was nonetheless 'a golden time of freedom and license to act and speculate', but he had a 'gloomy premonition' that it would be ended by an 'authoritarian reign of piety and iron'. We are not living in such a golden time; there are better grounds today for such gloomy premonitions. Public life is increasingly beset by elements of authoritarianism, some with a distinct proto-fascist tinge. But there is still space to think and speak critically, and we need to take full advantage of it.

To be sure, making the degeneration of public discourse and its consequences visible is not a simple matter, as Louis Mackay's cover for this, the 42nd volume of the *Socialist Register*, brilliantly captures, with its graphic representation of religious truths, corporate truths, bent truths, half-truths, and hidden lies. The essays in this volume are all sensitive to this, starting with a sober analysis of the 'cynical state' in the West, epitomized by the UK under New Labour, at the centre of the chronic mendacity we are living under. We then turn to a critique, based on the experience of democratization in Latin America in recent decades, of the term 'capitalist democracies', which argues that capitalist states are first and foremost capitalist and only contingently democratic.

Subsequent essays focus on the concealment of capitalist class interests behind the fig-leaf of the 'business community', the class war conducted in the name of 'welfare reform' and 'law and order', and the craven failure of the media to challenge official lies around Iraq. This is followed by an essay which describes how, G8 rhetoric on ending global poverty notwithstanding, the World Bank persists in using statistical measures that fail to reveal the extent of world poverty and the actual needs of the world's poor. Another essay shows how the world's most famous liberal economist, Joseph Stiglitz, while candidly expressing his disappointments at the World Bank, remains a prisoner of his discipline's utter failure to analyze the structural factors behind the maldistribution of political power and market information he complains of.

The abdication of so many left intellectuals from the vocation of telling the truth is surveyed in an essay which charts the rampant spread of postmodernism as both philosophy and 'habitus' in American academia. Postmodernism is one form of what the 1990 *Socialist Register* called 'the retreat of the intellectuals', and this was partly the result of political and intellectual shortcomings on the traditional left. One of these shortcomings is the subject of a wide-ranging and challenging essay which, starting with a critique of the position famously taken by E.P. Thompson in the 1965 *Register*, addresses a more long-standing retreat – from Marx to Rousseau – that has been at the core of the ambiguity about class in the socialist project from its inception. Intellectual retreats, especially when combined with complicity on the part of journalists with official mendacity, has often compelled artists to try to fill the gap. In this context we publish here our first ever essay on the politics of the theatre, which examines theatre's vital role, especially today, in 'playing with the truth'. Finally, the tensions between the aesthetic and the social, the elite and the mundane, postmodernism and socialism, as approaches to truth are addressed in a concluding essay which underscores the aims of the volume in saying that 'it is not power, but its victims who need the truth most urgently ... power does not need to be told the truth because it is in some ways irrelevant to it'.

At about this point in the *Socialist Register's* prefaces a paragraph usually appears that begins 'Among our contributors ...' and proceeds to describe the cast of characters in the order of their appearance. We have decided to break with this tradition and go back to the initial practice of the *Register* in 1964 and list the contributors alphabetically on a separate page in the conventional way. But, *nota bene*, all our contributors remain covered by our usual disclaimer that neither they nor we necessarily agree with everything in the volume; nor shall we neglect to thank them all here for their invaluable contributions. In addition to the thanks we also owe Adrian Howe and Tony Zurbrugg at Merlin Press, as well as Alan Zuege for his superb editorial assistance, we want to thank Atilio Boron and his colleagues at CLACSO for their remarkable achievement in translating, publishing and distributing the Register in Latin America, not only in Spanish but also in Portuguese. And we are grateful to Frederick Peters and his team of Aidan Conway, Tom Keefer and Marcel Nelson at York University for creating our new internet archive for all volumes of the *Socialist Register* from 1964 to 1999, and for making this available on our website: www.socialistregister.com.

Our contributing and corresponding editors around the world remain extremely important to the success of the Register. One of them, Diane

Elson, has retired, while generously offering her continuing support. On the other hand, we are delighted that the Marxist economist and Latin Americanist Alfredo Saad-Filho has agreed to join us as a contributing editor in London.

We should note, in conclusion, that we were very much saddened by the death in April 2005 of Andre Gunder Frank, a courageous internationalist who was a major formative influence on thinking about global development for almost four decade.

LP
CL
July 2005

# THE CYNICAL STATE

## COLIN LEYS

'Mendacity is a system that we live in'.
(Tennessee Williams, *Cat on a Hot Tin Roof*)

Governments have always lied. They naturally deny it, even long after it is abundantly clear that they have lied, trailing multiple red herrings, dismissing inconvenient evidence, implying that there is counter-evidence they are not free to produce. When a lie can no longer be credibly denied it is justified, usually by an appeal to the national interest. Governments of modern representative democracies are no different, even if they are more liable than dictators to be exposed. Half-truths and outright lies are routinely told. Facts are routinely concealed. Files are unaccountably lost. Tapes are mysteriously erased. Democratic checks and balances are rarely effective and the public's collective memory is short.

Even so, in recent years state cynicism has broken new ground. The British government's flagrant abuse of military intelligence to persuade parliament and the public to endorse its attack on Iraq was a dramatic case in point. In July 2003, soon after the official end of the war, a British government weapons expert, David Kelly, killed himself after being revealed as the source for a BBC report that the government's dossier outlining the intelligence had been knowingly 'sexed up'. The government appointed a reliable judge, Lord Hutton, to hold a public enquiry into Kelly's death. The evidence given to the enquiry showed that the Prime Minister's staff had been working flat out to make it appear that Saddam Hussein posed a threat to Britain that would justify invading Iraq. The government's intelligence 'dossier' was made to read much more alarmingly than the evidence produced by the intelligence services warranted. It claimed that Iraq had nerve gases, anthrax spores, ricin, botulinium toxin, mobile laboratories, nuclear materials and extended range rockets, none of which the intelligence service claimed as facts, and none of which later proved to be true. It also claimed several times that Iraq had weapons of mass destruction 'deployable within 45 minutes'. This claim was known to be vague, from an uncorroborated second-hand source, and to refer only to 'battlefield' weapons; and it too proved entirely unfounded. But more than any other piece of false information it was decisive in securing parliamentary and public acquiescence in the attack on Iraq.

The defence minister, Geoff Hoon, admitted to the Hutton enquiry that he knew the report referred only to battlefield weapons, not the long-distance missiles that most people assumed were meant by the expression 'weapons of mass destruction'. When asked why he had not corrected press reports that made this assumption he said his experience showed that correcting incorrect press reports was unprofitable. He was not challenged on this, or pressed to comment on the influence these reports had had on public opinion, although the record showed that the prime minister's staff were intently focused on ensuring that press headlines would be as alarming as possible. The evidence also showed that Hoon, Blair, and Blair's chief press officer Alastair Campbell had all subsequently told further lies about the compilation of the dossier. Campbell told Hutton that he had had no input into the dossier. The evidence showed he had had extensive input. Hoon told the parliamentary committee on defence that he had had nothing to do with it either. The evidence showed he had been involved as much as anyone. Most famously, Blair told the House of Commons that it was 'completely and totally untrue' that there was disquiet in the intelligence community over the 45-minute claim, but a senior intelligence officer told the enquiry that he and one of his colleagues had submitted a written report about their disquiet.[1]

Of course commentators who supported the attack on Iraq were willing to condone all this. But Lord Hutton condoned it absolutely too. The only behaviour he criticized in his final report was that of Andrew Gilligan, the BBC journalist who had broken the story, and the BBC director general and chairman who had backed him against furious attacks by the Prime Minister's office. All of them were forced to resign, while Blair and Hoon were totally absolved. John Scarlett, the senior intelligence official who had agreed to 'sex up' the intelligence service's original draft of the dossier at the behest of the Prime Minister's office, was promoted to be head of the secret service.[2] What is more, Hutton's decision to put all the evidence on the internet, but then to condemn the whistleblowers and exonerate the liars, meant that members of parliament and the electorate were being asked to become complicit in official mendacity. 'Transparent' government, he seemed to say, just means that MPs and voters must accept being lied to and that no one should be penalized for doing so.

As the occupation of Iraq dragged on, its apologists' indifference to the facts became more and more insulting to the intelligence of the public. In

March 2005 Gary Younge, a usually restrained commentator, summed up the general sense of disgust: 'We have entered a world where reality … is just a minor blockage in a flood of official, upbeat declarations … Each new dispatch from the departments of irony on both sides of the Atlantic suggests that truth can be created by assertion …'.[3]

Dissimulation is, of course, part of war, even if lying to your own electorate is a negation of democracy. But a cynical indifference to the truth is now hardly less common in domestic policy. For instance, in the Labour government's determination to 'marketize' health care it has shown itself equally willing to use flawed evidence. An article published in the authoritative *British Medical Journal* (*BMJ*) purported to show that an American Health Maintenance Organization or HMO, Kaiser Permanente, was more efficient than the National Health Service. The medical research community around the world immediately denounced the study as hopelessly flawed.[4] The government, however, adopted Kaiser Permanente as a model for the NHS to follow – citing it in policy documents and inviting Kaiser staff to advise the Department of Health.[5]

Another example was the government's decision to adopt a programme called 'Evercare' operated by another American HMO, United Healthcare. United Healthcare claimed that Evercare reduced the rate of emergency hospitalisation of frail elderly people by 50 per cent. United Healthcare had a notorious record of health care fraud in the USA, but its CEO gave $1.5 million to the 2004 Bush-Cheney election campaign and Bush's secretary for health recommended the company to the British secretary of state for health. In 2004 Simon Stevens, Blair's senior health policy adviser, resigned to become United Healthcare's new President for Europe, and secured a contract to introduce Evercare in Britain. A study of nine pilot schemes in the UK costing £3.4 million, however, showed that Evercare was unlikely to cut the rate of hospitalization by more than 1 per cent. Yet the government's primary care 'czar' declared that 'there is nothing in the research to make us have second thoughts about the strategy'.[6]

These stories, which could be replicated for almost any field of public policy in contemporary Britain, illustrate the emergence of a new, neoliberal policy regime that is more brazenly willing to dissemble, more indifferent to evidence, more aggressive towards critics and distinctly less accountable – to the point of being virtually unaccountable – than ever before. This policy regime is not peculiarly British. The old 'liberal/social democratic' policy regime which it has displaced did have distinctively British features. The new neoliberal policy regime is a more standardized affair. It not only spans the Atlantic but thanks to neoliberal globalization it is being gradually replicated, in essentials, throughout the world. Its key feature is that policy is now fundamentally about national competitiveness and responding to global market forces. The crucial roles are played neither by political parties nor by civil servants but by personnel seconded into the civil service from the private sector, a handful of 'special advisers' to the prime minister, a small group of certified market-friendly civil servants, and polling, advertising and media experts. Scientific evidence is still relied on, but only in so far as it serves competition policy; otherwise it is treated uncritically, if it helps the government, and dismissed if it does not. When this new policy regime is properly understood the lies about Iraq no longer appear as a special case, but only as a special dimension of a general one. Cynicism, we realize, is a necessary condition of neoliberal democracy.

## THE LIBERAL/SOCIAL DEMOCRATIC POLICY REGIME

Britain's previous liberal/social democratic policy regime combined elements of the Liberals' state reforms of the late nineteenth century with elements corresponding to the interventionist state of the twentieth. The Liberals created a higher civil service recruited competitively from the cleverest members of the same social class, and educated at the same elite private schools and universities, as the elected ministers they served. The idea was that officials of this calibre and background would be in a position to offer elected ministers honest advice and 'to some extent influence' them, in a shared 'freemasonry' of public service.[7] Because the emphasis was on social and political status, higher civil servants were, like almost all the ministers they served, 'generalists', relying for expertise on the advice of professional and technical civil servants – engineers, public health doctors, biologists, etc. For dealing with big issues of a politically sensitive nature they would recommend the establishment of Royal Commissions, composed of eminent experts with powers to commission research and call for expert evidence (between 1950 and 1980 one was appointed, on average, almost every year). For lesser issues that nonetheless called for additional expertise Departmental Enquiries could be set up, also with powers to draw on outside expertise.

With the advent of the Labour Party and an increasingly interventionist state agenda other elements were added to the mix. Innovating parties needed to develop policies out of office to present to the civil service when elected. The Labour Party had a research department that produced blueprints for new policies, as did the Trade Union Congress and the larger trade unions. The Fabian Society, established in 1884 with the aim of 'permeating' the main governing parties, became more and more linked to Labour and supplied it with a steady flow of reasonably well worked-out policy proposals. PEP (Political and Economic Planning), founded in 1931, and NIESR (the National Institute of Economic and Social Research), founded in 1938, were products of the depression and aimed in different ways to push social and economic reforms of a broadly liberal/social-democratic nature by publishing serious research on the issues. From 1929 onwards the Conservative Party also had a research department. Many leading politicians, from Cripps and Wilson to Macmillan and Heath, were intellectuals, often former academics and frequently authors of books and pamphlets on policy issues. The civil service existed to advise governments on the policy initiatives derived from all these sources, and turn them into practical plans and laws.

There were differences and tensions between the state and non-state components of this policy regime, but they shared a general commitment to a notion of objectivity, in the sense that policy proposals should be judged on the basis of rational argument and sound evidence. They all saw themselves as professionals, belonging to a 'public' domain, serving the public interest.

> The public domain ... was quintessentially the domain of ... professionals. Professional pride, professional competence, professional duty, professional authority and, not least, predictable professional career paths were of its essence. Professionals were the chief advocates of its growth; they managed most of its institutions, and they policed the frontier between it and the adjacent private and market domains. Above all, the values of the public domain were their values.[8]

The central tension in the liberal/democratic policy regime in the 1950s and '60s was due to the fact that the higher civil service, and especially its elite in the Treasury, which exercised considerable control over other departments' policies, was more inclined to be liberal than social-democratic. Moreover the 'freemasonry' which Gladstone's reforms had postulated between the higher civil service and ministers began to show cracks once the ministers were Labour MPs, with ideas and aims reflecting the party's roots in the labour movement and no longer predominantly educated at leading private schools or at Oxford or Cambridge.

Thomas Balogh, an economic adviser to the Labour prime minister Harold Wilson in the 1960s, voiced a growing impatience with the higher civil service's typically humanities-based education and pre-industrial social attitudes, denouncing it as 'the apotheosis of the dilettante'.[9] In 1966 Wilson created a Department of Economic Affairs to offset what was seen as the Treasury's bias for financial prudence over economic growth, and a Treasury departmental committee chaired by Lord Fulton (a university vice chancellor) recommended a reorganization of the higher civil service on technocratic lines. A Civil Service College was established, to emulate the French École

Nationale d'Administration, and a Civil Service Department took over the Treasury's management of recruitment, training and promotion.

Almost all these initiatives were neutralized, largely by the higher civil service itself. The Department of Economic Affairs was closed in 1969 after only three years. The Civil Service Department lasted longer, but was closed by Mrs. Thatcher in 1981. The Civil Service College survives, but only as a provider of short courses, with no prestige. The one significant innovation of the Wilson years that not only survived but flourished was the increased use of 'special advisers', brought in from outside to bolster ministers in face of what was seen as excessive civil service caution or conservatism. The Fulton Report had also recommended this, together with 'greater mobility between [the civil service] and other employments', including 'temporary appointments for fixed periods, short-term interchanges of staff and freer movement out of the Service', and giving further thought to 'hiving off' activities to non-departmental organizations. All of this prefigured the erosion of the boundaries between the public and private domains that was to take place under the neoliberal policy regime from the 1980s onwards.

But in retrospect it is easy to see that the issue was not merely changing class relations, or generalists versus technocrats; the fundamental tension within the old policy regime was the contradiction of social democracy itself. The real problem was that by the end of the 1960s British trade unions were unwilling to see the problems of British capitalism solved at their expense, while capitalists were unwilling to collaborate in any state-led economic strategy so long as the unions remained powerful, as even the Conservative prime minister Edward Heath discovered to his chagrin after taking office in 1970. (In 1973 he told a meeting of the Institute of Directors: 'When we came in we were told that there weren't sufficient inducements to invest, so we provided the inducements. Then we were told people were scared of balance of payments difficulties leading to stop-go. So we floated the pound. Then we were told of fears of inflation; and now we're dealing with that. And still you aren't investing enough!')[10]

The crisis came to a head in the winter of 1973-74. With the coal-miners 'working to rule' and the entire country limited to a three-day working week to conserve fuel, the head of the civil service, William Armstrong, had a nervous breakdown. The liberal/social democratic policy regime had collapsed. 'From that moment', Peter Gowan noted in a seminal article, 'a current within the Conservative Party … [was] working to make … [the Gladstonian civil service model] redundant by removing labour as a major force on the political scene, Americanizing the party system and state bureaucracy and breaking up the mandarinate'.[11]

The Labour Party returned to office in 1974 but crisis management became the overriding agenda. Domestic policy initiatives, from any source, were irrelevant unless they helped meet the conditions attached to the IMF loan that the Treasury mandarins and the Labour leadership decided they must accept, rather than embrace the socialist alternative advocated by the Labour Party's left wing. The IMF's conditions meant replacing Keynesianism by monetarism, opening the door to Thatcherism and the construction of a new, neoliberal policy regime.

## THE TRANSITION TO THE NEOLIBERAL POLICY REGIME

The starting-point for understanding the new policy regime is the ascendancy of capital that followed – and was meant to follow – from Thatcher's and Reagan's elimination of controls on cross-border capital movements from the early 1980s onwards. This allowed the financial markets and transnational corporations to set increasingly tight limits on the policies national governments could adopt.[12] These limits were registered in the political 'risk premium' that the markets placed on any government seen as liable to adopt policies – on taxation, on government spending, on labour regulation or environmental protection, etc. – that would reduce the profitability of capital, compared with governments elsewhere. In Britain before the 1992 election the risk premium for a possible Labour government was 2 per cent. To reduce this to 0.5 per cent (which they managed to do before the 1997 election), the new Labour leadership scrapped virtually all Labour's 'market unfriendly' policy commitments, deleted Clause Four (which still talked of public ownership) from the party's constitution, and adopted a new range of policies called for by the City of London (the heart of the country's financial sector), including handing over the setting of interest rates to the independent Bank of England and adopting the Conservatives' policy of having virtually all new public building financed and owned by the private sector.

Capital's political and social power had also been enormously increased by the Conservatives between 1979 and 1997, and Blair showed no inclination to challenge it. The chief executives of big companies continued to enjoy easy access to ministers and even the prime minister, and got respectful attention. This enabled them to overcome barriers intended to protect the public interest in one field after another – town planning legislation, GM food, the ownership of genes, the science research agenda of universities, etc. The trade unions, on the other hand, had been forced to accept an industrial relations regime that Tony Blair – who retained almost all of it – was pleased to call 'the most lightly regulated labour market of any leading economy in the world'.

The constantly-increasing power of capital also made private enterprise seem the natural order of things. Not only had Labour's post-war national-izations been undone, from electricity and gas to public transport, but many services that had always been public, such as prisons and airports, were now privately owned and run, while cultural and sporting events (and even police forces) increasingly relied on corporate sponsors until every dimension of daily life was tagged with their logos.

'New' Labour's strategists, the so-called 'modernizers', saw all this as 'the new reality'. Their idea was to win and hold power by not just fully accepting the new reality but accepting it so whole-heartedly that there would be no room left on that terrain for the Conservative Party, which would become as 'unelectable' as Labour had been from 1979 to 1994. This strategy meant insulating the Labour leader from pressure from the trade unions and party members. So the party's constitution was rewritten and the annual confer-ence emasculated as a policy-making (or even a policy-debating) forum. Of course the modernizers envisaged a 'third way', along which they would pursue whatever policies they considered progressive, in terms of what the new reality allowed; but they had no confidence that these would meet with the approval of the party rank and file and they were not disposed to have any public arguments about it.[13] Logically enough, too, the party's policy research capacity was also run down and eventually abolished. Blair declared that the party was now 'a party of business', and on that basis business could be asked to pay for whatever policy research the leadership wanted done.

Yet there was, obviously, still a need for policies – just within much narrower limits. With capital's freedom restored, the rules of policy-making changed. Major economic policies are still made, but in conformity with an overall agenda set by transnational corporations and the international and regional agencies they dominate. These *global market* policies involve adapting the British economy and Britain's socio-economic institutions (fiscal policy, aid to industry, education, training, the health and safety and labour market regulation, etc.) to compete successfully in the global marketplace. Since these policies are often electorally unpalatable they are made as far as possible out of the public eye – inside Whitehall or the European Commission, at the WTO – from where, once made, they appear as the impersonal and unavoid-able effects of the market. 'Treasury control' – the time-honoured principle that all departmental policies involving spending must be pre-approved by the Treasury – has acquired a new significance. Now all major expenditures also have to serve the government's overall competition strategy.

All this meant that by the turn of the century it was only in domain of *socio-cultural adjustment* policies that governments presented themselves in terms of having significant choices. Personal taxation, the scope and quality of public services, crime and 'security', immigration and 'identity politics' are the main terrains on which these policies are made. Here a wider range of options exists, but within limits that are broadly the same for all parties; and for much of this kind of policy-making it is pollsters, marketing experts and spin-doctors, as much as civil servants (let alone researchers), who are seen as having the required expertise to manage public opinion and adjust the electorate to the necessary consequences of global market policy-making.. The two sorts of policy are of course interdependent, and give rise to politically awkward dilemmas. To keep wages down immigrants are required, but immigrants are the right wing press' favourite scapegoats for every social ill; social services are popular, but the regressive tax system insisted on by the markets means that paying for them is politically unpopular; and so on. So what is the nature of the new neoliberal policy-making regime that these conditions entail?

## THE NEOLIBERAL POLICY REGIME

First of all, the civil service has been radically reorganized on business lines, following the doctrines of the 'new public management'. As many activities as possible have been transferred out of government departments into 'executive agencies', leaving a reduced policy-related higher civil service at the top. The slimmed-down departments have then been further slimmed down to achieve 'efficiency savings', and required to 'outsource' more and more of their routine functions to private companies, starting with cleaning and continuing with information technology, accounting, estate management, personnel, and so on. Government buildings are sold and leased back from private companies. Sometimes individual public services, such as various prisons or schools, or even a whole local education authority, are directly outsourced to be run by private companies.

But the role of those remaining at the top has changed too. Thatcher's ministers made it clear that dispassionate advice and careful argument were out. When she took office and started taking an unprecedented interest (for a prime minister) in higher civil service promotions, the quality she looked for was a capacity for vigorous implementation of her ideas. Early on she got into an argument about industrial relations, about which she had strong opinions but was poorly informed, with Donald Derx, a capable and dedicated civil servant. She went on and on until Derx finally said: 'Prime Minister, do you really want to know the facts?' – and promptly ended his prospects of promotion.[14] As David Marquand says,

> ... civil servants were no longer expected to tell the truth to power
> ... In a phrase coined by Lord Bancroft, head of the civil service

when Mrs Thatcher came to power, the 'grovel count' rose sharply. Those who could not bring themselves to grovel languished or left. Inevitably, those who grovelled internalized the crucial axioms of the government's new ideology and statecraft.[15]

New Labour showed no inclination to change this. They too wanted civil servants to be as like businessmen as possible. Thatcher's ministers told civil servants that they didn't want 'whingeing, analysis or integrity, that we must do as we are told and that they have several friends in the private sector who could do the job in a morning with one hand tied behind their back'.[16] Twenty-five years later Blair was telling them the same thing: 'Rigour about performance must be at the heart of a leaner, more efficient civil service … A culture of decision-making by committee, while ensuring all possible viewpoints are considered, leads to unnecessary delays and increased cost'.[17] In 2005 the head of the civil service, Sir Andrew Turnbull, very much 'on message', told a conference that 'the upper civil service had been forced to refocus its efforts from policy and management to an active role in the delivery of targets and key services. "The job is much more akin to being a chief executive officer than it has been in the past", he admitted'.[18]

But if senior civil servants are no longer primarily concerned with making policy, who is? Definitely not Royal Commissions. To 'conviction' politicians, 'ensuring all possible viewpoints are considered' seems a pointless diversion from where they are convinced the country should go, and neither Thatcher or Major appointed any Royal Commissions. In his first two years in office Blair appointed two, but rejected both their recommendations and never appointed another.[19] Even departmental enquiries, whose terms and proceedings can be much more closely controlled by ministers, have become relatively rare.[20] And policies emanating from party members and developed through internal party debates and compromises are definitely a thing of the past.

One obvious alternative source of policy-making that corresponds to this situation is 'think tanks', and it is certainly true that think tanks see themselves as playing a crucial policy-making role. But British think tanks are not the sort of intellectual powerhouse familiar in the USA, with massive private foundation funding.[21] Most British think tanks have only a handful of staff and budgets of a few hundred thousand pounds, and competition between them for funding – which is predominantly corporate – tends to make most of them more anxious to have media coverage than a reputation for serious research. As Andrew Denham and Mark Garnett note, it was Demos, 'the think tank with the flimsiest ideological attire' and a taste for 'back-of-an-envelope radicalism' (it first won attention with a pamphlet attacking the powers of the

Queen) that most appealed to New Labour in office, and its founding director Geoff Mulgan went on to become head of Tony Blair's Cabinet Office
Strategy Unit in 2003.[22] Even the more intellectually conventional Institute
for Public Policy Research (IPPR), whose director Matthew Taylor became
head of policy planning in the prime minister's Policy Directorate in 2003,
appears lightweight, at least by comparison with the think tanks founded in
response to the depression of the 1930s. Those earlier think tanks were 'at
least ... motivated by the hope that their findings would be educative, either
for policy-makers or for the public. Even on a charitable view, this urge
[now] seems lacking ...'.[23]

The characteristic claim of every new think tank is that there is a need for
'new ideas' – which indeed there is, since so many of the important ones have
been ruled out as unacceptable to the market, or politically risky. The trouble
is that in the narrow range that remains there are few useful new ideas to be
had. Catherine Bennett summed up the problem perfectly in 2002:

> If there is not already some sort of car boot sale where rejected or
> nearly-new thoughts can be bought, recycled, or exchanged for
> other unwanted policies, then it is high time one of the think-
> ers started one. With new tanks established almost daily, each one
> creating thousands of thoughts and papers, debates and alternative
> manifestos, each of which must be printed and circulated before
> it can be shelved, something has got to be done. Rubbish disposal
> experts estimate that getting rid of the IPPR's thought mountain,
> alone, already accounts for a landfill site the size of Croydon. Over
> at the government's Performance and Innovation Unit, John Birt's
> dedicated crater is said to be visible from space.[24]

The common overestimation of the influence of think tanks is largely
due to the fact that in the run-up to Thatcher's accession to power in 1979,
right-wing think tanks were an important source of neo-Conservative policy.
From 1955 onwards the Institute of Economic Affairs (IEA) had served as
a crucial base for 'organic intellectuals' of capitalism, sustaining and updat-
ing the strand of bourgeois thought that rejected the post-war compromise
with social democracy. As Richard Cockett showed in his book *Thinking the
Unthinkable*, when the contradictions of the post-war compromise finally
brought it to an end, allowing Mrs Thatcher to capture the leadership of the
Conservative Party in 1975 and win power in 1979, her principal lieutenants
at first drew heavily on the work of the IEA as well as the new Centre for
Policy Studies, founded in 1974, and the Adam Smith Institute, founded in
1977.[25] It was the apparent influence of these three think tanks during those

years that prompted the Labour leadership to create the IPPR in 1988, while they were in opposition, the Liberal Democrats (also in opposition) to create the Social Market Foundation in 1989; and the New Labour 'modernizers', on the eve of their capture of the party leadership, to found Demos in 1993. And these in turn prompted the formation of a rapidly proliferating medley of imitators, left and right, all striving for a place in the councils of power. To quote Bennett again:

> Once you add the product of all the other think tanks – Demos, Civitas, the Centre for Policy Studies, Localis, Policy Exchange, Reform, the Adam Smith Institute, NLGN, Politeia, the Foreign Policy Centre, the Social Affairs Unit, Catalyst, the Fabian Society, the Social Market Foundation, the racy new Do Tank and others too numerous to list, you are forced to think the unthinkable: who needs them?[26]

Who indeed? For the role played by the new right think tanks before Thatcher's 1979 election victory could not be repeated after it. Once neoliberal globalization had been accomplished, the scope for radical policy-making was drastically narrowed. Think tanks, which are not privy to much essential information about the global market forces involved in the making of economic policy, and which also depend on maximizing publicity to keep their funding coming in, cannot contribute significantly to economic policy-making, least of all for a party in office. That work must be done by true experts. Nor are think tanks well suited to helping to make the ongoing social and cultural policy adjustments that changing global markets require. Pollsters and marketing experts are the key to success there.

From time to time the government will toy with an obvious think-tank brain-child, such as 'citizenship ceremonies' for 18-year olds – usually to universal derision. 'Baby bonds' – a pet IPPR project for opening an account for every newborn infant into which the government would put some money, to give everyone some cash to do something with at 21 – did make it into Labour's pre-election budget in 2005, though to no great effect, at least electorally. In spite of their claims to the contrary it is hard to credit think tanks with being the source of any significant New Labour policy initiative.[27] Ministers and opposition leaders do use sympathetic think tanks as sounding-boards, making speeches or writing pamphlets under their auspices – which suggests that think tanks may do more to make market-driven policies palatable to voters than to turn popular sentiment into practicable policies.

Think tanks do serve as useful pools of political talent and ambition. On taking office in 1997 the Labour government doubled the number of ministers' 'special advisers' from 38 to 72, and many come from the think-tanks clustered around Westminster. Few of them bring relevant expertise from outside or carry intellectual weight inside. What most of them have is energy and a willingness to help work up solutions to whatever problems their minister is faced with. The key qualifications are loyalty and readiness to turn one's hand to whatever task is needed. Peter Hyman, a former special adviser to Tony Blair, says that a few advisers have their own ideas, which may be different from those of their ministers. But the 'vast majority', he reassures us, 'know they are there to serve the minister who employs them'.[28] Denham and Garnett concur, though with a different emphasis. 'At worst', they say, 'the current wave of apparatchiks seem to act as comfort blankets for ministers who have discarded their former idealism'.[29]

This leaves two significant sources of policy that are well attested, though virtually un-researched. One is the prime minister's 'senior' policy advisers. Thatcher appointed some prominent businessmen such as Sir Derek Rayner, a leading department store manager, and Sir Roy Griffiths, a leading supermarket manager, as special advisers to herself, and they were openly given more influence on policy than permanent civil servants. Blair followed suit, and under his personalized and highly-centralized system of government the influence of his senior policy advisers is very considerable – with sometimes disastrous results, since his choice of advisers has sometimes been lamentable. This was notoriously true of Andrew Adonis, his senior policy adviser on education, elevated to the peerage as Lord Adonis after the 2005 election and put in charge of schools policy in London. Adonis was one of the most widely-despised figures of Blair's court, credited with having got a series of disastrous education policies adopted through having the ear of the prime minister. The message would come to the department of education that 'Tony's office' was keen on 'specialist schools' or 'city academies', policies which were the brainchildren of Adonis, a journalist who had once written a book about social class in schools and was keen on private education. (Ted Wragg, a widely respected authority on education, and a comic script-writer on the side, created a fictional character called 'Tony Zoffis' whose ignorant prejudices successive education ministers had to swallow).[30]

Another example, in the other main field of social policy, health care, is Simon Stevens, mentioned earlier. Before his appointment as Blair's senior health policy adviser he had been a middle-level hospital manager. He believed strongly in replacing the national health service with a market open to private providers, and this is what happened, in spite of the fact that this policy was never openly acknowledged, let alone put before the electorate in any of Labour's manifestos, and in spite of its disastrous long-term implications.

The other significant source of policy, and perhaps the most significant change in the operation of the state under the neoliberal policy regime, is the employment in key civil service posts of senior staff on secondment from the private sector. In 2004 the head of strategy in the Department of Health, for example, was on secondment from the management consultancy PriceWaterhouseCoopers, a leading advocate of the privatization of public services, and especially health care. In some departments the circulation of personnel between the civil service and the private sector has become commonplace, and the delay required before civil servants can take up lucrative private sector posts, in which they can put their inside knowledge of government at the service of companies, has also been progressively shortened. This so-called 'revolving door' between the state and the private sector has long been notorious in the field of defence, which accounts for a huge share of public spending.[31] Now it is becoming more general throughout the higher civil service.[32]

The chief focus of critics hitherto has tended to be on the conflicts of interest involved in this, especially the extent to which the prospect of lucrative private employment may influence the judgment of senior civil servants who should be guided solely by the public interest, and this is certainly a serious issue.[33] But the role played by private sector personnel seconded to policy-making roles in government today is more far-reaching. Faced with the demand to become business-like, and to pursue business-friendly policies, senior civil servants understandably reach out to business for help. What they get may not in fact be great expertise, but it always involves the importation of the general world-view inculcated in American business schools and disseminated through global management teams and financial markets. And with the collapse of the idea of a distinctively public domain goes the disappearance of any clear concept of the public interest as something different from and deeper than the collective interest of the corporations that dominate the economy. In effect, the corporate agenda is installed in the state; or to put it another way, public policy-making itself is 'outsourced'.

## ENTREPRENEURIALISM AND THE USE OF EVIDENCE

Running through the history of the formation of the neoliberal policy regime is the emergence of a new ideal type, displacing that of the rational Weberian bureaucrat: the entrepreneur. What politicians admire, and want at the top of the state apparatus, are assertive, 'big' men (very rarely women), capable of some ruthlessness, strong on 'mission statements' and targets and impatient with detail, which they are apt to dismiss as the stock-in-trade of professional 'seers of difficulties' who will never accomplish anything. Civil servants have been seriously discouraged from playing their traditional role of screening out unworkable ideas. What is valued is a willingness to achieve whatever 'targets' the government decides it wants met, brushing aside obstacles and costs. The fact that so many 'can-do' businessmen of the kind politicians now hold up as models for senior civil servants to emulate — Gerald Ronson, Jim Slater, Jonathan Aitken, Robert Maxwell, Asil Nadir, John Gunn, Richard Brewster, David S. Smith, John Ashcroft — have eventually crashed spectacularly and/or gone to jail or been otherwise disgraced, losing (or in some cases stealing) the savings of thousands of people in the process, does not seem to dim their admiration.[34]

The result is a new attitude towards evidence. Evidence needed for policy-making relating to global market forces — statistical evidence on production, trade and finance, for example — is taken seriously. Evidence relating to socio-cultural adjustment policies is another matter (unless, of course, it is polling evidence on what voters are thinking and feeling, which is taken most seriously of all). Evidence that looks supportive of ideas to which the government is committed tends to be accepted uncritically. Contrary evidence tends to be dismissed. In Blair's entourage even pointing to the existence of contrary evidence comes to be treated as close to treason: 'critics of public-private partnerships, foundation hospitals and [university] tuition fees are branded not as participants in a reasonable debate about the direction of policy but relics of the party's dark ages, mad lefties jeopardizing the government's future'.[35] Outside Whitehall, consistently pointing to the existence of politically inconvenient evidence leads to professional marginalization or even — if the inconvenience is great enough — persecution. A cabal of obedient government backbenchers, for example, abused parliamentary privilege to make a scurrilous attack on the work of Professor Allyson Pollock, whose analyses of the private financing of hospital building had left that policy widely discredited.[36] Other examples of the persecution of critics, especially but not only by Blair's powerful spokesman Alastair Campbell, abound.[37]

That this should have become more or less normal, however, presupposes certain enabling conditions. Four stand out: the replacement of the culture of Royal Commissions by the culture of 'grey literature'; the loss of critical independence on the part of the academic research community; the de-politicisation of the electorate; and the return to respectability of irrational belief.

A lot of fun used to be had at the expense of Royal Commissions, seen as devices for indefinitely postponing action on controversial issues by appointing a group of the 'great and good' to mull them over inconsequentially for years. But Royal Commissions not only invited the best experts to give evidence, written and oral, but also commissioned research, and all of this was published in full, along with the Commissioners' final reports. Their recommendations could languish unimplemented, but the published research and evidence, publicly given and publicly interrogated, constituted a significant obstacle to the implementation of policies that flew in the face of the best evidence there was. Today, however, no one under the age of 45 has known the policy culture of which Royal Commissions were a significant part.

In place of the products of Royal Commissions there is 'grey literature'. Most definitions of grey literature focus on the idea that it is literature 'made available to the general public by public and private sector organizations whose function is not primarily publishing'.[38] And as governments cut back on free access to even routine official statistics, and as privatization makes more and more public activity 'commercially confidential', grey literature has acquired a sort of respectability by default. Journals and conferences are devoted to it. What strikes the enquirer concerned with truth, however, is that organizations that are not primarily publishers lack a strong interest in the validity of what they nonetheless publish. Whereas a non-fiction or journal publisher, or a serious newspaper, has a reputation for truth to protect, many if not most other organizations are not necessarily concerned with this. As anyone who has tried to use grey literature soon discovers, data and judgments that have not been peer-reviewed or otherwise tested for accuracy and reliability cannot be relied on. But grey literature is increasingly cited in support of government policy.

The use of bad evidence is also less subject to informed criticism by the scientific community than would have been the case twenty-five years ago. The corruption of research in the natural sciences by corporate funding is a well-known problem, yet science research is more and more dependent on corporate money.[39] And by a different route, university-based social science in Britain has now also become increasingly oriented to market values and interests. Unlike US social science, British social science has always been predominantly state-funded. Under the liberal/social democratic policy regime the funding was distributed through research councils run by social scientists, with substantial independence from the government. Nor have British social scientists experienced the pressures to conform from right-wing vigilantes that have reinforced the prevailing political conformity of American social science.[40] British social scientists might be 'pro-market', but there was no obvious career incentive to be so.

Under Thatcher, however, this began to change. General government funding of universities was put on a market-oriented footing. Every degree course now had to be justified by a 'business plan' showing how the cost of the staff needed to teach it would be met out of the student income it would earn, and the research funding that the staff could be expected to secure. Eventually, 'under-studented' departments were downsized or closed.

Government support for research through the universities' 'core funding' also declined (from 58.8 per cent of all research funding in 1984 to 35.1 per cent in 1997), and this support was now allocated on a selective basis. Under a periodic Research Assessment Exercise first introduced in 1986, departments with highly-ranked research output receive dramatically higher-than-average funding until the next 'RAE', while poorly-ranked departments receive dramatically less, or none at all. The share of research funding accounted for by work commissioned directly by either government departments or business rose from 15 per cent to 20.8 per cent of the total between 1984 and 1997, while the share coming from the government-funded research councils rose from 17.2 per cent to 24.1 per cent.[41]

In the case of the Economic and Social Research Council, reorganized under Thatcher in 1985, the bulk of its research funding was much more focused than before on themes seen as relevant to the promotion of national economic competitiveness.[42] Individual researchers could still get smaller grants for critical work, but the attractions of landing serious money – grants of several million pounds over five years are not uncommon – for major centres and programmes of applied research were obvious, and a new generation of well-funded academics emerged, wielding considerable patronage among younger researchers willing to work within the neoliberal paradigm.

The combined effect of all these changes has been to make research within that paradigm well rewarded, and therefore highly valued by university administrators, while effective public criticism of government policies is to say the least not warmly encouraged. As a result the topics chosen for study, and the questions asked, have undergone a significant shift. The quantity of research has risen but its analytic and critical quality has declined. This may be no truer of political science than of other social science disciplines, but it is especially obvious in the study of politics. Roelofs' critique of American political science now largely fits its British counterpart. To take just one example:

> Political scientists ... study parties and interest groups, yet the latters' creation and funding are usually neglected. The interlocking directorates among interest groups, foundations, and corporations are generally ignored. Professional associations, conferences of state officials, think tanks, and integrative organizations such as the Social Science Research Council and the American Council of Learned Societies are rarely examined in political science research. Thus indexes in American government textbooks sometimes list Ford, Betty, and omit the Ford Foundation.[43]

The same topics are also ignored, and the same questions are not asked, in Britain. Denham and Garnett, for example, the foremost academic experts on think tanks in Britain, make no effort to analyze the sources of their funding and the effect of this on what the tanks think about, and the conclusions they reach. There is a general de-politicisation of even political research.[44] Academic social scientists who offer informed public criticism of government policies have become an endangered species. It is more rewarding to engage in the kind of political punditry notably practised by Tony Giddens, the director of the London School of Economics (LSE) and high priest of the Third Way ('somewhere between the Second Coming and the Fourth Dimension');[45] or John Gray, an LSE professor of European political theory, once a Thatcherite and now a convert to oriental mysticism and animal liberation.[46]

The fact that few social scientists are serious critics of public policy facilitates the de-politicisation of the electorate. Britain has not undergone – yet – an intellectual takeover of the kind successfully carried out by the far right in the US since the late 1960s, at the cost of hundreds of millions of dollars a year, via the creation or capture of right-wing think tanks, magazines, newspapers, publishers, television channels, radio stations and even whole universities.[47] But three quarters of British national newspaper circulation has long been owned and controlled by right-wing press barons, often North American, and the popular titles are prone to extreme bias, if not outright lies.[48] And concessions by successive governments of both major parties to corporate media interests have steadily enlarged the scope for private broadcasters and forced public service broadcasters to compete for increasingly fragmented audience shares.[49] News and current affairs have been steadily cut back in favour of entertainment. The bizarrely misnamed 'reality TV' shows that dominated the schedules in the early 2000s were a sign of the times. The critical context for serious policy debate has been significantly eroded.

And then there is the general revival of irrational belief, entertainingly reviewed by Francis Wheen in *How Mumbo-Jumbo Conquered the World*. The publicly-owned public-service television channel, Channel 4, for example, ran a programme on nutrition hosted by a 'clinical nutritionist', complete with white coat, and continued it even when her credentials were exposed as worthless (the *Guardian*'s 'bad science' watchdog was able to buy her professional certificate for $60 for his deceased cat).[50] And the government's infatuation with business and businessmen meant that the cliché-ridden and unsubstantiated outpourings of business gurus would be taken seriously by the architects of public service 'reforms'. All this is bad enough. But what about 'alternative' medicine, advocated by the heir to the throne and adopted, partly as a sop to populism, by some parts of the National Health Service? Wheen's bracing comment that "'complementary" and "alternative" are essentially euphemisms for "dud"' would no doubt be dismissed by New Labour's boot boys as 'elitist'.[51]

Blair's deference towards mumbo-jumbo is usually attributed to the influence of his wife. Authors sympathetic to Cherie Blair, however, say that he shares her flakier interests.[52] If so, it helps to explain his refusal to condemn the teaching of creationism in a state secondary school in Gateshead that was captured by creationists. 'A more diverse school system', he said, 'will deliver better results for our children'.[53] The Blairs' spiritual tastes are perhaps more in tune with the zeitgeist than the scepticism of their critics, but it is not without consequences for public policy. Just as Thatcher had openly sympathized with the Ayatollah who called for Salman Rushdie to be murdered for writing *The Satanic Verses*, Blair's home affairs minister refused to condemn the violence by Sikh fundamentalists in Birmingham in late 2004 that succeeded in closing a play they found offensive, saying that 'both the theatre and the protesters had a right to free speech'.[54] On the contrary the government proposed to introduce legislation to make it a crime to 'incite to religious hatred'. (No law was proposed to criminalize the suppression by pharmaceutical companies of evidence showing that a profitable drug was dangerous, or the invention of evidence to win parliamentary assent to start a war.)

The influence of all these factors means that there is remarkably little adverse comment on the steep decline that has occurred since 1980 in the quality of government policy documents, whose level of argumentation and use of evidence is all too often inversely related to the quality of their presentation (in the style of corporate reports, complete with executive summaries and flashy graphics). They are designed to look principled, purposeful and rational. In reality what they constantly reveal is the subordination of policy to what are seen as market imperatives, presented as some sort of balance between principle and pragmatism, tradition and innovation. Stefan Collini's dissection of the Labour government's 2003 white paper on *The Future of Higher Education* could be replicated for a distressingly high proportion of them. He begins with a quotation from the white paper's introduction:

> We see a higher education sector which meets the needs of the economy in terms of trained people, research and technology transfer. At the same time it needs to enable all suitably qualified individuals to develop their potential both intellectually and personally, and to provide the necessary storehouse of expertise in science and technology, and the arts and humanities which defines our civilization and culture.

'It is hardly surprising', Collini comments,

> that universities in Britain are demoralized. Even those statements which are clearly intended to be upbeat affirmations of their importance have a way of making you feel slightly ill. It is not simply the fact that no single institution could successfully achieve all the aims crammed into this unlovely paragraph ... It is also the thought of that room in Whitehall where these collages are assembled. As the findings from the latest survey of focus groups come in, an official cuts out all those things which earned a positive rating and glues them together in a straight line. When a respectable number have been accumulated in this way, s/he puts a dot at the end and calls it a sentence.
>
> There are two sentences in that paragraph. The first, which is clear enough though not a thing of beauty, says that the main aim of universities is to turn out people and ideas capable of making money. The second, which is neither clear nor beautiful, says there are a lot of other points that it's traditional to mention in this connection, and that they're all good things too, in their way, and that the official with the glue-pot has been having a busy day, and that we've lost track of the subject of the verb in the last line, and that it may be time for another full stop.[55]

The unresolved conflict – at the level of discourse, that is – between market and non-market objectives, the interpenetration of electoral aims and public interest concerns, the loss of respect for (or even serious interest in) research and evidence, the waning of analytic skills and the apotheosis of the entrepreneur – combine to produce defective reasoning and exaggerated promises. Careful argument and the adducing of evidence give way to 'values', 'mission statements' and 'targets'.[56]

In the USA, the imperial heartland, indifference to evidence has been given an explicit imperial rationale. In 2002 Ron Suskind was told by one of Bush's 'senior advisers' that

> guys like me were 'in what we call the reality-based community', which he defined as people 'who believe that solutions emerge from your judicious study of discernible reality ... That's not the way the world really works anymore', he continued. 'We're an empire now, and when we act, we create our own reality ... We're history's actors ... and you, all of you, will be left to just study what we do'.[57]

This kind of lumpen-Hegelian rhetoric is perhaps a step too far for most apparatchiks of a sub-imperial power like Britain.[58] But it is the principle on which a great deal of policy is based.

## CONCLUSION: THE DEPENDENCY OF OUR TIME

Nothing described here is likely to be unfamiliar to anyone in the 'South', where national policy has almost always been largely driven by external market forces, backed by foreign political and military power. One could say that 'dependency' now affects all countries except the USA. Of course there are big differences of degree, but the policy regime of even a major post-industrial state like Britain is no longer as radically different from that of a 'banana republic' as most people in Britain imagine. The installation of management consultants in key government policy-making posts is not entirely unlike the installation of officers from the World Bank in the ministries of an African state. Structural adjustment is in progress in both.

Thanks to Thatcher and Blair, Britain has advanced farther and more willingly along this path than other west European countries, and since cultural change lags behind material change the gap between reality and official rhetoric may be larger than elsewhere. Perhaps inherited ideas and illusions about sovereignty, democracy and the public interest confront the new reality of global market forces and corporate power more starkly than in other comparable countries.[59] But all countries must now travel more or less the same path, for the same reason: policy-making must always try to conceal the basic fact that economic and social policy has to now be made on capital's terms. This is not something voters like to be told, and the policies capital demands are often electorally unpalatable. As far as possible, therefore, these policies are increasingly made in secret and their likely effects concealed.

The dismantling of the higher civil service inherited from the late nineteenth century corresponds to the substitution of the rationality of the market for the instrumental rationality of a bureaucracy. A preference for entrepreneurs – whether actual businessmen seconded in from the private sector, or civil servants with entrepreneurial personalities and outlooks – focused on 'getting things done', and an impatience with bureaucrats professionally concerned with the wider implications of policy ('ensuring all points of view are considered' with, no doubt, a sometimes irritating touch of *noblesse oblige*), makes sense in these terms.[60] The state becomes not just more and more responsive to capital, but more and more closely integrated with it. And the risks involved are not borne by the new entrepreneurs of the state – any more than they are in today's corporate world – but by the public.

NOTES

I am very grateful to Barbara Harriss-White for extensive and creative comments on an earlier draft of this essay.

1    Blair's statement to parliament no doubt relied on what his senior officials told him, so he may have told untruths unwittingly: but one of the noteworthy aspects of the whole affair was the way the responsibility that is supposed to be shouldered by ministers, and not least the prime minister, was constantly shuffled off onto officials – who also remained unpunished.

2    'Sexed up' was the expression allegedly used by David Kelly, the source for Gilligan's story. The expression preferred by the prime minister's office and Scarlett was 'presentational changes'.

3    'Never Mind the Truth', *Guardian*, 21 March 2005.

4    Richard G.A. Feachem, N.K Sekhri and K.L. White, 'Getting More For Their Dollar: A Comparison of the NHS with California's Kaiser Permanente', *BMJ*, 324, 2002, pp. 135-43. For the critiques see 'Rapid Responses' on the *BMJ*'s website, www.bmj.com, a selection of which was later printed in the *BMJ*, Vol. 324, 2002, pp. 1332-35.

5    The Kaiser article's authors declined to respond to the criticisms, and the *BMJ* declined to print a systematic critique. The reason for the latter decision remains obscure; it seemed to reflect the growing tendency of the medical establishment to make its peace with the government's determination to impose a market system on the National Health Service.

6    *Guardian*, 4 February 2005. 'Czar' was the popular name for a series of appointments of individuals to oversee the achievement of government targets in primary care, cancer care, drug abuse, etc.

7    The quoted expressions are from the famous Northcote-Trevelyan report adopted by Gladstone as prime minister and finally imposed throughout the civil service by the end of the nineteenth century.

8    David Marquand, *Decline of the Public: The Hollowing out of Citizenship*, Cambridge: Polity Press, 2004, pp. 53-54.

9    Thomas Balogh, 'The Apotheosis of the Dilettante', in Hugh Thomas, ed., *The Establishment*, London: Anthony Blond, 1959.

10    Quoted in Andrew Gamble, *Britain in Decline*, Fourth edition, London: Macmillan, 1994, p. 99.

11    'The Origins of the Administrative Elite', *New Left Review*, 162, 1987, p. 34.

12  This section draws on chapter 3 of my *Market Driven Politics: Neoliberal Democracy and the Public Interest*, London:Verso, 2000.

13  See Leo Panitch and Colin Leys, *The End of Parliamentary Socialism*, Second Edition, London:Verso, 2001, chapters 10 and 13.

14  Jim Prior, *A Balance of Power*, quoted in Peter Hennessy, *Whitehall*, London: Fontana, 1990, pp. 633-34.

15  Marquand, *Decline*, pp. 109-10. For a frankly embarrassing example of grovel see the speech given on September 10, 2003, by Sir John Bourn, the Comptroller and Auditor General, to the PPP [Public Private Partnerships] Forum, which represents the new industrial sector conjured into being by the private financing of public services. Bourn was nominally employed by parliament to check public spending, but he sounded exactly like someone hoping for a job with one of the companies involved.

16  Hennessey, *Whitehall*, p. 633, quoting an unnamed senior civil servant.

17  *Guardian*, 24 March 2004.

18  *Guardian*, 3 February 2005.

19  The government adopted the minority report of the two pro-market members of the Sutherland Commission on Care of the Aged, appointed in 1997, and balked completely at dealing with the compromise recommendations of the Wakeham Commission on the reform of the House of Lords, appointed in 1999.

20  Forty-seven significant departmental enquiries were appointed in the 1970s, 24 in the 1980s, and 13 in the 1990s (David Butler and Gareth Butler, *Twentieth-Century Century British Political Facts*, Basingstoke: Macmillan, 2000).

21  In the mid-1990s the Rand Corporation had 950 staff and a budget of $50-100 million, and four others had budgets of more than $10 million. The biggest British think tank, the Policy Studies Institute, with 54 staff and an annual income of $6.5 million in the late 1990s, was half as big as the fifth largest US think tank, the Heritage Foundation (see Andrew Denham and Mark Garnett, *British Think Tanks and the Climate of Opinion*, London: University College London Press 1988, p. 5).

22  Ibid., p. 244.

23  Ibid.

24  'Think Tanks? No Thanks', *Guardian*, 18 July 2002. Birt was a former Director General of the BBC brought into the prime minister's office to do 'blue skies thinking' – initially, apparently, about transport, a field in which he had no expertise at all.

25  Richard Cockett, *Thinking the Unthinkable: Think Tanks and the Economic Counter-Revolution, 1931-1983*, London: HarperCollins, 1995. See

also Radhika Desai, 'Second-Hand Dealers in Ideas: Think-Tanks and Thatcherite Hegemony', *New Left Review*, I/203, 1994.

26  Bennett, 'Think Tanks?'.

27  See Stephen Court, 'Think or Sink', *Public Finance*, 11 October 2002.

28  *1 Out of 10*, London: Vintage, 2005, p. 71.

29  Denham and Garnett, 'A "Hollowed Out" Tradition? British Think Tanks in the Twenty-First Century', in Diane Stone and Mark Garnett, eds., *Think Tank Traditions: Policy Research and the Politics of Ideas*, Manchester: Manchester University Press, 2004, pp. 232-46.

30  On Adonis' appointment as an unelected minister Francis Beckett catalogued the long series of disastrous educational policies for which he had been personally responsible: see 'The Rise of Tony Zoffis', *Guardian*, 11 May 2005.

31  This has been documented for the post-Cold War years by the UK Campaign Against Arms Trade, in *Who Calls the Shots? How Government-Corporate Collusion Drives Arms Exports*, London: February, 2005.

32  Peter Oborne thinks the critical turning point in the erosion of the boundary between the state and the private sector came with the appointment of Sir Andrew Turnbull as Cabinet Secretary in 2002. According to him, Turnbull's predecessor had fought hard to get a Civil Service Act passed, which would demarcate the boundary. 'One of Turnbull's first acts as Cabinet Secretary was to make it known that he did not believe that the Civil Service Act, and thus the protections it would have entrenched, were necessary' (*The Rise of Political Lying*, London: The Free Press, 2005, p. 189).

33  For examples of the effects of this see Allyson Pollock, *NHS plc: The Privatization of our Healthcare*, London: Verso, 2004, pp. 4-9.

34  This list is from Francis Wheen, *How Mumbo-Jumbo Conquered the World*, London: Harper Perennial, 2004, pp. 59-62, and refers only to fallen business idols in Britain. A list of fallen business idols in the US, such as Enron's Kenneth Lay, Jeff Skilling and Andrew Fastow, or WorldCom's Bernie Ebbers, would be a lot longer.

35  Anne Perkins, 'Regime Change or Climate Change, Tony?', *New Statesman*, 29 September 2003. Foundation hospitals – freeing the country's publicly owned hospitals from central government control and making them compete (or collaborate) with private ones – was the prelude to introducing a health care market. Introducing so-called 'top-up' fees for university students was another market-driven idea, deeply unpopular within the governing party.

36  For Pollock's account of this affair see *NHS plc*, pp. 209-13.

37  See Peter Oborne and Simon Walters, *Alastair Campbell*, London: Aurum Press, 2004.

38  Michael Quinion, 'Grey Literature' in World Wide Words, at http://www.worldwidewords.org

39  For a discussion of the capture of British university scientific research by corporations see George Monbiot, *Captive State*, Basingstoke: Macmillan, 2000 chapter 9.

40  Examples have recurred throughout the history of American social science, and not just in the McCarthy era. Two recent cases seem to be the result of efforts by pro-Israeli organizations to get rid of professors seen as pro-Palestinian: Joseph Massad at Columbia University, and Tariq Ramadan, a Swiss professor denied a visa to teach at Notre Dame. The case of the anthropologist David Graeber, 'let go' from Yale in 2005 on political grounds, is more typical.

41  Ted Tapper and Brian Salter, 'The Politics of Governance in Higher Education: The Case of the Research Assessment Exercise', OxCHEPS Occasional Paper No. 6, Oxford Centre for Higher Education Policy Studies, Oxford, May 2002, p. 29. The authors comment that 'in the age of global capital ... the market is becoming an increasingly significant player and the universities ... will have to determine what structures of governance they need to control its input' (p. 30). Their own view, however, is that all further developments in the research role of the universities will be determined by the government.

42  In 2001-2002 the Council had seven priority themes for centres and programmes in receipt of major funding, accounting for 63 per cent of its funding for specific research projects. They were: economic performance and development; social stability and exclusion; work and organization; knowledge, communication and learning; governance and citizenship; environment and human behaviour (Economic and Social Research Council *Annual Report 2001-2002*).

43  Joan Roelofs, *Foundations and Public Policy*, Albany, NY: State University of New York Press, 2003, p. 32.

44  Some American graduate students were recently invited to consider this question. They were highly intrigued. This, they said, was the sort of thing you get excited about when you are not 'doing political science'. In their own work they were using an 'actor-oriented stakeholder analysis', and were very much on their guard against 'left conspiracy theories'.

45  Wheen, *Mumbo-Jumbo*, pp. 224-25.

46  Before he was a Thatcherite Gray was a socialist, and between being a Thatcherite and an animal liberationist he was a traditional conservative.

His home page announces that he is available for long-term consultancies.

47  For a brilliant summary of this see Lewis Lapham, 'Tentacles of Rage: The Republican Propaganda Mill, A Brief History', in *Harper's Magazine*, September 2004, pp. 31-41.

48  The crude fabrications of the British tabloid press are periodically recorded by Roy Greenslade in the *Guardian's* weekly Media supplement.

49  See Leys, *Market Driven Politics*, chapter 5.

50  'You don't need to be human; you don't even have to be alive. No exam, no check-up on your qualifications and no assessment of your practice' (Ben Goldacre, reporting how his dead cat Henrietta became a certified member of the American Association of Nutritional Consultants, in *Guardian Life*, 19 August 2004).

51  Nick Cohen, *Pretty Straight Guys*, London: Faber and Faber, 2003, p. 28: 'Sceptics were elitist because they refused to share the people's authentic elation at the election of Tony Blair or grief at the death of Princess Di. Critics of business were elitist because they presumed to know better than hundreds of millions of consumers … The knowledgeable on any subject … were elitist because they knew more than the ignorant …'.

52  Francis Beckett and David Hencke, *The Blairs and Their Court*, London: Aurum Press, 2004, pp. 278-9.

53  Parliamentary response to Jenny Tonge MP, quoted in Wheen, *Mumbo-Jumbo*, p. 114.

54  Lee Glendinning, *Guardian*, 27 December 2004. The personal views of the minister in question, Fiona MacTaggart, are not known. Her comments sounded like a craven capitulation to violence – and the threats made to the playwright, herself a Sikh, and her family – in an effort to retain the Sikh vote.

55  'HiEdBiz', *London Review of Books*, 25(21), 6 November 2003.

56  The unfortunate British Prisons Service, hived off by the Conservatives as an 'executive agency', free – in theory – from day to day control by the Home Office, rejoiced in having 'one Statement of Purpose, one Vision, five Values, six Goals, seven Strategic Priorities and eight Key Performance Indicators' (Wheen, *Mumbo-Jumbo*, pp. 56-57).

57  'Without a Doubt', *New York Times*, 17 October 2004. Compare Hegel's *Philosophy of Right*: 'When philosophy paints its grey on grey, then has a shape of life grown old… The owl of Minerva spreads its wings only with the falling of the dusk'.

58  But Blair's right hand man Peter Mandelson is quoted as saying: 'our job is to create the truth' (Oborne, *The Rise of Political Lying*, p. 3).

59    A conjunctural factor of some importance in the British case was the determination of Blair, Brown and Mandelson to 'outspin' the right-wing media that had trashed the efforts of the party's former leader, Neil Kinnock, to return Labour to power in 1992. Although Oborne (in *The Rise of Political Lying*) is hostile witness, it is hard to dispute his judgment that what began as an understandable reaction to victimization ended up as 'the useful lies of the ruling class'.

60    Barbara Harriss-White suggests that 'perhaps the new entrepreneurial-ism is a transfer to the state of a social institution developed for the quite different "factor endowments" of the firm, where entrepreneurial behaviour is rewarded with monopoly rents; or is it perhaps a mask used cynically by both capital and the state because the 'rent' is the consolida-tion of a totalizing system?' (personal communication).

# THE TRUTH ABOUT CAPITALIST DEMOCRACY

## ATILIO A. BORON

Not long ago the celebration of capitalist democracies, as if they constituted the crowning achievement of every democratic aspiration, found legions of adepts in Latin America, where the phrase was pronounced with a solemnity usually reserved for the greater achievements of mankind. But now that more than a quarter of a century has elapsed since the beginnings of the process of re-democratization in Latin America, the time seems appropriate to look at its shortcomings and unfulfilled promises. Do capitalist democracies deserve the respect so widely accorded them? In the following pages we intend to explore what democracy means, and then, on the basis of some reflections on the limits of democratization in a capitalist society, go on to examine the performance of 'actually existing' democracies in Latin America, looking behind external appearances to see their narrow scope and limits.

## DEMOCRACY

Let us begin by remembering Lincoln's formula: democracy as the government of the people, by the people and for the people. Today this looks like the expression of an unreconstructed radical, especially in light of the political and ideological involution brought about by the rise of neoliberalism as the official ideology of globalized capitalism. Well before this, democracy had already become completely detached from the very idea, not to mention the agency, of the people. Lincoln's formula had long since been filed away as a dangerous nostalgia for a state of things irreversibly lost in the past. What replaced it was the Schumpeterian formula, whose deplorable consequences are still strongly felt in mainstream social sciences: democracy as a set of rules and procedures devoid of specific content related to distributive justice or fairness in society, ignoring the ethical and normative content of the idea of democracy and disregarding the idea that democracy should be a crucial component of any proposal for the organization of a 'good society', rather than a mere administrative or decisional device. Thus for Schumpeter it was possible to 'democratically' decide if, to take his own example, Christians should be persecuted, witches sent to the stake or the Jews exterminated. Democracy becomes simply a method and, like any other method, 'cannot be an end in itself'.[1] At the extreme, this approach turns democracy into a set of procedures independent of ends and values and becomes a pure decision-making model, like those which Peter Drucker proposes for the management of successful capitalist enterprises. It doesn't take a genius to realize that democracy is much more than that.

Moreover, the Schumpeterian paradigm also ignores the concrete historical processes that led to the constitution of 'actually existing democracies'. In proposing the abandonment of what he called the 'classical theory' of democracy Schumpeter projected a foolishly optimistic and completely unreal image of the historical sequences which, in a handful of nation-states, ended with the constitution of democracy.[2] The epic nature of the process of construction of a democratic order was movingly portrayed by Alexis de Tocqueville, as an 'irresistible revolution advancing century by century over every obstacle and even now going forward amid the ruins it has itself created'.[3] This assertion captures, as do many others by different authors in the classical tradition, the tumultuous and traumatic elements involved – even in the most developed, pluralistic and tolerant countries – in the installation of a democratic order. The blood and mud of the historical constitution of political democracies are completely volatilized in the hollow formalism of the Schumpeterian tradition. That is the reason why, as heirs of this legacy, Guillermo O'Donnell and Phillippe Schmitter warn, in the canonic text of 'transitology', that:

> One of the premises of this way of conceiving the transition [to democracy] is that it is possible and convenient for political democracy to be achieved without a violent mobilization and without a spectacular discontinuity. There is virtually always a threat of violence, and there frequently are protests, strikes and demonstrations; but once the 'revolutionary path' is adopted or violence spreads and becomes recurrent, the favorable outlook for political democracy is reduced in a drastic manner.[4]

A premise which is as forceful as it is false. In what country did the conquest of democracy take place in accordance with the stipulations set out above? Barrington Moore pointed out that without the 'Glorious Revolution' in England, the French Revolution and the US Civil War – all rather violent and blood-shedding episodes – it would be extremely hard to conceive the very existence of democracy in those countries.[5] Can we imagine the slave-owning society of the American South, or the English and French aristocracies, giving rise to democratic arrangements? Can we even conceive of democratization in these countries without a violent break with the past? And regarding our authors' concern with 'violence from below', what about 'violence from above' against democratization, systematically leading to state repression, summary executions and disappearances at the hands of paramilitary forces or death squads, military coup-mongering, let alone the structural violence embedded in grossly unequal societies? Isn't it time to ask ourselves who have been the principal agents of violence in Latin America? The exploited and oppressed classes, the strikers and demonstrators, or the forces determined to preserve their privileges and wealth at any price?

The 'Schumpeterian' perspective not only perverts the very concept of democracy but also poses an equally disquieting puzzle: if democracy is something as simple as a method of organizing collective decision-making, why is it that the overwhelming majority of mankind have lived for most of recorded history under non-democratic régimes? If it is something so elementary and reasonable, why has its adoption and effective implementation been so difficult? Why have some organizational formats – the capitalist company and the stock corporation, for instance – been adopted without significant resistance once the capitalist mode of production had been imposed, while the attempt to adopt the 'democratic form' in states has generated wars, civil strife, revolutions and counterrevolutions and interminable bloodbaths? Finally, why, if the capitalist mode of production is five hundred years old, is capitalist democracy such a recent and unstable achievement?

The ethical hollowing out of democracy by the Schumpeterian-based theories of democracy, and their radical inability to account for the process of construction of 'actually existing' democracies, call for an alternative theorization.

## CAPITALIST DEMOCRACY OR DEMOCRATIC CAPITALISM?

But this still requires a prior conceptual clarification. Indeed, if the use of the word 'democracy' is in itself distorting and plagued with ambiguities – democracy, 'by' whom, 'for' whom? – expressions like 'capitalist democracy' or 'bourgeois democracy' are no less contradictory and unsatisfactory. That is why the most rigorous and precise way of referring to the universe of the 'really existing' democracies is to call them 'democratic capitalisms'. Let us see why.

To speak of 'democracy' without any adjectives overlooks the enormous differences between: (a) the classical Greek model of democracy, immortalized in Pericles' celebrated Funeral Oration; (b) the incipient democratic structures and practices developed in some Northern Italian cities at the dawn of the Renaissance (later to be crushed by the aristocratic-clerical reaction); and (c) the various models of democracy developed in some capitalist societies in the twentieth century. Democracy is a form of organization of social power in the public space that is inseparable from the economic and social structure on which that power rests. The different modes of organization, both dictatorial and democratic, or the six classical forms of political power set out in Aristotle's *Politics*, take root in the soil of specific modes of production and types of social structure, so that any discourse that speaks of 'democracy' without further qualifications must necessarily be highly imprecise and confusing. Indeed, when political scientists speak of democracy, to what are they referring? A democracy based on slavery, as in classical Greece? Or that which prospered in urban islands surrounded by oceans of feudal serfdom, and in which the *populo minuto* strove to be something more than a manoeuvring mass under the oligarchic patriciate of Florence and Venice? Or the democracies of Europe, without even universal male suffrage, let alone the right of women to vote, prior to the First World War? Or of the 'Keynesian democracies' of the second post-war period, bearing the traces of what T.H. Marshall meant by social citizenship?[6]

Reacting against this disconcerting ambiguity, which also challenges the allegedly univocal nature of the expression 'bourgeois democracy', the Mexican essayist Enrique Krauze, an author with evident neoliberal inclinations, once made a passionate plea in favour of a 'democracy without adjectives'.[7] His exhortation, however, fell on deaf ears. A recent analysis of the literature carried out by David Collier and Steve Levitsky revealed the enormous proliferation of 'adjectives' (more than five hundred) that are employed in political science as qualifiers for the operation of democratic régimes, to the extent that more taxonomic pigeonholes exist than democratic régimes.[8] Despite this, plying democracy with adjectives – even if 'strong' terms are employed to this end, or ones highly loaded with signification, like 'capitalist' or 'socialist' – does not solve the essential problem but only serves to provide it with an elementary loincloth that fails to conceal the fact that the king is naked.

Let us take the expression 'capitalist democracy', frequently used by mainstream social scientists as well as by radical thinkers. What does it precisely mean? Some may believe that the problem is solved by adding the 'capitalist' qualifier to the word 'democracy' – which at least hints at the broader problem of the relations between capitalism and democracy and, more specifically, to the issue of the limits that the former sets on the expansiveness of democracy. Nevertheless, this standpoint is essentially incorrect: it rests on the assumption, quite clearly erroneous, that in this type of political régime the 'capitalist' component is a mere adjective that refers to a kind of economic arrangement that in some way modifies and colours the operation of a political structure that is essentially democratic. In reality the phrase 'capitalist democracy' is a sort of 'Hegelian inversion' of the proper relationship between the economy, civil society and the political realm, involving a subtle apology for capitalist society. For in this formulation democracy is presented as the substance of current society – routinely reasserted by numberless leaders of the 'free world', like George W. Bush, José M. Aznar, Tony Blair, etc., who define themselves as spokespersons of their own 'democratic societies'. Democracy is therefore qualified by an adventitious or 'contingent' feature – *merely* the capitalist mode of production! Capitalism is thus shifted to a discreet position behind the political scene, rendered invisible as the structural foundation of contemporary society. As Bertolt Brecht once observed, capitalism is a gentleman who doesn't like to be called by his name. But there is more. As the late Mexican philosopher Carlos Pereyra argued, the expression 'bourgeois democracy' is 'a monstrous concept' because it 'hides a decisive circumstance in contemporary history: democracy has been gained and preserved, to a greater or lesser extent in different latitudes, *against* the bourgeoisie'.[9]

A double difficulty exists, therefore, in the above-mentioned use of adjectives. In the first place, it gratuitously attributes to the bourgeoisie a historical achievement such as democracy, which was the work of centuries of popular struggles precisely *against*, first, the aristocracy and the monarchy, and then against the domination of capitalists, who tried hard to prevent or delay the victory of democracy, appealing to all imaginable means from lies and manipulation to systematic terror, epitomized by the Nazi State. Second, if the expression 'bourgeois democracy' is accepted, what is specifically 'bourgeois' becomes an accidental and contingent fact, a specification of an accessory kind with regard to a fetishized essence called democracy.

So how should democracy be properly conceptualized? Certainly, it is not a question of applying or not applying adjectives to a supposed democratic substance but of abandoning the neo-Hegelian inversion: that is to say, unlike the term 'bourgeois democracy', an expression such as 'democratic capitalism' recovers the true meaning of democracy by underlining the fact that its structural features and defining aspects – 'free' and periodic elections, individual rights and freedoms, etc. – are, despite their importance, only political forms whose operation and specific efficacy are unable to neutralize, let alone dissolve, the intrinsically and hopelessly anti-democratic structure of capitalist society.[10] This structure, which rests on a system of social relations centered on the incessant reproduction of labour power that must be sold in the marketplace as a commodity to guarantee the very survival of the workers, poses insurmountable limits for democracy. This 'slavery' of wage-earners, who must turn to the marketplace in search of a capitalist who may find it profitable to buy their labour-power, or otherwise try to eke out a dismal living as petty traders and scavengers in the slums of the world, places the overwhelming majority of contemporary populations, and not only in Latin America, in a situation of structural inferiority and inequality. This is incompatible with the full development of their democratic potential, while a small section of the society, the capitalists, are firmly established in a position of undisputed predominance and enjoy all sorts of privileges.

The result is a *de facto* dictatorship of capitalists, whatever the political forms – such as democracy – under which the former is concealed from the eyes of the public. Hence the tendential incompatibility between capitalism as a social and economic form resting on the structural inequality separating capitalist and workers and democracy, as conceived in the classical tradition of political theory, not only in its formal and procedural aspects, but grounded in a generalized condition of equality. It is precisely for this reason that Ellen Meiksins Wood is right when, in a magnificent essay rich in theoretical suggestions, she asks: will capitalism be able to survive a full extension of democracy conceived in its substantiality and not in its processuality?[11] The answer, clearly, is negative.

## OUTLINE OF A SUBSTANTIVE
## CONCEPTION OF DEMOCRACY

A comprehensive and substantive conception of democracy must immediately put on the table the issue of the relationship between socialism and democracy. It would be foolhardy on our part to attempt to broach this discussion here. Suffice it for the moment to recall the penetrating reflections of Rosa Luxemburg on this subject, including her democratic formula to the effect that 'there is no socialism without democracy; there is no democracy without socialism'.[12] Luxemburg emphasized the value of democratic capitalism without throwing the socialist project overboard. She did this by simultaneously pointing to the unjust nature of democratic capitalist societies. Her thinking avoids the traps of both vulgar Marxism – which in its rejection of democratic capitalism ends up spurning the very idea of democracy and justifying political despotism – and 'post-Marxism', and the diverse currents of neoliberal inspiration, that mystify democratic capitalisms to the point of treating them as paradigms of a 'democracy' without qualification.

Taking this reasoning into account it seems to us that a theorization aimed at overcoming the vices of Schumpeterian formalism and 'proceduralism' should consider democracy as a synthesis of three inseparable dimensions amalgamated into a single formula:

(a) Democracy presupposes a social formation characterized by economic, social and legal equality and a relatively high, albeit historically variable, level of material welfare, which allows the full development of individual capabilities and inclinations as well as of the infinite plurality of expressions of social life. Democracy, therefore, cannot flourish amidst generalized poverty and indigence, or in a society marked by profound inequalities in the distribution of property, incomes and wealth. It requires a type of social structure which can be found only exceptionally in capitalist societies. Despite all official claims to the contrary, capitalist societies are not egalitarian but profoundly inegalitarian. Egalitarianism is the ideology, class polarization is the reality, of the capitalist world. Political democracy cannot take root and prosper in a structurally anti-democratic society.

(b) Democracy also presupposes the effective enjoyment of freedom by the citizenry. But freedom cannot be only a 'formal right' – like those brilliantly incorporated into numerous Latin American constitutions – which, in practical life, does not enjoy the least likelihood of being exercised. A democracy that does not guarantee the full enjoyment of the rights it says it enshrines at the juridical level turns, as Fernando H. Cardoso said many years ago, into a farce.[13] Freedom means the possibility of choosing among real alternatives. Our 'free elections' in Latin America are limited to deciding which member of the same political establishment, recruited, financed and co-opted by the dominant classes, will have the responsibility of running the country.[14] What kind of freedom is this that condemns people to illiteracy, to live in miserable shacks, to die young for lack of medical assistance, depriving them of a decent job and a minimum standard of social protection in their old age? Are they free, the millions of jobless that in Latin America don't have even the couple of dollars needed to leave their homes to find some job, any job?

Moreover, while equality and freedom are necessary, they are not by themselves sufficient to guarantee the existence of a democratic state. A third condition is required:

(c) The existence of a complex set of institutions and clear and unequivocal rules of the game that make it possible to guarantee popular sovereignty, overcoming the limitations of the so-called 'representative' democracy and endowing the citizenry with the legal and institutional means of ensuring the predominance of the popular classes in the formation of the common will. Some scholars have argued that one of the central characteristics of democratic states is the 'relatively uncertain' character of the results of the political process, namely, the uncertainty of electoral outcomes.[15] But a warning should be issued about the risks of overestimating the true degrees of 'democratic uncertainty' found in today's democratic capitalisms. In actual fact there is very little uncertainty in them because even in the most developed ones, the most crucial and strategic hands in political life are played with 'marked cards' that consistently uphold the interests of the dominant classes. We repeat: not all hands, but definitively the most important ones – both at the electoral as well as at the decision-making level – are played with enough guarantees for the results to be perfectly foreseeable and acceptable to the dominant classes. This is the case, for instance, in the United States, where the major policy decisions and orientations of the two competing parties are almost identical, differing only on some marginal issues which do not threaten the rule of capital. Little wonder, then, that in no single capitalist country has the state ever called a popular plebiscite to decide if the economy should be organized on the basis of private property, popular economy or state-owned corporations; or, for example, in Latin America, to decide what to do about the foreign debt, the opening up of the economy, financial deregulation, or privatizations. In other words, uncertainty, yes, but only within extremely narrow, insignificant, margins. Elections, yes, but using all kind of resources, legal and illegal, to manipulate the vote and avoid having the people 'make a mistake' and choose a party contrary to the interests of the dominant classes. It isn't just that the games are played with 'marked cards'; other games aren't even played, and the winners are always the same.

To sum up: the existence of clear and unequivocal rules of the game that guarantee popular sovereignty is the 'political-institutional' condition for democracy. But, once again, this is a necessary but not sufficient condition, because a substantive or comprehensive democracy cannot sustain itself or survive for very long, even as a political régime, if its roots are deeply sunk in a type of society characterized by social relations, structures, and ideologies antagonistic or hostile to its spirit. 'To discuss democracy without considering the economy in which that democracy must operate', Adam Przeworski once wrote, 'is an operation worthy of an ostrich'.[16] Unfortunately, contemporary social sciences seem to be increasingly populated by ostriches. In real and concrete terms democratic capitalisms, even the most developed ones, barely fulfill some of these requirements: their institutional deficits are well known, their trends toward rising inequality and social exclusion are evident, and the effective enjoyment of rights and freedoms is distributed in an extremely unequal way among the various sectors of the population. Rosa Luxemburg was right: there cannot be democracy without socialism. We cannot hope to build a democratic political order without simultaneously waging a resolute struggle against capitalism.

## THE LATIN AMERICAN DEMOCRATIC EXPERIENCE

Let us imagine that Aristotle comes back to life, and we have the chance to ask him to look at the contemporary political scene in Latin America and pass judgment on the nature of the prevailing political regimes. Surely his conclusion would be that our capitalist 'democracies' are anything but democratic. Following his classic typology of political regimes he would certainly consider them as 'oligarchies' or 'plutocracies', that is, government of the rich exercised by somebody who is not necessarily rich but who rules for them. Looking at our political landscape one could say that our faulty democracies are governments of the markets, by the markets and for the markets, lacking all three of the conditions summarized above.

This is why, after more than two decades of 'democratization', the achievements of Latin American democratic capitalisms are so disappointing. Our societies today are more unequal and unjust than before, and our populations are not free, but enslaved by hunger, joblessness and illiteracy. If in the decades after 1945 Latin American societies experienced a moderate progress in direction of social equality, and if in that same period a diversity of political regimes, from variants of populism to some modalities of 'developmentalism', managed to lay the foundations of a policy that, in some countries, was aggressively 'inclusive', and tended towards the social and political 'enfranchisement' of large sections of our popular strata who had been traditionally deprived of every right, the period that began with the exhaustion of Keynesianism and the debt crisis has gone exactly in the opposite direction. In this new phase, celebrated as the definitive reconciliation of our countries with the inexorable imperatives of globalized markets, old rights – such as the rights to health, education, housing, social security – were abruptly 'commodified' and turned into unattainable goods on the market, throwing large masses of people into indigence. The precarious security nets of social solidarity were demolished *pari passu* with the social fragmentation and marginalization caused by orthodox economic policies and the exorbitant individualism promoted by both the 'lords of the market' and the political class that rules on their behalf.

Moreover, the collective actors and social forces that in the past voiced and channelled the expectations and interests of the popular classes – labour unions, left-wing parties, popular associations of all sorts – were persecuted by fierce tyrannies, their leaders jailed, massacred or 'disappeared'. As a result these popular organizations were disbanded and weakened, or simply swept aside. In this way the citizens of our democracies found themselves trapped in a paradoxical situation: while in the ideological heaven of the new democratic capitalism, popular sovereignty and a wide repertoire of constitutionally reasserted rights were exalted, in the prosaic earth of the market and civil society citizens were meticulously deprived of these rights by means of sweeping processes of social and economic disenfranchisement which excluded them from the benefits of economic progress and converted democracy into an empty simulacrum.

The result of the democratization process in Latin America having taken this form has been a dramatic weakening of the democratic impulse. Far from having helped to consolidate our nascent democracies, neoliberal policies have undermined them and the consequences are clearly felt today. Democracy has become that 'empty shell' of which Nelson Mandela has often spoken, where increasingly irresponsible and corrupt politicians run countries with total indifference to the common good. That this is so is proved by the enormous popular distrust of politicians, parties and parliaments, a phenomenon seen, with varying levels of intensity, in every single country of Latin America. Some recent empirical research provides interesting data on this.

## THE UNDP REPORT ON LATIN AMERICAN DEMOCRACY: A BALANCE SHEET

The UNDP's *Democracy in Latin America: Toward a Citizens' Democracy* is the most important and comprehensive comparative research on democratic capitalisms ever conducted in Latin America.[17] However, despite the immense efforts demanded by its realization, the severe flaws built into its theoretical apparatus and its methodology prevented it from producing a fully realistic portrayal of the situation of democracy in the region. The incurable problems of 'politicist' reductionism are evident from the very beginning of the thick volume. Thus the report starts by considering democracy as 'not only a political system but also a system of governance that permits greater public participation, thereby creating a favorable environment for societies to become involved in decisions that affect their development'.[18] Democracy, in sum, is a political thing having to do with voters, citizens and patterns of governance, in splendid isolation from the rest of social life. A research project with this starting-point (and punctuated here and there by occasional – but still highly significant – references to the contributions of Freedom House and the Heritage Foundation to the study of contemporary democracies) cannot go very far, no matter how many scholars are involved, or how large the budget.

Not surprisingly the report goes on to say that although '140 countries in the world today live under democratic regimes' – a fact that is seen as a major achievement – 'only in 82 of these is there full democracy'.[19] This gross exaggeration (no less than 82 full democracies!) is somewhat tempered when the authors warn the reader that authoritarian and undemocratic practices still persist under democratically-elected governments, and provide a convincing list of these. Nevertheless, this does not deter them from arguing that the eighteen Latin American countries included in the report 'fulfill the basic

requirements of a democratic regime; of these only three lived under democratic regimes 25 years ago'.[20]

To be sure, the report does not fail to notice that while 'the people of Latin
America consolidate their political rights they are faced with high levels of
poverty and the highest levels of inequality in the world'. This contradiction
moved the authors of the report to conclude, albeit somewhat enigmatically,
that 'there are severe tensions between the deepening of democracy and the
economy'. Thus while the report celebrates the main achievements of democracy in Latin America it doesn't fail to identify inequality and poverty as its
main weaknesses. Additionally, it urges the adoption of policies 'that promote
democracy in which citizens are full participants. Integral participation of
citizens means that today's citizens must have easy access to their civil, social,
economic and cultural rights and that all of these rights together comprise
an indivisible and interconnected whole'.[21] Unfortunately, the authors of the
report stop short of asking why is it that this whole set of rights, still granted
on paper by all capitalist states, is increasingly becoming little more than dead
letter everywhere in a neoliberal world. And why has access to those rights in
any case always been so limited in capitalist societies? Is it by chance, or due
to systematic class factors?

The report has no answer to these questions because the nature of the
contradiction between capitalism and democracy is not explored. In the 284
pages of the English version of the report the words 'capitalism' or 'capitalist'
appear just twelve times. The first mention comes only on page 51, surprisingly enough in a quotation from someone as inconspicuous a theorist of
capitalism as George Soros; indeed nine out of the twelve mentions appear
in quotations or in the bibliographic reference sector of the report. Only
three occur in the body of the text. Of course, this extreme reluctance to
talk about capitalism exacts a severe theoretical toll on the whole report. For,
how can one speak about democracy in today's world when one is reluctant
even to mention the word capitalism? How are we supposed to understand
the acknowledged 'tensions between the deepening of democracy and the
economy'? What features of the economy are to be blamed for this? Its technological base, its natural endowment, the size of the markets, the industrial
structure, or what?

The problem is not the 'economy' but the 'capitalist economy' and its
defining feature: the extraction and private appropriation of surplus value
and the ineluctable social polarization that springs up as a result. The tensions
are not between two metaphysical entities, 'democracy' and the 'economy',
but between two concrete historical products: the democratic expectations of the masses and the iron-like laws of capitalist accumulation, and the
contradiction exists and persists because the latter cannot make room for the

former, except in the highly devalued mode of the 'liberal democracy' we see all around us. He who doesn't want to talk about capitalism should refrain from talking about democracy.

## POPULAR PERCEPTIONS OF DEMOCRACY

One of the most useful components of the UNDP report is a comparative survey of public opinion conducted by Latinobarómetro with a sample of 18,643 citizens in 18 countries of the region. In broad terms, its findings are summarized as follows:

- The preference of citizens for democracy is relatively low;
- A large proportion of Latin Americans rank development above democracy and would withdraw their support for a democratic government if it proved incapable of resolving their economic problems;
- 'Non-democrats' generally belong to less educated groups, whose socialization mainly took place during periods of authoritarian-ism and who have low expectations of social mobility and a deep distrust of democratic institutions and politicians; and
- Although 'democrats' are to be found among the various social groups, citizens tend to support democracy more in countries with lower levels of inequality. However, they do not express themselves through political organizations.[22]

These findings aren't at all surprising. On the contrary, they speak very highly of the political awareness and rationality of most Latin Americans and their accurate assessment of the shortcomings and unfulfilled promises of our so-called 'democratic' governments. Let us push this line of analysis a little farther and look at the most recent data produced by Latinobarómetro in its 2004 international public opinion survey.[23] As expected, the empiri-cal findings show high levels of dissatisfaction with the performance of the democratic governments in their countries: whereas in 1997 41 per cent of the region's sample declared themselves satisfied with democracy, in 2001 this dropped to a 25 per cent, and rose again only slightly to 29 per cent in 2004, so that for the whole 1997–2004 period, there was a decline of 12 percent-age point in satisfaction with democracy in Latin America. The significance of this is enhanced by the fact that the starting-point in the comparison was far from reassuring, since even in 1997 almost 60 per cent were not satisfied with democracy. Only three countries deviated from this declining trend: Venezuela, ironically the favourite target of the 'democratic' crusade launched by the White House, where the percentage of people who declared themselves satisfied with the democratic regime increased by seven points; and Brazil and Chile, where the proportion rose by five and three percentage points respectively. The countries which showed the most dramatic declines in the index of democratic satisfaction were Mexico and Nicaragua, whose governments were very closely associated with the United States and loyal followers of the 'Washington Consensus'; there, satisfaction with democracy fell by almost 30 percentage points.

Let us look at things from another angle. In 1997 there were only two countries in which more than half of the population expressed satisfaction with the functioning of democracy. This rather modest mark of popular approval was achieved in Costa Rica, with 68 per cent, and Uruguay, with 64 per cent of the popular approval. Yet in 2004 not one country was over the 50 per cent mark. The disillusion with our 'actually existing democracies' left no country above 50 per cent: in Costa Rica the proportion had declined to 48 per cent while in Uruguay the index fell to 45 per cent. In Fox's Mexico, where such great hopes had been raised in a sector of the left intelligentsia, who naively believed that the victory of PAN would open the doors to an adventurous 'regime change' that would bring about full political democracy, only 17 per cent of the sample shared such rosy expectations in 2004. Lagos's Chile, in turn, presents a disturbing paradox for the conventional theory. The country regarded as the model of successful democratic transition, patterned after the equally-praised Spanish post-Francoist transition, reveals a high proportion of ungrateful citizens not persuaded by the applause of the social science pundits and the reassuring voices of the international financial institutions. Thus in 1997 only 37 per cent of Chileans declared themselves satisfied with the democratic, rational and responsible 'centre-left' government of the *Concertación*. After a sudden decline to 23 per cent in 2001, amidst anxieties over an economic downturn, the proportion rose to 40 per cent in 2004, a significant increase but, nevertheless, a figure that could hardly be regarded as healthy.

In the Brazil of Fernando H. Cardoso, a champion of Latin American democratic theory, the proportion of satisfied citizens fluctuated between 20 and 27 per cent during his two presidential terms, hardly a level to be proud of. After two years of Lula's government the proportion of satisfied citizens remained stable around the 28 per cent mark. In Argentina, in 1998, when the inebriating mist of the so-called 'economic miracle' (certified *urbi et orbi* by Michel Camdessus, then Director of the IMF) still prevented ordinary people from perceiving the approaching catastrophe, the proportion of the satisfied reached a record high of 49 per cent. By 2001, when the crisis was already three years old but the worst was still to come, this proportion would fall to 20 per cent, and in 2002 would fall further to reach a record low of

8 per cent after the confiscation of current account bank deposits and the massive street demonstrations that ousted the 'centre-left' De la Rúa government.

Given this disappointment with the performance of Latin American democratic governments, it is not surprising to learn that support for the *idea* of a democratic regime, as opposed to satisfaction with its concrete operation, also declined between 1997 and 2004. Whereas in 1997 62 per cent affirmed that democracy was to be preferred to any other political regime, by 2004 this had fallen to 53 per cent. And, in answer to a different question, no less than 55 per cent of the sample said they were ready to accept a non-democratic government if it proved capable of solving the economic problems affecting the country. In this framework of declining democratic legitimacy, prompted by the disappointing performance of supposedly democratic governments, an outstanding exception should be again underlined: the case of Venezuela, where support for the democratic regime climbed from 64 per cent to 74 per cent between 1997 and 2004. This country is now at the top of all countries in Latin America as far as support for the democratic regime is concerned, posing another distressing paradox for conventional theorists of democratization: how is it that Venezuela, repeatedly singled out by Washington for her supposed institutional weaknesses, the illegitimate nature of the Chávez government and other similar disqualifications, shows the highest support for democracy in the region?

We will pursue the answer to this below. But to sum up here, it is clear that the disillusionment with democracy prevailing in the region cannot be attributed to a distinctive authoritarian feature of societies fond of *caudillismo* and personalistic despotisms of all sorts. It is a rational response to a political regime that, in its Latin American historical experience, has given ample proof of being much more concerned with the welfare of the rich and the powerful than with the fate of the poor and the oppressed. When the same people in the sample were asked whether they were satisfied with the functioning of the market economy, only 19 per cent responded affirmatively, and in no country of the region did this figure reach a majority of the population. Few Latin American governments, of course, are very interested in knowing the reasons for this, let alone in calling for a public discussion of the issue. Nor are they remotely interested in calling referenda to decide whether or not such an unpopular economic regime deserves to be upheld against the overwhelming opinion of those who, supposedly, are the democratic polity's sovereign. That would be the only democratic response, but our 'democratic' governments do not dream of fostering such dangerous initiatives.

Where the number of those satisfied with the market economy is higher – not by chance Chile, the country most thoroughly brain-washed by the neoliberal virus – this proportion barely reaches 36 per cent of the national sample, a clear minority vis à vis those supporting alternative opinions. As long as Latin American democracies have as one of their paramount goals to guarantee the 'governability' of the political system, that is, to govern in accordance with the preferences of the market, nobody should be taken by surprise by these results. Dissatisfaction with the market economy would sooner or later spread to the democratic regimes. This was summed up in the widespread opinion among the general public that the rulers do not honour their electoral promises, either because they lie in order to win the elections or because the 'system' prevents them from doing so. But the public is only coming to realize what the real powers-that-be already know. Asked to identify who really exercises power in Latin America, a survey conducted among 231 leaders in the region (among whom were several former presidents, ministers, high-ranking state officials, corporate CEOs, etc.) 80 per cent of the sample pointed to big business and the financial sector, while 65 per cent pointed to the press and the big media. By comparison, only 36 per cent identified the figure of the President as somebody with the capacity to really wield power, while 23 per cent of respondents said that the American Embassy was a major wielder of power in local affairs.[24] Let us turn then to examining the real power structure in Latin America.

## FREE ELECTIONS?

Conventional social science argues that 'free elections' are a fundamental component of democracy. The UNDP Report defines as 'free' an election in which the electorate is offered a range of choices unrestricted by legal rules or restrictions operating 'as a matter of practical force'.[25] In the same vein, a report by the conservative think tank Freedom House, *Freedom in the World 2003*, asserts that an election can be considered free when 'voters can choose their authoritative leaders freely from among competing groups and individuals not designated by the government; voters have access to information about candidates and their platforms; voters can vote without undue pressure from the authorities; and candidates can campaign free from intimidation'.[26]

There are many problems with both definitions. To begin with, what constitutes 'a matter of practical force'? For the authors of the UNDP Report it is the imposition of certain restrictions on the political participation of particular parties in the electoral process. This argument is derived from the classic liberal premise that subscribes to a negative theory of freedom, according to which freedom only exists to the extent that external, governmental constraints are absent. In the ideological framework on whose basis liberal theory develops there are two separate social spheres: one, comprising civil society and markets, nurturing freedom; the other, embodied in the state, the home of coercion and restrictions. Therefore, 'forceful' restrictions on the free will of the citizenry can only come from the state. Consequently, examples of 'forceful' impediments are the legal proscription of the Peronista Party in Argentina, the APRA in Peru and the banning of the Communist parties throughout the region from the mid-forties to the early eighties. But this theorization is blind to other effective and lethal restrictions emanating from market power, in the form of economic blackmail, investment strikes, threats of capital flight and so on, that are not even mentioned in the Report and that decisively limit the decisional space of the sovereign people. These limitations and conditions are not construed as 'forceful' restrictions imposed on the will of the electorate but as healthy manifestations of pluralism and freedom.

Let us examine a concrete case: a little country like El Salvador, where almost one third of the population was forced to emigrate because of decades of civil strife and economic stagnation. As a result, El Salvador is heavily dependent on emigrants' remittances and on foreign investment, mainly from the United States. A few months before the last presidential election of 2004 major American firms established in El Salvador started to declare that they had already devised plans for quickly pulling out their investments and laying off employees in case the front-runner candidate of the Frente Farabundo Martí de Liberación Nacional (FMLN) won the elections. This statement created havoc in the already convulsed Salvadorean society, which was made worse when an official spokesperson of the US government warned that in such an eventuality the White House might step in to protect threatened US corporate interests, and would surely impose an embargo on remittances to El Salvador. It took less than two weeks to radically change the electoral preferences of the citizenry: the FMLN front-runner was pushed into second place, far behind the candidate supported by the establishment. After these announcements he appeared as the only one able to prevent the chaos that would surely follow the electoral victory of the 'wrong' candidate. Of course, these are little anecdotes that do not disturb the self-confidence of conventional political science, nor serve to exclude El Salvador from Freedom House's roster of the 'free countries' of the world.

In addition, to say that an election is 'free' ought to mean that there are real alternatives available to the electorate – alternatives, that is, in terms of policy options offered to the general public. A quite widespread formula adopted by the so-called Latin American 'centre-left' parties is 'alternation without alternatives', meaning the tranquil succession of governments led by different personalities or political forces but without attempting to implement any alternative policy agenda that might be labelled as an irresponsible political adventure leading in an undesirable post-neoliberal direction. Former

Brazilian president Fernando H. Cardoso used to say that 'within globaliza-tion there are no alternatives, outside globalization there is no salvation'. In which case, free elections mean very little.

Under the 'North Americanization' of Latin American politics, already discernible in the format as well as in the shallowness of electoral campaigns, party competition has been reduced to little more than a beauty contest or toothpaste advertising, in which 'images' of the candidates are far more important than their ideas. On the other hand, the parties' obsession with occupying the supposed 'centre' of the ideological spectrum, and the primacy of video politics with its flashy and incoherent speeches and its convoluted advertising styles, has reinforced the political mistrust of the masses and the indifference and apathy already promoted by market logic. This has long been typical of public life of the United States, and even might be said to have resulted from the conscious design of the founding fathers of the constitu-tion, who often advanced arguments on the desirability of discouraging, or preventing, too much participation by the 'lower classes' in the conduct of public affairs.

But there are further problems with electoral freedom in Latin America, having to do with the actual powers of the magistrate elected by the people to the presidency. Is the democratic sovereign electing somebody endowed with effective powers of command? Take the case of Honduras, regularly considered a democracy according to the Freedom House criteria prevail-ing in mainstream social sciences. The historian Ramón Oquelí has keenly observed that in the mid-eighties:

> (T)he importance of the presidential elections, with or without fraud, is relative. The decisions that affect Honduras are first made in Washington; then in the American military command in Panama (the Southern Command); afterwards in the American base command of Palmerola, Honduras; immediately after that in the American Embassy in Tegucigalpa; in fifth place comes the commander-in-chief of the Honduran armed forces; and the president of the Republic only appears in sixth place. We vote, then, for a sixth-category official in terms of decision capacity. The president's functions are limited to managing misery and obtaining American loans.[27]

Was the case of Honduras in the 1980s something special? Not really. Replace Honduras by almost any other Latin American country today, with the exception of Cuba and Venezuela, and a roughly similar picture will be obtained. In some cases, like Colombia, or the extreme case of Haiti, internal strife gives the military a crucial role in the decision-making process, lowering even further the importance of the presidency. This was the situation during the seventies and the eighties during the apogee of the guerrilla wars in Nicaragua, El Salvador and Guatemala, all countries in which there were democratically elected presidents. But for countries that do not pose a military threat to American interests, the central role rests in the hands of the US Treasury and the IMF, and the Latin American president can, in such cases, move up the decision ladder one or, at most two rungs.

For instance, the decision to adopt the Central American Free Trade Agreement, involving the Central American nations plus the Dominican Republic and the United States, is first of all made in the United States by the dominant imperial class and their subordinate allies in the periphery. This decision is then converted into an enforceable policy through the indispensable mediation of Washington, that is, the American state: principally the White House, the Treasury and State Departments, and the Pentagon.[28] Only then does it make its way to the international financial institutions, the 'guard dogs' of international capitalism with their paraphernalia of 'conditionalities' and expert missions and their repertoire of 'kid glove' extortions to ensure that the policy is carried out by the dependent states. In this particular phase the American embassies in the capital cities of the imperial provinces, the financial press and the local economic pundits that crowd the media play a critical role in pushing for the adoption of neoliberal policies, extolled as the only sensible and reasonable course of action possible and disregarding any other alternative as socialistic, populist or irresponsible. Then, the decision descends to a fourth rung: the offices of the ministers of economy and the presidents of the central banks (whose 'independence' has been actively promoted by the Washington Consensus over the past decades), where the incumbent heads and their advisers are usually economists trained in ultra-conservative American university departments of economics, and owe their professional careers to their loyalty to the big firms or international financial institutions in which they also work from time to time. These offices then communicate the decision to the supposedly 'first magistrate', the President, whose role is just to sign what already has been decided well above his competence and in a manner that does not even remotely resemble anything like a democratic process. Thus, our much-praised democracy is really only a particular political and administrative arrangement in which citizens are called on to elect an official who, in crucial decisions, is located at best on the fifth rung of the decisional chain. Senators and congressmen are even more irrelevant as expressions of popular will. If the country involved is riddled by civil strife and guerrilla warfare, like Colombia, for instance, then other wholly non-democratic military elements (like the Southern Command, the

American base and the local armed forces) intervene to reduce the relevance of the President even further.

Of course, there are some slight variations in this general model of economic decision-making. There are basically three factors that account for the variations:

(a) The relative strength and coherence of the peripheral state and the potency of the working class and popular organizations. Where the process of dismantling or destruction of the state has not progressed too far, and where popular organizations are able to resist the neoliberal encroachments, then the decisions made at the top cannot always be fully implemented;

(b) The interests of the local bourgeoisie, to the extent they are in conflict with the international ruling capitalist coalition. Where a local bourgeoisie still survives (not a national bourgeoisie in the classic sense – that is long gone in Latin America) with strong domestic interests and capacities for political articulation, then decisions made in the form suggested above do encounter some significant obstacles to their implementation – as is especially the case in Brazil today;

(c) The nature of the decision to be adopted. For instance, the forceful implementation of the Washington Consensus agenda in the Third World was jointly decided by 'the Wall Street-Davos lobby' and the G-7; or, in other words, by the international ruling classes and their political representatives in the core capitalist states. In matters more properly hemispheric the role of the European and Japanese members of the imperial triad is of much smaller importance and questions are mostly decided by the American ruling class. Moreover, some marginal decisions that do not affect the general course of capitalist accumulation are almost entirely made by the local authorities.

To sum up, democratically elected presidents in Latin America retain few functions, apart from the governance of misery. This is admittedly a crucial role that involves, on the one hand, begging for endless loans to repay an ever mounting external debt, and on the other 'keeping the rabble in line', to use Noam Chomsky's graphic expression; that is, steering the ideological and repressive apparatuses of the state to ensure the subordination of the majority and to see that capitalist exploitation proceeds along predictable lines. In order to perform this role labour has to be spatially immobilized and politically demobilized, while the unfettered mobility of capital has to be assured at all costs.

This downgraded role of the 'first magistrate' of Latin American democracies is quite evident in the day-to-day management of the state, and where it appears to be challenged by a new first magistrate, the formidable veto power acquired by ministers of the economy and presidents of central banks in Latin America comes into play, thus confining our 'democratically elected presidents' to a rather ornamental role in key decision-making areas. In Brazil, for instance, President Lula repeatedly said that the program Famine Zero would be his most important policy instrument in fighting poverty and social exclusion. To this end he set up an office directly dependent on the presidency under the direction of a Catholic priest, Frei Betto, a long-time friend of his. Yet Frei Betto was forced to resign after two years of futile efforts to get from the Minister of Economy, Antonio Palocci (a former die-hard Trotskyite, now converted into an ultra-orthodox neoliberal) the money needed to put the program on its feet. Why didn't Palocci supply the required financial resources? Simply because the request of the President didn't carry the same weight as the commands or even recommendations of international capital and its watchdogs. Since for the latter it is of crucial importance to guarantee a huge fiscal surplus to enable the prompt repayment of the external debt, and to acquire the coveted 'investment rating' that will, supposedly, release a flood of foreign capital into Brazil, decisions regarding social expenditures never reach the top of the list of budgetary priorities, no matter if it is a decision made by the democracy's 'first magistrate'. In sum: President Lula asked one thing and the Minister of Economy decided exactly the contrary, and prevailed. Lula´s friend had to leave, while the Minister received the applause of the international financial community for his unbending commitment to fiscal discipline. Similarly, Miguel Rosetto, the Minister of the Agrarian Reform, saw his budget, previously agreed upon with Lula, cut by more than half by a ukase of Palocci, again overruling a decision made by the President.

In Argentina, similarly, while President Néstor Kirchner delivers blazing speeches against the IMF and, more generally, international financial capital and neoliberalism, his Minister of Economy, Roberto Lavagna, makes sure that the incendiary prose of the President does not translate into effective policies and remains a rhetorical exercise destined only for internal consumption. Consequently, despite all the boastful official rhetoric suggesting otherwise, the Kirchner government actually has the dubious honour of being the government that has paid most to the IMF in all Argentine history.

## POPULAR REACTIONS

But the original promise of Lula, and the manoeuvrings of Kirchner, mean something nonetheless. They indicate not only that the limits of democratic capitalism are increasingly evident to the people of Latin America, but also that they are coming to expect something to be done about this. Recent developments in Bolivia, Ecuador and Uruguay need to be seen in this light.

These developments demonstrate, especially in the case of the Andean countries but not only there, the utter inability of the legal and institutional framework of Latin American 'democracies' to solve social and political crises within the established constitutional procedures. Thus, legal reality becomes illegitimate because our legality is unreal, not corresponding to the inner nature of our social formations. Popular upheavals toppled reactionary governments in Ecuador in 1997, 2000 and 2005, and in Bolivia the insurgence of large masses of peasants, aboriginal peoples and the urban poor overturned right-wing governments in 2003 and 2005. The 'constitutional' dictatorship of Alberto Fujimori in Peru was overthrown by a formidable mass mobilization during 2000, and in the next year Argentina's 'center-left' President Fernando de la Rúa, who had betrayed his electoral promises of a prompt and resolute abandonment of neoliberal policies, was rudely removed from power by an unprecedented popular outburst that took the lives of at least thirty-three people.

But these popular insurgencies also prove that this long period of neoliberal rule – with its paraphernalia of tensions, ruptures, exclusions and mounting levels of exploitation and social degradation – created the objective conditions for the political mobilization of large sections of Latin American societies. Are the above-mentioned plebeian revolts just isolated episodes, unconnected outbursts of popular anger and fury, or do they reflect a deeper and much more complex historical dialectic? A sober look at the history of the democratic period opened in the early eighties shows that there is nothing accidental in the rising mobilization of the popular classes and the tumultuous finale of so many democratic governments throughout the region. At least sixteen presidents, the majority of them obedient clients of Washington, were forced to leave office before the completion of their legal mandates because of popular revolts. Some went at the end of the 1980s, like Alfonsín in Argentina, who had to relinquish his powers to his elected successor six months ahead of schedule because of an intolerable combination of social unrest, popular riots and hyperinflation. In this he was following Siles Suazo of Bolivia, who was forced to call early presidential elections in 1985, being unable to reach the full completion of his term in office. Brazil's Fernando Collor de Melo, in 1992, and Venezuelan Carlos Andrés Pérez, in 1993, were both impeached and ousted from office on charges of corruption amidst a wave of popular protests. The rest were overthrown amidst severe social and economic crises. In addition, referenda called to legalize the privatization of state enterprises or public services invariably defeated the expectations of the neoliberals, as in the cases of Uruguay (on water supply and port facilities) and Bolivia and Perú (over water resources). On top of that, impressive social uprisings took place to nationalize oil and gas in Bolivia; to oppose the privatization of oil in Ecuador, the telephone company in Costa Rica, the health system in several countries; to put an end to the plunder of foreign banks in Argentina; and to stop programmes of coca eradication in Bolivia and Peru.[29]

Two lessons can be drawn from all these political experiences. First, that the popular masses in Latin America have acquired a novel ability to remove anti-popular governments from office, rolling over the established constitutional mechanisms that not by chance have a strong elitist bias (politics is an elite affair, and the populace should not mingle with the gentlemen in charge). But, on the other hand, the second lesson is that this salutary activation of the masses fell short of building a real political alternative leading to the overcoming of neoliberalism and the inauguration of a post-neoliberal phase. These heroic uprisings of the subordinate classes had a fatal Achilles heel: organizational weakness, as expressed in the absolute predominance of spontaneism as the normal mode of political intervention. Suicidal indifference towards the problems of popular organization and the strategy and tactics of political struggle became crucial factors explaining the limited achievements of all those upheavals. True, neo-liberal governments were replaced, but only by others like them, less prone to use neo-neoliberal rhetoric but loyal to the same principles. The impetuous mobilization of the multitude vanished in thin air shortly after the presidential reshuffling without being able to create a new political subject endowed with the resources needed to modify, in a progressive direction, the prevailing correlation of forces. Not unrelated to these unfortunate results is the astonishing popularity gained especially among political activists by new expressions of political romanticism, such as Hardt and Negri's exaltation of the virtues of the amorphous multitude or Holloway's diatribes against parties and movements that, supposedly unwilling to learn the painful lessons of twentieth century social revolutions, still insist on the importance of conquering political power.[30]

Disillusionment with neoliberalism has helped to accelerate the decline of optimism about democratization that was clearly predominant only a few years ago. Nevertheless, it must be borne in mind that the weakness of the popular impulse at the time of building an alternative was not only visible during 'extra-constitutional' transfers of power. It has also been clearly seen in the case of governments elected in accordance with the Schumpeterian prescriptions of the experts in 'democratic transition' after the economic collapse of neoliberalism. The cases of Kirchner in Argentina, Vázquez in Uruguay, and especially Lula in Brazil, clearly illustrate the powerlessness of the subordinate classes to impose a post-neoliberal agenda even in governments popularly elected with that paramount purpose. If in the political turbulences the masses overthrow the incumbent governments and then demobilize and withdraw, in the cases of constitutional governmental replacements the political logic has been surprisingly similar: the masses vote but then go home, letting the people who supposedly 'know' how to run the country and manage the economy do their job. As in the cases of presidential replacement via popular revolt, the outcomes could not be more disappointing.

Yet, despite all these shortcomings the unprecedented capacity of the popular masses in Latin America to oust anti-popular governments has introduced a new factor into the political scene. The formidable resurgence of the popularity of the Cuban Revolution and its leader, Fidel Castro, throughout Latin America, and the newly-won reputation of Hugo Chávez, his Bolivarian Revolution, his permanent recourse to referenda and elections to prove his popular legitimacy as a means of restoring to the presidency the prerogatives of the 'first magistracy', and his permanent assertions that the solution of the evils of the region can only be found in socialism, not capitalism – a bold statement that had disappeared from public discourse in Latin America – are clear signs of the changing popular mood in the region.

Moreover, Chávez's strong bet in favour of participatory democracy and his repeated popular consultations – general elections, constitutional reforms, referenda, etc. – have nurtured the development of a new political consciousness among large sections of the working classes who now see in the political initiatives of Caracas a door wide open to the exploration of new forms of democracy, far superior to the empty formalism of the 'representative democracy' prevailing in the other Latin American countries. It is still too soon to tell whether the radical democratic stirrings that today shape Venezuelan politics will be imitated elsewhere, or if the Bolivarian experiment will finally succeed in overcoming the narrow limits of democratic capitalism and tempting others to follow the same path. But so far its overall impact, within Venezuela as well as abroad, can hardly be overestimated. A good indication of this is provided by the inordinate attention – and the enormous resources in time, personnel and money allocated to 'fix' the situation – that the Venezuelan political process commands in Washington.

The formidable obstacles that Chavez still faces – undisguised harassment by the US domestically and abroad, attempted coup d'états, international criminalization, economic sabotage, media manipulation, etc. – and that radical democratic projects elsewhere in Latin America today would have to face as well, ranging from brutal IMF and World Bank 'conditionalities' to every kind of economic and diplomatic pressure and blackmail, should also not be underestimated. In Latin America, the progress, however modest, in the process of democratization is likely to unleash a blood-bath. Our history shows that timid reformist projects gave way to furious counter-revolutions. Will it be different now?

## LIMITS OF DEMOCRATIC CAPITALISM

All things considered, the balance-sheet of Latin American democracies reveals the severe, incurable limitations of capitalist democracy and the formidable obstacles that arise in the periphery to the full development of the democratic project.

A careful inspection of the international political scene shows that there are four possible levels of democratic development conceivable within a capitalist social formation. A first level, the most rudimentary and elementary, could be called an 'electoral democracy'. This is a political regime in which elections are held on a regular basis as the only mechanism for filling the post of the chief executive and the representatives in the legislative branch of the state. To some extent this first and most elementary level of democratic development is a simulacrum, an empty formality devoid of any meaningful content. There is, certainly, 'party competition': candidates can launch intensive campaigns, elections can be doggedly contested and public enthusiasm in the run-up to, and on, election day can be high. Yet this is an isolated gesture because the outcome of this routine changes nothing in terms of public policies, citizenship entitlements or the promotion of the public interest. It is the 'degree zero' of democratic development, the most elementary starting-point and nothing else. As George Soros warned before the election of Lula, Brazilians can vote as they please, once every two years, but markets vote every day, and the incoming president, whoever it is, will surely take note of this. 'Markets force governments to make decisions that are unpopular but indispensable', Soros noted in an interview. 'Definitively, the real meaning of the states today rest on the markets'.[31] The incurable misery of democratic capitalism is coldly expressed in his words. Markets are the real thing, democracy just a convenient ornament.

There is, though, a second level that can be called 'political democracy'. This implies moving a step further than electoral democracy through the establishment of a political regime that allows for some degree of effective political representation, a genuine division of powers, an improvement in the mechanisms of popular participation via referenda and popular consultations, the empowerment of the legislative bodies, the establishment of specialized agencies to control the executive branch, effective rights of public access to information, public financing of political campaigns, institutional devices to minimize the role of lobbies and private interest groups, etc. Needless to say, this second kind of political regime, a sort of 'participatory democracy', has never existed in Latin American capitalisms. Our maximum achievement has been only the first.

A third level can be called 'social democracy'. It combines the elements of the previous two levels with social citizenship: that is, the granting of a wide spectrum of entitlements in terms of living standards and universal access to educational, housing and health services. As Gösta Esping-Andersen has observed, a good indicator of the degree of social justice and effective citizenship in a country is given by the extent of 'de-commodification' in the supply of basic goods and services required to satisfy the fundamental human needs of men and women. In other words, 'de-commodification' means that a person can survive without depending on the market's capricious movements and, as Esping-Andersen notes, it 'strengthens the worker and debilitates the absolute authority of employers. This is, precisely, the reason why employers have always opposed it'.[32]

Where the provision of education, health, housing, recreation and social security – to mention the most common elements – are freed from the exclusionary bias introduced by the market we are likely to witness the rise of a fair society and a strong democracy. The other face of 'commodification' is exclusion, because it means that only those with enough money will be able to acquire the goods and services which are inherent in the condition of citizen.[33] Therefore, 'democracies' that fail to grant a fairly equal access to basic goods and services – that is to say, where these goods and services are not conceived as universal civil rights – do not fulfill the very premises of a substantive theory of democracy, understood not only as a formal procedure in the Schumpeterian tradition but as a definite step in the direction of the construction of a good society. As Rousseau rightly remarked:

> If you would have a solid and enduring State you must see that it contains no extremes of wealth. It must have neither millionaires nor beggars. They are inseparable from one another, and both are fatal to the common good. Where they exist public liberty becomes a commodity of barter. The rich buy it, the poor sell it.[34]

The situation in Latin America fits exactly the model of what Rousseau saw as a feature 'fatal to the common good', and this was not the result of the play of anonymous social forces but the consequence of a neoliberal project to reinforce capitalism imposed by a perverse coalition of local dominant classes and international capital. Until recently, the Scandinavian countries and Latin America have illustrated the contrasting features of this dichotomy. In the former, a politically effective citizenry firmly devoted to the universal access to basic goods and services and incorporated into the Nordic countries' fundamental 'social compact' (and, in a rather more diluted way, into that of the European social formations in general). This amounts to a 'citizen's wage' – a universal insurance against social exclusion because it guarantees, through 'non-market' political and institutional channels, the enjoyment of certain goods and services which, in the absence of such insurance, could be acquired only in the market, and only by those whose incomes allowed them to do so.[35] In sharp contrast, democratic capitalisms in Latin America, with their mixture of inconsequential political processes of political enfranchisement co-existing with growing economic and social civic disenfranchisement, wound up as an empty formality, an abstract proceduralism that is a sure source of future despotisms. Thus, after many years of 'democratic transition' we have democracies without citizens: free market-democracies whose supreme objective is to guarantee the profits of the dominant classes and not the social welfare of the population.

The fourth and highest level of democratic development is 'economic democracy'. The basis of this model is the belief that if the state has been democratized there are no reasons to exclude private firms from the democratic impulse. Even an author as identified with the liberal tradition as Robert Dahl has broken with the political reductionism proper to that perspective by arguing that 'as we support the democratic process in the government of the state despite substantial imperfections in practice, so we support the democratic process in the government of economic enterprises despite the imperfections we expect in practice'.[36] We can, and should, go one step further and assert that modern private firms are only 'private' in the juridical dimension which, in the bourgeois state, upholds existing property relations with the force of law. There ends these firms' 'private' character. Their awesome weight in the economy, as well as in the political and ideological realms, makes them truly public actors that should not be excluded from the democratic project.

Gramsci's remarks on the arbitrary and class-biased distinction between public and private should be brought to the fore once again. An economic democracy means that the democratic sovereign has effective capacities to decide upon the major economic decisions influencing social life, regardless of whether these decisions are originally made by, or will affect, private or public actors. Contrary to what is maintained by liberal theories, if there is one thing more than another that is political in social life it is the economy. Political in the deepest sense: the capacity to have an impact on the totality of social life, conditioning the life chances of the entire population. Nothing can be more political than the economy, a sphere in which scarce resources are divided among different classes and sections of the population, condemning the many to a poor or miserable existence while blessing a minority with all kind of riches. Lenin was right: politics is the economy concentrated. All neoliberal talk about the 'independence' of central banks, and neoliberal reluctance to accept the public discussion of economic policies more generally – on the grounds that the latter are 'technical' matters beyond the scope of competence of laymen – is just an ideological smoke screen to ward off the intrusion of democracy into the economic decision-making process.

## CONCLUSION

After decades of dictatorship involving enormous spilling of blood, the social struggles of the popular masses brought Latin America back – or in some cases for the first time – to the first and most elementary level of democratic development. But even this very modest achievement has been constantly besieged by opposing forces that are not ready to relinquish their privileged access to power and wealth. If capitalist society has everywhere proved to be a rather limited and unstable terrain on which to build a steady democratic political order, Latin America's dependent and peripheral capitalism has proved to be even more unable to provide solid foundations for democracy. And it is proving highly resistant to the strong popular desire and pressures that are manifest today for opening great new avenues of mass political participation and self-government and which might lead on to the full realization of democracy. Some particular experiences – like the 'participatory budgeting' originally tried under the leadership of the PT in Porto Alegre, Brazil, the reiterated calls to popular referenda in Venezuela, and 'grassroots' democracy in Cuba, based on high levels of political involvement and participation at the workplace and the neighbourhood – are significant steps in this direction. The traditional model of 'liberal democracy' faces an inevitable demise. Its shortcomings have acquired colossal proportions, and its discontents are legion, in the advanced capitalist nations as well as in the periphery. A new model of democracy is urgently needed. True: the replacement is still in the making, but the first, early signs of its arrival are already clearly discernible.[37]

Contrary to what is asserted by many observers, the crisis of the democratization project in Latin America goes well beyond the imperfections of the 'political system' and has its roots in the insoluble contradiction, magnified in the periphery, between a mode of production that, by condemning the wage-labour to find somebody ready to buy its labour power in order to ensure its mere subsistence, is essentially despotic and undemocratic; and a model of organization and functioning of the political space based in the intrinsic equality of all citizens. The formalistic democracies of Latin America are suffering from the assault of neoliberal policies that amount to an authentic social counter-reformation, determined to go to any extremes to reproduce and enhance the unfettered dominance of capital. 'Market-driven' politics cannot be democratic politics.[38] These policies have caused the progressive exhaustion of the democratic regimes established at a very high cost in terms of human suffering and human lives, making them revert to a pure formality deprived of all meaningful content, a periodical simulacrum of the democratic ideal while social life regresses to a quasi-Hobbesian war of all against all, opening the door to all types of aberrant and anomalous situations.

But this is not only a disease of 'low-intensity' democracies at the periphery of the capitalist system. In the countries at the very core of that system, as Colin Crouch has observed, 'we had our democratic moment around the mid-point of the twentieth century' but nowadays we are living in a distinctively 'post-democratic' age. As a result, 'boredom, frustration and disillusion have settled in after a democratic moment'. Now 'powerful minority interests have become far more active than the mass of ordinary people …; political elites have learned to manage and manipulate popular demands; … people have to be persuaded to vote by top-down publicity campaigns' and global firms have become the major and unchallenged actors in democratic capitalisms.[39]

This is especially true in societies in which national self-determination has been relentlessly undermined by the increasing weight that external political and economic forces have in domestic decision-making, to the point that the word 'neo-colony' describes them better than the expression 'independent nations'. This being the case, in Latin America the question is increasingly being posed: to what extent is it possible to speak of popular sovereignty without national sovereignty? Popular sovereignty for what? Can people subjected to imperialist domination become autonomous citizens? Under these very unfavourable conditions only a very rudimentary democratic model can survive. Thus is it becoming clearer that the struggle for democracy in Latin America, that is to say, the conquest of equality, justice, liberty and citizen participation, is inseparable from a resolute struggle against global capital's despotism. More democracy necessarily implies less capitalism. What Latin America has been getting in the decades of its 'democratization' has been precisely the opposite – and that is what people across the region are increasingly now rising up against.

## NOTES

I want to express my gratitude to Sabrina González for all her assistance during the preparation of this paper. It goes without saying that all mistakes and errors are the exclusive responsibility of the author.

1    Joseph Schumpeter, *Capitalism, Socialism and Democracy*, New York: Harper, 1947, p. 242.

2    Under the 'classical theory' Schumpeter lumped together the teachings of such diverse authors as Plato, Aristotle, Machiavelli, Rousseau, Tocqueville and Marx, among others.

3    Alexis de Tocqueville, *Democracy in America*, Garden City: Doubleday, 1969, p. 12.

4    Guillermo O'Donnell and Phillippe Schmitter, *Conclusiones Tentativas Sobre las Democracias Inciertas*, Buenos Aires: Paidós, 1988, p. 26.

5    Barrington Moore, Jr., *Social Origins of Dictatorship and Democracy: Lords and Peasants in the Making of the Modern World*, Boston: Beacon Press, 1966.

6    T.H. Marshall, *Class, Citizenship and Social Development*, New York: Anchor Books, 1965.

7    Enrique Krauze, *Por una Democracia sin Adjetivos*, Mexico City: Joaquín Mortiz/Planeta,1986, pp. 44-75.

8    David Collier and Steve Levitsky, 'Democracy with Adjectives: Conceptual Innovation in Comparative Research', Working Paper #230, Kellogg Institute, University of Notre Dame, August 1996.

9    Carlos Pereyra, *Sobre la Democracia*, México: Cal y Arena, 1990, p. 33.

10   Atilio A. Boron, *State, Capitalism and Democracy in Latin America*, Boulder and London: Lynne Rienner Publishers, 1995, pp. 33-68.

11   Ellen Meiksins Wood, *Democracy Against Capitalism: Renewing Historical Materialism*, Cambridge: Cambridge University Press, 1995, pp. 204-37. On this see also Arthur MacEwan, *Neoliberalism or Democracy?*, London: Zed Books, 1999; and Atilio A. Boron, *Tras el Búho de Minerva. Mercado contra Democracia en el Capitalismo de Fin de Siglo*, Buenos Aires: Fondo de Cultura Económica, 2000.

12   It goes without saying that our agreement extends to her entire statement and not only to its second part, although it is this that we are concentrating on here.

13   Fernando Henrique Cardoso, 'La Democracia en las Sociedades Contemporáneas', *Crítica y Utopía*, 6, 1982 and 'La democracia en América Latina', *Punto de Vista*, 23, April 1985.

14   The situation is not so different in most of the rest of the world. Indeed, as Noam Chomsky observed, in the last presidential elections the American people were offered a nice democratic menu: they could either elect one multimillionaire, already in office, or elect another multimillionaire, already in the Senate, both of which, in turn, had as their running mates two other multimillionaires. This was the choice in what is considered,

by mainstream social science, as one of the most perfected models of democratic development in the world!

15   Adam Przeworski, *Capitalism and Social Democracy,* Cambridge: Cambridge University Press, 1985, pp. 138-45.

16   Adam Przeworski, *The State and the Economy under Capitalism*, New York: Harwood Academic Publishers, 1990, p. 102.

17   United Nations Development Program, *Democracy in Latin America: Towards a Citizens' Democracy*, New York: UNDP, 2004.

18   Ibid., p. 25-6.

19   Ibid., p. 25.

20   Ibid., p. 26. The three democratic countries were Colombia, Costa Rica and Venezuela.

21   Ibid., p. 26.

22   Ibid., p. 29.

23   Cf. www.latinbarometro.org. The countries included in the study are Argentina, Bolivia, Brazil, Chile, Colombia, Costa Rica, Ecuador, El Salvador, Guatemala, Honduras, México, Nicaragua, Panamá, Paraguay, Perú, República Dominicana, Uruguay and Venezuela.

24   United Nations Development Program, *Democracy*, p. 155. Figures do not add to 100 because the respondents could identify more than one factor.

25   Ibid., p. 79.

26   Cf. Freedom House, *Freedom in the World 2003: Survey Methodology*, http://www.freedomhouse.org/ratings/, p. 7.

27   Quoted in Agustín Cueva, 'Problemas y Perspectivas de la teoría de la Dependencia', in *Teoría social y procesos políticos en América Latina,* Mexico: Editorial Edicol Línea Crítica, 1986, p. 50.

28   This key role of the US state has been forcefully demonstrated in Leo Panitch and Sam Gindin, 'Global Capitalism and American Empire', in *Socialist Register 2004: The New Imperial Challenge.*

29   James Petras, 'Relaciones EU-AL: Hegemonía, Globalización e Imperialismo', *La Jornada,* Mexico, 10 July 2005. See also, CLACSO's journal OSAL, the Social Observatory of Latin America, with in-depth coverage of social conflicts and protests movements in Latin America since 2000.

30   Michael Hardt and Antonio Negri, *Empire*, Cambridge: Harvard University Press, 2000; John Holloway, *Change the World Without Taking Power*, London: Pluto, 2002. We have examined these problems at length in Atilio A. Boron, *Empire and Imperialism: A Critical Reading of Michael Hardt and Antonio Negri* [2001], Translation by Jessica Casiro, London and New York: Zed Books, 2005; 'Civil Society and Democracy: The Zapatista

Experience', *Development,* Society for International Development, 48(2), 2005; and 'Der Urwald und die Polis. Fragen an die politische Theorie des Zapatismus', *Das Argument,* 253, 2003.

31    George Soros, 'Entrevista', *La República,* Rome, 28 January 1995.

32    Gösta Esping-Andersen, *The Three Worlds of Welfare Capitalism,* Princeton: Princeton University Press, 1990, p. 22.

33    A subtle analysis of this process of commodification in the United Kingdom, in public health and public television, and its deleterious impact on democracy, is found in Colin Leys, *Market-Driven Politics,* London: Verso, 2001.

34    Jean-Jacques Rousseau, *The Social Contract and Discourse on the Origin of Inequality,* New York: Washington Square Press, 1967, p. 217.

35    Samuel Bowles and Herbert Gintis, 'The Crisis of Liberal Democratic Capitalism: The Case of the United States', *Politics and Society,* 2(1), 1982.

36    Robert A. Dahl, *A Preface to Economic Democracy,* Los Angeles: University of California Press, 1986, p. 135. See also Carnoy Martin and Dereck Shearer, *Economic Democracy: The Challenge of the 1980s,* Armonk: M.E. Sharpe Inc., 1980, pp. 86-124 and 233-76.

37    The recent writings of Boaventura de Sousa Santos provide an insightful perspective on the 're-invention' of democracy. A summary of his major findings can be found in Boaventura de Sousa Santos, *Reinventar la Democracia: Reinventar el Estado,* Buenos Aires: CLACSO, 2005.

38    Leys, *Market-Driven Politics.*

39    Colin Crouch, *Post-democracy,* Cambridge: Polity Press, 2004, pp. 7, 18-9.

# THE 'BUSINESS COMMUNITY'

## DOUG HENWOOD

The US may be populated by nearly 300 million isolated monads, but do we ever love the word 'community'.[1] On the left, it's never 'blacks' or 'Jews', it's 'the black community' and 'the Jewish community'. Presumably there's something abrupt and almost impolite about simple monosyllabic nouns, so the addition of a few Latinate syllables softens the blow. But there's a way in which the use of the word reads like a wish fulfillment, a hope that a community that doesn't really exist in any for-itself sense can be created in the act of naming it.

But, beyond the left, it's also a popular formulation in mainstream American speech. Examples I've collected over the years include the reality TV community, the military community, the air-hijacking community, the mortgage community, the Alzheimer's community, the cybernerd community, the Phish community, and the copyright community. Of particular interest to readers of this volume might be one of the more ubiquitous examples: 'the business community'.

Just what is the business community? The media can use it to mean anything from Main Street store-owners to Fortune 500 CEOs – and even the global worthies who gather every January at the World Economic Forum in Davos. But whatever the slipperiness of the signifier, or the internal divisions within the signified, the business community – which I take as a euphemism for capital and capitalists – shows a lot more coherence and power than many of the other notional communities I listed.

Raymond Williams said that a community is created through communication. There are few social formations with richer networks of communication than the big owners and top managers of large corporations. They congregate in 'peak associations' like the Business Roundtable and the World Economic Forum, and in the myriad trade associations and lobbying groups that populate Washington. Some actively support think tanks, from relatively centrist ones like The Brookings Institution to aggressively ideological ones like the Club for Growth. Business has its own media – daily newspapers, weekly magazines, entire cable TV channels – produced mainly by loyal hired hands

paid far less regally than the CEOs they write about. The business community articulates productively with the state, frequently exchanging personnel,
pushing political agendas. The cybernerd community rarely does.

As with all communities, there is variation among its members. On its
left, by generous definition, are the 'enlightened' entities that like to give the
appearance of doing well by doing good, as the socially responsible sorts like
to say. An example of this can be found on the website of the Pew Center on
Climate Change, an elite environmental organization based ultimately on an
oil fortune. It reports on the efforts of the 'business community' to do something about global warming.[2] Reading below the headline, we learn that
these green-minded businesses are those belonging to its Business Environmental Leadership Council, which include BP, DuPont, Royal Dutch/Shell,
Toyota, and Weyerhaeuser. It is very difficult to imagine any of them leading
us to a more sustainable form of economic life; they operate under the ster-
nest disciplines to ruin more than they regenerate. But Pew's use of the term
'business community' invokes a warm feeling of high-minded corporate citizens transcending their base economic interests in the name of the higher
good. This is advertising, not politics.

At the right end of the spectrum, Milton Friedman spies a 'suicidal impulse'
among the business community.[3] Supporting the public schools (rather than
their privatization), encouraging antitrust prosecution of Microsoft (rather
than letting the market take its course), and contributing to environmental
organizations may all sound good, but runs the severe risk of inviting government regulation. (In truth, this behaviour is not so common. Wal-Mart, for
instance, has been aggressive in funding school privatization efforts.) Friedman
mulls over several reasons for this odd impulse. He dismisses Schumpeter's
theory that corporations breed a socialist – bureaucratic culture. He considers the possibility that businesspeople are simply amateurs at politics, who
don't really understand what they're up to. In the end, he confesses that he
has no good explanation, but urges the Cato community to figure it out. It
doesn't seem to occur to Friedman that the business community is nowhere
near as enamoured of Manchester liberalism as he is. Capitalists operating in
the real world want the state to do their bidding.

Friedman's blind spot about the corporate urge to do good, or at least
appear to do good, demonstrates the historical amnesia and social isolation
characteristic of academic economists. If we turn to a book like Roland
Marchand's *Creating the Corporate Soul,* we can learn a lot about the origins of
these impulses in the need to fight the labour unrest and political threats of
the early 20th century as the modern large corporation was in formation.[4]

AT&T, terrified of the example of public ownership of telephone companies in Europe and suffering from a miserable public image, embarked on one of the first image-making campaigns in the history of public relations. Over the course of decades, it advertised aggressively not just to sell its services, but to sell the very idea of private monopoly in telephony, and, ambitiously, even to make the company 'loveable'. In an early instance of the fraudulent deployment of a very loaded word, Ma Bell, as AT&T would later be known, tried to position the telephone not merely as an engineering marvel, but as a device enabling the transformation of the vast area of the United States into a single 'community' or 'neighbourhood'. Commenting on this, Claude Fischer noted that AT&T was manipulating 'these value-laden terms in ways that evaded their basic meanings'.[5] But it mostly worked. AT&T successfully staved off the threat of nationalization, and managed to survive the scrutiny of trustbusters until it was finally broken up in 1984. And there are probably a few people who are still nostalgic for the days of the old Phone Company more than twenty years after its breakup.

Corporate PR is, of course, pervasive, even though the old threats – unionization, trustbusting, nationalization – have largely disappeared. It's so much part of our mindscape these days that many people don't even notice it, or dismiss it all as slick bullshit, but the endless onslaught of image advertising, logos, and invocations of corporate personality almost certainly helps keep the threats at bay. Even if you can't measure the effects of a single ad, or even a single ad campaign, the endless cascade of brand-building doubtless has a cumulative effect. Early image advertisers loved to illustrate the size of the corporation – Pillsbury the world's largest flour mill, AT&T its continental network, Metropolitan Life its pioneering skyscraper – but today the ubiquity of image-making evokes something of a capitalist sublime, which inspires deferential awe.

But the material reality has changed enormously. Creating the soulful corporation meant hiding the centrality of profit-making and foregrounding instead an ethic of service, when memories of the robber barons' arrogance – like Vanderbilt's 'the public be damned' – were still fresh. We still see traces of that today, for sure; Hewlett-Packard would love for us all to believe that it exists to make its engineers happy and its customers more productive. But Milton Friedman's once-revolutionary idea that the only responsibility of a corporation was to make a profit has become common wisdom among a lot of Americans. (Efforts to spread this gospel beyond the borders of the United States have yet to be fully successful.) Executives say things openly today that they probably wouldn't have in the 1930s or 1960s. Despite tight oil markets and the highest prices in decades, the oil industry has been reluctant to spend more money on exploration. Why? A very succinct answer came from ExxonMobil president Rex Tillerson, who told the *Wall Street Journal*,

'You give me a choice of producing more barrels, or making more money, I am going to make more money every time'.[6]

Early corporate soul-creators were big on corporate paternalism – recreational outings, employee housing, and the like – as long as it didn't threaten work discipline or the bottom line. Not now; today's corporations are frankly making no such efforts, and talk openly about the need to maximize shareholder value. Yet miraculously, there's been no return of the old threats from labour or the state that first motivated the PR offensive a century ago.

Even more remarkable, the bear market of 2000-2002 and the corporate scandals that were its accompaniment, resulted in almost no measurable backlash against corporate power. The bull market of the 1990s was fuelled by lots of expensive hype: propaganda from the dot.coms, cheerleading by Wall Street analysts whose banking colleagues were underwriting the shares they were shaking their pom-poms for, and great energy thrown into the manufacture of brand identities. It became fashionable during the late 1990s boom to speak of brands as a 'new religion', a source of 'meaning', with 'spiritual dimensions'; prominent among them, according to the ad agency Young & Rubicam, are Calvin Klein, MTV, and Gatorade.[7] Star accounting theorist Baruch Lev made great advances in attempting to put a dollar value on brands (and other intangibles, like 'ways of doing business') so they could appear on New Age balance sheets.[8] It's notable that the star radical economics book of the 1990s was Naomi Klein's *No Logo:* even critiques of corporate power make their first engagement at the level of brand identity.

But corporations aren't really about catchy graphic design and the propagation of spiritual meaning. They're ultimately institutions of class power (the populist critique made in the film *The Corporation* evades this point by fetishizing the legal form of the institution). Profits ultimately redound to people, not legal fictions.

How does that work exactly? In the 1983 edition of *Who Rules America,* William Domhoff argued that the upper class WASPs listed in the *Social Register* (no relation to this publication) were the core of the American ruling class, meritocratically augmented with the cream of the corporate crop. This peak status was earned through ownership of corporate stock and exercised through their domination of elite think tanks (through board connections) and the political process (through campaign contributions). Certainly there's a lot about this that's still true; politicians would be lost without the professionals who think for them, and broke without a continuing stream of cheques from the various personifications of capital.

But that WASP ruling class now looks dissipated. Its fortune has been sliced into too many parts over the generations to be meaningful in a US stock market now capitalized at nearly $12 trillion. The *Social Register* is a shell of its former self; it's now published by a fairly *nouveau* outfit, Forbes.[9] Aside from libraries, it's available only to listees, for $125. The 2005 edition lists just 25,000 families – down from 30,000 in the mid-1990s – with a quaint geographical distribution: 27 per cent from the New York area, 11 per cent, in Pennsylvania, 10 per cent in Massachusetts, and just 8 per cent in California. According to Forbes Media's advertising tip sheet, half attended Ivy League universities, 77 per cent own multiple homes (25 per cent own three or more) but only 400 own yachts. (There's a yacht index for the readers who see the world that way. There are also indexes of descendants of passengers on the *Mayflower*, of signers of the Declaration of Independence, and of members of the Sky Castle French Hounds, a Pennsylvania hunt club.).[10] An ad page goes for $11,500, and promises access to the 'top echelon of power and wealth in America', and an 'opportunity to align with one of America's most prestigious luxury brands'. It does look like Domhoff's core of the ruling class has degenerated into a niche market – a well-appointed niche for sure, but not what it once was.[11]

Other institutional expressions of Domhoff's ruling class are in much better shape. The Council on Foreign Relations, for example, is thriving; with an imposing headquarters on Manhattan's Park Avenue, it has $205 million in assets (and just $9 million in liabilities).[12] But its deliberative style is out of fashion in the Bush years. It has, to be sure, brought some right-wingers into its orbit: Max Boot – enthusiastic celebrant of the American imperial role, signatory to the Project for a New American Century manifesto, and *Weekly Standard* contributing editor, is a national security fellow. Despite such adaptations, however, it's no longer at the centre of foreign-policy-making. It could reclaim that role someday, especially should the occupation of Iraq turn out to be an incurable disaster.

The WASP elite used to find political expression in the pre-Reagan Republican party, the party of Taft and Rockefeller; now all that's left of that are pathetic remnants like Sen. Lincoln Chafee. Writers on the left often like to focus on the rightward move of the Democrats, but the transformation of the Republican party is far more profound.[13] As Jeffrey M. Stonecash shows in *Class and Party in American Politics,* in the 1950s and 1960s the two parties were surprisingly similar, with liberal and conservative wings, and a lot in between. Among northern electoral districts, party allegiance was less correlated with income than it is today. An exception was the South, where poorer districts were heavily Democratic, but in a special way for a special reason: blacks couldn't vote and many poor whites didn't register, meaning that the party's regional base was among conservative, better-off whites.[14] Over time, white Southern Democrats evolved into Republicans, reducing the weight of the right in the Democratic party while increasing it in the

Republicans. Yes, the Democrats have moved to the right in some ways, but no Democrat today would filibuster a civil rights bill. By contrast, as a black friend once told me, most African-Americans look at a Republican and see a Klansman's bedsheet.

But since the early post-World War II decades, the Republican party has transformed itself into one of the most right-wing mainstream parties in the world, with a base now in the South and West. This reflected the revival of the right, beginning in the mid-1950s, after the losses of the 1930s and 1940s. Of course, some business interests, especially smaller ones, never accepted the New Deal, but Wall Street and the Fortune 500 had largely made peace with it.

The rebellion against this compromise was initially confined to a very marginalized right, consisting of a subset of the petite bourgeoisie and a new crop of conservative intellectuals gathered around William Buckley's *National Review* (founded in 1955). In Buckley's famous formulation, the agenda of the magazine and the movement was to stand athwart the tracks of history and yell 'Stop!' The movement gathered strength with Barry Goldwater's 1964 presidential campaign, which was an electoral disaster, but a symbol of the rising strength of the right within the Republican party. I can speak from personal experience, as a member of the Party of the Right at Yale in 1971-72, that it was still extremely odd to be a serious conservative in elite circles. There was an air of fatalism about the movement; we all took inspiration from Whittaker Chambers' remark that '[i]t is idle to talk of preventing the wreck of Western Civilization, it is already a wreck from within'.[15] Creeping socialism would continue its course until the final expropriator had been expropriated, though we wouldn't have put it quite that way.

As the 1970s progressed, however, it got progressively less weird to be on the right in elite circles. As Thomas Ferguson and Joel Rogers demonstrate in *Right Turn,* while the public had moved right on some issues, like crime and welfare, there was certainly no mandate for the sort of ruling class offensive ultimately mounted by Ronald Reagan when he took office in 1981. The driving force was the rightward move within the corporate elite, which was distressed by the collapse in corporate profitability from the Golden Age highs into the 1970s doldrums, and a general erosion of bourgeois authority that took economic form as rising inflation and bear markets in stocks and bonds, and political form in wildcat strikes, sabotage on the line, and Third World demands for a new, redistributionist global economic order.

An important part of the class war was conducted by the Republican party and Reagan, an old corporate tool of General Electric and a posse of Southern California businessmen. (Interestingly, though, the deregulation of crucial sectors like transport and communications began under Jimmy Carter,

Reagan's Democratic predecessor, with some of the intellectual energy for the movement coming out of the office of liberal stalwart Sen. Ted Kennedy.) The Reagan Democrats who voted Republican in 1980 – as some kind of phantasmic assertion of race privilege and masculine toughness – didn't expect the deep recession of 1981-82 and the union-busting agenda initiated by the mass firing of striking air traffic controllers, but they got it anyway. That agenda was greatly aided by the high-interest rate policies instituted by Paul Volcker, when he took over at the Federal Reserve in 1979 with the announcement that the American standard of living had to decline. Volcker was appointed by Carter, deepening the bipartisan roots of the late 1970s/early 1980s crackdown, but it's highly unlikely that a Democratic president would have broken a union, lowered taxes on the rich so deeply, or cut domestic spending as harshly as Reagan.

Volcker's interest-rate squeeze was broadly supported by the 'business community', and not just by financial interests, as populists sometimes claim. Central banking is one of the means by which business interests can run state policy to their advantage, largely immune to democratic accountability or even full public understanding. But there were many changes in the financial markets in the 1980s that greatly transformed class relations.

As with transport deregulation, the financial transformation had its roots in the 1970s. A milestone was Wall Street's Mayday – the May 1 1975 deregulation of commissions. That formal change helped usher in a new regime on Wall Street: the relationship gave way to the transaction. The pre-Mayday Wall Street was dominated by connections: industrial firms always dealt with the same banker, and bankers were recruited on the basis of prep school and other social connections. Fixed commissions stabilized those arrangements, as price competition was kept in check. The demise of fixed commissions, however, introduced competition into Wall Street's previously clubby world. Competition, ever the revolutionary principle of capitalism, transformed the business community.

One way to think about what's happened with the business branch of the ruling class is to extend to a social structure the formula that's often applied to the transformation of Wall Street over the last three decades (a transformation that began with the abolition of fixed commissions): the transaction has replaced the relationship. And the old model that John Kenneth Galbraith described in *The New Industrial State* – of a largely vestigial shareholding class passively assenting while professional mangers ran large businesses while aspiring mainly to a regime of secure mediocrity – has given way to a far more intense and demanding regime of profit maximization.

In the classic version of managerial capitalism first outlined by Adolph Berle and Gardiner Means in their 1932 classic, *The Modern Corporation and*

*Private Property,* shareholders had become largely incapable of influencing corporate management. Their complaints were truly heart-rending: managers could waste resources on high pay, generous staffing levels, and excessive product quality, thereby cheating shareholders out of their money. Even though share ownership was highly concentrated among the very rich, there were still too many shareholders to speak with one voice. Thirty years later, Galbraith developed this model, pronouncing profit maximization a thing of the past. Corporations were no longer run by capitalists, but by a technostructure of professional managers and engineers. In a preface to the 1967 reissue of *The Modern Corporation,* Berle described the new system as one of 'collective capitalism' – not socialism, by any means, but neither was it private enterprise as it was once understood. Keynes's goal, the euthanasia of the rentier, had been largely achieved.

No doubt this was an exaggeration; the PR that created the 'soulful corporation' had won over the liberal bourgeoisie and its intellectuals. Still, there was something to it; Wall Street was relatively quiet, and the 'business community' was dominated by the senior executives of the industrial giants.

All that came apart in the 1970s. Profit rates plummeted, inflation rose, and both the First World working class and the commodity exporters of the Third World openly resisted prevailing lines of authority. Alarmed, by the end of the decade, the vestigial stockholders of liberal mythmaking were up in arms, having lost all patience with their managers' complacent mediocrity. With the 1980s came the unleashing of the leveraging mania and the declaration of a new era of shareholder rights. For much of the decade, what Alan Greenspan once called 'unaffiliated corporate restructurers' launched attacks on established corporations that were deemed insufficiently profitable. Using billions in borrowed money, individuals like Carl Icahn and partnerships like Kohlberg Kravis Roberts either bought stakes in firms with sagging stock prices or took entire companies private.[16] Faced with outside pressure from purely financial interests to maximize profits, firms cut costs by downsizing and outsourcing, sold or shut unprofitable divisions, and in general smashing the old Galbraith paradigm. The manoeuvres typically involved lots of debt, which promoters described as a great incentive to slash spending and sell off assets, but it left corporate America in a weakened state when the boom ended in 1989.

Wall Street continued to shake up what it calls the real sector in the 1990s by switching from debt to shareholder activism, led by public pension funds like the California Public Employees Retirement System (CALPERS), which made up hit-lists of faltering corporations and pressed them to get their act together. Though the approach was different from that of the 1980s, the expectations were the same: cut costs, raise profits, and get the stock price up. To press the point, top managers were increasingly paid in stock options rather than direct salaries, in order to get them to think and act like shareholders.

It all worked, in a way. Stockholder rebellion was a major reason for the intensification of economic life from the early 1980s onwards, and the increased pressure on the world's working classes. Though it began with Wall Street attacks on managerial privilege, it ended with both branches of the capitalist family, financiers and managers, in agreement about the need to keep costs low and profits high. After a steep decline in corporate profitability between 1997 and 2001, managers were able to squeeze costs and restore profits, mainly by keeping wages and employment down. As of mid-2005, total employment in the US was about 10 million below where it would have been had the recovery/expansion followed historical averages.[17] From the recession trough through the first quarter of 2005, corporate profits rose over five times as much as employee compensation; in previous cycles, the average ratio was less than two to one.

As the bust of the early 2000s revealed, managers still had plenty of stubborn resourcefulness in them: to get profits and stock prices up, they frequently lied, and sometimes massively. They got away with it for a few years because Wall Street often believes what it wants to be true; stock buyers had every incentive to believe inflated profit reports. But, remarkably, the reforms after the bust were minimal; their legislative centerpiece was the Sarbanes-Oxley Act, which essentially required managers to swear that the financial statements are true. Complaints about onerous and expensive compliance requirements of the Act filled the business press in 2004 and 2005. In May 2005, Bush essentially fired Securities and Exchange Commission head William Donaldson for excessive zeal in policing the financial markets, and replaced him with a right-wing Republican Congressman, Christopher Cox. Donaldson was one of the founders of elite investment bank Donaldson Lufkin Jenrette, and a member of Bush's famed Yale secret society Skull and Bones; despite that establishment pedigree, he had made enemies by tightening up on mutual and hedge funds. Cox was the author a 1995 bill (passed over Clinton's veto) that made it much harder for lawyers and shareholders to sue corporations – a gift especially to high-tech companies, at the expense of entrepreneurial attorneys and activist pension funds.[18]

What does this say about the inner workings of the business community? Though the Cox-for-Donaldson trade looks like a tilt towards management and away from Wall Street, even Wall Street wasn't fond of Donaldson's oversight, and there hasn't been much complaint about his departure. Wall Street is mostly back to believing what it wants to believe. An index of 'earnings quality' compiled by Merrill Lynch, which compares managers' versions of corporate profits with underlying economic reality, is at the low end of its historical range – and, as of June 2005, getting worse – exceeded by only the worst two years of the bubble.[19] There's comity in the business community, and little overt worry about the fiscal stability or the international standing of the United States.

With the WASP elite having faded since the 1970s, what has been taking its place? Certainly, as has long been pointed out, the old northeastern WASP elite has been supplemented by forces from the South and West, who are, at least on the surface, sometimes hostile to their class elders. George W. Bush, from high-end Yankee stock, nonetheless keeps his distance from Yale to boost his Texas credentials. His father's handlers made it known that the president loved to snack on pork rinds, an incredible piece of public relations designed to convince voters he was a man of the people. His son, who pronounces 'insurance' with the accent on the first syllable, and 'vehicle' with the accent on the second, seems to need no such PR, though it's hard to believe he learned these habits at Andover, Yale, or Harvard.

But it's not just symbolism; there were real interests behind his rise from Texas to the national scene. In Texas, his prominent early supporters included some oilmen, who knew him from his failed attempts to make a living exploring for hydrocarbons in the 1980s, and Richard Rainwater, the former investment manager for the Bass brothers, the Fort Worth-based billionaires. Though Bush showed little aptitude for much beyond drinking at the time, his backers were charmed by his being the son of the vice president, and by the mid-1990s they were ready to support his bid for governor. While governor, Bush did several favours for Rainwater and his business interests. Rainwater was a founder of Columbia/HCA, a for-profit hospital chain; in 1995, Bush vetoed a Patient Protection Act that was fervently opposed by the firm. In 1997, Bush proposed privatizing Texas's state mental hospitals, while Rainwater was busy building a for-profit mental health care enterprise. Among his other crucial business supporters were Thomas Hicks, chair of Hicks, Muse, Tate, and Furst, a prominent leveraged-buyout firm, and top executives of Enron.[20] Now that George W. Bush is president, extractive and military industries seem to have a special place in the administration's heart. The oil connection is obvious; the reason that Cheney wants to keep the names of his energy advisors secret is that they all come from the industry.

Curiously, though, it doesn't seem that the oil industry was hot to start a war with Iraq.[21] But the spike in oil prices that the war contributed to has done wonders for energy sector profits.[22] And the administration's relentless efforts to lift environmental regulation have deeply pleased not only oil industry executives and shareholders, but also other rapacious industries like mining and logging. Bush has also continued to promote private medical-industrial complex interests, with the pharmaceutical industry playing an important role. Though a Kerry administration would never have proposed some kind of national health insurance scheme, Democrats are generally more likely to try to control the prices of prescription drugs, and to allow the importation of cheaper drugs from Canada, two things that drive Big Pharma crazy. Before becoming Secretary of Defense, Donald Rumsfeld was CEO of the giant drugmaker Searle.

Bush has also made lots of friends on Wall Street. Surprisingly, investment bankers have historically been an important Democratic business constituency. No longer. Wall Street swung heavily into the Republican column in 2004. Goldman Sachs, which produced former Clinton Treasury Secretary Robert Rubin as well as Jon Corzine, the New Jersey Democrat who is one of the Senate's most liberal members, is now run by a Republican, Hank Paulsen. The major reason seems to be Bush's finance-friendly tax cuts.[23] By contrast, Kerry had much thinner support from the business community. His big-money support came mostly from lawyers, who hate the Republicans for trying to make it harder for citizens to sue businesses for damages; from lobbyists with historic ties to Democratic administrations; and from Hollywood, which hates the Republicans for their puritanism. It looks like the business community's interest in the 2004 election was driven less by matters of macro policy and more by specific sectoral and personal interests.

Under Bush, there's been one major victory in a long-standing struggle by business interests: a major 'reform' of the US bankruptcy code. For most of its history, the US has been a debtor-friendly regime. With the explosion of consumer credit in the 1980s and 1990s, the number of Americans filing for bankruptcy rose dramatically – from around 300,000 a year in the early 1980s to over a million by 1996. The credit industry grew ever-more agitated by the insolvency boom. Instead of reflecting on the contribution of their aggressive marketing and usurious interest rates to the situation, they blamed an indulgent legal system and an erosion in morals, and began an intense lobbying campaign to tighten the law. Although a reform bill got through Congress in 2000, Clinton vetoed it in the last weeks of his term. But in 2004 a substantially similar bill – which, for the first time, applied an income test to those seeking to have their debts wiped away – was signed by Bush.

The finance sector hasn't done so well with another of its long-term obsessions: privatization of the Social Security system. Though it looked for a while like it might be smooth sailing for privatization in the first year of Bush's second term, the scheme attracted surprising popular opposition. As privatization became more politically radioactive, a number of brokerage houses dropped out of the lobbying effort. It's reassuring to see that business interests can't shove just anything down the public's throat.

When looked at from some angles, you'd think that Wall Street might have problems with part of the Bush program. Fiscal policy has been disastrous. According to Congressional Budget Office estimates, Washington went from a structural surplus of 1.6 per cent of GDP (i.e. adjusted for the stage of the of the business cycle) to a deficit of 3.0 per cent of GDP in 2004, a shift of 4.6 percentage points, far bigger than the shift during the Reagan years (though that deterioration was from small deficits becoming very large ones). There's little hope of improving the fiscal position – and it could get worse, if the administration and Congress indulge their desires for more tax cuts.

You might think that a serious bourgeoisie would be alarmed at this accumulation of debt. You might even think that the investors who own over $4 trillion in outstanding US Treasury obligations might be nervously annoyed to hear the President dismiss the Treasury bonds held by the Social Security trust fund as mere pieces of paper – it almost makes you wonder if the unilateralists in the administration would deal with any serious dollar crisis by defaulting. But that hasn't happened. You might also think that US multinationals might be disturbed that Bush's foreign policy is doing some collateral economic damage (something that's has been covered assiduously in London's *Financial Times*, but hardly at all in the American papers). Harassment of foreign students is discouraging them from studying at US universities, even though they're normally good both for university incomes and for intellectual life. Visa restrictions are hurting the import of skilled workers, and several Chinese firms pulled out of the annual Consumer Electronics Show in Las Vegas because Washington wouldn't give them visas. That came a month after a third of Chinese applicants for visas to attend an economics conference in Seattle were denied entry. None of this can be helpful for commerce in conventional terms, and it doesn't sound good for the culture either.

And US multinationals also seem to be suffering from the US's declining image in the world, especially in Old Europe. American names like Coca-Cola, McDonald's, GM, Disney, Wal-Mart, and The Gap all reported declines in European sales as 2004 progressed – and among the hardest-hit was that iconic product intimately associated with the lone cowboy, Marlboro. The companies prefer to attribute this to 'nonpolitical' factors, like unemployment, taxes, and regulation (as if those were nonpolitical), but the breadth of the declines looks like more than coincidence. Keith Reinhard, chair of advertising giant DDB Worldwide, told the *Financial Times* that his sense is 'we are seeing a transfer of anger and resentment from foreign policies to things American'. Pollster John Zogby detects 'growing hostility towards American products'.

Bush's focus on military and political power, and his relative lack of interest in global economics, has also allowed substantial bits of Latin America to wander off the neoliberal path. Argentina successfully cut payments to its private bondholders with no retribution. In Venezuela, Hugo Chavez survives US efforts to undermine him, and the Organization of American States has resisted Washington's attempts to isolate his regime. Uprisings in Ecuador and Bolivia have toppled neoliberal governments. Nothing like the Clinton administration's tireless campaign to open foreign financial and product markets has been mounted by Bush. His economic appointments have all been somewhere between mediocre and terrible.

The American bourgeoisie, or at least its business class, doesn't seem to have a problem with any of this. It was solidly behind Bush's re-election campaign. Questioned at an October 2004 election-themed event at the Council on Foreign Relations, JP Morgan Chase chief economist John Lipsky said he wasn't worried about the deficit because he thought a second Bush adminis-tration could make the necessary spending cuts to solve the problem.[24] That's delusional; it would be politically impossible – and almost mathematically impossible – for that to happen, and it's a bit shocking to hear someone of Lipsky's presumed sophistication say something so nonsensical. There's just not enough civilian discretionary spending in the federal budget to cut. But, as of mid-2005, Wall Street was remarkably sanguine about the US fiscal deficit (and the current account deficit as well, but that's another story).

Why? Shouldn't Wall Street be worried about Bush's fiscal recklessness? In the short to medium term, finance houses have an interest in an expand-ing quantity of US Treasury paper; it gives them more inventory to trade and repackage creatively. But over the longer term, adherents to almost any school of economics, except maybe the dreamier post-Keynesian ones, view chronic deficits as dangerous to an economy's health (and even its political stability).

A provisional answer might be that the distinction between the 'business community' and the ruling class has largely disappeared, and that policy is now made through a Wall Street lens of maximizing profits over the next few quarters, and the long term can take care of itself. I say provisional because things could change, and because socialists should be careful about thinking they could offer capitalists better strategies for running capitalism. It must be admitted that the capitalists have longevity and success on their side. But nothing, and no one, is perfect, and it's worth thinking about this.

Let's take a look at Alan Greenspan's Federal Reserve, an institution that is supposed to be an executive committee of the bourgeoisie *par excellence*.[25] Greenspan's reputation is that of a candidate for sainthood on Wall Street. No wonder; his tenure has been one of relentless indulgence of bank mergers and speculative manias, and the rapid mounting of a bailout when things go wrong. His aggressive support after the 1987 stock market crash, understandable in itself, gave the green light to the last two years of the leveraging mania of the 1980s – massive and pointless hostile takeovers, balance sheet 'restructurings' that fed cash to shareholders financed by large servings of fresh debt, the final *jouissance* of the savings and loans. When that mania went off the rails, leading to the long recession of the early 1990s and the first 'jobless recovery', Greenspan lowered interest rates dramatically and kept them there. While that too was understandable, it laid the foundation for the long speculative mania of the late 1990s. Greenspan did worry publicly about 'irrational exuberance' in December 1996 – burying the phrase in the midst of a tedious speech on central banking with the phrase itself buried in a tortured question – and after taking loads of heat, he didn't speak publicly again about the market for months. When he did resume talking about the market, it was mainly to dismiss worries about a bubble and celebrate the productivity miracle of a New Economy.[26]

Anyone who was awake during the bubble years remembers well the 'Greenspan put' – the widespread belief that the Fed would put a floor under stock prices.[27] And when that mania went off the rails, Greenspan again lowered interest rates hard and long. Low rates helped keep the economy from imploding, but the bubble's hangover (excessive investment, especially in high-tech equipment; ravaged balance sheets; and badly bruised animal spirits) were a heavy drag on recovery. But even as the supply side of the economy was stagnating, with the second-worst GDP growth performance and the worst rate of job growth of ten post–World War II expansions, low rates ignited another mania: speculation in residential property. House prices in hot metropolitan areas exploded, and US consumers borrowed $2.2 trillion against rising home equity between 2000 and 2004.[28] Any decline in house prices or serious rise in interest rates could put millions of households in financial hot water – but, once again, Greenspan has denied that there's a housing bubble.

You could argue that Greenspan had little choice but indulgence after the panics of 1987, 1990, and 2000, but as Hyman Minsky used to say, stability is destabilizing. Every bailout emboldens speculators during the next upswing. In his seventeen-year tenure, Greenspan has done little to dampen speculation, through either policy or speech (or even, it seems, through private suasion). Such indulgence is totally out of character for a central banker. In the 1960s, then-Fed chair William McChesney Martin – famous for remarking that his job was to remove the punchbowl just as the party was getting going – held that widespread talk of New Eras was a sign that speculation was getting dangerously out of control. Greenspan cheers on New Eras. They're lots of fun if you're one of the winners. But something has changed when a central banker considers it his job to spike the punchbowl, and administer hair of the dog if revellers wake up the next morning feeling a little rocky.

This isn't an endorsement of the traditional sado-monetarism of central bankers, an approach that lives on at the European Central Bank, which maintains its anti-inflation vigilance with half the continent's economies in or near recession. But it does suggest that the distinction between the American ruling class and its business community – with the ruling class presumably operating on a time scale of decades rather than quarters – has largely collapsed.

Another piece of evidence supporting this hypothesis is the reaction to Bush's tax cuts. In the late 1990s, a union economist recounted a conversation he'd had with two Fortune 500 CEOs. After reminding them that profitability was the highest it had been since the 1960s, the stock market in the midst of a seemingly endless bull run, and the political environment exceedingly friendly towards corporate interests, he asked them why they hated Clinton so much. Their answer was simple: 'He raised our taxes'. And he had. According to Congressional Budget Office estimates, the average effective tax rate on the top 1 per cent of the income distribution rose from 25.5 per cent in 1986 to 36.0 per cent in 1996 – an increase of roughly $100,000. Bush's cuts knocked their tax rates back to nearly 1986 levels (26.7 per cent in 2004).[29] Tax cuts for those at less elite levels, those with incomes in the low- to mid-six figures, were less dramatic, but still not insignificant: almost $7,700 for the top quintile, those with average incomes of $183,000. This helps explain both Bush's strong support from the 'business community' and his increased electoral support among affluent households: he carried voters with household incomes above $100,000 by 11 percentage points in 2000 – and 17 points in 2004.

Tax cuts and deregulation have been like psychotropic drugs for the American business class and the households who live on returns to capital. But the economic model has an unsustainable look about it. US net foreign debt was 34 per cent of GDP in the first quarter of 2005; it was just 18 per cent in 2000, 10 per cent in 1990, roughly 0 per cent in 1980 – a sharp contrast with the surplus of 3 per cent in 1969.[30] It cannot keep running huge fiscal and current account deficits forever. That's not to say the US is headed for some sort of major smashup, as many leftists (and Hayekians) argue. But it does mean a retrenchment – some sort of homegrown structural adjustment program – that the present business community and its political system seem incapable of conceiving, much less imposing. The reaction to Social Security privatization suggests that smooth political sailing is hardly guaranteed. Maybe the historical task of Hillary Clinton – former corporate lawyer, former Wal-Mart director – will be to calm the waters as the austerity program is launched.

## NOTES

1    This is almost entirely about the US business community. That's embar-
     rassingly provincial, but writing about something more global would be
     too ambitious. While it's true that the upper reaches of the American
     bourgeoisie have substantially internationalized, their political engage-
     ment is heavily domestic.

2    Pew Center on Climate Change website www.pewclimate.org/what_s_
     being_done/in_the_business_community/, accessed on April 24, 2005.

3    Milton Friedman, 'The Business Community's Suicidal Impulse', Cato
     Policy Report, March/April 1999, www.cato.org/pubs/policy_report/
     v21n2/friedman.html.

4    Roland Marchand, *Creating the Corporate Soul: The Rise of Public Relations
     and Corporate Imagery in American Big Business*, Berkeley: University of
     California Press, 1998.

5    Quoted in Ibid., p. 74.

6    Bhushan Bahree and Jeffrey Ball, 'Oil Giants Face new Competition for
     Future Supplies', *Wall Street Journal,* 19 April 2005, p. A1.

7    Richard Tomkins, 'Brands Are the New Religion, Says Ad Agency',
     *Financial Times*, 1 March 2001, p. 4, and Rochelle Burbury, 'Mind Games',
     *The Fin* (supplement to the weekend *Australian Financial Review*), 21-22
     July 2001, p. 5.

8    See the discussion of Lev in Doug Henwood, *After the New Economy*,
     New York: New Press, 2005, chapter 1.

9    On the recent fate of the *Social Register,* see Cecil Adams, 'How do you
     get listed in the Social Register?', www.straightdope.com/classics/
     a5_032.html; Shelley Emling, 'Social Register less influential in egali-
     tarian times; Directory's "days not numbered", Forbes insists', *Atlanta
     Journal-Constitution*, 21 June 2002, p. 2E; and Ruth La Ferla, 'Courting
     Park Avenue, One Socialite at a Time', *New York Times*, 6 February 2005,
     section 9, p. 1.

10   The *Social Register* rate card is at www.forbesmedia.com/pdf/
     socregistertoolkitsheet.pdf

11   A personal anecdote: my mother-in-law, who is from an upper-class
     WASP family in Baltimore, says her mother took the *Social Register* very
     seriously, and urged her daughter to fill out the information card that
     would assure her listing. She refused, thinking the whole thing a cross
     between a relic and a joke.

12   Council on Foreign Relations, *2004 Annual Report*, p. 74. The operat-
     ing budget for *Foreign Affairs* alone in 2004 was $5.2 million – but the
     magazine is impressively profitable, since revenue was $6.6 million on a

circulation of 134,000. By contrast, *The Weekly Standard,* the magazine that thinks for the Bush administration, survives only on subsidies from its owner, Rupert Murdoch.

13  Narratives of the Democrats' rightward move often play down the role of business interests in the party. In *Right Turn,* Ferguson and Rogers emphasize the importance of capital-intensive internationalizing business interests in the New Deal; opposition to Roosevelt came heavily from low-wage, low-margin businesses, who hated unions and minimum wage laws. The Kennedy and Johnson administrations were richly involved with the business community; names like Harriman and Dillon are shared by investment banks and 1960s Democratic cabinet members.

14  Jeffrey M. Stonecash, *Class and Party in American Politics,* Boulder: Westview, 2000, p. 45.

15  The full quote is wonderfully over the top: 'It is idle to talk of preventing the wreck of Western Civilization, it is already a wreck from within. That is why we can do little more now than snatch a fingernail of a saint from the wrack, or a handful of ashes from the fagots, and bury them secretly in a flower pot against that day, ages hence, when a few men begin again to dare to believe that there once was something else, that something else is thinkable, and need some evidence of what it was, and the fortifying knowledge that there were those who, at the great nightfall, took loving thought to preserve the tokens of hope and truth'. As a measure of the change in the ideological atmosphere, the quote now appears on the website of Rep. John Linder, a Georgia Republican, http://linder.house.gov.

16  Early in the decade, large investors shunned the leverage artists, considering them dangerous and unseemly. But as the decade progressed, public pension funds and insurance companies happily invested in buyout and restructuring funds.

17  This somewhat shocking deficiency of 10 million jobs is based on comparing recent history (from November 2001 through May 2005) to an average of nine earlier post-World War II recovery/expansion cycles. Average employment gain 42 months after a trough (which is what May 2005 was) +9.8 per cent, compared with just 1.9 per cent through May 2005. Translated into numbers, that gap amounts to 10.3 million.

18  Litigators and public pension fund managers lean Democratic, so Cox's bill and Clinton's veto were part of a partisan war.

19  Merrill Lynch, '"GAAP Gap" Update – EPS Quality Deteriorates Slightly More', *U.S. Strategy Update,* 13 June 2005.

20  Background on Bush's Texas supporters comes from Center for Public

Integrity, 'How George W. Bush Scored Big With The Texas Rangers', 18 January 2000, and Center for Public Integrity, 'The Buying of the President 2000', 5 January 2000.

21   Raad AlKadiri of PFC Energy, a Washington-based consultancy, said the industry did not support the war, in an interview on my radio program, 'Behind the News' WBAI, New York, 3 April 2003; archived at www.leftbusinessobserver.com/Radio_1.html#030403.

22   Though one can never know for sure, the oil spike is probably the result of a combination of factors: anxiety about the war; generalized political anxieties about the region; strong demand growth from China, India, and the US; and tight supplies, thanks in part to low exploration budgets (kept low under pressure from Wall Street to pass the cash along to shareholders instead).

23   Though this is a rather sensitive area, a lot of Democratic support on Wall Street came from Jews, who feel an affinity with the party's cultural liberalism, and who historically felt snubbed by the old, heavily Republican, WASP elite.

24   This observation occurred during the question and answer session following the regular presentation. While a transcript of the regular session is available on the CFR website http://cfr.org/pub7466/daniel_k_tarullo_john_p_lipsky_stephen_roach_peter_hooper/world_economic_update.php, the Q&A isn't. I was there and heard the remark.

25   Christopher Rude, formerly an economist at the Federal Reserve Bank of New York, once told me that within the Fed it's thought that politicians and bankers come and go, but central bankers are supposed to do the long-term thinking for the class.

26   The 'irrational exuberance' speech is at www.federalreserve.gov/boarddocs/speeches/1996/19961205.htm. For typical Greenspan comments on the bubble, see www.federalreserve.gov/boarddocs/testimony/1999/19990617.htm and www.federalreserve.gov/boarddocs/speeches/1999/19990827.htm

27   A 'put' is an option to sell a stock or other security at a given price for a given time. For example, an IBM April 70 put would give you the right to sell shares of IBM at $70 a share between now and next April. The simplest use of a put is to buy one to offset the risk of a decline in a security's price; much more complex uses are possible.

28   The estimate of home equity withdrawal comes from Goldman Sachs, *Daily Economic Commentary*, 14 March 2004.

29   Average income in the top 1 per cent was $1,050,000 in 2001.

30   These estimates come from the Federal Reserve's flow of funds accounts

www.federalreserve.gov/releases/z1/, table L.1. Adding net holdings in foreign direct investment and foreign equities reduces the depth of the red ink somewhat, but doesn't reduce the trend of substantial deterioration.

# THE TRUTH ABOUT WELFARE REFORM

## FRANCES FOX PIVEN
## AND BARBARA EHRENREICH

For nearly three decades, most Republicans, conservative think tanks, the right-wing media, the Christian right, and even a good many Democrats have been fulminating about a program known in the United States as 'welfare'. The numbers of people on the program rise and fall, the actual name of the program changes, but the fixation on welfare does not much change. Presumably, overly generous cash assistance to poor women and their children coddles these women, leading to a host of social problems, ranging from idleness to out-of-wedlock births and broken families, crime and truancy, and even poverty itself.

In fact, even at its peak, the program that provided cash assistance to the very poor was quite small, reaching fewer than 5 million families, or 5 per cent of the population, two-thirds of them children. The costs were low, about one per cent of the federal budget, and perhaps three to four per cent of most state budgets. With welfare 'reform' in 1996, those already low numbers declined dramatically, to the point where there are only two million families in the program.

Yet the hullabaloo continues. In early 2004, Nexis listed 21 times as many articles in major newspapers on 'welfare' as on 'unemployment insurance' and 68 times as many hits as a search under 'Family and Medical Leave Act' and 'paid family leave'.[1] And the congress continues to try to toughen the already draconian conditions for assistance. Republicans are pushing for more required working hours for mothers on the program, and for reduced block grants to the states so that less money is available to support working mothers with benefits such as childcare. Why has this small program become so focal in American politics?

The answer, we think, is that the organized right made welfare and welfare recipients into a foil to cover their real targets: (1) the larger programs, including medicaid and unemployment insurance which benefit far larger numbers of Americans, and social security which benefits almost all Americans; and (2) the political culture undergirding those programs, with its implicit ideals of social cohesion and mutual responsibility. There were good reasons for this strategy. The people on welfare were already marginalized, and vulnerable. Paupers have always been a despised caste in western societies. Add to this longstanding distaste the fact that, in the wake of the mass migration of African Americans from the rural south to the urban north and the protests that ensued in the 1960s, welfare had become a disproportionately black and Hispanic program (although the plurality of recipients were non-Hispanic whites.) The presidential campaigns of Barry Goldwater and George Wallace registered this fact and demonstrated the political uses of racism even in the north. 'Welfare' became a code-word to evoke and mobilize rising white racial hatreds.

At the same time, changes in sexual mores and family structure were stirring a backlash of popular anxieties, anxieties that were fuelled even more by the rise of the feminist movement. Since most recipients were single mothers in what was judged to be the 'matriarchal' subculture of the poor, they were easily deployed as a symbol of all that was wrong with America. Ronald Reagan made the image of the 'welfare queen' a staple of American popular culture; and right-wing intellectuals agonized over the presumed promiscuity of welfare recipients. This was the politics of spectacle, a spectacle designed to evoke and intensify popular antipathies against Democrats, against blacks, against liberals, against unruly and 'licentious' women, and against government, or at least those parts of government that provided support to poor and working people. In the background and out of the spotlight was the longer term campaign of the organized right to defeat and dismantle the New Deal/Great Society political order.

## THE WINNING OF THE NEW DEAL/GREAT SOCIETY ORDER

The New Deal/Great Society order was established during the middle decades of the twentieth century, from the 1930s until the 1970s, when the United States developed something approaching a modern European-style welfare state. Two great episodes of protest punctuated the era. It began with the social movements of labour, the aged and the unemployed in the 1930s, and it ended when the protest movements of African Americans, the urban poor, women and environmental activists of the 1960s and early 1970s subsided.

In the 1930s, new programs were inaugurated that provided cash income and 'in-kind' supports such as housing for the poor. In 1935, the federal government threw its support behind collective bargaining, and unions grew, especially in the mass production industries. A minimum wage was legislated, along with a maximum hours law that guaranteed many workers higher overtime pay. The transactions of banks and investors were subject to closer regulation. To be sure, all these programs were flawed. The aged who depended on social security were still poor, many of them subsisting on day-old bakery goods. Little low-income housing was actually built. Workplaces were still not really safe, and in any case, the regulations ignored the physical dangers of new occupations. Innovative schemes for financial manipulation evaded static regulations. And so on. Still, life for most Americans became a little more secure, a little less dangerous.

The resurgence of protest movements in the 1960s led to the resurgence of welfare state initiatives. The protests were spearheaded by the black freedom movement which began in the South as a movement for civil rights, and then spread to the cities of the North where it became a kind of poverty rights movement. A vulnerable Democratic administration responded with the liberalization of the 1930s programs, as well as the creation of new programs that provided nutritional supplements, health care, and subsidized housing for the poor. Moreover, the black freedom movement became a template for other movements, among women, environmentalists, and youth. Industry was required to meet environmental and workplace safety standards, and even hiring practices were regulated to reduce racial and gender discrimination.

When the smoke had cleared, the accomplishments of the movements could be tallied. Between 1930 and the 1970s, income and wealth concentration had plummeted by half.[2] Racial discrimination certainly did not disappear, and African Americans lagged sharply behind whites economically. Their unemployment rates remained twice as high, they were much more likely to be poor, and their net worth was a small fraction of their white counterparts.[3] But however precariously, a good number of blacks were making their way into the middle class, and they had also become voters and acknowledged participants in American political and cultural life.[4]

Even limited and conditional programs contributed to an ongoing transformation in American political culture. The large role that the national government had tried to play in coping with the Great Depression, and especially its initiatives in extending assistance to the poor and working class, changed the way that people thought about government, and therefore changed the basis of their political allegiance. In the nineteenth century, American political parties had perfected the tribalist and clientelist strategies that mobilized high levels of popular electoral participation while insulating voters from the central policy issues of the day. In the New Deal/Great Society order,[5] however, voter support depended less on tribalist and clientelist appeals, and more on assessments of whether the regime was contributing to widespread economic well-being. This was no small achievement. The public held elected officials responsible for their economic well-being, and the initiatives of the 1960s strengthened that strand in popular thought. Political scientists began to take for granted that election results could be predicted from indicators like unemployment rates, or social security benefit levels, or changes in personal income.[6] The phenomenon was called, somewhat disparagingly, 'pocket-book politics'. But pocket-book politics, if it meant the pocketbooks of all the people, was a step toward a more democratic society.

There was also a collectivist dimension to the new political culture. The very fact that popular economic well-being was now considered a government responsibility – as opposed to the personal responsibility embedded in the Protestant ethic, and later celebrated in the propaganda of the organized right – implied as much. This idea of mutuality, of collective responsibility, was underlined by programs like social security where the payroll taxes of active workers literally paid the pensions of those workers who had retired. And imagine, the program was wildly popular! A degree of mutuality and collective responsibility was also reflected in the growth of non-governmental insurance schemes like Blue Cross and employment-based pension plans.

## THE CAMPAIGN TO DEMOLISH
## THE NEW DEAL/GREAT SOCIETY ORDER

American business and its allies on the organized right had always opposed these initiatives. But the catastrophe of the Great Depression, the political exposes of business wrongdoing to which it led, and the tumult and threat power of the protest movements of the decade combined to strip business of much of its influence in the 1930s.[7] Subsequently the extraordinary profits that American business enjoyed during and after World War II helped to relax opposition to the New Deal programs. After all, the US was the only major industrial power to emerge from the war relatively unscathed, and for 25 years American corporations dominated world markets. To be sure, in the absence of protest, prosperity did not lead to the expansion or improvement of New Deal initiatives. Income support programs remained meagre, and the legislative protections of unions were rolled back with the Taft-Hartley and Landrum-Griffith Acts. Harry Truman's proposal for national health insurance was killed by the American Medical Association, and subsidized housing programs shrank.

Still, this low intensity war notwithstanding, the New Deal order was not dismantled, and in fact those working people who were in the unionized mass production industries did well, which is why the period is often characterized as an era of 'labour accord', or the era of the American social compact. Moreover, when riots spread across American cities in the 1960s, business also went along with the expansion of the American welfare state.

On November 8, 1954, Dwight Eisenhower had written to his brother Edgar Newton Eisenhower:

Should any political party attempt to abolish social security, unemployment insurance, and eliminate labor laws and farm programs,
you would not hear of that party again in our political history.
There is a tiny splinter group, of course, that believes you can do
these things. Among them are H.L. Hunt (you possibly know his
background), a few other Texas oil millionaires, and an occasional
politician or business man from other areas. Their number is negligible and they are stupid.[8]

As Eisenhower indicated, business opposition to the New Deal was muted,
for a time. But as the movements of the 1960s subsided, longstanding nascent
business opposition to the New Deal/Great Society order reemerged.

It was not just that the movements were no longer a threat. American business was in trouble. As Europe and Japan recovered, American corporations
faced the unfamiliar prospect of tight competition with goods manufactured
elsewhere, and this at a time when they were carrying the costs of the higher
wages, more generous social programs, and workplace and environmental
regulation which the turbulent 1960s had produced. By the early 1970s, with
profit margins narrowing and the memory of the tumultuous sixties fading,
the sorts of business leaders that Eisenhower had disparaged as marginal and
stupid were leading a conservative counter-assault that, as it gained momentum, threatened to wipe out the reforms of both the New Deal and the
Great Society.

The agenda of the campaign is by now familiar: shift the brunt of taxation
from business and the affluent to working people, and from capital to wages;
dismantle the environmental and workplace regulations that so irritated business and also cost them money; reduce worker power by weakening unions,
eviscerating regulatory protections of workers, largely through non-enforce-
ment; and roll back income support programs so as to drive more people into
the labor force and the scramble for work, and also keep them anxious and
vulnerable about their jobs and their wages.

Wage cuts and social benefit cuts obviously drive more people to seek
work, often as part-timers or temps. Immigration policies that leave the
borders relatively open, but bar immigrants from social welfare protections,
also contribute to an abundance of workers, even though the administration that presides over these policies simultaneously indulges the vigilante
Minutemen who recently undertook to patrol the Mexican border. So does
the assault on pensions enlarge the numbers looking for work. As the private
plans won by unionized workers from their employers after World War II
were shifted from defined-benefit pensions to lower cost undefined ones
(401Ks), employers saved money but pension benefits shrank. At the same

time, employer-controlled pension funds became the target of plunder by management. As retirement benefits plummet, inevitably more of the old will continue to work.[9]

Over time, as the campaign gained momentum and scored successes, the agenda became more ambitious, and greedier. Not only were the social programs to be slashed, but what remained of them was targeted as another arena for profitability through publicly subsidized privatization. Families squeezed between stagnant wages and rising costs resorted increasingly to borrowing, and record numbers were driven into bankruptcy. Then, in an effort spearheaded by the banks and credit card companies, even the protections to ordinary families offered by bankruptcy law were rolled back.

The agenda was promoted by a multi-pronged strategy including the buildup of the lobbying capacity of business through the creation of new peak organizations, the revival of sleepy older organizations like the Chamber of Commerce and industry trade groups, and the buildup of a business political war machine on Washington D.C.'s K Street. The campaign also worked hard, and more or less successfully, to fold in a growing populist right based in the fundamentalist churches. The emergence of the Christian right and affiliated movements to outlaw abortion and encourage gun ownership were rooted in anxieties provoked by cultural changes associated with the 1960s. But as a matter of practical politics, those anxieties and the political energies they generated were largely put to work in the campaign to dismantle the New Deal/Great Society order.

The message machine created by the campaign helped to seal this odd alliance. The organized right, it is often said, launched a war of ideas, and the main ideas were a hybrid of market fundamentalism and Christian fundamentalism. Market fundamentalism is of course simply old-fashioned laissez faire, a doctrine in which the individual stands naked and unprotected before market forces and market 'law'. Christian fundamentalism also strips the individual of communal and political supports, although now the individual stands naked and unprotected before God, and God's law. Industrial Areas Foundation community organizer Mike Gecan writes:

> The religious resonance is reinforced by an economic resonance that is also deep and powerful. The president's 'ownership society' is based on a vision of an individual who is capable of having a direct and personal relationship with the market. An individual should have control over his or her own economic destiny – should be able to own a home rather than renting, work for a private business rather than for the government, save money for retirement rather than expecting the government or an employer to make

the arrangements …. The president is asserting that the individual person or family doesn't need mediating institutions and programs …. [T]hese institutions and programs have disrupted the development of the hoped-for relationship between the person and the market, just as many believers feel that denomination and religious bureaucracies impede the growth of the personal relationship with God.[10]

While confounded liberals often mourn that the right had new ideas, neither of these tenets was actually new at all, of course. What was new was the deliberate and strategic creation of an apparatus to promulgate these ideas. With a handful of small right-wing foundations in the lead, a new infrastructure of think tanks, public intellectuals, periodicals, societies, right-wing media and university outposts was constructed. New media outlets were established, and mainstream media journalists and executives were harassed and intimidated, charged with being 'liberal', or more recently, insufficiently patriotic.[11] The rhetoric of welfare reform, with its signature slogan of personal responsibility, played a significant role in this campaign. Some of the best known luminaries in the pantheon of right-wing conservative intellectuals made their name through diatribes against welfare, including George Gilder, Charles Murray, and Marvin Olasky.

Together, this alliance of business and the populist right took over the Republican party, pouring new money into the electoral campaigns of hard-right candidates, and pushing older-style conservatives to the margins. But the real measure of its political success was in its influence on the Democratic party that had, for all its internal conflicts, and however reluctantly, championed the New Deal/Great Society order. Franklin Delano Roosevelt had talked of 'strong central government as a haven of refuge to the individual'.[12] But in the 1990s, the Democrats jettisoned this key tenet of the New Deal/Great Society – largely because of the success of the right-wing campaign against welfare.

That campaign had succeeded in turning welfare into a metaphor for African Americans, sexual license, and liberalism. In 1992, Bill Clinton made his bid for the presidency on the slogan of 'ending welfare as we know it', and when the Republicans held his feet to the fire with their proposal for rolling back welfare called the Personal Responsibility and Work Opportunity Reconciliation Act, he followed the advice of his pollsters and consultants and signed the measure. This was in 1996, when Clinton campaigned again for the presidency, following the advice of his consultant Dick Morris to 'fast-forward the Gingrich agenda'.[13] 'Progressives', argued Clinton pollster Stanley B. Greenberg, 'needed to transcend welfare politics'.[14] The Democratic strategy, in a nutshell, was to beat the Republicans by adopting their positions.

The new welfare legislation essentially turned the administration of welfare over to the states, with the proviso that welfare receipt was limited to five years in a lifetime, and that at least half of the women on the rolls were also working. More important, since federal funding was now in the form of a lump-sum block grant, the states had a financial incentive to limit access to welfare assistance. This they did. Under the banner of 'work first', access to benefits was made more difficult,[15] and staying on the rolls was also harder since the sanctions of benefit cuts or termination were freely used to punish recipients and their children for one or another sort of transgression of increasingly complex rules, or for failing to meet the terms of individualized 'contracts' they were required to sign.[16]

Welfare reform itself was cruel, but its impact was necessarily limited, because few families had been long term welfare recipients in the first place. The message about the degraded, even pathological, character of the people who depended on welfare had a far wider reach, however. For example, the theme of 'personal responsibility' resurfaced in early 2005 in the build-up to the passage of a new bankruptcy law which eliminates the possibility of a fresh start for debtors in the poor and middle classes (unsurprisingly, the law leaves loopholes for wealthy debtors).

With its emphasis on 'personal responsibility' as opposed to the supposedly degrading forms of 'dependency', welfare reform was an attack on the New Deal/Great Society ideas of collective responsibility, and smoothed the way for the agenda of upward income redistribution that was always the goal of the right's campaign. The harping on welfare helped to discredit other and bigger income support and in-kind programs, including unemployment insurance, old age and disability insurance, nutritional and health supports, and housing subsidies. Simultaneously of course it served to discredit 'liberalism' and the Democratic party that had once been its champion.

## THE VICIOUS CIRCLE OF RIGHT WING POLICIES

The results are obvious. Income and wealth inequality are soaring. The top one per cent grabbed 38.4 per cent of the total increase in income between 1979 and 2000. The bottom 20 per cent took home 0.8 per cent. In 2001, the richest one per cent owned 44.8 per cent of all common stock (excluding pensions); the poorest 80 per cent owned 5.8 per cent. Since then, the Bush tax cuts have channelled more money to the very rich. The purchasing power of the minimum wage is worth 25 per cent less than in 1967, and more than one in four workers are earning less than a poverty wage. But CEO pay has soared,[17] and so have profits. The United States is far more class-polarized, certainly in income terms, than other industrial nations.[18] Moreover, it is on the low end of international comparisons of social mobility.[19]

Class polarization, abetted by Republican anti-welfare-state policies, has the effect of further undercutting the old ideals of collective responsibility and mutual assistance. Rather than rub shoulders with the increasing impoverished working class, the upper middle class tend to retreat into their own world of privatized goods and services. They send their children to private schools, to avoid both the crumbling public schools and the impecunious children who crowd them. They avoid public transportation and parks. They even shop in different settings, as the mass market of the postwar years has segmented decisively into discount stores, on the one hand, and luxury purveyors on the other. As the wealthy withdraw from public services and spaces, they come to resent supporting such social goods through their taxes. It's hard to feel solidarity with people you do not normally encounter, unless as servants, or that you encounter uneasily and even fearfully.

The Republican answer to rising poverty and widening class divisions is to promote what they call the 'ownership society', in which risks are not shared but confronted individually. This goal is expressed in their efforts to replace public pensions with private investment accounts, and health insurance with 'medical savings accounts', or subsidized rental housing with home ownership. The ownership society is also a justification for the spread of various stock ownership pension schemes. One consequence is obviously to put at risk the benefits that workers and the poor were more or less guaranteed under New Deal/Great Society programs. But there is another perhaps more insidious consequence as workers with pitifully small stock accounts are encouraged to turn away from collective efforts to improve pensions or health care or housing programs in favour of playing in a market in which they are unlikely to survive, much less grow rich.

So the policy direction initiated by welfare reform has set in motion a vicious cycle: cuts in social spending, along with upwardly redistributive tax policies, exacerbate the poverty of the poor and a large portion of the working class, deepening the rift between the classes and further weakening appeals to collective responsibility. Instead of public spending for social welfare, we get ever-rising spending for law enforcement and prisons to house the noncompliant poor. The result is a society increasingly divided between gated communities, on the one hand, and trailer parks and tenements on the other – a society in which traditional notions of the 'common good' can only seem quaint.

Growing hardship among the lower classes, combined with the ever-present spectacle of enormous wealth, might be expected to lead to political unrest and even insurgency. The American working class has seen its real wages decline since the turn of the century; more families are dependent on two wage-earners for survival; and more wage-earners – 90 per cent more since 1973 – must hold more than one job. Welfare reform, combined with cuts in other social services, guarantee that there is no way out for hard-pressed families at the bottom: they must exemplify the Protestant work ethic even more than the upper classes who most vigorously espouse it – and usually at the expense of any kind of family involvement. Multiple jobs, lack of adequate childcare, and long commutes from neighbourhoods containing (barely) affordable housing to distant work sites generate a host of problems from routine sleep deprivation to child neglect.

## RELIGION AND THE WELFARE STATE

But economic misery does not necessarily translate into progressive political activism. As organizations like unions and local Democratic Party clubs have declined, hard-pressed Americans have turned to religion, and especially to politically right-leaning evangelical and often fundamentalist Protestant churches. The Bush administration sees the evangelical churches as a central source of political support, and worked strenuously to mobilize their membership for the 2004 election. Through the administration's 'faith-based' social service initiatives, individual churches receive public money to expand their social services and hence their membership. In turn, church leaders urge their parishioners to vote Republican or at least to vote against candidates who favour abortion and gay rights, meaning of course Democrats. So another vicious cycle has been set in motion: declining public services push people toward the churches, which in turn promote a political agenda involving still further decreases in public services. As this process continues, the outcome – which would seem to contradict the outlook of secular advocates of untrammelled free enterprise – is that a increasingly free market economy combines with a compensating form of religiosity that reflects an intellectually, artistically and sexually repressive culture.

It might have been expected that in the aftermath of the 2004 election, centrist Democrats, rather than attribute their defeat to being out-of-touch on 'faith' issues, and thus conceding the 'moral values' edge to the party that brought us Abu Ghraib, would have re-examined their affinity for candidates too mumble-mouthed and compromised to articulate poverty and war as the urgent moral issues they are. These are issues, after all, on which it is not hard for even secular liberals to claim that Jesus is on their side. Policies of pre-emptive war and the upward redistribution of wealth are inversions of the Judeo-Christian ethic, which is for the most part silent, or mysteriously cryptic, on gays and abortion. With their craven, breast-beating response to Bush's electoral triumph, leading Democrats only demonstrate how out of touch they really are with the religious transformation of America. Where secular-type liberals and centrists go wrong is in categorizing religion as a form of 'irrationality', akin to spirituality, sports mania and emotion generally. They fail to see that the current 'Christianization' wave bears no resemblance to the Great Revival of the early nineteenth century, an ecstatic movement that filled the fields of Virginia with the rolling, shrieking and jerking bodies of the revived. In contrast, today's right-leaning Christian churches represent a coldly Calvinist tradition in which even speaking in tongues, if it occurs at all, has been increasingly routinized and restricted to the pastor.

What these churches have to offer, in addition to intangibles like eternal salvation, is concrete, material assistance in the form of childcare, after-school programs, support groups for battered women, and help for the unemployed – all permeated with proselytizing messages. Some churches even offer occasional cash hand-outs to members facing eviction or medical debts. They have become an alternative welfare state, whose support rests not only on 'faith' but also on the loyalty of the grateful recipients. For example, just a short drive from Washington D.C., in the Virginia suburbs, is the McLean Bible Church, spiritual home of Senator James Inhofe and other prominent right-wingers. On any given weekday night there, dozens of families and teenagers enjoy a low-priced dinner in the cafeteria; a hundred unemployed people meet for prayer and job tips at the 'Career Ministry'; divorced and abused women gather in support groups. Among its many services, MBC distributes free clothing to 10,000 poor people a year, has helped start an inner-city ministry for at-risk youth in the District of Columbia, and operates a 'special needs' ministry for disabled children. MBC is a mega-church with a parking garage that could serve a medium-sized airport, but many smaller evangelical churches offer a similar array of services – childcare, after-school programs, ESL lessons, help in finding a job, not to mention the occasional cash handout. Nor is the local business elite neglected by the evangelicals. Throughout the Republican 'red states' – and increasingly the Democratic 'blue ones' too – evangelical churches are vital centers of 'networking', where the carwash owner can schmooze with the bank's loan officer. Some churches offer regular Christian businessmen's 'fellowship lunches', where religious testimonies are given and business cards traded, along with jokes aimed at Democrats and gays.

The lesson is clear. Got a drinking problem, a vicious spouse, a wayward child, a bill due? Find a church. The closest analogy to America's bureaucratized evangelical movement is Hamas, which draws in poverty-stricken Palestinians through its own miniature welfare state. While Hamas operates in a nonexistent welfare state, the Christian right advances by attacking the existing one. Mainstream, even liberal, churches also provide a range of

services, from soup kitchens to support groups. What makes the typical evangelical church's social welfare efforts sinister is their implicit – and sometimes
not so implicit – linkage to the destruction of public and secular services. In
the 2004 election year the connecting code words were 'abortion' and 'gay
marriage': to vote for a candidate who opposed these supposed moral atroci-
ties, as the Christian Coalition and so many churches strongly advised, was to
vote against public housing subsidies, childcare and expanded public forms
of health insurance. Of course, Bush's faith-based social welfare strategy only
accelerates the downward spiral toward theocracy. Not only do the right-
leaning evangelical churches offer their own, shamelessly proselytizing social
services; not only do they attack candidates who favour expanded public
services – but they stand to gain public money by doing so.

It is this dangerous positive feedback loop, and not any new spiritual or moral
dimension of American life, that the Democrats have failed to comprehend:
the evangelical church-based welfare system is being fed by the deliberate
destruction of the secular welfare state. What the American political system
needs, at the very least, is a political alternative that offers a firm commitment
to public forms of childcare, healthcare, housing and education – for people
of all faiths and no faith at all. At the same time, progressives should perhaps
rethink their own disdain for service-based outreach programs. Once it was
the left that provided 'alternative services' in the form of free clinics, women's
health centers, food co-ops and inner-city multi-service storefronts. Enterprises like these are not substitutes for an adequate public welfare state, but
they can become the springboards from which to demand one.

This is especially important now when there are growing signs that the
agenda put in motion by welfare reform may be about to unravel. It was
one thing to attack the relatively marginalized group of welfare recipients;
quite another to take on the fifty-odd million elderly people who depend on
public pensions and health insurance. Bush's drive to privatize or otherwise
eliminate Social Security has won no converts, and served only to contribute
to his declining approval ratings. At the same time, declining public support
for higher education, combined with sky-rocketing college costs, is forcing
middle-class families to reflect on the role of government as a provider of
social welfare. For all but the wealthy, health insurance is becoming inadequate or out of reach, especially as rates of job turnover increase. In the
desolation left by six years of extreme right-wing economic and social policy,
values such as collective responsibility and the common good may be beginning to regain their lustre.

NOTES

1   Heather Boushey, 'A House Divided: How Welfare Reform Pits Working
    Families Against the Non-Working Poor', *New Labor Forum*, 13(3), Fall
    2004, p. 28.

2   For a discussion, see Alexander Hicks, 'Back to the Future? A Review
    Essay on Income Concentration and Conservatism', *Socio-Economic
    Review*, 1, 2003, pp. 271–88.

3   For a discussion, see Herbert J. Gans, 'Race as Class', *Contexts*, November
    2005. The median white household earned 62 per cent more income
    and possessed twelve times the wealth of the median black household.
    See Melvin Oliver and Thomas Shapiro, *Black Wealth/White Wealth: A
    New Perspective on Racial Inequality*, New York: Routledge, 1997, pp. 86–
    90, 96–103.

4   The shift in public opinion is notable. In 1944, only 45 per cent of
    Americans agreed that African Americans should have as good a chance
    as white people to get any kind of job. Three decades later, 97 per cent
    agreed. Benjamin I. Page and Robert Y. Shapiro, *The Rational Public:
    Fifty Years of Trends in Americans' Policy Preferences*, Chicago: University of
    Chicago Press, 1992, pp. 63; 68–71.

5   Plotke calls this a 'Democratic political order', but means essentially the
    same thing. 'From the 1930s through the 1960s, it dominated American
    political life. By political order I mean a durable mode of organizing and
    exercising political power at the national level, with distinct institutions,
    policies and discourses'. See David Plotke, *Building a Democratic Political
    Order*, Cambridge, UK: Cambridge University Press, 1996, p. 1.

6   Edward R. Tufte initiated this interpretation with his argument that
    politicians standing for election tried to coordinate the business cycle
    with the election cycle. See his *Political Control of the Economy*, Princeton:
    Princeton University Press, 1978. Thomas Ferguson offers an analysis
    that shows that in the 2004 election, voters in states with sharp increases
    in inequality did go for Kerry. At the same time, his argument posits that
    increasing inequality is associated with increased religiosity, strength-
    ening conservative forces. See 'Holy Owned Subsidiary: Globalization,
    Religion, and Politics in the 2004 Election', in William Crotty, ed., *A
    Defining Election: The Presidential Race of 2004*, Armonk: M.E. Sharpe,
    2005.

7   Economic collapse discredited business, at a time of widespread social
    unrest to which national political leaders had to respond. Moreover,
    the structural power that business usually wields through the threat of
    disinvestments in a decentralized system was reduced both by economic

slowdown, and by the growing role of the national government. For an extended discussion, see Jacob S. Hacker and Paul Pierson, 'Business Power and Social Policy: Employers and the Formation of the American Welfare State', *Politics and Society,* 30(2), June 2002, pp. 277-325.

8    Presidential Papers of Dwight D. Eisenhower, Document 1147, http://www.eisenhowermemorial.org

9    For a discussion see William Greider, 'Riding Into the Sunset', *The Nation,* 27 June 2005.

10    Mike Gecan, 'Taking Faith Seriously', *Boston Review,* April/May 2005.

11    See Robert Parry, 'The Answer is Fear', *The Progressive Populist,* 11(12), 1 July 2005.

12    The quotation is from a speech to the Commonwealth Club in 1932. See Aaron Singer, ed., *Campaign Speeches of American Presidential Candidates,* New York: Frederick Ungar, 1976, cited in Ronald Schurin, 'A Party Form of Government', Ph.D. dissertation completed at the Graduate School of the City University of New York, 1996. Schurin argues that this definition of the role of government was a strong and consistent theme in Roosevelt's public addresses.

13    See Jonathan Schell's review, 'Master of All He Surveys', *The Nation,* 21 June 1999, of two Morris books, *The New Prince: Machiavelli Updated for the Twenty-first Century,* and *Behind the Oval Office: Getting Reelected Against All Odds.*

14    This is from Stanley B. Greenberg's reminiscence, 'How We Found – and Lost – a Majority', *The American Prospect,* 16(6), June 2005. Greenberg's 1991 article, 'From Crisis to Working Majority', *The American Prospect,* 2(7), September 1991, was considered a key guide for the Clinton 1992 campaign.

15    For a detailed discussion, see Evelyn Brodkin, Carolyn Fuqua, and Elaine Waxman, 'Accessing the Safety Net: Administrative Barriers to Public Benefits in Metropolitan Chicago', May 2005, www.povertylaw.org.

16    For data on the varied fate of welfare 'leavers', see Gregory Acs and Pamela Loprest, *Leaving Welfare: Employment and Well-Being of Families that Left Welfare in the Post-Entitlement Era,* Kalamazoo: W.E. Upjohn Institute for Employment Research, 2005.

17    See Lawrence Mishel, Jared Bernstein, and Sylvia Allegretto, *The State of Working America, 2004-2005,* Ithaca: Cornell University Press, 2005. See also Michael D. Yates, 'A Statistical Portrait of the U.S. Working Class', *Monthly Review,* 56(11), April 2005.

18    See Alex Hicks, 'Back to the Future? A Review Essay in Income Concentration and Conservatism', *Socio-Economic Review,* 1, May 2003, pp. 271-88. Hicks reviews data presented by T. Piketty and E. Saez that

shows dramatically less household income concentration at the upper level in France in the 1980s and 90s, and considerably less even in the United Kingdom. 'Income Inequality in the United States, 1913-1998', Working Paper 8467, Cambridge: National Bureau of Economic Research, 2001 (http://www.nber.org/papers/4867.pdf).

19  See 'A Commentary on Excess', 2 May 2005, available from toomuch@app.topica.com.

# THE 'SCHOLARLY MYTHS' OF THE NEW LAW AND ORDER DOXA

## LOÏC WACQUANT

The moral panic that has been raging through Europe in recent years about 'street violence' and 'delinquent youth,' which allegedly threaten the integrity of advanced societies and call in turn for severe penal responses, has mutated, since the French presidential elections of 2002, into a veritable *law-and-order pornography*, in which everyday incidents of 'insecurity' are turned into a lurid media spectacle and a permanent theatre of morality. The staging of 'security' (*sécurité, Sicherheit, seguridad*), henceforth construed in its strictly criminal sense – after crime had itself been reduced to street delinquency alone, that is to say, in the final analysis, to the turpitudes of the lower classes – has the primary function of enabling leaders in office (or competing for it) to reaffirm on the cheap the capacity of the state to act at the very moment when, embracing the dogmas of neoliberalism, they unanimously preach its impotence in economic and social matters.[1] The canonization of the 'right to security' is the correlate of, and a fig leaf for, the dereliction of the right to work, a right inscribed in the French Constitution but flouted daily, on the one side by the persistence of mass unemployment in the midst of national prosperity and, on the other by the growth of precarious wage labour that denies any security of life to the growing numbers of those who are condemned to it.

At the beginning of 2002, as the presidential election campaign commenced, all the mainstream media and political parties in France chose to focus to the point of obsession on the supposed increase in 'insecurity,' in spite of the *decrease* in street crime recorded during that year. Driven by the logic of commercial and electoral competition, no one thought it worthwhile to pay the slightest attention to the results of a series of solidly documented reports produced by INSEE (the National Institute for Economic and Statistical Studies) on the inexorable rise of casual employment, the tenacity of mass unemployment in the urban periphery, and the consolidation of a vast sector of the 'working poor' – according to the new label freshly imported from America – along with the policies of industrial withdrawal and economic deregulation that fuel their ranks. Witness a hardly noticed survey, soberly entitled 'Sensitive Urban Areas: The Rapid Increase in Unemployment between 1990 and 1999', which reveals that job precariousness and social insecurity became generalized and concentrated during that decade, notwithstanding renewed economic growth and a decrease in the official jobless figures at the national level.[2] Thus the share of precarious workers – those employed on short-term contracts, as temporary staff, in subsidized jobs and government-sponsored training programs – rose from one in eleven in 1990 (or 1.98 million people) to one in seven in 1999 (3.3 million). Among the 4.7 million residents of the 750 'sensitive urban areas' designated as such by the 1996 Urban Renewal Pact – amounting to one out of every thirteen French inhabitants – the proportion of those in precarious positions bordered on 20 per cent.

So much to say that, for youths lacking recognized educational credentials living in France's neighbourhoods of relegation, insecure wage work is no longer a deviant, temporary and atypical form of employment, but the modal path of entry into a world of work now haunted by the spectre of impermanence and unlimited flexibility.[3] And this is for those 'privileged' enough to get paid employment, since at the same time unemployment among 15-24 year-olds in these districts kept on climbing: between 1990 and 1999 the proportion of youths who looked in vain for a job rose from 19.9 per cent to 25.6 per cent nationwide; for their compatriots living in those urban areas coyly labelled 'sensitive,' the increase was much sharper, from 28.5 per cent to nearly 40 per cent. If one adds those in precarious work to those out of work, it turns out that 42 per cent of the youths in these dispossessed districts were thus marginalized in 1990, and that this figure had jumped to some 60 per cent by 1999 – before unemployment resumed its relentless forward march to push it higher still. In light of these statistics, attesting to the silent normalization of social insecurity under a so-called Left government, one can better understand the pitiful electoral score achieved among the working class by the Socialist Party candidate who boasted at his campaign meetings of having slain the dragon of unemployment and who, ignoring the spectacular deterioration of the (sub)proletarian condition during his term in office, was promising the imminent return of 'full employment' by the end of the next term – a truly obscene slogan for the residents of housing estates subjected for two generations to the rampant de-socialization of wage work.[4]

On the main television channels the eight o'clock news has mutated into a chronicle of run-of-the-mill crimes that suddenly seem to teem and threaten on every side – here a paedophile school teacher, there a murdered child, somewhere else a city bus stoned or a tobacconist insulted. Special broadcasts multiply at peak listening times, such as an episode of the programme 'This Can Happen To You' which, under the rubric of 'school violence,' unwinds the tragic story of a child who committed suicide as a result of a racket in the playground of his primary school – a completely aberrant case, but instantly converted into a paradigmatic one for the sake of boosting audience ratings. Magazines are full to bursting with features about 'the true figures,' the 'hidden facts' and assorted 'explosive reports' on delinquency in which sensationalism vies with moralism, and periodically draw up the fearsome cartography of 'no-go areas' and tender essential 'practical advice' for dealing with dangers decreed omnipresent and multiform.[5]

On all sides one hears the obsessive lament about the idleness of the authorities, the ineptitude of the justice system, and the fearful or exasperated indignation of ordinary folk. At the beginning of 2002, the Plural Left government multiplied conspicuous measures for repressive show that even its most obtuse members could hardly fail to realize would have no traction whatsoever on the problems these measures were supposed to treat. One example that verges on the caricatural: the ruinous purchase of a bullet-proof vest *for every single gendarme and police officer* in France, when upwards of 90 per cent of them never encounter an armed villain in the course of their entire career, and when the number of law-enforcement agents killed on duty has decreased by half in ten years. The right-wing opposition was not to be outdone on this front, and promised to do exactly the same as the government on all counts, only faster, stronger, and tougher. With the exception of the non-governmental Left and the Greens, all the candidates for elected office thus promoted 'security' to the rank of absolute priority for public action and hurriedly proposed the same primitive and punitive solutions: to intensify police operations; to zero in on 'youths' (working-class and immigrant youths, that is), 'recidivists' and the so-called hard core of criminals encrusted in the outer suburbs (which conveniently excludes white-collar crime and official corruption); to speed up judicial proceedings; to make sentences tougher; and to extend the use of custody, including for juveniles, even though it has been demonstrated time and again that incarceration is eminently criminogenic. And, to make it all possible, they demanded in unison an unlimited increase in the means devoted to the enforcement of social order by the law. The head of state himself, Jacques Chirac, a multi-recidivist offender responsible for the organized looting of hundreds of millions in public funds while Mayor of Paris for two decades, impervious to all sense of shame, dared to call for 'zero impunity' for minor offences perpetrated in the dispossessed neighbourhoods whose residents, precisely, have taken to nicknaming him '*Supervoleur*' ('Super-thief') in reference to the multiple scandals in which he has been directly implicated.[6]

But this new political-discursive figure of 'security' that unites the most reactionary Right and the governmental Left in all the major countries of Europe is not content to merely reiterate the 'old persistent and indestructible myth' of modern society, described by Jean-Claude Chesnais in his *History of Violence in Western Society from 1800 to Our Times*, which recurrently depicts violence as a phenomenon resulting from a long-term evolution but at the same time as something always totally unprecedented, springing up suddenly, and intrinsically urban.[7] Its originality resides in drawing most of its force of persuasion from those two contemporary symbolic powers that are science and America – and, better yet, from their cross-breeding, that is, American science applied to American reality.

Just as the neoliberal vision in economics rests on models of dynamic equilibrium constructed by an orthodox economic science 'made in the USA', the country that holds a near-monopoly over Nobel prizes in that discipline, so the law-and-order vulgate of the turn of the century presents itself in the guise of a scholarly discourse purporting to put the most advanced 'criminological theory' at the service of a resolutely 'rational' policy, a policy deemed ideologically neutral and ultimately indisputable since it rests on pure considerations of effectiveness and efficiency. And, like the doctrine of generalized subordination to the market, the new security doxa comes directly from the United States, which, since the abrupt collapse of the Soviet empire, has become the beacon-country of all humanity, the sole society in history endowed with the material and symbolic means to convert its historical particularities into a trans-historical ideal and then to make that ideal, come true by transforming reality everywhere in its image.[8]

And so it is to New York that over the past several years French politicians (as well as their English, Italian, Spanish, and German colleagues), of the Left as well as the Right, have travelled as one on a pilgrimage, to signify their newfound resolve to crush the scourge of street crime and, for this purpose, to initiate themselves into the concepts and measures adopted by the US authorities. Backed by the science and policy of 'crime control' tested in America, the new one-track 'securitythink' that now rules in most of the countries of the First World, and many of the Second, presents itself in the form of a concatenation of '*scholarly myths*,' that is to say, a web of statements that intermingle 'two principles of coherence: a proclaimed coherence, of scientific appearance, which asserts itself by proliferating outward signs of scientificity, and a hidden coherence, mythic in its principle.'[9] One can examine its texture and take apart its mechanisms in four steps.

## 1. HOW 'SUPERCRIMINAL' AMERICA WAS PACIFIED
## AND OVERTAKEN BY FRANCE

According to the first media-political myth, until recently the United States was ravaged by astronomic levels of crime but, thanks to exacting innovations in policing and punishment, it has 'solved' the crime equation after the manner of New York City. During the same period, owing to their laxity, the countries of old Europe have let themselves be caught in a lethal spiral of 'urban violence' that has caused them to suffer from an uncontrolled epidemic of crime on the American pattern. Thus, such a self-styled 'expert' on the question as Alain Bauer, the chief executive officer of Alain Bauer Associates, a 'security consulting' firm, who happens to be an influential adviser to French socialist cabinet members and a Grand Master of the Grand Orient (the main French masonic order), could announce with fanfare in a leading national newspaper that, following a 'historic cross-over of the curves' depicting the crime statistics of the two countries in 2000, 'France is more criminogenic than the US'.[10]

This astonishing 'revelation', instantly propagated by all the mainstream media (Agence France Presse, France-Info, the main commercial television channel TF1, etc.), demonstrates that on the question of 'insecurity' one can say anything and everything and be taken seriously, so long as one intones the catastrophic and repressive refrain of the day. In reality, thanks to the International Crime Victimisation Survey (ICVS),[11] it has been well-established for at least *a good ten years* that the United States has entirely ordinary rates of crime when these are measured by the *prevalence of victimization* – rather than by the statistics of crimes reported to the authorities, which are not constructed and collated on the same basis across countries, and which, as all 'specialists' worthy of the name know, are a better indicator of the activity of the police than of criminals. The US rates have long been comparable to, and even generally lower than, those of a good many other advanced countries, with the notable and readily explicable exception of homicide.[12] Thus, among the eleven post-industrial nations covered by the ICVS in 1995, that is to say before the full-scale implementation of 'zero tolerance,' the US came in second after England for vehicle thefts and robberies as well as for serious bodily harm; tied third with France, and far behind Canada and England, on the burglary scale; seventh, trailing Switzerland, Austria and Holland, among others, for sexual offences; and right at the tail of the pack (ninth) for the incidence of simple theft, with a score half as high as that of the Netherlands. In all, a combined index of victimization covering eleven types of offence puts the *US of 1995 in seventh position* (with 24.2 per cent of its residents having suffered from one or several crimes during the past year), well below Holland (31.5 per cent) and England (30.9 per cent), but also behind Switzerland, Canada, and France (fifth with 25.3 per cent).[13] The least 'criminogenic' countries then were, and by a wide margin, Ireland (16.9 per cent) and Austria (18.9 per cent). Yet it is to New York City, and not Dublin or Vienna, that the politicians and the new experts in crime control rushed from across Europe in search of the holy grail of security.

Only its stupendous homicide rate distinguishes America from the countries of western Europe: with ten murders for every 100,000 inhabitants at the beginning of the last decade, and six per 100,000 in 2002, that level remains nearly five times higher than those of France, Germany or England. It is for this reason that the legal scholars Franklin Zimring and Gordon Hawkins entitled their canonical work on the criminal question in the US, *Crime is Not the Problem: Lethal Violence in America*:[14] America has a highly specific problem of *deadly violence by firearms*, highly concentrated in its urban ghettos and linked, on the one hand, to the free possession and circulation of some 200 million guns and handguns (four million Americans carry one on a daily basis and half of all households have one at home); and, on the other, to the weakness of the social-welfare system, rigid racial segregation, and the deep rooting of the illegal street economy in the impoverished districts of its major cities.[15]

If America is not the 'supercriminal' society it is commonly believed to be, neither does the trend-line in violent crime in France, and more generally in Europe, converge with that of the United States, dominated as it is by deadly violence. Indeed, the rate of homicides and attempted homicides (taken together) in France *fell* by one-fifth during the last decade, from 4.5 per 100,000 inhabitants in 1990 to 3.6 in 2000. It is true that cases of '*vols avec violence*' (corresponding roughly to robbery and assault) increased noticeably during these years but, far from striking 'everyone and everywhere', as the media would have us believe, offences against persons are rare (they befall about 2 per cent of the population in any given year); they remain heavily concentrated among the young working-class population residing in the country's urban periphery; and they are in the main relatively benign: the 'assaults' reported to the authorities are exclusively *verbal* in half of all cases, and they entail physical injury in only one incident out of four (they lead to hospitalization or a work-leave in only one case in twenty). As for burglary and thefts from and of vehicles, which are vastly more common than offences against people, they have fallen steadily since 1993.[16]

These trends revealed by official French statistics are confirmed by the ICVS survey: between 1996 and 2000, that is, in the very period when the catastrophic discourse on the 'explosion' of criminality swelled to the point of saturating France's political and journalistic field, the cumulative incidence of victimization for ten categories of offence *fell* from 43 to 34 per 100,000, corresponding to a decrease superior by one-fifth to the decline in crime recorded by the US (from 47 per cent to 40 per cent).[17] This drop occurred in all types of offences except for assault and battery, which as we have already seen are typically much less serious than this designation suggests, and are moreover relatively rare (the incidence of vehicle theft is six times higher than that of robbery, which affects only 1.8 in every 100 residents). Thus, with 34 offences per 100 in the year 2000, France registered an overall victimization rate close to that of Denmark (35 per cent) and Belgium (33 per cent), placing it behind the United States and Canada (39 per cent), and far to the rear of Holland (48 per cent) and England (54 per cent).

So the assertion that America was 'supercriminal,' but is so no longer since the coming of 'zero tolerance,' while France is infested by crime (understand: because it failed to import this policy with all due urgency), does not pertain to criminological argumentation but to ideological claptrap. This does not stop Alain Bauer, its author, giving lessons in 'methodology' to the French authorities who consult him with deference (as evidenced by his testimony before the Senate information commission on crime on 28 March 2000); or enjoying the reputation of being a rigorous 'criminologist' (no joke intended) among supposedly trustworthy journalists (such as those of *Le Monde*, who regularly quote him as an authority); or being the sitting President of the Oversight Committee of the National Crime Observatory recently created by Interior Minister Nicolas Sarkozy.

## 2. IT IS THE POLICE WHO MAKE CRIME MELT AWAY

A recent report by the Manhattan Institute – a major promoter of the 'class cleansing' of the streets and nerve centre of the worldwide campaign to penalize poverty[18] – asserts this with emphasis: the sustained drop in the statistics of crime in the US over the past decade is due to the energetic and innovative action of the law-enforcement forces, after they were finally freed from the ideological taboos and legal yokes that previously constrained them. The paradigmatic case for this is offered by the spectacular turn-around achieved in New York by the Republican mayor Rudolph Giuliani under the leadership of his master police chiefs William Bratton and William Safir.[19] But there is a catch: here again facts are more stubborn than ideology, and all scientific studies converge in concluding that the police did not play the key determining role that the advocates of the penal management of social insecurity assign to it as a matter of *petitio principii* – far from it.

The first proof is that the drop in criminal violence in New York began *three years before* Giuliani ascended to power at the end of 1993, and continued at the same rate after he assumed office. Better still: the incidence of homicides committed without the use of firearms in the city has been falling slowly but steadily *since 1979*; only gun-related murders declined sharply after 1990, after having taken off between 1985 and 1990 due to the spread of the crack trade; and neither of these two curves displays any particular inflection under Giuliani.[20] The second proof is that the ebbing of criminal violence is just as marked *in cities that did not adopt* the New York policy of 'zero tolerance,' including those that opted for a diametrically opposed approach, such as Boston, San Francisco or San Diego – where so-called problem-solving policing strives to establish ongoing relationships with residents aimed at preventing offences, rather than dealing with them *ex post* by all-out penal repression.[21] In San Francisco, a policy of systematic 'diversion' of delinquent youth towards job-training programmes, counselling and social and medical treatment made it possible to cut the number of jail admissions by more than half while reducing criminal violence by 33 per cent between 1995 and 1999 (compared with a 26 per cent drop in New York City, where the volume of jail entries swelled by a third during the same period). And for third proof, from 1984 to 1987 New York Mayor David Dinkins had already implemented an aggressive and assiduous law-enforcement policy similar to that deployed after 1993, under the code name 'Operation Pressure Point', which was accompanied by a sharp *increase* in criminal violence, and especially homicides.[22] Whence it emerges that, contrary to the claims of the promoters and importers of the 'Bratton model,' the policing strategy adopted by New York during the 1990s is *neither necessary nor sufficient* to account for the crime drop in that metropolis.

The comparison with Canada, a neighbouring country endowed with a similar economic, demographic, and political structure, and whose overall level of crime is practically identical (with the notable exception of the incidence of murders, which is three times lower), confirms this conclusion. Indeed, with a few rare exceptions, between 1991 and 2001 all the regions of Canada recorded a marked decline in homicides, armed robberies, and burglaries of the same magnitude as that observed in the United States, even though the practices of the law-enforcement forces, judicial expenses, and resort to confinement remained unchanged there. Indeed, owing to fiscal constraints, the ratio of police supervision in Canada (given by the number of police divided by the total population) *fell* by 9 per cent, and the country's incarceration rate sagged by 7 per cent, against increases of 10 per cent and 47 per cent respectively in the United States during the same period. As criminologist Marc Ouimet notes, 'such a similarity of trends for different kinds of crime, for different regions in the same country, and for two different countries, supports resorting to general explanations to account for the declines,'[23] and he points toward two exogenous forces driving this remarkable parallelism between the US and Canada: the one-fifth drop in the number of people in the 20- to 34-year age bracket on both sides of their common border, and the marked decrease in unemployment in both countries, which allowed unskilled lower-class youths to find work and thus encouraged them to withdraw from the criminal economy.

In point of fact six factors, *all of them independent of the activity of the police and the justice system*, have combined to sharply curtail the incidence of violent offences in the large cities of the US in the 1990s. First, *flourishing economic growth*, unparalleled in the country's history in its scale and duration, effectively provided jobs and supplied incomes to millions of youths hitherto doomed to idleness or illegal trades, including in the ghettos and barrios where unemployment retreated noticeably.[24] But the boom did not for all that dent the endemic poverty of the segregated neighbourhoods of the American metropolis, because most of these new jobs remained casual and underpaid: the official poverty rate in New York City remained unchanged at 20 per cent throughout the whole decade of the 1990s. In fact, it was above all young Latinos who directly benefited from the improvement in the state of the deskilled labour market. For blacks, the euphoric economic climate acted indirectly by raising their hopes for future mobility and by encouraging a growing fraction of teenagers to pursue post-secondary schooling, which greatly reduced their probability of being involved in violent street crime, either as victims or as perpetrators.[25] Notwithstanding the persistence of under-employment and the extremely low level of wages in the new service sectors, detailed statistical studies suggest that the direct and indirect impact of the rapid decline in aggregate unemployment explains 30 per cent of the decrease in the national crime rate.[26]

The second factor is the *twofold transformation of the drug economy*. To begin with, the retail trade in crack in impoverished neighbourhoods gained structure and stability, so that resort to violence as a means of regulating competition between rival gangs receded abruptly.[27] At the end of the 1980s this trade experienced explosive growth and, given that barriers to entry were virtually non-existent, new entrepreneurs, often young and independent, were constantly coming forward to engage in deadly territorial struggles: in 1991, 670 of the 2,161 homicides recorded in New York City were linked to narcotics trafficking. A decade later, demand had settled down and the sector had become 'oligopolized', so that the number of dealers fell and relations between them were less conflictual. This translated into a precipitous plunge in the number of drug-related homicides – it dropped below the one-hundred mark in 1998 – since the greater part of that criminal street violence is violence *between criminals*.[28] Next, crack lost favour with consumers, who returned to other opiates and narcotics, such as marijuana (consumed in the form of a cigar called a 'blunt'), heroin, and methamphetamines, the trade in which generates less extortion because it is dominated by retail sellers operating within networks of mutual acquaintances rather than through anonymous exchanges in public places.[29]

Next, as noted earlier, the *number of young people* (especially those between 18 and 24) shrank, which translated almost mechanically into a decline in street crime, since these are the age categories that are, always and everywhere, most inclined to violent law-breaking. This demographic evolution alone accounts for at least one-tenth of the drop in offences against persons during the period under consideration.[30] To which one must add, in the case of New York City, the ghoulish statistic of candidates for crime put out of commission by the AIDS pandemic among heroin users (19,000 deaths recorded between 1987 and 1997), those killed by drug overdoses (14,000), gangsters slain by their colleagues (4,150) or put behind bars or deported (5,250), making a total of some 43,000 'trouble-makers' eliminated over a decade, equal to the number of prisoners sent from the city every year to expiate their misdeeds in the penitentiaries that dot the upstate countryside.[31] The recessive effect of the decrease in the young and criminal population was moreover amplified by a strong *upsurge in immigration*, especially of predominantly feminine migration streams coming from countries such as the Dominican Republic, China, and Russia. Emigrants from these countries arriving in New York during the decade of the 1990s had access to 'ethnic niches' that facilitated their entry into the local economy so that, thanks to their commercial activity and consumption, they revitalized declining districts on the edges of the large black ghettos, enabling their inhabitants to 'reclaim public space and deter outdoor criminal activity'.[32]

But economic and demographic causes are not the only ones operating, and one must include, among the forces that have cut crime in the United States, a *learning effect*, christened the 'little-brother syndrome' by criminologists, by virtue of which the new generations of youths born after 1975-1980 drew away from hard drugs and the dangerous life-style associated with them in a deliberate refusal to succumb to the macabre fate they had seen overtake their older brothers, cousins, and childhood friends, fallen on the front line of the 'street wars' of the end of the 1980s: uncontrolled drug addiction, imprisonment for life, violent and premature death.[33] Witness the 'truces' and 'peace treaties' signed by the gangs that controlled the ghettos of Los Angeles, Chicago, Detroit, and Boston in the early 1990s, which sharply reduced the number of homicides of young, poor males. For their part, organizations located inside the zones of relegation of the US metropolis, such as churches, schools, the gamut of associations, neighbourhood clubs, collectives of mothers of child victims of street killings (such as MAD, Mothers Against Drugs, in Chicago, and Mothers ROC, Mothers Reclaiming Our Children, in Los Angeles),[34] have mobilized and exercised their capacity for informal social control wherever they still could. Their *awareness and prevention campaigns*, such as operation 'Take Back Our Community' organized by the Grand Council of Guardians (the black police association of New York City), have accompanied and bolstered the spontaneous withdrawal of youths from the predatory economy of the streets. One should underline here, with Benjamin Bowling, the fact that, like the improvement of the economy, these collective initiatives of the residents of poor neighbourhoods have been totally blacked out in the dominant discourse on the fall in criminality in the US, and have even been virulently denigrated by Rudolph Giuliani and William Bratton.[35]

Finally, the levels of criminal violence recorded by the US at the beginning of the 1990s were *abnormally high* and were therefore very likely to turn downwards again, thanks to the statistical law of regression towards the mean, inasmuch as the factors that had stimulated them to jump outside the norm (such as the initial takeoff in the crack trade) could not persist. By replacing it in the *longue durée* of the twentieth century, the historian Eric Monkkonnen has shown how the period 1975-1990 was atypical of the basic trends in violent crime in New York City: between 1900 and 1960 the homicide rate in America's symbolic capital was a notch below the national average; it left this bracket after the race riots of the 1960s to come to rest at three times the country-wide figure, due to the lightning development of a drug economy regulated by armed confrontation; the swift ebb of the decade of the 1990s simply brought it back to around the country average where it had been a quarter of a century earlier.[36]

The conjunction of these six factors is amply sufficient to explain the decrease in violent crime in the US over the past dozen years. But the long and slow pace of scientific analysis is not the rapid and spasmodic tempo of politics and the media, and Giuliani's propaganda machine pounced on the inevitable lag in criminological research to fill the explanatory gap with its prefabricated discourse on the efficacy of police repression, disinterred as the sole remedy for the congenital carelessness of the dangerous classes. A seductive discourse, since, being framed in the trope of 'responsibility,' it echoes the individualistic and utilitarian thematics carried by the neoliberal ideology now hegemonic on both sides of the Atlantic. But let us admit, for the sake of argument, that the police have indeed had a discernible impact on crime in New York City. The whole question remains to know *how* it could have produced this outcome.

### 3. BEHIND 'ZERO TOLERANCE,' BUREAUCRATIC REORGANIZATION

According to the planetary mythology diffused by neoliberal think-tanks and their allies in the political and journalistic fields, the New York police laid low the hydra of crime by implementing a very particular policy, called 'zero tolerance', which professes to pursue without fail or respite the most minor infractions committed in public space. Thus since 1993 anyone caught panhandling or loitering in the city, playing their car stereo too loudly, throwing away empty bottles or writing graffiti on the streets, or even violating a mere municipal ordinance, is supposed to be automatically arrested and immediately dispatched behind bars: 'No more D.A.T.s [desk appearance tickets, requiring one to report later to the local police station where charges may then be laid]. If you peed in the street, you were going to jail. We were going to fix the broken windows [i.e., punish the slightest external indicators of disorder] and prevent anyone from breaking them again'. This strategy, claimed its mastermind William Bratton, 'would work in any city in America' and it would work just as well 'in any city in the world'.[37]

In reality, this policing slogan of 'zero tolerance' – which has gone all the way around the world when, paradoxically, it is scarcely used any longer as a law-enforcement strategy in the US, where even conservative politicians deem it offensive: in New York officials use the more polite expression '*quality-of-life policing*' – is what Kenneth Burke calls a 'terministic screen' that conceals, by the very fact of amalgamating them, several concurrent but quite distinct transformations in day-to-day law-enforcement.[38] The New York police department effectively underwent four sets of parallel changes:

(1) a sweeping bureaucratic restructuring, entailing the decentralization of services, the flattening out of hierarchical levels, the lowering of the age of its managers through the on-the-spot firing of three out of every four top-ranking officers, and the devolution of direct responsibility to precinct captains, whose remuneration and promotion depend partly on the crime 'figures' they produce (which creates strong pressure to manipulate statistics, for example by multiplying the number of false arrests);

(2) a stupendous expansion of human and financial resources: the number of uniformed officers leaped from 27,000 in 1993 to 41,000 in 2001, amounting to half as many police as the whole of France for only eight million residents! This growth in personnel was only possible thanks to an increase in the police budget of 50 per cent in five years, which allowed it to top 3 billion dollars in 2000, despite massive cutbacks in local government spending (during the same period, funds for the city's social services were slashed by 30 per cent);[39]

(3) the deployment of new information technologies, including the famed Compstat programme (a scientific-sounding acronym that tritely means 'computer statistics'), an electronic information and data-sharing system making it possible to track the evolution and distribution of criminal incidents in real time so as to reallocate police forces at top speed to the affected areas; and, finally,

(4) a thoroughgoing review of the objectives and procedures of every service, according to schemas worked out by consultants in 'corporate reengineering,' and the implementation of targeted 'action plans' focused on the possession of firearms, drug dealing in public places, domestic violence, traffic violations, etc.

All in all, a bureaucracy rightly reputed to be cowardly, puffing, and passive, as well as notoriously corrupt and set in the habit of waiting for crime victims to come and file complaints, which it was content to merely record, with a constant concern to make the least possible waves in the media and the courts – this bureaucracy was transmogrified into a veritable simile of a zealous 'security firm,' endowed with colossal human and material resources and an offensive outlook. This much one can grant without contest. But if this bureaucratic mutation had a pronounced impact on crime – and no one has so far succeeded in demonstrating any[40] – this impact has nothing to do with the particular policing *tactics* adopted by the police at ground level.

## 4. FROM 'BROKEN WINDOWS' TO 'BREAKING BALLS'

The last worldwide security myth to come from America is no less droll than the previous three. This is the idea according to which the policy of 'zero tolerance,' supposedly responsible for the policing triumph of New York City, rests on a *scientifically proven criminological theory*, the celebrated 'broken-windows theory.' The latter postulates that the immediate and stern repression of the slightest violations or nuisance on the streets stems the onset of major criminal offences by (re)establishing a healthy climate of order – a queer illustration of the popular French adage 'he who steals an egg steals an ox' – by reasserting the norm and dramatizing respect for the law. Now, this so-called theory is in no way scientific, insofar as it was formulated twenty years ago by the ultra-conservative political scientist James Q. Wilson and his acolyte George Kelling (the former chief of police of Kansas City, since converted into a Senior Fellow at the Manhattan Institute) in the form of a short text of nine pages published, not in a criminological journal subject to peer review by competent researchers, but in the cultural magazine *The Atlantic Monthly* (which did not prevent it from being published in French translation in the official journal of the Institut des Hautes Études de la Sécurité Intérieure in 1999).[41] And it has never received even the beginnings of an empirical verification since then.

In support of the 'broken windows theory,' its advocates cite as if by rote the book *Disorder and Decline*, published in 1990 by the Chicago political scientist Wesley Skogan, which traces the causes of, and evaluates the remedies for, social and ecological dislocations in urban areas on the basis of a battery of surveys in forty neighbourhoods in six US cities. But, upon close reading, it turns out that this work shows that it is poverty and racial segregation, and not the climate of 'urban disorder,' that are the most potent determinants of crime rates in the metropolis. Moreover, its statistical conclusions have been invalidated due to an accumulation of measurement errors and missing data; and its author himself grants the illustrious 'broken windows theory' the status of a mere 'metaphor'.[42] Indeed, no study designed to verify the 'ratchet effect' postulated by the said theory (according to which the suppression of minor offences would limit the incidence of major ones), such as the survey carried out by Albert Reiss in Oakland, California, and that of Lawrence Sherman in the federal capital Washington, has succeeded in turning up evidence for it. The comparative analysis of systematic data collected in 196 districts of Chicago on the basis of interviews and daily video recordings has even conclusively shown that there exists no statistical relation between the visible indicators of 'disorder' in a given area and its crime rates (with the possible and partial exception of burglary).[43]

When all is said and done, at the end of a painstaking examination of the question, the legal scholar Bernard Harcourt argues that, if the New York police department contributed to the decline in crime, it was not by re-establishing civility and communicating a message of stern refusal of impunity, but by the simple fact of having massively increased the intensity of the surveillance it wields: in 1990 Giuliani's city had thirty-eight police for every 100,000 inhabitants, as against twice that number ten years later, and their action was strongly targeted on dispossessed populations and districts.[44] In short, it is the *accentuation and concentration of police and penal repression*, and not the moral mechanism of the restoration of the norm postulated by the so-called theory of Wilson and Kelling, that would account for police effectiveness in the case – itself still hypothetical – where policing would have played a significant role.

But there is a still more comical side to this tale: the adoption of permanent police harassment of the poor in public space by the city of New York had, *on the admission of its own inventors, no link whatsoever with any criminological theory*. The famous 'broken-windows theory' was in reality discovered and invoked by city officials only *a posteriori*, in order to dress up in rational garb

measures that were popular with the (mostly white and bourgeois) electorate, but fundamentally discriminatory in both principle and implementation,
and to give an innovative spin to what was nothing more than a reversion to
an age-old police recipe, periodically put back to work and in fashion. Jack
Maple, the 'genius of the war against crime'[45] and Bratton's right-hand man,
who was the initiator of 'quality-of-life policing' in the subway before it
was extended to the streets, says so explicitly in his autobiography published
in 1999 under the cowboyish title *Crime Fighter*: '"Broken Windows" was
merely an extension of what we used to call the "Breaking Balls" theory',
issued from conventional police wisdom, which stipulates that if the cops
persistently go after a notorious offender for pecadillos he will, for the sake
of peace and quiet, end up leaving the neighbourhood to go and commit his
lawbreaking somewhere else, so that the local level of crime will diminish.
Maple's innovation consisted in 'modernizing' this notion as 'Breaking Balls
Plus' (to use his expression), by linking identity checks to judicial data-bases
so as to arrest the maximum number of villains sought for other offences or
already under judicial supervision via probation or parole.[46]

The architect of Giuliani's policing policy openly sneers at those who
believe in the existence of 'a mystical link between minor incidents of disorder and more serious crimes.' The idea that the police could reduce violent
crime by cracking down on incivilities seems to him plainly 'sad', and he
gives a wealth of examples giving the lie to this preposterous notion, drawn
from his professional experience in New York and New Orleans. He even
compares a mayor who would adopt such a policing tactic to a doctor who
'give[s] a face-lift to a cancer patient', or an underwater hunter who catches
'dolphins instead of sharks.' And, to avoid all ambiguity, Maple hammers
the point home: '"Quality-of-Life Plus" is not "zero tolerance"'. Quite the
contrary, it implies precisely directing *police activity to those social categories
presumed to be crime vectors* to avoid wasting finite resources of time and law
enforcement personnel.[47]

As Maple puts it in his book,

> [Following] reports of a dramatic drop in violent crime [in New
> York], many people credited the 'Broken Windows' notion that
> the crooks had suddenly taken to the straight and narrow because
> they had picked up on the prevailing civility vibe. That's not how
> it works. Rapists and killers don't head for another town when
> they see that graffiti disappearing from the subway. The average
> squeegee man doesn't start accepting contract murders when-
> ever he detects a growing tolerance for squeegeeing. Panhandling
> doesn't turn a neighbourhood into Murder Central.... Quality-

of-life enforcement works to reduce crime because it allows the cop to catch crooks when the crooks are off-duty, like hitting the enemy planes while they're still on the ground.[48]

Jack Maple would no doubt be astonished to read the following state-ment in 'Memorandum No. 31', drafted by the 'experts' of the very official Institut des Hautes Études de la Sécurité Intérieure, the pseudo-research arm of the French Ministry of the Interior charged with conducting studies justifying the punitive turn of the Plural Left government, to guide mayors in elaborating 'local security contracts' in their city:

> American studies have shown that the proliferation of incivilities is nothing but the advance warning sign of a general rise in crime. The initial deviant behaviors, no matter how minor they seem, inasmuch as they become general, stigmatise a neighbourhood, attract other forms of deviance into it, and herald the end of every-day social peace. The spiral of decline is set off, violence takes root, and with it every kind of crime: assaults, burglaries, drug traffick-ing, etc. (see J. Wilson and T. [sic] Kelling, 'The Broken Windows Theory').
>
> It is on the basis of these research findings that the New York chief of police put in place a battle strategy called 'zero tolerance' against the authors of incivilities, which seems to have been one of the causes of the very marked reduction of crime in that city.[49]

One finds it hard to curb a mounting *sentiment of incredulity* in the face of such an outpouring of falsehoods, to not say transatlantic tripe, and the shameful credulousness to which they attest. For the tactic of permanent police persecution of the poor in the streets implemented in New York is nothing other than the systematic and deliberate application of folk 'theo-ries' based on the professional common sense of policemen. It pertains not to criminology but to 'crookology,' as Jack Maple would say (he was fond of defining himself as a 'crookologist'). But, precisely, such common sense does not, in this instance, make much sense. A rigorous and thorough evaluation, by two of the country's best specialists, of the scientific inquiries conducted in the US over the past twenty years, with the aim of testing the effective-ness of the police in the fight against crime, concludes, soberly, that neither the number of officers thrown into the battle; nor internal changes in the organization and culture of law-enforcement agencies (such as the introduc-tion of community policing); nor yet strategies that target places and groups with a strong criminal propensity (with the 'possible and partial exception' of programmes aimed at outside drug trafficking) have by themselves any impact on the evolution of offences.[50] In a final irony, among all the various police tactics reviewed, the authors spotlight 'Compstat' and 'zero tolerance' as 'the least plausible candidates for contributing to the reduction of violent crime' in urban America, and they conclude: 'There is one thing that is a myth: [that] the police have a substantial, broad, and *independent* impact on the nation's crime rate'.[51]

Like Russian dolls, these four scholarly myths from across the Atlantic nest into each other so as to form a kind of logical chain, with the air of a syllogism, making it possible to justify without resistance the adoption of an aggressive policy of 'class cleansing' of city streets. This policy is fundamentally discriminatory in that it rests on an equivalence between behaving outside the norm and being an outlaw, and it targets neighbourhoods and populations suspected beforehand, if not held guilty on principle, of moral deficiencies, nay legal offences. If it is true that US society, for so long 'supercriminal,' has been pacified by the action of the police just when other countries have been struck full force by an 'explosion' of crime; and that New York City, the Mecca of the new US policing religion, has crushed criminal violence thanks to its policy of 'zero tolerance'; and that this policy itself was articulated in conformity with a sound criminological theory ('broken windows'); then indeed how could one not rush to import these notions and instigate the measures for which they seemingly supply a rational foundation? In reality the four key propositions of the new 'made-in-USA' security vulgate are devoid of any scientific validity, and their practical efficacy rests on a collective faith without foundation in reality. But, strung to one another, they function as a planetary launching pad for an intellectual hoax and an exercise in political legerdemain which, by giving a pseudo-academic warrant to sweeping police activism, contribute powerfully to legitimating the shift towards the penal management of social insecurity that is everywhere being generated by the social and economic disengagement of the state.

NOTES

This text is abridged and adapted from chapter 8 of Loïc Wacquant, *Punishing the Poor: The New Government of Social Insecurity*, Durham and London: Duke University Press, in press.

1    Loïc Wacquant, 'The Penalisation of Poverty and the Rise of Neoliberalism,' *European Journal of Criminal Policy and Research*, special issue on 'Criminal Justice and Social Policy,' 9(4), Winter 2001, pp. 401-412; and the issue of *Déviance et société* on the theme of 'Urban Disorders: Sociological Perspectives,' December 2000, pp. 24-4.

2    Jean-Luc Le Toqueux and Jacques Moreau, 'Les zones urbaines sensibles. Forte progression du chômage entre 1990 et 1999,' *INSEE Première*, October 2000, p. 334.

3    For a gripping account of the conditions of routine superexploitation of the 'floating' labour force, read Daniel Martinez, *Carnets d'un intérimaire*, Marseilles: Agone, 2002; on the repression by employers of the attempts at mobilization of this deskilled workforce, young and often issued of recent immigration, see Abdel Mabrouki and Thomas Lebègue, *Génération précaire*, Paris: Le Cherche-Midi, 2004.

4    On the social and political bases of the growing split between the governmental left and the working-class electorate, read Olivier Masclet, *La Gauche et les cités. Enquête sur un rendez-vous manqué*, Paris: La Dispute, 2003.

5    Annie Collovald, *Violence et délinquance dans la presse. Politisation d'un malaise social et technicisation de son traitement*, Paris: Editions de la DIV, 2000, and Serge Halimi, 'L'insécurité' des média,' in Gilles Sainati and Laurent Bonelli, eds., *La Machine à punir*, Paris: L'Esprit frappeur, 2001, pp. 203-234.

6    [Translator] '*Supervoleur*' is a derivation of '*Supermenteur*' ('Superliar'), the television character decked out in cape and mask featuring Chirac as an inveterate liar on the daily political muppet show *Les Guignols de l'Info* (shown daily at 8 pm on the main cable station Canal Plus).

7    Jean-Claude Chesnais, *Histoire de la violence en Occident de 1800 à nos jours*, Paris: Pluriel, 1981, p. 431.

8    See the two issues of *Actes de la recherche en sciences sociales* devoted to 'L'exception américaine' (nos. 138 and 139, June and September 2001).

9    Pierre Bourdieu, *Ce que parler veut dire*, Paris: Fayard, 1982, p. 228.

10   The title of the article in *Le Figaro*, 18 June 2001, deserves to be quoted in full: 'The stunning results of a comparison between the criminal statistics of the [French] Ministry of the Interior and those of the FBI: France is more criminogenic than the United States.' Stunning indeed since this comparison is devoid of validity – a fact that even Bauer implicitly acknowledges when he concedes that 'the statistical design [used] is random, relative, partial, fragmented, and biased'! On the rise of these new consultants-advisers on security, bogus researchers and true

propagandists and salesmen, see Pierre Rimbert, 'Les nouveaux managers de l'insécurité: production et circulation d'un discours sécuritaire,' in *La Machine à punir*, op. cit., pp. 161–202.

11   The International Crime Victimization Survey (of whose existence Alain Bauer, like the leading government experts on this matter, seems utterly unaware) is a questionnaire survey of households conducted about every four years since 1989 by criminologists at the University of Leiden under the aegis of the Dutch Ministry of Justice and the United Nation's Interregional Criminological Justice Research Institute (based in Rome). It measures and compares the prevalence, incidence, and evolution of rates of victimization in some fifteen advanced countries.

12   This point is underlined by Leena Kurki, 'International Crime Survey: American Rates About Average,' *Overcrowded Times*, 8(5), 1997, pp. 4–7, and Michael Tonry and Richard S. Frase, eds., *Sentencing and Sanctions in Western Countries*, New York: Oxford UP, 2001, pp. 12–14.

13   John van Kesteren, Pat Mayhew and Paul Nieuwbeerta, *Criminal Victimisation in Seventeen Industrialized Countries: Key Findings from the 2000 International Crime Victims Survey*, The Hague: WODC, Ministry of Justice, 2000.

14   Franklin E. Zimring and Gordon Hawkins, *Crime is Not the Problem: Lethal Violence in America*, New York: Oxford UP, 1997.

15   Douglas Massey, 'Getting Away with Murder: Segregation and Violent Crime in Urban America,' *University of Pennsylvania Law Review*, 143(5), May 1995, pp. 1203–1232; Lauren Krivo and Ruth D. Peterson, 'Extremely Disadvantaged Neighbourhoods and Urban Crime,' *Social Forces*, 75(2), December 1996, pp. 619–50; and Garen Wintenmute, 'Guns and Gun Violence,' in Alfred Blumstein and Joel Wallman, eds., *The Crime Drop in America*, New York: Cambridge UP, 2000, pp. 45–96.

16   Laurent Mucchielli, *Violences et insécurité. Fantasmes et réalités dans le débat français*, Paris: La Découverte, 2001, pp. 67 and 61.

17   See van Kesteren, Mayhew and Nieuwbeerta, *Criminal Victimisation in Seventeen Industrialized Countries*, op. cit., Table 2, pp. 180–1. Incidence is measured by the total number of victimizations reported per 100,000 residents; it is superior to prevalence (the percentage of inhabitants who have suffered at least one attack), since the same person may have been the victim of several crimes in the course of the year.

18   It is this neoconservative institute, founded by Anthony Fischer (Margaret Thatcher's mentor), that canonized the 'broken-windows theory' and the policy of 'zero tolerance,' and then pushed for their export to Europe and Latin America, after having (successfully) campaigned for

the dismantling of public aid during the 1980s (Loïc Wacquant, *Les Prisons de la misère*, Paris: Raisons d'agir Éditions, 1999, pp. 14-22).

19    George L. Kelling and William H. Souza, *Does the Police Matter? An Analysis of the Impact of NYC's Police Reforms*, New York: Manhattan Institute, Civic Report no. 22, December 2001.

20    Jeffrey Fagan, Franklin Zimring and June Kim, 'Declining Homicide in New York City: A Tale of Two Trends,' *Journal of Criminal Law and Criminology*, 88(4), Summer 1998, pp. 1277-1324; and Alfred Blumstein and Richard Rosenfeld, 'Explaining Recent Trends in U.S. Homicide Rates,' ibid., pp. 1175-1216.

21    Judith A. Greene, 'Zero Tolerance: A Case Study of Police Policies and Practices in New York City,' *Crime and Delinquency*, 45(2), April 1999, pp. 171-187; Khaled Taqi-Eddin and Dan Macallair, *Shattering 'Broken Windows': An Analysis of San Francisco's Liberal Crime Policies*, Washington: Justice Policy Institute, 1999; and Loïc Wacquant, 'Mister Bratton Goes to Buenos Aires. Prefacio à la edición para América latina,' in *Las Cárceles de la miseria*, Buenos Aires: Ediciones Manantial, 2000, pp. 11-17.

22    Benjamin Bowling, 'The Rise and Fall of New York Murder: Zero Tolerance or Crack's Decline?,' *British Journal of Criminology*, 39(4), Autumn 1999, pp. 531-54; Robert Panzarella, 'Bratton Reinvents "Harassment Model" of Policing,' *Law Enforcement News*, 15-30 June 1998, pp. 13-15.

23    Marc Ouimet, 'Oh, Canada! La baisse de la criminalité au Canada et aux États-Unis entre 1991 et 2002,' *Champ pénal*, 1(1), January 2004 (available at http://champpenal.revues.org/document11.html)

24    Richard B. Freeman, 'Does the Booming Economy Help Explain the Drop in Crime?,' in *Perspectives on Crime and Justice: 1999-2000 Lectures Series*, Washington: US Department of Justice, 2000.

25    Andrew Karmen, *New York Murder Mystery: The True Story Behind the Crime Crash of the 1990s*, New York: New York UP, 2001, pp. 209-13.

26    Jared Bernstein and Ellen Houston, *Crime and Work: What We Can Learn from the Low-Wage Labor Market*, Washington: EPI Books, 2000.

27    One will find a gripping description of the day-to-day operation of the crack trade in East Harlem in Philippe Bourgois, *In Search of Respect: Selling Crack in El Barrio*, New York: Cambridge UP, 1995, and, from the viewpoint of the police, in Robert Jackall, *Wild Cowboys: Urban Marauders and the Forces of Order*, Cambridge: Harvard UP, 1997.

28    Bruce A. Jacobs, *Robbing Drug Dealers: Violence Beyond the Law*, New York: Aldine de Gruyter, 2000.

29  Daniel Cork, 'Examining Space-Time Interaction in City-Level Homicide Data: Crack Markets and the Diffusion of Guns Among Youth,' *Journal of Quantitative Criminology*, 15, 1999, pp. 379-406; Benjamin Bowling, 'The Rise and Fall of New York Murder,' op. cit.; and Bruce D. Johnson, Andrew Golub and Eloise Dunlap, 'The Rise and Decline of Hard Drugs, Drug Markets, and Violence in Inner-City New York,' in Blumstein and Wallman, *The Crime Drop in America*, op. cit., pp. 164-206.

30  James Alan Fox, 'Demographics and U.S. Homicide,' in Blumstein and Wallman, *The Crime Drop in America, op. cit.*, pp. 288-317.

31  Karmen, *New York Murder Mystery*, op. cit., pp. 242-3.

32  Ibid., p. 225:'The largely unplanned social experiment in multiculturalism of bringing together people speaking 121 different languages seems to have worked out very well, in the sense that it put a brake on spiraling crime rates and even helped turn the tide.'

33  Richard Curtis, 'The Improbable Transformation of Inner-City Neighbourhoods: Crime, Violence, Drugs, and Youth in the 1990s,' *Journal of Criminal Law and Criminology*, 88(4), Summer 1998, pp. 1233-76; and Johnson, Golub and Dunlap, 'The Rise and Decline of Hard Drugs, Drug Markets, and Violence in Inner-City New York,' op. cit.

34  Mary Pattillo, 'Sweet Mothers and Gangbangers: Managing Crime in a Black Middle-Class Neighbourhood,' *Social Forces*, 76(3), March 1998, pp. 747-74, and Ruth Wilson Gilmore, 'You Have Dislodged a Boulder: Mothers and Prisoners in the Post-Keynesian California Landscape,' *Transforming Anthropology*, 8(1/2), 1999, pp. 12-38.

35  Bowling, 'The Rise and Fall of New York Murder,' op. cit.

36  Eric Monkkonen, *Murder in New York City*, Berkeley: University of California Press, 2001.

37  William W. Bratton and Peter Knobler, *Turnaround: How America's Top Cop Reversed the Crime Epidemic*, New York: Random House, 1998, pp. 229 and 309. *Turnaround* is the 'autobiography' in which Bratton offers a paean to his own life with the help of a journalist specialized in rose-coloured biographies of sporting and political stars, and for which he received the tidy advance of $375,000. After being fired unceremoniously by Rudolph Giuliani (who deemed the popularity of his chief of police excessive in relation to his own), Bratton converted into an international 'consultant in urban security' in order to better sell his expertise in the four corners of the planet to which he was summoned by politicians anxious to demonstrate publicly their resolve to combat crime. In 2002, he was named Chief of the Los Angeles Police Department but, curiously, 'zero tolerance' is invisible in his reorganization of policing there.

38   E.B. Silverman and P. O'Connell, 'Organizational Change and Decision Making in the New York City Police Department,' *International Journal of Public Administration*, 22(2), 1998, pp. 217-259, and Karmen, *New York Murder Mystery*, op. cit., chapter 3.

39   Citizens Budget Commission, *New York City and New York State Finances, Fiscal Year 1999-2000*, New York: Five-Year Pocket Summary, CBC, 2000. During his second term of office, for example, Rudolph Giuliani allocated $80 million to a programme called 'Operation Condor' that allowed city police to work a sixth day of overtime every week. Meanwhile the municipal libraries cut back their opening hours and services due to a budget shortfall of $40 million (equivalent to one-sixth of their funding).

40   Based on a painstaking examination of all available police and court data Karmen found, for instance, that contrary to the claims of city officials, the new police tactics implemented under Giuliani did not produce an increase in arrests for firearms possession nor a rise in the rate of clearance of crime complaints, any more than they led to an improvement in other commonly used indicators of the preventive or repressive efficacy of the police (Karmen, *New York Murder Mystery*, op. cit., pp. 263-4).

41   James Q. Wilson and George Kelling, 'Broken Windows: The Police and Neighbourhood Safety,' *Atlantic Monthly*, 249, March 1982, pp. 29-38.

42   Loïc Wacquant, 'Désordre dans la ville,' *Actes de la recherche en sciences sociales*, 99, September 1993, pp. 79-82 (a critical dissection of Wesley Skogan, *Disorder and Decline*, New York: Free Press, 1990); Bernard E. Harcourt, 'Reflecting on the Subject: A Critique of the Social Influence Conception of Deterrence, the Broken Windows Theory, and Order-Maintenance Policing New-York Style,' *Michigan Law Review*, 97(2), November 1998, pp. 291-389; Wesley G. Skogan, 'Review of George Kelling and Catherine M. Coles, *Fixing Broken Windows: Restoring Order and Reducing Crime in Our Communities* (1996),' *American Journal of Sociology*, 103(2), September 1997, pp. 510-2.

43   Albert J. Reiss, Jr., *Policing a City's Central District: The Oakland Story*, Washington: National Institute of Justice Research Report, April 1985; Lawrence Sherman, 'Police Crackdowns: Initial and Residual Deterrence,' *Crime and Justice: A Review of Research*, 12, 1990, pp. 1-48; Robert J. Sampson and Stephen W. Raudenbush, 'Systematic Social Observation of Public Spaces: A New Look at Disorder in Urban Neighbourhoods,' *American Journal of Sociology*, 105(3), November 1999, pp. 603-51.

44  Bernard Harcourt, *Illusions of Order: The False Promise of Broken Windows Policing*, Cambridge: Harvard UP, 2001.

45  According to the title conferred by Rudolph Giuliani at the official funeral given by the city to Jack Maple: 'Master Crime Fighter Given Eulogy to Match his Success,' *New York Times*, 10 August 2001.

46  Jack Maple and Chris Mitchell, *The Crime Fighter: How You Can Make Your Community Crime-Free*, New York: Broadway Books, 1999, pp. 152-3.

47  'The units enforcing quality-of-life laws must be sent where the maps [distributing the statistics of recorded offenses] show concentrations of crimes and criminals, and the rules governing the stops have to be designed to catch the sharks and not the dolphins' (Maple and Mitchell, *Crime Fighter*, op. cit., pp. 154-5).

48  Ibid., p. 154-5.

49  Institut des Hautes Études de la Sécurité Intérieure, *Guide pratique pour les contrats locaux de sécurité*, Paris: La Documentation française, 1997, pp. 133-4. 'Local security contracts' are compacts made by a city with the central government to activate and coordinate crime prevention and repression strategies in targeted domains and neighbourhoods.

50  John E. Eck and Edward R. Maguire, 'Have Changes in Policing Reduced Violent Crime?,' in Blumstein and Wallman, *The Crime Drop in America*, op. cit., pp. 207-65, who insist: 'The most plausible hypothesis is that these police actions interacted with other criminal justice policies (such as imprisonment) and social forces (such as the aging of the population or the decline of outside retail drug markets)…. Some form of interaction is more plausible than a claim that changes in policing were the sole or greatest contributor to the drop in violent crime' (pp. 245 and 248).

51  Ibid., p. 249.

# TELLING THE TRUTH AT A MOMENT OF TRUTH: US NEWS MEDIA AND THE INVASION AND OCCUPATION OF IRAQ

## ROBERT W. McCHESNEY

> A popular Government, without popular information, or the means of acquiring it, is but a prologue to a farce or a tragedy; or, perhaps, both. Knowledge will forever govern ignorance; and a people who mean to be their own governors must arm themselves with the power which knowledge gives. (James Madison[1])

The notion of a free press, of an institution that monitors those in power and those who wish to be in power, that ferrets out truth from lies, that draws public attention to the pressing issues of our times, is a cornerstone of liberal democratic theory. In practice, even in liberal democratic capitalist societies, press systems have never accomplished these laudable goals, though certain press systems, usually through progressive activism and reforms, have come much closer than others. The primary internal impediments to a viable free press have been private ownership of the media, and the drive to maximize profit, often through selling advertising. The primary external barriers are the difficulty of promoting a participatory democratic political culture in a class-divided society, as well as the constant pressure, direct and indirect, that elites put on the press to have it support elite aims. Radical press criticism, beginning most notably in the work of Marx, has never rejected Madison's notion of a free press.[2] To the contrary, the gist of radical press criticism has emphasized the irreconcilable nature of the free press ideal with a capitalist society.

The greatest test of a press system is how it empowers citizens to monitor the government's war-making powers. War is the most serious use of state power, organized sanctioned violence; how well it is under citizen review and control is not only a litmus test for the media but for society as a whole. Those in power, those who benefit from war and empire, see the press as arguably the most important front for war, because it is there that consent is manufactured, and dissent is marginalized. For a press system, a war is its moment of truth.

With regard to the United States, it would be difficult to exaggerate how deeply concerned the founders were with limiting the war-making power of the government, of keeping the president in particular under strict control by Congress. The founders were no friends of egalitarianism or democracy – but they were resolutely opposed to tyranny. All of them learned from Montesquieu that history from Greece and Rome to modern times had repeatedly demonstrated that a state's existence as a self-governing republic was incompatible with becoming a militaristic empire defined by secrecy and hierarchy. And they understood that a viable free press was the only mechanism that could provide citizens with the precious commodity most frequently denied them by their governors: the information necessary to control those with the power to send the nation's children to their deaths on distant killing fields.

It is the press that is singularly responsible, therefore, for the maintenance of civilian control over the military, and the prevention of empire run amok. When the US Supreme Court considered the meaning of freedom of the press in the Pentagon Papers case in 1971, Justice Potter Stewart wrote: 'In the absence of governmental checks and balances present in other areas of our national life, the only effective restraint upon executive policy and power in the areas of national defense and international affairs may lie in an enlightened citizenry – in an informed and critical public opinion which alone can here protect the values of democratic government'. Such great words and sentiments notwithstanding, the track record of the US media over the past century in relation to US overseas wars, and the broader role of the United States in the world, has been dreadful. Time and time again the system has spread lies and half-truths and crushed dissent, which more often than not proved to be justified by the facts. In the United States, honest reflection is always done with hindsight, premised on the notion that we have learned from the past and that these problems in the media have been eliminated. After putting this pattern in historical perspective, this essay analyzes the US media coverage of the invasion and occupation of Iraq in 2003-2005. As we shall see, in this moment of truth for a free press, the truth was almost nowhere to be found.

## MANUFACTURING CONSENT FOR WAR

Beginning with the 1898 Spanish-American War, the United States has engaged in scores of foreign military operations and several major wars involving the deployment of US troops. In nearly all of these major wars – the Spanish-American War, World War I, World War II, Korea, Vietnam, the Central America proxy wars of the 1980s, and the first Gulf War – a clear pattern emerged: the President wished to pursue war while the American people had severe reservations. In nearly every case the White House ran a propaganda campaign to generate public support for going to war, a campaign that bent the truth in line with the view that the ends (war) justified the means (lies). This is not to say that all of these wars by definition were improper. A powerful case, for example, can be made for US participation in World War II. But even in that case, President Roosevelt was concerned that the American people would not fall in line no matter how strong the evidence. So, as the saying goes, he 'lied' us into war.

The news media were placed in a recurring dilemma in each of these wars. The administration was pursuing aggressive propaganda campaigns to whip up popular support for war, and a key battleground was winning favourable press coverage. The news media in each case were presented with the dilemma of either challenging the administration pro-war line, demanding hard evidence for claims, digging deep to see that the full story was put before the American people, or going along more or less with the pro-war line. In principle, credible journalism should hold the nation's rulers to the same evidentiary standards it holds the enemies of the nation's rulers. We take no pleasure in reporting that the news media in nearly every case opted for Plan B. In the case of Vietnam, where the Pentagon Papers and the taped sessions in President Johnson's office document the shameless duplicity of the government, the willingness of the news media to parrot administration lies was a thorough abrogation of the requirements of a free press, with disastrous consequences for millions of lives. At journalism schools, these episodes are considered embarrassing moments in the history of US journalism, and not dwelt upon in the curricula. What is dwelt upon is the reporting that challenged official fiction years after the lies were told and the lives were lost.

The explanation of why the news media fail to get the fundamental facts before the American people concerning the decision of whether to go to war, be it in 1917, 1941, 1950, 1964, or 2003, are deep-seated. One could argue that the patriotic impulse is such that any journalism will have the strong tendency to 'root for the home team', as some have put it. But this analysis begs the question of why the patriotic impulse exists in different forms at different times, why some in society express it more fervently than others, how the patriotic impulse is enforced, how it manifests itself through media institutions and professional practices, and how we explain the exceptions. In short, the patriotic impulse explanation leads to far more questions than answers.

To explain the woeful coverage of US wars requires a look at the broad crisis in journalism I have analyzed at length elsewhere.[3] By the early 20th century and thereafter, major news media were large commercial organizations and therefore tended to be conservative institutions. Those who owned and managed these firms tended to be comfortable with the world view of those atop the social structure, because that is where they also resided, and were supportive of government policies that were understood to advance those interests. Moreover, most media owners did not want to be accused of being unpatriotic or treasonous. The system had done well by them. From a structural or sociological perspective, one would not expect that commercial news media organizations would pose a critical challenge to a strong pro-war campaign.

But what about the editors and working journalists who composed and edited the news? Some of them proudly hailed from the working class. Certainly they had no similar allegiance to the policy imperatives of the elite. To the extent that they had a certain autonomy from the implicit and explicit institutional prerogatives of the owners, the nature of press coverage was far less certain. Here we might even expect some stubborn interrogation of the powers-that-be. Regrettably, that has only rarely been the case. The primary problem has been the emergence of what is called 'professional journalism', which coincided with the emergence of the United States as a global military power. All of the limitations of the version of professional journalism that solidified its hold on newsrooms in the United States by the 1940s – reliance on official sources, fear of context, and the unstated 'dig here, not there' mandate – worked in combination to make professional journalism a lapdog more than a watchdog as the drums of war beat louder.

The factor most scholarship emphasizes in this regard is professional journalism's reliance upon official sources. If people in power are debating an issue, journalists have some wiggle room to root around and explore it. If people in power agree on an issue, presuppose it, or do not seriously debate it, it is almost impossible for a journalist to raise it without being accused of partisanship and pushing an ideological agenda. So it is rarely done, and when it is done it is dismissed as bad journalism.

The ability of official sources to determine the range of legitimate debate is a regrettable tendency for most political stories, but it is nothing short of a disaster for the coverage of the US role in the world. For here ordinary citizens rely to an even greater extent upon the media than they do for domestic politics, where their daily experience can provide some corrective to skewed press coverage. Moreover, there is typically a greater consensus among 'official sources' on the US's benign role in the world than there is on any other issue, except, perhaps, the greatness of US-style capitalism as the only legitimate way to organize an economy.

There are two fundamental presuppositions – actually, articles of faith – that guide US foreign policy. They are accepted by 'official sources' in both political parties, and they are almost never questioned in major US news media. The first presupposition is the notion that the United States is a benevolent force in the world and that whatever it does, by definition, is ultimately about making the world a more just and democratic place. This is a pleasing assumption, and it puts a necessary fig leaf over what may be less altruistic aims. This presupposition also makes it possible for there to be almost no debate or discussion of the actual role of the United States in the world. Many Americans accept the official story that the United States is a benevolent giant, attacked on all sides by powerful evil-doers. That the United States accounts for almost half of all military spending in the world; that US military spending dwarfs the second largest military power by a factor of eight; that the United States has hundreds of foreign military bases in literally scores of nations: all of this is largely unmentioned and unknown to Americans. It is simply assumed away. And that leaves most Americans largely clueless about how the United States is perceived in the rest of the world.

The second article of faith that is generally unquestioned by the American media is the notion that the United States, and the United States alone, has a '007' right to invade any country it wishes. The United States also reserves the right to 'deputize' an ally to conduct an invasion if it so desires. Otherwise other nations are not permitted to engage in the invasion business. This presents a small problem for the political elite and for the news media. After all, the UN Charter and a number of other treaties signed by the United States prohibit the invasion of one nation by another unless it is under armed attack. Moreover, the US constitution characterizes treaties as the highest law of the land, so that if the United States violates international law, it arguably warrants presidential impeachment. To top it off, in popular discourse the United States proudly promotes itself as favouring the rule of law, and a main argument against all of its adversaries is invariably that they ignore treaties they have signed. That is, in fact, sometimes used as a rationale for a US invasion.

This is not to say that there is not highly competent and quality reporting on US foreign policy, only that it tends to stay within the parameters of what official sources consider legitimate. The truly great reporting, from people like I.F. Stone and Seymour Hersh, went boldly outside these parameters. (And some of the best reporting on the United States role in the world, not surprisingly, comes from American reporters working outside the United States, where reliance upon US official sources as the basis for legitimate news and opinion plays a much more limited role.)

In combination, the limitations of professional journalism, the influence of owners, the linkages of media institutions to the power structure of society, and the internalized elite presuppositions, have led to what can only be characterized as a palpable double standard in coverage of the US role in the world. None have demonstrated this more convincingly than Edward S. Herman and Noam Chomsky in *Manufacturing Consent*.[4] Stories that support the aims of US policymakers get lavish and sympathetic treatment; stories of similar or greater factual veracity and importance that undermine US policy goals get brief and unfavourable mention. As Howard Friel and Richard Falk have demonstrated in their research, the US news media, including the most respected newspapers like *The New York Times*, turn a blind eye to US violations of core international law, while having no qualms about playing up the violations of adversaries. It would be nearly impossible for the coverage to be more unprincipled.[5]

## THE CONTEMPORARY CRISIS IN JOURNALISM

The problems with US media coverage described above were evident from the 1960s into the 1980s, the so-called golden age of professional journalism. Press coverage exhibited severe flaws even when the newsrooms were relatively flush with resources and had as much autonomy as they ever would. The main developments in journalism over the past two decades that have eroded professional journalism – corporate consolidation and organized right-wing attacks on the 'liberal media' – have only made the situation worse.

The corporate downsizing and cutback epidemic has been especially hard on international coverage. The sharp reduction in the number of foreign correspondents working for US news media has been a familiar story over the past two decades. These are positions that cost a lot of money, and to the managers in charge they don't seem to generate any black ink on their corporate balance sheets. Moreover, managers argue that people don't seem to care if there is less international coverage, or if what passes for international coverage has less to do with politics and more to do with easy-to-report natural disasters and plane crashes. So from the corporate worldview, axing these positions is a no-brainer.

The resulting problem with not having many foreign correspondents with a familiarity with the language, history and customs of the regions they are covering has become painfully clear over the past fifteen years. When conflicts break out in the Balkans, Africa, South Asia or elsewhere, US news media have few if any reporters on the ground to provide context for the story. This means that there is less capacity for journalists to provide a counterbalance to whatever official story Washington puts forward. At its worst, foreign reporting becomes celebrity journalists and anchors being airdropped into a crisis area and shepherded around by representatives of the US government. This is not a recipe for independent journalism.

The right-wing critique of the 'liberal' media has not helped matters either.

Anti-war criticism of a Democratic war-maker from the right, though rare, is kosher if framed in hyper-nationalist terms. Thus Sean Hannity attacked Clinton's Kosovo war in terms he later characterized as treasonous when they were used by others about President Bush's Iraq war. A constant theme of the right-wing critique of the 'liberal' news media is that journalists are insufficiently patriotic; this translates into journalists being extra-sensitive to prove their nationalist credentials. Again, this is not conducive to critical analysis of foreign wars.

The combined effect of commercial and conservative attacks on professional journalism is to undermine the formal adherence to a neutral and non-partisan position. This does not mean mainstream media can become explicitly partisan to the left; that is more unthinkable then ever. Nor does it mean that most news media have dropped their formal commitment to political neutrality. It means that there are a growing number of media that push a partisan pro-Republican political agenda, often under a thin veneer of being 'fair and balanced'. So the Fox News Channel, Sinclair Broadcasting, the *New York Post*, the *Washington Times*, the editorial page of the *Wall Street Journal*, and most of talk radio, all serve as standard-bearers for the Republican right. They aggressively promote right-wing policies and bash Democrats who get in the way. In coverage of Republican wars this translates into aggressive pro-war posturing and wholesale rabid condemnation of anti-war criticism as unpatriotic or treasonous. Because the rest of the news media tend to be timid by comparison, this right-wing phalanx sets the tone for coverage to an extent that is out of proportion to its size. And the rest of the press becomes even more hesitant to contradict the government line.

All of this came together in the coverage of the terrorist attacks of September 11, 2001, and the subsequent invasion and occupation of Afghanistan. Despite the massive amount of attention the news media devoted to the topic – it was arguably the biggest US news story in a half-century – coverage was heavily propagandistic. Elementary questions about the administration's performance in failing to prevent the attack were not pursued. Hard looks at the relationship of the Bush Administration, the US government, Al Qaeda and other Mideast governments were all but non-existent. Even to broach the question of why the terrorists attacked the United States – as if there might be a rational explanation beyond the idea that these were madmen who hated us 'because of our freedoms' – was dismissed as implicitly condoning the attack and mass murder.

Guided by the Bush Administration and 'official sources', within hours of the 9-11 attacks, these terrorist acts had been converted from vicious crimes against humanity, from criminal acts of terror, to acts of war. The War on Terrorism entailed a push for a broad militarization of society and, immediately, for the invasion and bombing of Afghanistan, a nation that did not attack the United States on 9-11.

The truth about 9-11 is still largely unknown. But what pieces have emerged, mostly in the margins, and with all too little pressure from mainstream media, suggest that much of what was presented as received wisdom in the months following the 9-11 attacks was incorrect, if not nonsense. The testimony of Richard Clarke as well as the report of the 9-11 Commission both highlight the negligence of the administration in failing to stop the terrorist attack or in addressing it properly afterwards. One can only imagine what mainstream media, egged on by Fox News, the *Wall Street Journal* editorial page, talk radio, and the *New York Post*, would have done to a President Gore or a President Clinton in a similar situation. In the immediate aftermath of the 9-11 attacks, courtesy of a hyperventilating press, President Bush was reborn as a cross between Abraham Lincoln and Winston Churchill.

The press was eating out of the Bush administration's bowl. If media truly constituted the most important front in modern war, the stars were in alignment for a bold invasion that had been atop the wish list of the main Bush foreign policy advisors for years, but was once thought too politically controversial to accomplish: the invasion of Iraq.

## BUILD-UP TO THE INVASION OF IRAQ

It was in this environment that the United States was able to launch an invasion and occupation of Iraq on entirely bogus grounds. The three major justifications offered explicitly and implicitly by the Bush Administration to generate public support for the war were: (1) that Iraq illegally possessed weapons of mass destruction and was poised to use them on the United States in the immediate future; (2) that Iraq had been somehow connected to the attacks on 9-11, so pursuing Saddam Hussein was a rational next step in the campaign against bin Laden; and (3) Iraq was the leading terrorist state, 9-11 notwithstanding, so the War on Terror had to go through Baghdad.

The second and third claims were unsubstantiated on their face, and borderline preposterous. The Bush Administration was careful about making these claims in any official setting, but utterly shameless about turning to these claims to win support on the home front. The legal case the United States made for a 'pre-emptive' invasion of Iraq was the issue of Iraq's possession of weapons of mass destruction capable of being used against the United States. This case was made with considerable fanfare, both for domestic audiences and to generate global support, but there was significant evidence undermining its credibility. As is now established beyond any and all doubt: there were no weapons of mass destruction in Iraq, the Bush administration pushed its claims with little concern for evidence, and the news media participated in this fraud to an appalling extent. (The May 2005 disclosure of the pre-invasion British intelligence Downing Street memo that provided damning evidence about how the United States was cooking intelligence to justify the invasion of Iraq – the 'smoking gun memo' – was the final nail in a well shut coffin.) This episode has been diagnosed in detail, and is now considered one of the darkest moments in the entire history of US journalism.

Omitted, too, in the coverage was the inescapable fact that the US invasion of Iraq violated international law.

The media institutions themselves were hawkish. The *Columbia Journalism Review* subsequently reviewed the editorial pages of the six top dailies that influence public opinion – including the *New York Times,* the *Washington Post,* the *Wall Street Journal* and *USA Today* – and determined that all of them failed to hold the Bush administration to an adequate standard of proof. *Editor & Publisher* determined that of the top 50 daily newspapers in the nation, not a single one was strongly 'anti-war' on its editorial page.

The reliance upon official sources to frame the debate and set the agenda is mostly responsible for the disgraceful press coverage of Bush Administration lies. As Jonathan Mermin put it in a brilliant essay in *World Policy Journal,* conventional journalism means 'journalists continue to be incapable of focusing on an issue for perspective on US foreign policy that has not been first identified or articulated in official Washington debate'. Here it is important to note that most Democratic leaders did not assume an anti-war position, so there was little countervailing framing coming from officialdom. Mermin scoffs at the idea that elite consensus justifies journalists regurgitating the government position uncritically: 'The absence of opposition to a Republican military intervention among Democratic politicians is not persuasive evidence that the policy is sound, or even that presumptively informed and thoughtful people believe it sound'. What it adds up to, in clear contradiction to the spirit and intent of the First Amendment, is 'if the government isn't talking about it, we don't report it'.[6]

A comprehensive analysis of the sources used on TV news in the weeks leading up to the US invasion – when a significant percentage of the US population was opposed to an invasion – showed that 3 per cent of the US sources employed were anti-war, and over 70 per cent were decidedly pro-war. A Fairness and Accuracy in Reporting (FAIR) survey of nightly news coverage on NBC, ABC, CBS, PBS, CNN and Fox during the first three weeks after the invasion found that pro-war US sources outnumbered anti-war sources by 25 to 1. Moreover, the on-air experts that TV news relied upon were generally 'establishment' figures and so by definition uncritical.[7]

Press coverage reached its nadir immediately preceding the invasion. In February 2003 Colin Powell went before the United Nations to make the definitive case for invading Iraq. Powell provided little verifiable evidence for his extravagant claims. Six months later, Associated Press correspondent Charles J. Hanley fact-checked Powell's speech, and 'utterly demolished' it, as *Editor & Publisher* put it.[8] Regrettably the best journalism all too often tends to be in post-mortems, when the political consequences are minuscule. At the time of Powell's speech, when the fate of peace hung in the balance and when independent experts were puncturing most of his claims, the news media regurgitated Powell's points and praised them for their veracity in a manner that could not have been exceeded by Stalin's stooges. Gilbert Cranberg, formerly of the *Des Moines Register*, has compiled a comprehensive study of the press coverage of Powell's speech. Among the terms used by the leading American papers to describe the merits of Powell's case: 'a massive array of evidence'; 'a sober, factual case'; 'an overwhelming case'; 'a smoking fusillade … a persuasive case for anyone who is still persuadable'; 'an ironclad case… incontrovertible evidence'; 'an accumulation of painstakingly gathered and analyzed evidence'; 'succinct and damning evidence … the case is closed'.[9]

In past wars like Vietnam, apologists for gullible press coverage could argue that the news media had no way of knowing that the Johnson Administration was lying to them, and that the Gulf of Tonkin incident was a ruse. Such was not the case with Iraq. At every step of the way there was an impressive amount of material in the international press and on the internet that contradicted the Bush administration's line. (For example, consider the powerful and immediate rebuttal to Powell's UN speech by Glen Rangwala of Cambridge University.)[10] It was all but ignored. Former Marine and Republican weapons inspector Scott Ritter – who spent years on the ground in Iraq – carefully repudiated all of the Bush Administration claims;[11] as a result he was subject to a character assassination campaign that made it easier for a news medium to turn to celebrities like country music singer Lee Greenwood, action movie star Chuck Norris or ex-football player Mike Ditka as if they were credible experts. A journalist did not have to be I.F. Stone to see that there was something fishy about the official story; all she had to do was keep her eyes open and her critical faculties working.

Moreover, unlike Vietnam, the invasion of Iraq was met by a massive anti-war movement in the United States *before* any bullets were expended. Hundreds of thousands of Americans took to the streets in February 2003 to protest the planned invasion of Iraq. Following the familiar pattern for dissident opinion, press coverage was minimal and dismissive.

## MANAGING THE HOME FRONT DURING WAR

Perhaps the most striking development in press coverage of the invasion and war was the policy of 'embedding' journalists with military units, so they could see first-hand how the war was developing. Proponents of the policy argued it would protect journalists from enemy fire and make it possible for them to get stories that would be otherwise unattainable.

Embedded reporting in combination with full throttle jingoism on US television news made it difficult for journalists to do critical work. 'I think the press was muzzled, and I think the press was self-muzzled', stated CNN's Christine Amanpour, arguably the most respected foreign correspondent on US television, a few months later. 'I'm sorry to say, but certainly television and, perhaps, to a certain extent, my station was intimidated by the administration and its foot soldiers at Fox News. And it did, in fact, put a climate of fear and self-censorship, in my view, in terms of the kind of broadcast work we did'.[12]

The problems continued after the formal defeat of Saddam Hussein's army during the liberation that immediately became an occupation. The US news media were caught entirely by surprise. Indeed, the term 'occupation' had never been used prior to the invasion. Mermin quotes PBS's Jim Lehrer, who defended this omission: 'The word occupation ... was never mentioned in the run-up to the war. It was liberation. This was [talked about in Washington as] a war of liberation, not a war of occupation. So as a consequence, those of us in journalism never even looked at the issue of occupation'.[13]

At the same time, it was imperative for the Bush Administration that the best possible spin be put on the war, that it be regarded at home as a success, especially with an election coming up. The one great advantage the Bush Administration had was that it could use its power to heavily promote stories that painted the picture it wanted to be seen, and by remaining quiet it could pour water on those stories it did not wish to see developed. When information continued to emerge discrediting the Bush administration's rationale for the war, and the nature of the 'liberation', like the 'Downing Street memo' of British intelligence, the White House sealed its lips, Democrats meekly obliged, and reporters had little to work with. As a result journalistic mountains were converted into molehills.

Conversely, stories like the toppling of the Saddam Hussein statue in Baghdad, President Bush dressing up in flight-suit drag and appearing below a giant 'Mission Accomplished' banner, the 'rescue' of Jessica Lynch, as well as the capture of Saddam Hussein and the Iraqi election of early 2005, all got lavish attention at the time such attention was needed. Each of these was held up as a critical juncture, the moment the tide was turning and the Bush administration's policies were being proven 'right'. But, in each instance, the passage of only a few days or weeks would reveal that the tide had not turned – and that the administration's approach remained as ill-fated as ever.

Consider the prison torture scandal at Abu Ghraib prison. Award-winning Associated Press reporter Charles Hanley broke a story on US torture of Iraqi prisoners in fall 2003, but, as Mermin notes, it 'was ignored by the major American newspapers'. Hanley explained to Mermin that his 'was not an officially sanctioned story that begins with a handout from an official source', noting at the same time the 'very strong prejudice toward investing US official statements with credibility while disregarding statements from almost any other source'.[14] Hanley's story featured Iraqis recounting their personal experience at Abu Ghraib. It did not provoke a Bush photo-op in a warden's costume in front of Abu Ghraib, or a steady stream of official press releases drawing attention to it. When it finally was broken with photo-graphic evidence by Hersh and CBS News in the US, the story received plentiful coverage. But it was a classic case in which the line of investigation stopped at low levels, and exonerated those in charge of the overall policy. Without any push from official sources the story faded away. Indeed, it went unmentioned during the 2004 presidential campaign debates.

One year after the Abu Ghraib story broke, Seymour Hersh reflected on the whitewash of extensive and persistent US war crimes, which he among others has documented, and the role the US media played. 'It's a dreary pattern', Hersh wrote. 'The reports and subsequent Senate proceedings are sometimes criticized on editorial pages. There are calls for a truly independent investigation by the Senate or the House. Then, as months pass with no official action, the issue withers away, until the next set of revelations revives it'. There were ten official military inquiries into Abu Ghraib, but they 'are all asking the wrong questions … The question that never gets adequately answered is this: what did the president do after being told about Abu Ghraib?'[15]

A major area of tension between the Bush Administration's wish to paint the rosiest possible picture and the responsibility of reporters to present a more accurate picture of what is transpiring in Iraq is the reporting of the war's toll in human lives. The US government wishes to minimize the public's awareness of the human cost of the war, both to the Iraqis and to US soldiers. Wary of Vietnam-like images, the Bush Administration fought to keep this information strictly out of public view. Iraqi casualties were not recorded, and reporters have been unable to get to the places where most of these casualties occur. As a result, Michael Massing notes, journalists have been 'exceedingly cautious' in making estimates.[16] While few US journalists had any interest in this subject, the respected British medical journal *The Lancet* published a study by Johns Hopkins University scholars who estimated the Iraqi civilian death toll at 100,000 in October 2004, before the second siege of Falluja, with a majority of the deaths due to US military actions.[17] The report caused a tempest for a day or two, as it exceeded the figures accepted by US news media by a factor of seven or eight. But the issue died quickly enough, as no US official source wished to dwell on this topic. This lack of interest in keeping an accurate accounting of Iraqi civilian deaths tends to undermine the official claim that this war is motivated by a great concern for the welfare of the Iraqi people.

## MEDIA MOMENT OF TRUTH

Although US journalism, especially in coverage of wars, tends to run in packs, it is not monolithic. Even at its worst there is usually an exception that proves the rule. In addition, among the ranks of journalists are many highly principled and courageous reporters, who entered the profession not to serve as a conduit for those in power, but to shine a light on those in power on behalf of the citizenry. As the dissonance grew between the official story offered by the White House and largely regurgitated in the media and the actual horror story on the ground in Iraq, many journalists took a hard look at media performance and the state of the profession. By the end of 2003 the *Columbia Journalism Review*, *Editor & Publisher* and other leading industry publications or journalism reviews – not to mention the first rate work done by groups like FAIR and publications like the *New York Review of Books* and *The Nation* – had presented probing criticisms of media coverage of the war.

In early 2004 the *New York Times* made the unprecedented gesture of offering a mea culpa for its flawed coverage of the weapons of mass destruction controversy, while the *Washington Post* allowed its media reporter, Howard Kurtz, to write an extended critique of its coverage.[18] Each newspaper implicitly acknowledged its role in leading the nation to war on bogus grounds, yet neither explicitly took responsibility. The confessions were halting and unenthusiastic, but, in a field where admissions of fundamental error are about as welcome as getting root canal surgery without a painkiller, they sent a powerful shot over the bow of journalism nationwide. This occurred on the heels of Howard Dean's rise to the top of the Democratic field, running on an essentially anti-war platform, and when observers were beginning to use words like 'quagmire' to describe the US occupation of Iraq. The apologias were the tip of the journalistic iceberg. Many journalists were appalled by the war, humiliated by the poor performance of the news media, and frustrated by the Bush Administration's deception. Some critics predicted that the working press would get a wake-up call from the scandalous coverage of the Iraq war and turn its anger on Bush in advance of the November election. If there was going to be room for more independent and critical coverage of the US war on Iraq, in early 2004 conditions in newsrooms were as ripe as they ever would be.

Alas, it would not come to pass. The impulse for media self-criticism is quickly tempered by the deeply ingrained institutional realization that it is not healthy to encourage the public to keep the hood up any longer than necessary so they can inspect the engine. Few other major media took the bait and pursued the issue of how the media were complicit in sponsoring a devastating and illegitimate war. It was difficult to avoid Danny Schechter's conclusion that the mainstream press made minimum concessions on its Iraq coverage as a form of damage control. It had no interest in laying out the whole truth.[19]

The *New York Times* certainly wanted to get the incident in its rear view mirror as quickly as possible. The *Times* quietly removed Judith Miller (the reporter whose uncritical and whole-hog reliance on extremely dubious sources in 2003 gave tremendous legitimacy to the Bush Administration's lies about Iraq possessing weapons of mass destruction) from her beat, but she was not formally censured. Miller herself was unapologetic. 'My job isn't to assess the government's information and be an independent intelligence analyst myself', she is quoted by Mermin as saying. 'My job is to tell readers of the *New York Times* what the government thought about Iraq's arsenal'.[20]

The way journalists adapted to the coverage of the occupation of Iraq was not to tell the truth and let the chips fall where they might. As one Baghdad correspondent for a large US newspaper told Massing in October 2004, 'the situation in Iraq was a catastrophe', a view shared 'almost unanimously' by his colleagues. A widely circulated email that September by Farnaz Fassihi, a Baghdad correspondent for the *Wall Street Journal*, was a devastating critique of the US war, 'a foreign policy failure that will haunt the United States for decades to come'. Fassihi concluded: 'The genie of terrorism, chaos and mayhem has been unleashed onto this country as a result of American mistakes and it can't be put back into the bottle'. Massing notes that other US correspondents in Baghdad were startled at the attention Fassihi's email received. 'Everyone was marveling and asking what we were doing wrong if that information came as a surprise to the American public', one of them told Massing.[21]

Such a candid view of conditions in Iraq was regarded by the evolving conventions of professional journalism as partisan, unprofessional and not objective – regardless of whether or not it was true – because it was a thorough repudiation of the Bush administration position. It was not *balanced*, 'balance' being defined not by the evidence but by accommodation to powerful interests. This point cannot be overemphasized: the balance editors employed had nothing to do with the evidence, and everything to do with keeping the Bush administration and the political right off their backs. 'Every story from Iraq is by definition an assessment as to whether things are going well or badly', a US newspaper correspondent in Baghdad told Massing. 'Editors are hypersensitive about not wanting to appear to be coming down on one side or the other'.[22] (There is little evidence that appearing too pro-administration on the war caused many editors to shudder in fear.) Once Fassihi's email was spread across the Internet, the *Wall Street Journal* received pressure to remove her from the beat because she could no longer be regarded as 'objective'. Fassihi was immediately sent on a vacation until after the November US election, though the *Journal* stated that this had nothing to do with her email.

Edward Wasserman reflected upon this conundrum in the *Miami Herald*. 'I can only imagine the current mind-set of supervising editors: If we give prominence to this story of carnage in Iraq, will we be accused of anti-administration bias? And – here it gets interesting – will we therefore owe our readers an offsetting story, perhaps an inspirational tale of Marines teaching young Iraqis how to play softball?' So by following the obsession with balance, the news reports presented a confusing and skewed picture of the reality on the ground in Iraq. And it meant that the logical hard questions that would emerge from tough-minded reporting – like what on earth accounts for this mess? – got lost in the contradictory and incoherent picture provided by 'balanced' reporting.[23] 'Balance' did mean that a number of quality reports could get through, especially in the print media. In the months before the November election, there were several first-rate examinations in the main-stream press of the failures of the US occupation. But the TV news coverage was far more pro-war, generally dismissing or ignoring facts that got in the way, with Fox News the exemplar, though far from alone in its patriotic charge.

It did not help matters that John Kerry and leading Democrats did not oppose the war per se, but only how it was being executed. Kerry was no anti-war candidate, and the war, amazingly enough, was not a defining issue in the 2004 campaign. This meant there was no 'official' anti-war source to embrace what critical reporting there was, draw voter attention to it, and encourage journalists to do more of the same. Not surprisingly, public opinion surveys indicated that in the fall of 2004 a significant percentage of Americans – and most Bush voters – still believed Iraq possessed weapons of mass destruction and that Saddam Hussein was shown to have been a major supporter of Al Qaeda, and hence lurked behind the 9-11 attacks. In view of how much media coverage was devoted to these issues, a more thorough repudiation of the press could barely be imagined. (What would people have thought of the US media system if in 1944 a survey had found that a majority of Americans thought China was responsible for the attack on Pearl Harbor?)

## DEMOCRACY INVARIABLY ASCENDANT

Because the core articles of faith remain inviolable in US journalism and politics, US media coverage of American foreign wars inexorably slides into providing a view compatible with those atop society. Despite the thorough invalidation of every official reason provided by the Bush Administration to invade and occupy Iraq, journalists made almost no effort to locate more plausible explanations for such a major war. It would not have taken long for an inquiring reporter to find serious experts able to discuss the following factors: the imperial drive encouraged by the existence of a massive military-industrial complex; the geopolitical and economic advantages of having permanent military bases and a client regime/friendly ally in the heart of the Middle East; the domestic political advantages for a President to have the populace whipped into wartime fervour; the security needs of Israel, a close ally of the United States; and, of course, oil. Such explanations can be found in elite journals, in the business press, in intelligence reports and in academic studies. Such an approach is applied in popular analyses of the motives of any other nation throughout history, but such inquiry was and is off-limits in US politics and in US mainstream journalism. To leading American politicians and journalists, the United States is a benevolent nation, always working with the ultimate objective of promoting democracy.

When the United States finally convened an election in Iraq on January 30, it was trumpeted with a massive PR blitz by Washington, and the media obediently responded. The election was regarded as a wondrous democratic moment and viewed without criticism in the news media. Finally, the war was won! And, finally, too, the real reason why the United States had invaded and occupied Iraq could be declared: to bring democracy to the entire Middle East – and, of course, to liberate the women! This explanation was embraced across the political spectrum, as it tapped into the core presuppositions about the US role in the world. But empirical support for the democratic claim also evaporated as the situation in Iraq grew even more grim for the US forces and the elected government by mid-2005.[24]

As the United States celebrated the triumph of freedom and democracy, elementary questions went unasked. On what grounds should the US claim to be concerned with democracy be taken seriously? Is the United States a purely philanthropic power that has no military or economic designs? Why did US occupation authorities in Iraq work so hard to delay elections? If the US favours democratic rule, why ignore the fact that most Iraqis voted for parties calling for an early or even immediate end to the US occupation? Is it legitimate to invade a nation to install democracy? If it is legitimate, is every non-democracy in need of an invasion or just some? Which ones? Is Iraq just the first nation on a list of those that should be invaded? What about

Pakistan? Or Saudi Arabia? Or Kuwait? And who makes the decision about which country to invade, and who does the invading? If the United States can do it to Iraq, can India do it to Pakistan? Can Russia invade Uzbekistan? Can Venezuela invade Colombia? These are the kinds of questions that must be answered if the invasion of Iraq is to be justified in terms of 'democracy'. Otherwise it is just the law of the jungle, with all talk about democracy so much bunkum. In the US media system, these questions almost never get asked; the subject never gets sustained attention.

The problems besetting US journalism are deep-seated and will not go away unless there is structural change in the media system, such that truthful reporting on affairs of state can be a rational expectation. This requires immediate political organizing to change the policies upon which the media system is based, and it requires making media reform part and parcel of broader movements for peace and social justice. In the end, media reform and social justice will rise or fall together. We need a press system that tells the truth.

NOTES

1    Letter to W.T. Barry, 4 August 1822, in Philip R. Fendall, ed., *Letters and Other Writings of James Madison*, Volume III, Philadelphia: Lippincott, 1865, p. 276.

2    See Saul K. Padover, editor and translator, Karl Marx, *On Freedom of the Press and Censorship*, New York: McGraw-Hill, 1974.

3    See Robert W. McChesney, *The Problem of the Media*, New York: Monthly Review Press, 2004, ch. 2.

4    Edward S. Herman and Noam Chomsky, *Manufacturing Consent: The Political Economy of the News Media*, New York: Pantheon, 1988.

5    Howard Friel and Richard A. Falk, *The Paper of Record: How the New York Times Misreports U.S. Foreign Policy*, New York: Verso, 2004.

6    Jonathan Mermin, 'The Media's Independence Problem', *World Policy Journal*, 21(3), Fall, 2004, p. 69.

7    Steve Rendall and Tara Broughel, 'Amplifying Officials, Squelching Dissent: FAIR Study Finds Democracy Poorly Served by War Coverage', *Extra!*, May/June, 2003, http://www.fair.org/extra/0305/warstudy.html

8    'Watchdogs of War', *Editor & Publisher*, 8 September 2003; Greg Mitchell, 'Why We Are in Iraq', *Editor & Publisher*, 8 September 2003.

9    Cited in Eric Alterman, '"Case Closed"', *The Nation*, 25 April 2005.

10   Glen Rangwala, 'Claims in Secretary of State Colin Powell's UN

Presentation Concerning Iraq, 5th Feb 2003', http://middleeastreference.org.uk/powell030205.html.

11  See for example Scott Ritter, 'Is Iraq a True Threat to the US?', *Boston Globe*, 20 July 2002, http://www.commondreams.org/views02/0721-02.htm.

12  Antonia Zerbisias, 'The Press Self-muzzled Its Coverage of Iraq War', *Toronto Star*, 16 September 2003.

13  Mermin, 'The Media's Independence Problem', p. 67.

14  Ibid.

15  Seymour Hersh, 'The Unknown Unknowns of the Abu Ghraib Scandal', *The Guardian*, 21 May 2005.

16  Michael Massing, 'Iraq, the Press and the Election', *New York Review of Books*, 16 December 2004.

17  L. Roberts et al., 'Mortality Before and After the 2003 Invasion of Iraq: Cluster Sample Survey', *The Lancet*, 364(9448), pp. 1857-64. It should be noted that the figure of 100,000 deaths was a controversial one, arrived at by extrapolating from a comparison of prewar and wartime mortality rates in a sample of Iraqi neighbourhoods. For a critique see Fred Kaplan, '100,000 Dead – or 8,000. How Many Iraqi Civilians have Died as a Result of the War?', 29 October 2004, http://slate.msn.com/id/2108887. The effort to produce an accurate casualty estimate continues today. British and American researchers in the Iraq Body Count project maintain a database at http://www.countthecasualties.org.uk/ of media-reported civilian deaths in Iraq resulting from the military invasion and occupation. It estimates the casualties, in the period of 1 January 2003 to 15 June 2005, to be between 22,248 and 25,229.

18  Howard Kurtz, 'Paint by Numbers: How Repeated Reportage Colors Perceptions' (Media Notes), *The Washington Post*, 12 July 2004.

19  Danny Schechter, 'Is Our Media Covering Its Errors or Covering Them Up?', *CommonDreams.org*, 16 August 2004, http://www.commondreams.org/views04/0816-04.htm.

20  Mermin, 'The Media's Independence Problem', pp. 67–8.

21  Statements quoted in Massing, 'Iraq, the Press and the Election'. See also Michael Massing, 'Now They Tell Us', *New York Review of Books*, 26 February 2004.

22  Massing, 'Iraq, the Press and the Election'.

23  Edward Wasserman, 'Cowardice in the Newsrooms', *Miami Herald*, 6 September 2004.

24  Andrew Ackerman, 'War Reporters at ASNE Say Iraq Remains Frightening', *Editor & Publisher*, 15 April 2005.

# PROPAGANDA-MANAGED DEMOCRACY: THE UK AND THE LESSONS OF IRAQ

## DAVID MILLER

During the 2005 election campaign in the UK, the Conservative party adopted a strategy of describing Blair as a 'liar' over Iraq. Some critics regarded this as counterproductive.[1] It was seen as harming the Tories electorally, but there was also an implication that this was not quite the done thing, as if it breached the protocols of dignified politics. Blair himself has repeatedly stated that he doesn't mind people disagreeing with him just as long as they don't attack 'my conduct and integrity'.[2]

The extraordinary thing about these events is that it should be thought that lying was the worst thing that Blair had done. The degraded quality of political debate is such that the ultimate prize is to catch one's political opponents in a falsehood. Political success is reduced to the outcome of a linguistic battle. This illustrates a wider problem: the notion that words and deeds are separate, or at least separable things – that for political success one does not need to act consistently or honourably, one just has to ensure that what one says can be said to be consistent or honourable.

This divorce between words and deeds closely – and not accidentally – parallels a similar divorce at the core of the belief systems promoted by the powerful. The gap between words and deeds has widened in recent years, with Iraq merely providing the defining moment in which this is seen clearly by millions of people. But the lies go much deeper than the convenient rationale for an unpopular invasion. They are actually a key and necessary part of the neoliberal period.

In the real world, where most of the world's population still has to live, there is an inescapable connection between saying and doing. And in the real world the opprobrium of millions towards Blair (and Bush and the rest) is based on the fact that he lied for a purpose. That purpose was the pursuit of US imperial interests. In that purpose he broke international law and helped to kill tens of thousands of civilians in the process. This makes Blair something worse that being a common or garden liar. The charge sheet also includes murder and war crimes.

## LIVING IN THE MATRIX

The separation between words and deeds, or rhetoric and reality, is increasingly recognized in every sphere of public life, from the inappropriately-named 'reality TV' shows and the hyper-unreality of advertising, to election razzma-tazz, corporate spin and government propaganda. We live in a period where we must recognize what John Kenneth Galbraith, in *The Economics of Inno-cent Fraud*, describes as a 'continuing divergence' between 'approved belief' and reality.[3] We live in the age of the fake.[4] For many, the lies around Iraq crossed a line and revealed concerted government lying which was seen as comparatively new. In my view it is new in the sense that we are in a new, neoliberal period which stands in marked contrast to the period of social democracy (roughly 1945-1979) when the gap between words and actions was of necessity narrower. The compromise between capital and labour forced the creation of a common language. This had its limits, but at least in key aspects of domestic policy the gap between rhetoric and reality was narrower. There was less need to lie, less need to attempt to align capital-ist interests with general interests because there was some compromise and mediation of interests.

Under neoliberalism, the gap between the interests of the elite and the general interest widens dramatically, and is exacerbated by the gap in social experience created by increasing economic inequality. A whole new machin-ery of propaganda was called for and could be seen in the rise of the PR industry, and in the overhaul of state propaganda.[5] After 9/11, the assault on Iraq involved a huge propaganda build up, both organizationally and ideologically.[6] It is in the ideological campaign to sell the invasion that we can best see our rulers in action, both because this was a crucial period for them and because we now have access to some of the key documents which recorded their thinking.

## 'A CLEVER PLAN': IRAQ

The assault on Iraq was a long-term plan of the US right, but it was 9/11 that provided the opportunity to put it into action. In early 2001 Bush administra-tion officials had been candid that Iraq was not a threat. 'He [Saddam Hussein] is unable to project conventional power against his neighbors', Colin Powell said in February 2001.[7] 'The truth is', noted one of UK Foreign Secretary Jack Straw's advisers, that what had changed was 'not the pace' of Saddam Hussein's WMD programmes, 'but our tolerance of them post-11 Septem-ber'.[8] Between September 2001 and the spring of 2002 the plan to invade

Iraq was developed by the Bush administration and by March 2002 the Blair administration was fully on board. The message delivered to Condoleezza Rice in the second week of March by Blair's most senior foreign affairs adviser, Sir David Manning, was that Blair 'would not budge in [his] support for regime change'.[9]

The Americans pressed on with their policy, but recognized the need for a political strategy to deliver it. So as Richard Dearlove, the head of MI6, put it, 'the intelligence and facts were being fixed around the policy'.[10] British officials regarded this strategy, which included attempting to link Al Qaeda and Iraq, as 'frankly unconvincing'. They conveyed to the US administration the support of the UK government, but alerted it to the difficulties faced by the British. Manning told Rice that Blair 'had to manage a press, a Parliament and a public opinion that was very different than anything in the States'. As Christopher Meyer, the British Ambassador to the US, put it, the management of dissent required a 'plan' that 'had to be clever' and 'would be a tough sell for us domestically'.[11]

According to a Whitehall briefing paper for the Prime Minister's meeting on 23 July 2002, the 'conditions necessary' for military action included 'justification/legal base; an international coalition; a quiescent Israel/Palestine; a positive risk/benefit assessment; and the preparation of domestic opinion'.[12] There were two key elements to the plan. The first was to use the United Nations to 'wrong foot' Saddam Hussein into delivering a *casus belli*.[13] In other words, the UK government persuaded the US government that by manipulating the UN to provoke a war, they could gain greater legitimacy for the invasion.[14] The second element was to play up the threat from Iraq. This was necessary to prepare 'domestic opinion'. According to the Cabinet Office this would involve the following:

> Time will be required to prepare public opinion in the UK that it is necessary to take military action against Saddam Hussein. There would also need to be a substantial effort to secure the support of Parliament. An information campaign will be needed which has to be closely related to an overseas information campaign designed to influence Saddam Hussein, the Islamic World and the wider international community. This will need to give full coverage to the threat posed by Saddam Hussein, including his WMD, and the legal justification for action.[15]

The organizational apparatus to conduct this campaign was thoroughly overhauled by the US and UK governments after September 2001 and co-ordinated by the Office of Global Communications created by Bush in July

2002.[16] Only the content of the campaign remained to be worked out. This was prepared and launched two months later involving the full weight of US and UK government resources and a wide range of government departments, PR consultancies, think tanks and intelligence agencies. The US government focused on the alleged (and quite false) connection between Iraq and 9/11 or at least 'terrorism' in general. This was so successful that by the end of 2002 two thirds of US citizens believed that Iraq was involved in September 11 attacks.[17] By contrast, in the UK more weight was laid on the alleged threat posed by Iraq. 'To get public and Parliamentary support for military options', wrote Jack Straw's adviser, we have to be 'convincing' that 'the threat is so serious/imminent that it is worth sending our troops to die for'; and that 'it is qualitatively different from the threat posed by other proliferators who are closer to achieving nuclear capability (including Iran)'.[18]

In order to show this, the UK government launched a massive 'information' campaign, at the centre of which was the dossier on Weapons of Mass Destruction.[19] This contained a litany of lies about Iraq's weapons capability. The most discussed claim, though by no means the only deception, was that WMD could be 'ready within 45 minutes of an order to use them'. The dossier claimed that 'much information about Iraqi weapons of mass destruction is already in the public domain from UN reports and from Iraqi defectors. This points clearly to Iraq's continuing possession, after 1991, of chemical and biological agents' and Iraq has 'continued to produce chemical and biological agents'. But the UN reports and information from the key defector, Hussein Kamel, showed that there was no evidence that the Iraqi government had engaged in new production, and that it had verifiably destroyed 90–95 per cent of its chemical and biological agent. Any that remained (including Anthrax and VX nerve agent – with the single exception of mustard gas) was in a form which would have degraded to 'useless sludge' (within the 10 years that had elapsed), to use the words of Scott Ritter, the former weapons inspector. So the evidence on which the dossier relied did not support its account. Therefore, the government knew that there was no threat.[20]

On the possibility of using the weapons within 45 minutes the dossier claimed that Iraq 'can deliver chemical and biological agents using an extensive range of artillery shells, free-fall bombs, sprayers and ballistic missiles ... The Iraq military are able to deploy these weapons within 45 minutes of a decision to do so'.[21] This neatly conflates the alleged 'intelligence' on 45 minutes with long range ballistic missiles. In fact, Iraq did not have any such missiles, and according to John Scarlett of the Joint Intelligence Committee the original intelligence assessment was only that 'battlefield mortar shells or small calibre weaponry' could be deployed in 45 minutes. Again, both Blair and Campbell were in a position to know this since it was their own intel-ligence. In other words, the 45 minute claim involved at least three separate deceptions: on the existence of agents in weaponized form; on existence of the delivery mechanism; and on the application of the 45 minute claim to long-range delivery systems.

Peter Oborne, of the conservative *Spectator* magazine, declares that it is 'amazing' that there is a 'group of shameless habitual liars at the centre of power'.[22] But it is not terribly surprising, nor is it terribly new, for the politi-cal elite to believe it is their right to lie in defence of their interests. What is perhaps novel is that elements of the elite now subscribe to a belief system that is unable to comprehend the difference between truth and lies. This collapse of the distinction between truth and interests is a characteristic of the neo-conservative movement in the US and has striking parallels in the development of New Labour in the UK.

## THE RISE OF THE 'SHAMELESS HABITUAL LIAR'

Peter Oborne's book, *The Rise of Political Lying*, provides a good analysis of the trajectory of new labour deception. It focuses on the role of key opera-tives like Geoff Mulgan and Charlie Leadbetter and their use of relativist and post-structuralist conceptions of narrative to suggest that there are only versions of truth. Both Mulgan and Leadbetter were linked with the *Marxism Today* project around Stuart Hall and Martin Jacques which paved the way for New Labour ideology.[23] Oborne notes how this fits well with the neo-conservative analysis derived from Leo Strauss that democracy and truth were irreconcilable.[24] As the prominent neo-conservative, Irving Kristol, has put it: 'the notion that there should be one set of truths available to everyone is a modern democratic fallacy'.[25]

But Oborne does not delve into the history of lies and propaganda and underestimates the historic depth of the contemporary pattern of deception. The weakest part of his analysis is his explanation of the reasons for the rise of spin. He describes a 'massive change in British political culture in the past few decades'. This, he believes, rather than 'internal or external pres-sures', has produced the 'catastrophic' decline in standards of 'truth telling'.[26] He mentions the contributory role of technological developments in mass communication and points to the application of advertising and market-ing techniques; the 'hard sell' instead of 'humanity, complexity and truth'.[27] While his account is an accurate, if brief, description of the transformation of the culture, it fails to explain why the culture would change, except under the influence of technology. But the adoption of the techniques of market-ing and advertising industry is not the inevitable result of neutral transfer of knowledge from one part of society to another, but actually a key indicator of the rise of corporate power.

Oborne dates the malaise to the Major government and says it has accelerated under New Labour. Thatcher's propagandists by contrast, made 'the most' of her 'triumphs' and played down 'her mistakes and failures' but 'never departed' from the 'common sense' that they must present what they saw as the truth.[28] Oborne adds to this that some Labour ministers do not lie. It is as if the propensity to lie is partly related to questions of character.

In fact the neoliberal revolution and its promotion of corporate power is the key to the convergence of the parties (to 'factions of the business party'), the downgrading of parliament, the increase in inequality and the rise of PR and lobbying. Since the onset of the neoliberal revolution, initiated by the Thatcher and Reagan administrations, the sweep of privatization and neoliberal reform has occurred unevenly. The US has always been a more market oriented society and more advanced 'propaganda-managed' democracy than European countries, where the UK has been at the forefront of this process. The apparatus of lying has developed faster in the UK than in continental Europe, covering the gamut of communicative spheres (corporate PR, political communications, lobbying and civil society spin techniques).

The export of US (read neoliberal) techniques of electioneering has been rapid if also uneven.[29] The same is true of the growth of the PR industry. This has been particularly marked in the UK, whose PR industry has been the main economic engine for the expansion of techniques of propaganda control. The UK PR industry is the second largest in the world after the US, larger than that in Japan and twice the size of that in France and Germany (in 2002).[30] The PR industry had been lobbying for thirty years with some success for the increased use of PR consultancies by government, but it took the Phillis inquiry, which reported in 2004, to really open the floodgates to the use of private sector PR to sell government policy.[31] In the US this process was much more advanced, and became a political scandal in 2004/5 with the revelation that fake 'news' had been constructed for US government departments by PR companies.[32]

## THE ORIGINS OF PROPAGANDA–MANAGED DEMOCRACY

However much the neoliberal period has involved a marked increase in the technology of propaganda control, the gap between words and deeds is not new. In this respect, it resembles the period in which modern democracy was born, when the threat from the masses led to a huge upsurge in the machinery of propaganda. The theory and practice of a propaganda-managed democracy were developed between 1880 and 1920.

In the UK, the threat of democracy was a keen concern of the business, political and intellectual elites. Graham Wallas, whose key contribution to the theory of propaganda-managed democracy is largely forgotten, was a one time member of the Fabian Society who grew sceptical of the ability of the people to rule. His book, *Human Nature in Politics*, first published in 1908, advanced the argument that 'human intellectual limitations' meant the possibility of the 'manipulation of the popular impulse' and therefore that the scope of popular democracy should be restricted so as to leave out 'those questions … which cause the holders of wealth and industrial power to make full use of their opportunities'.[33] This could be achieved thanks to the fact that 'the art of using skill for the production of emotion and opinion has so advanced, that the whole condition of contests would be changed for the future'.[34] Wallas' contribution is largely forgotten. There is little awareness that there was a concerted movement in Britain to 'take the risk out of democracy' as Alex Carey has memorably put it.[35]

After Wallas lectured in the US in 1910, his work was taken up enthusiastically by Walter Lippman, himself a former member of the Socialist Party USA, and widely recognized on the left as an important intellectual progenitor of the theory and justification of a propaganda-managed democracy. It was essential, he wrote, that 'the public be put in its place' so that 'each of us may live free of the trampling and the roar of a bewildered herd'.[36] Lippmann thought that the 'manufacture of consent' was both necessary and possible. 'Within the life of the generation now in control of affairs, persuasion has become a self conscious art and a regular organ of popular government'.[37]

Back in the UK, the business classes were already organizing to buy insurance against democracy by the late 19th century. The Engineering Employers Federation was a key capitalist lobby group set up in 1896. By 1911 a hugely important and now largely forgotten activist for big business, going by the delightful name of Dudley Docker, was organizing corporate propaganda outfits known as 'Business leagues' under the slogan 'pro patria imperium in imperio' (for our country a government within a government) – in other words, business rule. 'If our League spreads', wrote Docker in 1911, 'politics would be done for. This is my object'.[38] In 1916 he was founding president of the Federation of British Industries. By 1918, when universal suffrage was (almost) fully instituted for the first time, corporate propaganda was in full swing – organized by a group of business activists (including Docker) around the British Commonwealth Union. Their intent can be understood by the names they gave themselves – the 'London imperialists' and the 'diehards'. Their project was business rule and in the 1918 election they fielded nearly 50 covert candidates, whose ostensible party loyalty was a cover for business loyalties.[39] In 1919 they launched a powerful new organization whose name unblushingly revealed its purpose: 'National propaganda'. They went into action almost straight away during the 1919 Rail Strike in close collaboration with the Prime Minister, Lloyd George, who granted them access to all special branch and intelligence files on the left. They later played a pivotal role in the 1926 General Strike, by which time they had changed their name to the Economic League. Their principal role in this period was propaganda intended to undermine the democratic process and especially the labour movement.

This story has been almost entirely suppressed.[40] Since then, the power of business lobbyists has waxed and waned, and taken on new guises, such as Aims of Industry, set up in 1942 to counter Labour's nationalization plans. But there is an unmistakeable continuity between these early business practitioners of propaganda-managed democracy, and today's.

## TODAY'S SUCCESSORS OF WALLAS AND LIPPMAN

The concerns about the unleashed power of the masses which the rise of organized labour and the campaign for universal suffrage raised in the early 20th century are back again. The social democratic and liberal left, or rather the ex-liberal left, appears to be particularly exercised by this. In Britain the *Guardian* has featured a succession of commentators blaming the public for what they see as the malaise of the political system. Polly Toynbee epitomizes this when she writes: 'It is salutary to be reminded how much sheer pig-headed ignorance, nastiness, mean-spiritedness and rudeness politicians encounter every day. Trying to squeeze votes out of people who can't be bothered to inform themselves of the most basic facts is wearying work'.[41] Elsewhere she denounces the media for attempting to 'Get the politicians, catch the government lying, denigrate, mock, kill. Never mind the substance of a policy'. This, she write 'is political decadence', which 'is in danger of making the country nearly ungovernable'.[42]

The same line could be heard from Blair aides such as Geoff Mulgan, who denounced 'the lack of a strong ethic of searching for the truth in much of the media'.[43] The most extended attack on the media in this vein has come from John Lloyd, a former *New Statesman* editor, who claimed the media were undermining democracy.[44] His point of departure was the BBC report by Andrew Gilligan which exposed the 'sexing up' of the dossier on Weapons of Mass Destruction. Lloyd asserted that the Gilligan story 'wasn't true'.[45] But this assertion was categorically wrong. The published evidence clearly shows that the story was true. Downing Street repeatedly intervened to 'sex up' the dossier – or to give 'presentational advice', as Alastair Campbell laughably put it – and was key to the strategy of selling the policy of regime change by lying about it. Whether or not all the evidence was available at the time of Gilligan's report, his story was true, as the government's weapons expert, David Kelly, had intimated to him and other journalists. Lloyd and the rest exhibit the standards of journalism and evidence typical of the political elite in general. They are simply unable to write the truth about their political masters, being lost in the same matrix of deception and self-deception. They betray an abject supplication before our rulers.

As Marx and Engels put it in the German Ideology:

> The division of labour,... manifests itself ... in the ruling class as the division of mental and material labour, so that inside this class one part appears as the thinkers of the class (its active, concep-tive ideologists, who make the perfecting of the illusion of the class about itself their chief source of livelihood), while the others' attitude to these ideas and illusions is more passive and receptive, because they are in reality the active members of this class and have less time to make up illusions and ideas about themselves.[46]

Lloyd fits this description well, as do so many other journalists and the staff-ers in Downing Street who helped their masters concoct the lies in question around Iraq. The outpourings of Lloyd and other apologists for neoliberal-ism in the UK bear a striking resemblance to those uttered by the neo-con followers of Leo Strauss. Irving Kristol notes that the truth must not be uttered in front of the masses in case 'the popularization ... of these truths might import unease, turmoil and the release of popular passions ... [with] mostly negative consequences'.[47]

## THE LESSON OF IRAQ

The lesson of Iraq is that the gap between elite belief systems and the truth has widened. This is a development grounded in material changes. Winning support for the idea that profits are legitimate and wages are fair is more diffi-cult under neoliberal conditions than it was under social democracy, hence the need to lie and fabricate more than before in order to align dominant class interests with popular aspirations becomes a structural condition of the neoliberal period. In other words, the exponential growth of lying and of the apparatus for constructing lies is fundamentally connected to the freeing of capital from democratic control.

We should beware of those accounts which argue that our leaders have always lied or that there is nothing new in their contemporary lies. Such accounts fail to account for lying as an outcome of concrete material proc-esses. Propaganda-managed democracy is hardly a matter of innocent fraud. The necessity for propaganda is created by the narrowing social basis of neoliberal rule. This type of rule depends more on propaganda as the gap between class and general interests grows. But propaganda becomes ever more fragile as a mechanism of control as the divergence is experienced and understood by the people. The global justice and anti-war movements are both an expression of that fragility. Our rulers know this, and the fear it causes pushes them on to ever more extravagant lies.

## NOTES

1    For example, Melanie Phillips: 'His repeated taunt that Mr. Blair was a liar rebounded badly; British voters don't like their politicians to trade insults, even if they agree with them'. 'Stuck in the Middle with You', *Wall Street Journal Europe*, 9 May 2005.

2    Philippe Naughton, 'Blair Dismisses Iraq Row as a Distraction', *Times Online*, 25 April 2005.

3    J.K. Galbraith, *The Economics of Innocent Fraud*, London: Penguin, 2005.

4    David Miller, 'The Age of the Fake', *Spinwatch*, 14 March 2005.

5    David Miller and William Dinan, 'The Rise of the PR Industry in Britain 1979-1998', *European Journal of Communication*, 15(1), 2000, pp. 5-35.

6    David Miller, 'The Propaganda Machine', in David Miller, ed., *Tell Me Lies: Propaganda and Media Distortion in the Attack on Iraq*, London: Pluto, 2004.

7    John Pilger, 'Pilger Film Reveals Colin Powell said Iraq was No Threat', *Daily Mirror*, 22 September 2003; and see Secretary Colin L. Powell, 'Press Remarks with Foreign Minister of Egypt Amre Moussa', Cairo, Egypt (Ittihadiya Palace), 24 February 2001, http://www.thememory-hole.org/war/powell-cairo.htm.

8    Memo from Peter Ricketts, Political Director, Foreign & Commonwealth Office, to the Foreign Secretary, Jack Straw, dated 22 March 2002, http://www.david-morrison.org.uk/other-documents/ricketts020322.pdf.

9    David Manning to Tony Blair, 'Your Trip to the US', 14 March 2002, http://www.david-morrison.org.uk/other-documents/manning020314.pdf.

10   Matthew Rycroft to David Manning, 'Iraq: Prime Minister's Meeting: 23 July' [The Downing Street Memo], published by the *Sunday Times*, 1 May 2005.

11   Christopher Meyer to David Manning, 'Iraq and Afghanistan: Conversation with Wolfowitz', 18 March 2002, http://www.david-morrison.org.uk/other-documents/meyer020318.pdf.

12    Cabinet Office paper, 'Conditions for Military Action', published in the *Sunday Times*, 12 June 2005.

13    Meyer's words in Meyer to Manning, 'Iraq and Afghanistan'.

14    For the documents in full and an analysis of them, see David Morrison, *Blair's Big Lie*, A Labour and Trade Union Review pamphlet, London: Bevin Books, April 2005; and 'More on Blair's Big Lie', May 2005, http: www.david-morrison.org.uk/iraq/bn-blairs-big-lie-more.htm.

15    Cabinet Office paper, 'Conditions'.

16    David Miller, 'The Propaganda Machine'.

17    Laura Miller, John Stauber and Sheldon Rampton, 'War is Sell', in David Miller, *Tell me Lies*.

18    Ricketts' memo to Jack Straw.

19    *Iraq's Weapons of Mass Destruction: The Assessment of the British Government*, 24 September 2003, http://www.number-10.gov.uk/output/Page271. asp.

20    See the forensic deconstruction of these claims on Glen Rangwala's site: http://www.middleeastreference.org.uk.

21    *Iraq's Weapons of Mass Destruction*, p. 17.

22    Peter Oborne, *The Rise of Political Lying*, London: Free Press, 2005, p. 244.

23    Greg Philo and David Miller, *Market Killing*, London: Longman, 2001.

24    Peter Oborne, *Rise of Political Lying*, p. 218.

25    Quoted in Ronald Bailey, 'Origin of the Specious: Why do Neoconservatives Doubt Darwin?', *Reason*, July 1997; See also Jim Lobe, 'Leo Strauss' Philosophy of Deception', *AlterNet*, posted 19 May 2003, http://www.alternet.org/story/15935.

26    Peter Oborne, *Rise of Political Lying*, p. 123.

27    Ibid., p. 125.

28    Ibid., p. 141.

29    In the rather 'tepid' debate on the 'professionalization' of political communications study after study demonstrates that US techniques of spin are being exported all round the world, although they meet greater resistance in some states than in others. See Gerry Sussman, *Global Electioneering: Campaign Consulting, Communications and Corporate Financing*, Lanham: Rowman and Littlefield, 2005; David Miller, 'System Failure: It's Not Just the Media – The Whole Political System has Failed', *Journal of Public Affairs*, 4(4), 2004, pp. 374-83.

30    Miller and Dinan, 'The Rise'.

31    David Miller, 'Phillis Report Signals End Of UK Public Service Information', *Spinwatch*, 2 February 2004; David Miller, 'Privatising Spin', *Spinwatch*, 18 May 2004, http://www.spinwatch.org.

32  Source Watch, 'Fake News', consulted 6 July 2005, http://www.source-watch.org.

33  Cited in Terence H. Qualter, *Graham Wallas and the Great Society*, New York: St. Martin's Press, 1979, p. 134.

34  Graham Wallas, *Human Nature in Politics*, Lincoln: University of Nebraska Press, 1962, p. 29.

35  Alex Carey, *Taking the Risk Out of Democracy: Corporate Propaganda Versus Freedom and Liberty*, Sydney: University of New South Wales Press, 1995.

36  Walter Lippmann, *Public Opinion*, London: Allen and Unwin, 1921.

37  Ibid., p. 158. 'The crowd is enthroned' PR pioneer Ivy Lee had written in 1914, calling for professional propagandists to act as modern 'courtiers' to 'flatter and caress' the crowd. See Ray Eldon Hiebert, *Courtier to the Crowd: The Story of Ivy Lee and the Development of Public Relations*, Ames: Iowa State University Press, 1966.

38  R.P.T. Davenport-Hines, *Dudley Docker: The Life and Times of a Trade Warrior*, Cambridge: Cambridge University Press, 2002, pp. 70, 74.

39  J.A. Turner, 'The British Commonwealth Union and the General Election of 1918', *English Historical Review*, 93, July 1978, pp. 528-59.

40  But see Mike Hughes, *Spies at Work*, Bradford: 1 in 12 Publications, 1994.

41  Polly Toynbee, 'Voting's Too Good for 'em: The Public Cavil Endlessly at Politicians while Wallowing in Wilful Ignorance and Bitter Prejudice', *The Guardian*, 4 June 2004.

42  Polly Toynbee, 'Breaking News', *The Guardian*, 5 September 2003.

43  Geoff Mulgan, 'The Media's Lies Poison Our System', *The Guardian*, 7 May 2004.

44  John Lloyd, *What the Media are Doing to Our Politics*, London: Constable Robinson, 2004.

45  John Lloyd, 'Dishonest? Take a Look at Your Own Deeds, Greg', *Observer*, 24 October 2004, p. 8.

46  Karl Marx, 'Ruling Class and Ruling Ideas', in *The German Ideology*, Moscow: Progress Publishers, 1968, p. 64.

47  Quoted in Bailey, 'Origin of the Specious'.

# CORRECTING STIGLITZ:
# FROM INFORMATION TO POWER
# IN THE WORLD OF DEVELOPMENT

## BEN FINE AND ELISA VAN WAEYENBERGE

Over the past decade Joseph Stiglitz has acquired a considerable reputation for radicalism. It began with his launching of the post Washington Consensus after his appointment as Chief Economist at the World Bank, and was then reinforced by his subsequent 'resignation' from that post in 2000, followed by his extensive critique of the IMF, above all in his best-selling book, *Globalization and Its Discontents*.[1] But on closer examination Stiglitz's trajectory reveals a number of telling truths, not so much about himself, as about the World Bank's policies and ideology, the influence on the Bank of the US government (most sharply revealed in the recent appointment of Wolfowitz as President of the Bank), and the dismal science of the Bank's economics – from which Stiglitz has in some respects at most marginally departed. In reality the Bank has responded to its crisis of legitimacy in the early 1990s by de-emphasising neo-liberal theory in principle whilst supporting private capital ever more strongly in practice. Ideologically, this has been marked by a number of shifts in World Bank parlance, from 'good governance' to 'poverty alleviation', and especially its most recent claim to be first and foremost a 'knowledge bank'. Tellingly, these elements are in fact entirely consistent with Stiglitz's scholarly work and were, indeed, strongly endorsed by him during his time at the Bank. Only after he was forced out of the Bank was he forced to accept, however partially, unconsciously and implicitly, that the world – including the Bank – has to be understood in ways that depart from the scholarly tradition he has sought to promote.

### THE POST WASHINGTON CONSENSUS AND THE
### REDISCOVERY OF DEVELOPMENT AT THE BANK

Just over a decade ago the Bretton Woods institutions were marking, if hardly celebrating, their fiftieth anniversary. At that time they were under heavy criticism from all sides, not least because of the appropriately named 'lost

decade' of the 1980s during which the Washington Consensus had dominated development policy. The Bank and the IMF were condemned from the
extreme right for providing any aid at all to corrupt and inefficient governments. A more effective critique came from those who attacked the Bank's
dogmatic 'market versus state' agenda.

In response, the Bank and the IMF adopted a raft of concepts and policy
stances that played a major role in deflecting criticism and restoring a degree
of legitimacy. Governments were now required to be partners in, to 'own',
the policies that were attached as conditions to loans. 'Good governance' was
emphasized. The Bank's Comprehensive Development Framework inspired a
new-found commitment to, and partnership with, the IMF for poverty alleviation, allowing the marginal differences between them to be buried in the
formulation of Poverty Reduction Strategy Papers (as the economic assessments for countries receiving loans have become known since 1999). The
Washington Consensus was now admitted to have had an excessive macro
bias towards stabilization, and a restricted micro agenda of price incentives. A
'broader' understanding of development was now advocated.

A set of intellectual advances within mainstream economics provided a
helpful context within which the Bank and the IMF undertook this reinvention. A 'newer' development economics had emerged in the late 1980s,
with the 'rediscovery' of the singularity of development. In contrast to the
neo-liberal 'new' development economics, it emphasized market (and institutional) *imperfections*.[2] On the one hand, it reflected attempts to incorporate
realism into economic analysis, including such factors as economies of scale,
imperfect information or even the lack of markets; on the other it reflected
an ambition to account for features traditionally beyond the realm of mainstream economics – history, institutions, social networks, etc.

The Bank's desire to engage with these developments was realized through
the appointment of Stiglitz as Chief Economist. Much as the Bank had gained
intellectual leadership during the rise to prominence of the 'mono-econom-
ics' of the Washington Consensus, whereby the problem of development
had been reduced to the rational responses of economic agents to price
incentives, failure to engage with a shifting paradigm risked threatening that
position. Stiglitz's appointment also offered the opportunity to demonstrate
that the Bank was responsive to criticisms of the Washington Consensus for
its extreme pro-market stance and its poor outcomes in practice.

Initially, Stiglitz fulfilled expectations. Most memorably, shortly after his
appointment, he called for his post Washington Consensus, the main elements
of which were endorsed in the Comprehensive Development Framework
subsequently put forward by Bank's President, James Wolfensohn. A broader

framework for development was outlined, based on objectives of environmental sustainability, equity and democracy:

> We seek sustainable development, which includes preserving
> natural resources and maintaining a healthy environment. We seek
> equitable development, which ensures that all groups in society, not
> just those at the top, enjoy the fruits of development. And we seek
> democratic development, in which citizens participate in a variety
> of ways in making the decisions that affect their lives.[3]

This suggested that the Bank was abandoning neo-liberalism and adopting
a more moderate and broader approach to development than simply relying
to the maximum possible extent on market forces. The Bank's re-emphasis
on its developmental role also had implications for its relationship with the
IMF. While the era of structural adjustment had entailed important overlaps, making the two institutions into what some observers saw as identical
rather than 'fraternal' twins,[4] the Bank's new agenda sought to reassert the
conventional demarcation between the Fund's predominantly short-term
macroeconomic focus and the Bank's longer-term structural focus.

Yet, since the Stiglitz-sponsored discursive innovations increasingly
offered a platform for opposition to policies particularly cherished by the US
Treasury, and successfully promoted by the IMF, Stiglitz's diligence quickly
turned from asset to liability. He had taken issue with the IMF's handling of
the series of financial crises that marked the late 1990s (East Asia 1997-98,
Russia 1998, Brazil 1999) and with its promotion of hasty privatizations
in the former command economies. In Stiglitz's thinking the IMF rapidly
emerged as the evil twin, the embodiment of pernicious monetarist ideology
and, ultimately, an obstacle to development.[5]

Such a high-profile insider assault on one of the pillars of a carefully
US-guarded international financial set-up did not go down well with the
US financial establishment. The response from then US Treasury Secretary
Lawrence Summers, himself previously Chief Economist at the Bank, was
unequivocal: if Wolfensohn wanted a second term, Stiglitz had to go.[6] Once
freed from his official straitjacket, however, Stiglitz continued to infuriate the
US financial establishment. Significantly, in an article in the *New Republic*, he
called the IMF staff 'third rank students from first rate universities' and for
the first time identified vested financial interests as the reason why particular
policies had been imposed on the crisis-stricken economies,[7] a theme further
pursued in his international best-seller, published in 2002.

## GLOBALIZATION AND LIMITED DISCONTENT

In *Globalization and Its Discontents*, Stiglitz was able to make his case against the Washington Consensus unencumbered by the constraints of holding office at the Bank. Nonetheless, he did so in ways that differ only marginally from the positions he took before his departure. Stiglitz's criticisms are, and always have been, standard criticisms, and had been made by progressive scholars, albeit from different perspectives, for a decade or more before being adopted, pretty much without acknowledgement, by Stiglitz himself – in conformity with the Bank's practice of never acknowledging that its shifting rhetoric may have been anticipated, let alone prompted, by external critics. Specifically, Stiglitz is concerned that the policies being imposed by the neo-liberal Washington Consensus as conditions attached to loans have been disastrous. They include, for example, a fiscal austerity that deflates the economy and provokes economic and social instability; high interest rates that also deflate and force businesses into bankruptcy; trade liberalization that undermines domestic industries before they are established competitively; financial liberalization that crowds out local banking more attuned to domestic needs; and premature and inappropriate privatization before the requisite institutions for implementation and regulation are in place.[8]

But where Stiglitz really moves beyond his pre-sacking posture is in the ferocity of his indictment of the IMF as being primarily responsible for poor and failed policy. Why the Bank should be less to blame is unclear, other than as a reflection of a lingering loyalty on Stiglitz's part, and his belief that the Bank is frustrated by the IMF. His charge against the IMF goes beyond that of poor economics and, hence, poor policy. Rather, these are themselves explained by two further factors, conjured up as *dei ex machina*: ideology and self-interest. He sees the Washington Consensus as driven by a dogmatic belief, against all the evidence, in the virtues of free markets. This belief has been effectively demolished, as far as Stiglitz is concerned, by his own approach to economics: 'More recent advances in economic theory ... have shown that whenever information is imperfect and markets incomplete, which is to say always, *and especially in developing countries*, then the invisible hand works most imperfectly'.[9]

Significantly, the imperfect information/markets approach that has exclusively informed Stiglitz's scholarly work is otherwise notable for its virtually total absence from his best-selling book. Its absence seems due not so much to a desire to popularize his account (although it no doubt helps), but to a shift in what he sees as key explanatory factors. For in addition to deploring the role of neo-liberal ideology he argues that the Washington Consensus has been driven and accepted by those whom it most benefits, allowing the interests of the Western financial community to prevail over those of the world's poor.

Yet this view of the ideology and interests of the financial community represents a remarkable and generally unobserved contradiction in Stiglitz's analytics. For it is inconsistent with the references he makes to advances in economic theory (in which Stiglitz is largely referring to his own work), according to which *individuals rationally* pursue their own interests, as they do in all mainstream economic theory. For if things like ideology and a community of (financial) interests are causal, this is something on which Stiglitz has no analytical purchase. Instead, he represents the problem as one of a moral failing on the part of the IMF and its supporters. And whilst he is sufficiently critical of neo-liberal globalization to be counted as a prominent dissident, his critique rarely extends to the Bank, especially if it could be unshackled from the IMF. But the evolving position of the Bank before, during and after Stiglitz's reign suggests that it is more important to look at both ideologies and conspiracies of interests than at the imperfect workings of more or less invisible hands. In other words, Stiglitz's work ends at the point where it should just be beginning.

## RHETORIC, SCHOLARSHIP AND POLICY AT THE BANK

As much, then, as Stiglitz's contributions helped the Bank's much-needed reinvigoration, his commitment to the policy implications of his own scholarship, evident in his increasingly vociferous critique of the IMF, could not be reconciled with the holding of office within the Bank and ultimately led to his removal. It is against this background that the putative shift to a more state- and poor-friendly stance on the part of the Bank needs to be carefully deconstructed, by looking closely at its shifts on privatization, aid and knowledge.

Although the Bank had fanatically pursued privatization in the past, its new position is highlighted in a heading in a recent comprehensive Report endorsed by the current Chief Economist, Francois Bourgignon: 'Privatization Has Been Oversold and Misunderstood'. The Bank's previous stance had been underpinned by free market dogma and the judicious selection and interpretation of evidence. In contrast, its latest offering accepts that there can be a case for continuing public ownership in principle, despite 'the fact that state ownership is flawed', and offers the case of the Brazilian hydro. It concedes that more and better evidence is needed on the welfare impact of privatization. And whilst, as always, falling short of self-criticism, it allows the Wall Street Journal to speak on its behalf in this respect:

> The World Bank, the apostle of privatization, is having a crisis of faith. What seemed like a no-brainer idea in the 1990s – that developing nations should sell off money-losing state infrastructure to efficient private investors – no longer seems so obvious … Consumers, feeling deceived, increasingly associate privatization with higher rates for them and higher profits for foreign companies and corrupt officials. The unexpected turn of events has left privatization enthusiasts at the World Bank wondering what went wrong.[10]

So there seems to be a shift in principle towards a more tempered position on privatization, and from dogma to a more scholarly approach, much in Stiglitz manner. The situation with respect to policy in practice is, however, open to an entirely different interpretation. This can be seen by reading between the lines of the Report itself. For its thesis is not about accepting that privatization has gone too far, and that it is time to give state enterprise another chance. To the contrary, most of the Report is concerned to identify what pre-conditions, of regulation and competition, the state must put in place in order that privatization can be renewed and be successful. There is no consideration of state enterprise as an alternative, nor any measured consideration of whether the resources, efforts and capacity-building needed to ensure successful privatization might not be better spent promoting and improving the performance of state enterprise.

Further, the Report is conscious of the extent to which privatization has stalled in practice, especially in Africa, as a result of opposition from government, popular movements and – though more by way of passive resistance – private (foreign) capital. The latter is rarely interested in investing in socio-economic infrastructure, such as water provision, with impoverished customers and uncertain returns. The result is that the Report offers a pecking order of infrastructure targeted for privatization – running from the attractive fields of telecommunications and energy, through transport, to the dead ducks of water and sewerage.

In short, the Bank has taken an apparently more cautious approach to privatization in principle, as the means by which to try and push more of it through in practice, with a focus on sectors where there may be more chance of success. State activity is needed to make privatization happen. Significantly, the Bank has sought to transfer billions of dollars of infrastructural financing from the public to the private sector, from International Development Assistance (IDA), which makes concessional loans to governments, to the International Financial Corporation (IFC), which lends exclusively to the private sector.[11]

There are more general lessons to be learned from this account, for it reveals that there is considerable dissonance between the scholarship, the rhetoric and the policy of the Bank. As argued elsewhere, the ways in which they are (in)consistent with one another varies over time and across issues.[12] At the most general level, for example, the neo-liberal rhetoric of the Washington Consensus is pure fantasy, serving to justify or to conceal extensive discretionary intervention, not least in the conditionalities imposed with adjustment loans. By contrast, the new rhetoric is equally discretionary in its policy interventions, but now provides a different rationale for them. In light of 'a variety of country characteristics both observable and unobservable, including institutional capacity, business culture, nature of organized interest groups, patterns of social conflict, and codes of conduct ...', it now declares, '[t]here is no universally appropriate model'.[13] In this way, not only has the Bank's apparent distancing of itself from neo-liberalism enhanced its legitimacy and consistency, it has also provided a rationale for a broader scope of intervention in both economic and social policy, as markets both have to be made to work and their imperfections have to be corrected through the non-economic factors that underpin them.

## KNOWLEDGE OF AID AND IN AID OF KNOWLEDGE

A close inspection of the Bank's rhetoric and practices around aid further illustrates these issues. For when Stiglitz arrived at the Bank in 1997, ready to infuse it with his own brand of thinking, the operational realities around aid had been taking a particular form. After more than fifteen years of experience with adjustment lending and much debate inside and outside the Bank a consensus had emerged within the institution, evident in its 1994 report on Africa,[14] that adjustment had promoted 'sound' policies, but had not necessarily produced very strong results in terms of growth or poverty reduction. As the Bank understood it, implementation problems carried the entire brunt of inadequate economic performance, and local 'ownership' of its reform programme became a perceived precondition for the economic success of assistance packages. Following this, the ambition to exercise greater selectivity in the allocation of aid flows gained currency. Instead of imposing conditions to be achieved in response to the receipt of loans, loans were to become conditional on what had been achieved beforehand. Furthermore, countries that had not yet sufficiently 'improved' their policies or governance were to benefit from ideas (mainly transferred through policy dialogue and advisory services) rather than loans, as the pedagogical role of the Bank moved centre stage: '(a)id can nurture reform in even the most distorted environments – but it requires patience and a focus on ideas, not money'.[15]

The core of the Bank's performance-based allocation system is the annual

Country Policy and Institutional Assessment, CPIA. This involves the attribution of a score on a scale from 1 to 6 for sixteen criteria.[16] Necessarily, the ratings carry the Bank's judgement on which policy and institutional environment is best suited to development, and are built around readily recognisable precepts: low inflation; budget surplus; minimal restrictions on trade and capital flows; flexible goods, labour and land markets; market-determined interest rates; prohibition of directed credit; and competition policies guaranteeing equal treatment of foreign and domestic investors, accompanied by 'virtually' complete capital account convertibility. To temper the Washington Consensus taste of this approach, the CPIA also comprises criteria projecting concerns for equity – limited to the targeting of public expenditure and social safety-nets, the environment, and gender; a recognition of the importance of human resource development (health, education, nutrition); and 'governance', meaning the property and contract rights regime, transparency of government, corruption prevention, the organization of the civil service, and the quality of budgetary and financial management.[17] The allocation formula deployed by the Bank ensures that the level of resource allocation rises faster than the rating of performance so that there is a considerable reward for countries at the upper end of the CPIA scale. This translated, in the Bank's last aid allocation exercise, into a distribution of resources in which countries in the top performance quintile received on average five times as much per capita as countries in the bottom quintile.[18]

The CPIA exercise emblematically illustrates how in practice Bank assistance remains conditional in an even more stringent manner on a core set of neo-liberal policies, with a veneer of social and governance concerns. This combines with its commitment to country 'ownership' through Poverty Reduction Strategy Papers (PRSPs). The latter come about through close collaboration between recipient/debtor and the Bank/IMF, wrapped in a compulsory 'participation' procedure in which CPIA results serve as beacons indicating areas on which the PRSP should focus.[19] The recipient country facilitates a policy framework, developed according to Bank/IMF priorities, that ties certain aspects of social policy formation to the well-known neo-liberal macroeconomic framework.[20]

The proposal to allocate aid selectively to countries characterized by 'good' policies and institutions came to be formally supported by a set of arguments regarding the relationship between aid, conditionality and macroeconomic performance. These are mainly attributed to a few individuals (Paul Collier, David Dollar and Craig Burnside) who were active in the Bank's research department when Stiglitz was Chief Economist. Their main argument, which forms the core message of the two main Bank reports on aid and conditionality, is simplistic and predictable.[21] Aid only affects the

growth rate of recipient economies positively if the 'right' policies/institu-
tions prevail and aid conditionality has no effect on the policy environment,
with the concomitant policy rationalization that aid should be (re)allocated
towards those countries characterized by a 'good' policy/institutional environment. This crude thesis rapidly acquired scientific status, notwithstanding
the seriously flawed nature of the research that underlay it.[22] Its deficiencies
range from weaknesses of model specification to the misuse of data and case
material, raising serious questions about the Bank's academic standards and
intellectual honesty – especially significant, given the Bank's command over
massive research resources, and its current claim to command and disseminate knowledge.[23] Interestingly, Stiglitz endorsed this research on various
occasions, even if the macroeconomic stance it embodies directly contradicts
his post Washington Consensus.[24]

The projection of this particular understanding of the dynamics of aid
and conditionality was furthermore conveniently linked to the Bank's new
emphasis on 'knowledge'. At the 1996 Annual Meeting Bank President
James Wolfensohn initiated a whole set of initiatives to operationalize his
'Knowledge Bank' vision.[25] Of course, the Bank has always exercised a
knowledge role, with a variety of contradictory elements, the more so as
it became leader of the aid regime when, during the 1980s, policy-based
lending expanded rapidly.[26] The current explicit promotion of a knowledge
mission for the Bank, however, took on specific significance as it reflected
particular shifts within the World Bank Group, already alluded to above.

Over the last two decades, the Group has witnessed the very rapid expansion of its private sector arm, the International Finance Corporation.[27] This
has been accompanied by steady declines in the operations of its traditional
non-concessional lending window, the International Bank for Reconstruction
and Development (IBRD), which, in 2002, for the first time registered negative lending, and a significant fall, by one third over the last decade, in donor
contributions to the aid window of the Bank, the IDA.[28] Meanwhile, all the
current activities of the Bank are strongly driven by the strategic priority of
private sector development.[29] These trends highlight the use of the Bank's
financial resources, at subsidized rates, to support corporate investment, as
against its supposed mission, as a public international financial institution,
to promote development and combat poverty. The 'knowledge' mission can
hardly repair this disconnection but it has served to draw attention away
from the Bank's financial role by emphasizing its supposedly unique ability to
share decades of learning about economic development with clients around
the world.

The promotion of a knowledge mission for the Bank was accompanied by
a set of analytical arguments on why the Bank should be so engaged. Stiglitz,

in particular, contributed to these, keen to impose his own analysis on the new subject area. 'Knowledge' emerges as another factor of production, with poor countries now differing from rich ones 'not only because they have less capital, but because they have less knowledge'.[30] Furthermore, 'knowledge' tends to be a public good. Stiglitz explains:

> Most knowledge is a global public good: a mathematical theorem is as true in Russia as in the US ... The problems that economics deals with, such as scarcity, are ubiquitous, and accordingly the laws of economics are universally applicable even if idiosyncratic institutions exist within each country.[31]

And he continues:

> Much of the knowledge that is required for successful development is not patentable, it is not the knowledge that underlies new products or processes. Rather, it is equally fundamental knowledge: how to organize firms, how to organise societies, how to live healthier lives in ways that support the environment. It involves knowledge that affects fertility and knowledge about the design of economic policies that promote economic growth.[32]

The supply of such a public good will be deficient without active public support. Here then is a central role for the Bank:

> The accumulation, processing, and dissemination of knowledge in development, as well as working more broadly to close the knowledge gap, is the special responsibility of the World Bank. The two activities of the Bank are complementary. Knowledge, particularly knowledge about the institutions and policies that make market economies work better, leads to higher returns and better allocation of capital ... The World Bank has a role to play in providing such advice that extends beyond the public-good nature of knowledge. It is, and is widely perceived to be, an honest broker.[33]

Apparently characterized by economies of scale and scope in knowledge, the Bank has a unique capacity to analyze, codify and disseminate development experience around the world. The Bank research alluded to above regarding aid and conditionality is a case in point: 'One example of how economies of scope work in favour of Bank research is a report entitled "Assessing Aid". Macroeconomists, public finance analysts and poverty experts worked on different aspects of the impact of aid, and these analyses were then brought together to construct an integrated view of what works, what does not and why'.[34]

Never mind the fact that this research failed to sustain its own conclusions, and flagrantly violated the basic rules of scholarly research.[35] Could particular imperatives have steered its conclusions, in a crass example of 'crony intellectualism'? Of course not: the Bank's knowledge is 'neutral', particularly in the context of the recent changes in the study of development, with the (Stiglitzian) intellectual project of the New(er) Development Economics providing an opportunity for the Bank to restyle itself comfortably on 'knowledge' lines. Moreover, with the end of the Cold War the grand ideological battles are apparently over, with now 'almost universal agreement' that markets should be at the centre of any 'vital' economy.[36] Government plays a role in complementing markets, ensuring their proper functioning.[37] Within this broad agreement, the continuing debates are 'over more *technical* matters, such as how to respond to economic crisis, how to undertake financial reform, and what is the proper sequencing of privatisation'.[38] Hence, finally, while nations in the developing world have of course had to struggle to overcome their colonial heritage, Stiglitz counsels that 'it is not necessarily the case that everything that the colonists left behind – including their economic theories – was flawed; and it is not necessarily the case that the economic theories of those that supported the struggle for independence were sound'.[39]

This is surely a manifesto for neo-colonialism in the realm of economics, and is anchored in a dramatically reductionist understanding of knowledge.[40] The socio-historical, political and economic context in which knowledge comes about and is put to use, is entirely disregarded, combined with a glaring absence of critical reflection on how the Bank is governed and its implications for norms of 'scientific' acceptability, strongly affected by the leading role of economics at the Bank and the particular state of the discipline.[41] As others have noted, the claim of the Bank to be the major repository for and distributor of knowledge about development merely entrenches and reinforces global power relations.[42]

Illustrative are issues raised by the Global Development Network (GDN).[43] The idea for this emerged out of an effort by the Bank to broaden its regional approach to policy and research networks.[44] It was initiated by Stiglitz and was assured of strong support from Wolfensohn.

The GDN is explicitly intended to be a forum for Southern knowledge-sharing through the organization of conferences, collaborative research, research awards, etc. While the Knowledge Bank 'scans globally' for best practice, the GDN partners are to 'reinvent locally', with local adaptations amounting to the 'reinvention' of 'best practice' for the new context by local research and policy institutes.[45] Where previously policy 'advice', backed up by conditionality, attempted to bring a country to implement 'best-practice recipes', often without 'ownership' of or support for the reforms, now local policy and research institutions can adapt and prepare a 'transplanted policy initiative' to 'better survive and perhaps thrive in the local environment'. As a result of this process of 'adaptation', which often involves 'reinventing the idea', government officials should no longer see policy reform as a foreign imposition 'but as a local product that addresses their needs and which they can sponsor'.[46] Thus, especially in the context of a persistent decline in national institutes of research in developing countries over the last two decades, the GDN comes to play an important role in structuring the supply of development thinking ('knowledge') within developing countries, strengthening the advocacy and agenda-setting capacities of certain think-tanks and amplifying one (economic) discourse in preference to alternative voices. Certain policy approaches are reinforced by the multiplication of organizations at a domestic level and, although alternative perspectives on development and grass-roots knowledge are not necessarily excluded in either the Bank or the GDN, their influence is much more tenuous.[47]

## THE LIMITS OF ORTHODOX DISSENT

The relationship between Stiglitz's analytical ventures and the Bank's self-reinvention is obviously more complicated than can simply be inferred from his ejection from the Bank. The previous discussion of privatization, aid as reward for good (neo-liberal) policies, and knowledge as aid, reveals the complexity of Stiglitz's role. For as we have seen this fierce critic of (premature) privatization and neo-liberal macroeconomics condoned performance-based aid and has positively embraced the idea of knowledge as aid. This mixed response is a consequence of his needing to conform to the policy dictates of the Bank while he was working there, but also of the limitations of his own economics. What is the substance of Stiglitz's economics, and does it go any way towards justifying his reputation for radicalism?

Stiglitz understands the (capitalist) economy through the idea that exchanges take place between agents who are imperfectly and asymmetrically informed.[48] Consequently, markets work imperfectly, leading them to be inefficient in respect to the volume of trade, perpetuating imbalances between supply and demand, or even to be absent altogether. From his information-theoretic approach to market imperfections, Stiglitz draws Keynesian conclusions for macroeconomic policy (a critique of monetarism).[49] He seeks an appropriate balance between market and state in microeconomic policy and, for developing countries, safety nets for the poor, and a proper sequencing and regulation of financial liberalization in particular, and other policies in general, as opposed to neo-liberal shock therapy.

In these respects, as revealed time and again in his publications, whether policy documents, textbooks or pure research, the outstanding feature is a profound orthodoxy, judged on a number of criteria. For example he defines economics 'as the study of scarcity, how resources are allocated among competing uses',[50] echoing the definition notoriously adopted by Lionel Robbins during the Great Depression (when resources were clearly *not* being allocated among competing uses). Methodologically, he remains committed to the central tenets of the orthodoxy, drawing almost exclusively upon methodological individualism, as optimising individuals are organized by the market in equilibrium, for better or worse. He also accepts the distinction between positive and normative economics, even if he recognizes that ideology inevitably enters economics because evidence is insufficient to discriminate between competing theories.[51]

Furthermore, like the vast majority of mainstream economists, Stiglitz reveals scant knowledge of the history of economic thought or of political economy. And both his post Washington Consensus and Wolfensohn's Comprehensive Development Framework are notable for their neglect of the literatures that have forced them to be adopted – whether on the developmental state, or 'adjustment with a human face', or the critiques of neo-liberalism and modernization/and development as growth.

This is indicated by the absence from Stiglitz's work of numerous crucial variables developed by, and common to, the social sciences in general, and political economy in particular. For Stiglitz, for example, the response to the suggestion that exchanges (between capital and labour or landlords and peasants, for example) might be 'contested', is to place 'power' into a nebulous category that can be set aside in deference to sounder economic argument: 'There are good economic reasons, beyond the exercise of "power" (whatever that much-used term means) for the existence of hierarchical relationships'.[52] This attitude to power and the like is indicative of a fundamental schizophrenia within Stiglitz's world view, for he needs to appeal to such factors whenever his own theoretical approach fails, as it inevitably does, to capture the factors he sees are at work.

In addition, in the absence of the concepts of power, conflict, etc., although emphasis on market failure is the distinguishing mark of Stiglitz's economics, he continues to favour markets and competition as the core, if not the only, significant element needed for an understanding of the economy and its effective functioning. In his view, 'despite the presence of imperfect competition, imperfect information, externalities, and public goods, the basic competitive model continues to provide important and powerful insights'. Although this provides the point of departure for his 'richer, more complete model of the modern economy', he suggests that 'by and large, private markets allocate resources efficiently'. Consequently he can claim that 'both individuals and countries gain from voluntary trade', although this is later qualified, if not contradicted, by the suggestion that 'While all countries benefit from free trade, some groups within a country may be adversely affected'. He sees the state as essentially benevolent, a special institution (all belong and it can compel) for the correction of market failures and undesirable social outcomes. This implies a weak role for the state but, equally, a weakened understanding of it:

> There are three basic reasons why the government intervenes in the economy: (1) to improve economic efficiency by correcting market failures; (2) to pursue social values of fairness by altering market outcomes; and (3) to pursue other social values by mandating the consumption of merit goods (such as education) and outlawing the consumption of merit bads (such as illicit drugs).[53]

This hardly captures the nature of the state in developing and transitional economies, even if it could be accepted as anything other than an imaginary ideal of the state in developed economies. The possibility that the state might be captured by, or representative of, vested interests, with corresponding ideologies and powers, is precluded, together with any proper treatment of historical specificity and context.

Such limited analytical principles are cruelly exposed by big questions. Historical events such as the Great Plague, for example, become accidents or random events. For development, the question is posed of why 'developed and less developed countries are on different production functions'. One answer is that:

> We emphasize that accidents of history matter ... partly because of pervasive complementarities among agents ... and partly because even a set of dysfunctional institutions and behaviors in the past can constitute a Nash equilibrium from which an economy need not be inevitably dislodged.[54]

In less technical terms, 'Gaps in knowledge and organization, both between more and less developed countries and within developed countries, account for much of the differences in income'.[55] In this light, Stiglitz might better have stuck to his 1991 judgement that as far as development is concerned he was far from 'sanguine' about 'the future success of our profession'.[56]

Significantly, throughout his work, there is little or no reference to globali-zation. The same even remains true, despite its title, of his best-selling book *Globalization and Its Discontents*, in which there is scarcely a concept, let alone a theory, of globalization (other than as a reduction in transport and commu-nication costs).

In his own professional experience, he is then confronted with an insolu-ble paradox. If the world is populated by optimising individuals, and the state is essentially benevolent, how do we explain the persistent adoption of bad policies, and the enforced departure from governmental posts of those who pursue good ones? Thrust, at the most personal of levels, into the real world, Stiglitz abandons his analytical principles and appeals to some combination of irrationality, ideology, and organized vested interests. His colleagues at the IMF are berated for being of low quality. If the state is needed to act on behalf of individuals who do not know what is best for them,[57] what if such individuals take control of the state? Deregulation, corruption, austere macr-oeconomic policies and financial booms and busts featured during Stiglitz's time at the World Bank and as advisor to Clinton (to whom he remains endearingly loyal, in the belief that Clinton was betrayed by his other advis-ers). These things lead him to suspect the presence of entrenched financial interests and ideologies.

Remarkably, as already indicated, his critical accounts of his experiences draw on these things, plus incompetence, for their causal content, with little or no reference to information-theoretic economics, and certainly none of the theorems that are reputed to exude from him on an hourly basis.[58] But from where do these vested interests and their ideologies come, and why does incompetence prevail when, where and how it does? The guns of the Nobel scientist fall silent, although it is always possible to see such things as the path-dependent consequences of the pursuit of individual self-interest, as imperfect markets and institutions have evolved in response to random shocks. Such analytical acrobatics, however, at most indicate the parallel universe in which Stiglitz's economics serve a rhetorical and ideological fig-leaf for the darker side of the Bank's practice.

## CONCLUDING REMARKS

Given all this, how can Stiglitz be considered a radical? During his tenure at the Bank he scarcely ever alluded to ideology and vested interests. This helps to explain the directions, and limitations, of his contributions at that time. Knowledge as aid is fully compatible with his 'asymmetric information' approach; indeed, differences in knowledge are deemed to explain differ-ences in levels of development. Without any hint that the Bank might itself be subject to ideology and vested interests (despite its record prior to his arrival, against which he was reacting), he held that it makes sense for it to purvey its knowledge. Targeted aid makes sense in the same way, in view of the incentive-compatibility problems involved (how do we make recipients do what they should). Privatization is subject to criticism if not properly sequenced and regulated. But, as with macro-policy if taken to neo-liberal extremes, his criticism is restricted to the IMF and to the shock treatments imposed on the former Soviet Union and elsewhere.

Thus, Stiglitz's departure from orthodoxy in scholarship remains as limited as his attitude to inadequate Bank rhetoric and practice is complacent. Yet he has displayed considerable intellectual and personal integrity by remaining committed to what he sees to be the implications of his economics for policy – there are pervasive market and institutional imperfections and these must be addressed, rather than wished away by neo-liberal virtualism. For taking his scholarship into the policy arena, in particular with regard to inappropriate macroeconomic recommendations in the wake of the various financial crises and the hasty privatizations undertaken across the developing and transition economies, he was ousted from the Bank – despite the continuing role that his discourse plays there (and, increasingly, within the IMF as well). Indeed the Bank's report on privatization, discussed earlier, comfortably cites Stiglitz to support its latest rethink![59]

Second, Stiglitz's reputation for radicalism reflects profound shifts over the course of his career in the ideology of those amongst whom he moves – whether academic economists or policymakers. He is a Keynesian, with a profound belief in the imperfect workings of the economy at macro and micro levels. As such, he would have been unremarked, except for his prolific academic output, during and immediately after the post-war boom. But now, in the era of neo-liberal hegemony, he seems like a breath of fresh, radical air. This is implicitly recognized by Stiglitz himself. He has set up a campaign for alternative economics (although he has rarely engaged with anything outside the mainstream).[60]

Third, the nature and scope of economics have shifted in ways, partly promoted by Stiglitz himself, that propel mainstream economists more into the public eye. Unlike the vast majority of his Keynesian predecessors, who concerned themselves with, and confined their analytical principles to, the imperfect workings of the markets of the advanced economies, the information-theoretic approach broadens its compass to incorporate all economic and social relations. Such 'economics imperialism' means that economists can now freely talk about politics, customs, institutions, history, culture and so on, in ways that are readily communicable to non-economists and that appear to be less reductionist.[61]

This is why Stiglitz's scholarship and rhetoric is conducive to restoring and to sustaining the legitimacy of the Bretton Woods institutions, even if his own policy conclusions proved so unpalatable in practice. Some people see his approach as scarcely distinguishable from the Washington Consensus. Williamson, who gave the Consensus its name, complains that 'I once attempted to engage Stiglitz in a debate about the Washington Consensus. He declined to participate on the grounds that he and I disagree little about substance as opposed to semantics and he did not consider semantics to be worth debating.'[62]

The basic idea of correcting market and institutional imperfections when that offers better outcomes than leaving things to the market, hardly represents a deep understanding of development, nor a recipe for promoting it. Its affinities with the Washington Consensus are at least as striking as its differences. It does not even go so far as to restore the central pillars of the pre-Washington Consensus of the McNamara period, with its emphasis on a central role for the state through welfarism, modernization and Keynesianism.[63] In lieu of these, we are offered limited aid but fulsome knowledge – to what effect?

Perhaps the most important conclusion to be drawn from the curious case of Stiglitz is just how limited is the scope for criticism and change within the World Bank. There was no problem with his economics. Indeed within a year of his resignation he was awarded the Nobel Prize in economics, and Stiglitz-speak continues to underpin Bank (and, increasingly, IMF) rhetoric. But as soon as that economics was perceived to challenge policy (and ideology and vested interests) in practice, it was abruptly excised. Once outside the Bank, Stiglitz does seem to have learned what many of us had already learned from that same vantage point – that mainstream economics, even with informational, market and institutional imperfections, must give way to a political economy of historically and ideologically vested interests (of which western finance is at most a good starting point). It remains to be seen whether this truth eventually predominates over the post Washington Consensus that he promoted whilst at the Bank, and which he has inconsistently and unfortunately continued to promote even after he discovered that vested interests and ideology might be of more significance. Whilst Stiglitz proved his intellectual integrity in the struggle against the rhetoric of neo-liberalism, his work has been deployed to limit the progressive reaction against it, and to mask the continuing divorce between ideology and practice in the business of knowledge, aid and development.

NOTES

1    Joseph E. Stiglitz, *Globalization and Its Discontents*, New York: W.W. Norton and Co, 2002.

2    For the new and newer development economics, see Ben Fine and K. S. Jomo, eds., *The New Development Economics: A Critical Introduction*, Delhi: Tulika, and London: Zed Press, 2005, forthcoming.

3    Joseph E. Stiglitz, 'More Instruments and Broader Goals: Moving Toward the Post Washington Consensus', the WIDER Annual Lecture, Helsinki, 7 January 1998. This and subsequent contributions in the same vein are collected in Ha-Joon Chang, ed., *Joseph Stiglitz and the World Bank: The Rebel Within*, London: Anthem Press, 2001.

4    Paul Mosley, Turan Subasat and John Weeks. 'Assessing Adjustment in Africa', *World Development*, 23(9), 1995, p. 1459.

5    Reflecting back on the tasks ahead of him as he joined the World Bank, Stiglitz commented: 'I knew the tasks were difficult, but I never dreamed that one of the major obstacles the developing countries faced was man-made, totally unnecessary, and lay right across the street – at my "sister" institution, the IMF'. See Stiglitz, *Globalization and Its Discontents*, p. 25.

6    For a good account see Robert Wade, 'Showdown at the World Bank', *New Left Review*, II/7, 2001, pp. 124-29. Technically speaking Stiglitz resigned as the Bank's Chief Economist in November 1999, but stayed on as Wolfensohn's own 'special advisor' until April 2000 – when he was also forced out of that role.

7    Joseph E. Stiglitz, 'What I Learned at the World Economic Crisis', *New Republic*, 17 April 2000.

8    See Stiglitz, 'More Instruments'.

9    Stiglitz, *Globalization and Its Discontents*, p. 73.

10   World Bank, *Reforming Infrastructure: Privatization, Regulation, and Competition*, Washington: The World Bank and Oxford University Press, 2004, p. 259; for the quotations in the previous paragraph see pp. 4, 8, 15, 43.

11   K. Bayliss and D. Hall, 'A PSIRU Response to the World Bank's "Private Sector Development Strategy: Issues and Options"', University of Greenwich, http://www.psiru.org/reports/2001-10-U-wb-psd.doc, 2001, accessed November 25th.

12   Ben Fine, *Social Capital versus Social Theory: Political Economy and Social Science at the Turn of the Millennium*, London: Routledge, 2001.

13   World Bank, *Reforming Infrastructure*, pp. 8-9.

14   World Bank, *Adjustment in Africa: Reforms, Results and the Road Ahead*, Washington, DC: World Bank, 1994.

15   World Bank, *Assessing Aid. What Works, What Doesn't and Why*, Published for the World Bank by Oxford University Press, 1998, p. 4.

16   The CPIA-practice has been heavily promoted by the Bank across the donor community and is rapidly becoming a standard. See Barry Herman,

'How Well Do Measurements of an Enabling Domestic Environment for Development Stand up?', UNCTAD, Meeting of the Group of 24, 2004, http://www.g24.org/003gva04.pdf.

17    http://siteresources.worldbank.org/IDA/Resources/CPIA2003.pdf.

18    IDA, 'Allocating IDA Funds Based on Performance', March 2003, http://siteresources.worldbank.org/IDA/Resources/PBAAR4.pdf, p. 8.

19    For a critical commentary on the nature of the 'participation' characterizing the PRSP process see Frances Stewart and Michael Wang, 'Do PRSPs Empower Poor Countries and Disempower the World Bank, or Is It the Other Way Round?', QEH Working Paper Series, http://www.eurodad.org/uploadstore/cms/docs/WBevalMay03.pdf, 2003. In general, groups disagreeing with the neo-liberal point of departure and issuing alternatives tend to be excluded from the debate on the ground that they do not comprehend economics.

20    Tellingly, the joint IMF/WB 2003 Progress Report on PRSP called for a stricter commitment in the PRSPs to macro-economic 'discipline': 'although most PRSPs affirm the importance of low and stable inflation in their efforts to reduce poverty, there is little evidence of an explicit consideration of the inflationary implications of monetary financing'. See International Monetary Fund and International Development Association, 'Poverty Reduction Strategy Papers – Progress in Implementation', http://www.imf.org/external/np/prspgen/2003/091203.pdf, 2003, p. 5.

21    World Bank, *Assessing Aid*; Devarajan Shantayanan, David Dollar and Torgny Holgren, eds., *Aid and Reform in Africa*, Washington: World Bank, 2001.

22    For critical deconstruction of the Collier-Dollar-Burnside thesis see Jonathan Beynon, 'Policy Implications for Aid Allocations of Recent Research on Aid Effectiveness and Selectivity', paper presented at the Joint Development Centre/DAC Experts Seminar on 'Aid Effectiveness, Selectivity and Poor Performers', Paris, http://www.oecd.org/dataoecd/15/62/2664833.pdf, 2001.

23    Research at the Bank benefits from an average annual budget of well over US$100m, dwarfing the resources available to any other single institution concerned with development research. See World Bank, *Report on the World Bank Research Program Fiscal 2000 and 2001 and Future Directions*, Washington: World Bank, 2002, p. 15.

24    Joseph E. Stiglitz, 'Can Aid Facilitate Development', *OECF Journal of Development Assistance*, 3(2), 1998, pp. 10-4; 'The World Bank at the Millennium', *Economic Journal*, 109(November), 1999, p. 590; and 'Scan Globally, Reinvent Locally. Knowledge Infrastructure and the

Localisation of Knowledge', in Diane Stone, ed., *Banking on Knowledge*, London: Routledge, 2000, pp. 25-6. This lends support to comments by Bank staff, even those sympathetic to Stiglitz's views, that he treated the Bank much like a travel agency, neglecting his internal roles of mentoring staff or of directing the research complex. See Robert Wade, 'Showdown', p. 129.

25  For a comprehensive account of the various initiatives of the Knowledge Bank, see Kenneth King and Simon McGrath, *Knowledge for Development. Comparing British, Japanese, Swedish and World Bank Aid*, London: Zed Books, 2004, especially pp. 55-98.

26  While under its auspices indicators of economic performance changed little if they did not worsen, the intellectual milieu and terms of debate were radically transformed. See Ben Fine and Colin Stoneman, 'Introduction: State and Development', *Journal of Southern African Studies*, 22(1), March, 1995, pp. 5-14; Peter Gibbon, 'The World Bank and the New Politics of Aid', *European Journal of Development Research* 5(1), 1993, pp. 35-62.

27  IFC investments increased four and a half times in real terms between 1980 and 2000, and its share (together with that of the Multilateral Investment Guarantee Agency) in total Bank Group financial products increased more than seven times, from 3.3 per cent in 1980 to 25 per cent in 2000. See World Bank, 'Private Sector Development Strategy – Directions for the World Bank Group', http://www.wds.worldbank. org/servlet/WDS_IBank_Servlet?pcont=details&eid=000090341_ 20030812143402, p. 22.

28  It should be noted that the size of the tri-annual IDA-replenishment has more or less remained the same over the last ten years as the IDA increasingly relies on its own resources (mainly reflows and investment income) to finance its activities. The latter have risen from 10 percent as a share of total replenishment for IDA-10 (1993-1996) to over 40 percent for IDA-13 (2002-2004).

29  See World Bank, 'Private Sector Development Strategy'.

30  World Bank, *World Development Report 1998/9. Knowledge for Development*, Oxford: Oxford University Press, 1998, p. 1.

31  Joseph E. Stiglitz, 'Knowledge as a Global Public Good', in Inge Kaul et al., eds., *Global Public Goods*, Oxford: Oxford University Press, 1999, pp. 310-1.

32  Ibid., p. 318. See also Christopher Gilbert, Andrew Powell and David Vines, 'Positioning the World Bank', *Economic Journal*, 109(November), 1999, p. 563.

33  Stiglitz, 'The World Bank at the Millenium', 1999, p. 590.

34    Lyn Squire, 'Why the World Bank Should Be Involved in Development Research', in C. Gilbert and D.Vines, eds., *The World Bank: Structures and Policies*, Cambridge: Cambridge University Press, 2000, p. 118.

35    To the contrary, it is claimed that the 'return' of this research is '120000 per cent of the return on the typical aid dollar', which moreover is an 'under-estimation' as knowledge can be used year after year with no additional knowledge generation costs, see David Dollar, 'Some Thoughts on the Effectiveness of Aid, Non-Aid Development Finance and Technical Assistance', *Journal of International Development*, 13(7), 2001, p. 1004.

36    Joseph E. Stiglitz, 'Knowledge for Development: Economic Science, Economic Policy and Economic Advice', in Joseph E. Stiglitz and Boris Pleskovic, *Proceedings of the Annual Bank Conference on Development Economics,* Washington: World Bank, 1999, p. 14.

37    See World Bank, *The State in a Changing World*, New York: Oxford University Press, 1997.

38    Stiglitz, 'Knowledge for Development', 1999, p. 14, our emphasis. For Stiglitz, if ideological differences persist, such as the unfortunate insistence by the IMF and US Treasury on capital account liberalization, then 'science' is the strongest antidote.

39    Joseph E. Stiglitz, 'Introduction', in C. Gilbert and D. Vines, eds., *The World Bank*, 2000, p. 4.

40    On how the concept of knowledge as implied by Stiglitz's analysis is a-historical and a-political see Lyla Mehta, 'From Darkness to Light? Critical Reflections on the World Development Report 1998/99', *Journal of Development Studies*, 36(1), 1999, pp. 151–61.

41    On how the high percentage of Bank staff educated in the US contributes to the amplification of US influence, see Devesh Kapur, 'The Changing Anatomy of Governance of the World Bank', in J. Pincus and J. Winters, eds., *Reinventing the World Bank*, Ithaca: Cornell University Press, 2002, p. 65. On the degree of Americanization of economics, see Ben Fine and Dimitri Milonakis, *Economic Theory and History: From Classical Political Economy to Economics Imperialism*, London: Routledge, 2006, forthcoming.

42    See Joel Samoff and Nelly P. Stromquist, 'Managing Knowledge and Storing Wisdom? New Forms of Foreign Aid?', *Development and Change*, 32, 2001, especially pp. 639–42; and Lyla Mehta, 'The World Bank and Its Emerging Knowledge Empire', *Human Organization*, 60(2), 2001, pp. 189–95.

43    www.gdnet.org

44    See Diane Stone and Erik Johnson, 'The Genesis of the GDN', in D.

Stone, ed., *Banking on Knowledge*, London: Routledge, 2000.

45  Stiglitz, 'Scan Globally', p. 31.

46  Ibid., p. 33.

47  Diane Stone, 'The "Knowledge Bank" and the Global Development Network', *Global Governance*, 9, 2003, p. 20. See also Diane Stone, 'Think Tank Transnationalisation and Non-Profit Analysis, Advice and Advocacy', *Global Society*, 14(2), 2000, especially pp. 170-71.

48  In his *Whither Socialism?*, Cambridge: MIT Press, 1994, Stiglitz explains its flaws and collapse through purely speculative reasoning based on his information-theoretic approach.

49  Although he accepts its fundamental concept of the natural rate of unemployment, Joseph E. Stiglitz, 'Reflections on the Natural Rate Hypothesis', *Journal of Economic Perspectives*, 11(1), 1997, pp. 3-10. See also his *The Roaring Nineties: Seeds of Destruction,* New York: W. W. Norton and Co, 2003, where it is necessarily accepted that monetarism might work temporarily and by way of exception.

50  Joseph E. Stiglitz, *Economics of the Public Sector,* Third Edition, New York: Norton & Company, 2000, First Edition of 1986.

51  Joseph E. Stiglitz, 'Another Century of Economic Science', *Economic Journal*, 100(1), January, 1991, p. 131.

52  In debate, Joseph E. Stiglitz, 'Post Walrasian and Post Marxian Economics', with Samuel Bowles and Herbert Gintis 'The Revenge of Homo Economicus: Contested Exchange and the Revival of Political Economy', *Journal of Economic Perspectives*, 7(1), 1993, pp. 109-14 and pp. 83-102, respectively.

53  Joseph E. Stiglitz and Carl E. Walsh, *Economics,* Third Edition, New York: Norton & Co, 2002, p. 338. For the quotations in the previous paragraph see pp. 229, 58 and 378.

54  Joseph E. Stiglitz and Karla Hoff, 'Modern Economic Theory and Development', Symposium on Future of Development Economics in Perspective, Dubrovnik, 13-14th May 1999.

55  Joseph E. Stiglitz, 'Democratizing the International Monetary Fund and the World Bank: Governance and Accountability', *Governance*, 16(1), 2003, p. 123.

56  Stiglitz, 'Another Century', p. 140, and 'The New Development Economics', *World Development*, 14(2), 1986, pp. 257-65.

57  Stiglitz, *Economics of the Public Sector*, p. 90.

58  Paul Samuelson, 'A Small Pearl for Doctor Stiglitz's Sixtieth Birthday: When Risk Averters Positively Relish "Excess Volatility"', in Richard Arnott et al., eds., *Economics for an Imperfect World: Essays in Honor of Joseph E. Stiglitz*, Cambridge: MIT Press, 2003, p. 14.

59  World Bank, *Reforming Infrastructure*, p. 259, citing Joseph E. Stiglitz, 'Whither Reform? Ten Years of the Transition', Keynote Address, Annual World Bank Conference on Development Economics, 29–30th April 1999, Washington, DC.

60  Check out the Initiative for Policy Dialogue at www-1.gsb.columbia. edu/ipd.

61  See Fine and Milonakis, *Economic Theory and History*.

62  John Williamson, 'Appendix: Our Agenda and the Washington Consensus', in Pedro-Pablo Kuczynski and John Williamson, eds., *After the Washington Consensus: Restarting Growth and Reform in Latin America*, Washington: Institute for International Economics, 2003, p. 326.

63  Ben Fine 'Introduction', and 'The New Development Economics', in Fine and Jomo, eds., *The New Development Economics*.

# COUNTING THE POOR:
# THE TRUTH ABOUT WORLD POVERTY
# STATISTICS

## SANJAY G. REDDY

K nowing the extent of acute deprivation in the world, and how far it is changing over time, is crucial to assessing the state of the world, and the appropriateness of the policies currently being followed by states and international institutions. This explains the widespread interest that has attended the strenuous debate which has emerged in the last four years concerning the present extent and recent trend of poverty in the world. This debate centres, in particular, on the validity of the global poverty estimates produced by the World Bank. It is entirely uncontroversial that the extent of absolute deprivations is centrally relevant to assessing the state of the world. Thus, the fact that the Bank's global poverty estimates have been questioned from all sides is very significant. In particular, the controversy is relevant to assessing progress toward the first of the so-called Millennium Development Goals (adopted by the United Nations as a governing framework for development policy), which calls for halving poverty (as estimated by the Bank on the basis of its one dollar a day concept, discussed further below) by 2015.

The production of global poverty statistics is a relatively recent activity. Until around 1980 there had been no effort to produce internationally comparable poverty statistics or comprehensive regional and global poverty estimates. Beginning around 1980, both the Bank and the UN Economic Commission for Latin America made initial efforts to do so. However, the first significant global poverty estimates were those published in 1990 in the Bank's flagship *World Development Report*. Since then, the Bank has periodically updated these. Until very recently, the Bank was the sole producer of global poverty estimates. As public debates on the effects of liberalization and globalization have become more heated, interest has grown in estimates of global poverty and their relevance to assessing the present form of globalization.[1]

Some critics of the Bank who are proponents of the prevalent mode of private property-entrenching market-oriented liberalization claim that the

Bank's estimates of global poverty *understate* the rate of reduction of poverty in recent years.[2] They argue that poverty reduction has been substantial, and that it can be attributed to the economic reforms recently undertaken by developing countries. This is a position that they share with the outgoing president of the World Bank, Jim Wolfensohn, who, citing the Bank's poverty statistics, claimed that: 'over the past few years [these] better policies have contributed to more rapid growth in developing countries' per capita incomes than at any point since the mid-1970s. And faster growth has meant poverty reduction'.[3] Other critics question the methodology employed both by the Bank and by its critics on the right.[4] It is far from clear to non-technical observers which descriptions of the world are most in keeping with 'the truth'. The reasons for the confusion are deep-seated and are ultimately rooted in the lack of transparency and accountability of international institutions.

## THE MONEY-METRIC APPROACH TO GLOBAL POVERTY ESTIMATES

The method of global poverty estimation adopted by the Bank as well as by almost all of its recent critics may be described as a 'money-metric' approach. The phrase 'money-metric' is used here to signify that the international poverty line is defined in relation to a money amount rather than an explicit conception of human well-being. The money-metric approach to global poverty estimation consists of four steps. In the first step, an international poverty line (or IPL) is defined. The IPL is defined in terms of a certain number of notional 'international' currency units (or so-called PPP dollars) deemed 'equivalent' in purchasing power to the US dollar in a specific base year. In the second step, the IPL is translated spatially into some number of units of each local currency, with respect to which it is deemed to possess an 'equivalent' amount of purchasing power in the base year. The conversion factors used for these spatial translations are purchasing power parity conversion factors (or PPPs) calculated on the basis of price data in all countries. In the third step, the IPL is translated temporally into some number of units of each local currency in the year in which the poverty assessment is being undertaken. Typically, a country's consumer price index is used to judge what constitutes the rate of 'equivalence' between purchasing power in the base year and in the assessment year. In the fourth step, the resulting poverty line expressed in terms of local currency units is used to undertake a poverty assessment. A household survey is used to identify the number of individuals whose level of disadvantage (understood in terms of the monetary value ascribed to their consumption or their income) falls beneath the level of the poverty line, as well as the extent of such disadvantage in the case of each such individual.

The Bank's most recent global poverty estimates are based on a lower IPL of 'one dollar per day' (actually $1.08) and a higher IPL of 'two dollars per day' (actually $2.16) of 1993 international dollars (deemed equivalent in purchasing power to US dollars). On the basis of these IPLs the Bank concludes that in the most recent year for which it has produced estimates (2001) the share of the developing world population living under the lower (one dollar per day) poverty line was 21.1 per cent, amounting to 1,092.7 million people. This is, according to the Bank, a reduction from the 1990 level of 1218.5 million and even more from the 1981 level of 1,481.8 million.[5] Whereas the most prominent recent critics of the Bank's estimates (who claim that poverty has been falling more rapidly than the Bank estimates) adopt methodologies which differ from that of the Bank in certain respects, they share the money-metric framework, and indeed they present themselves as adopting poverty lines which are identical or at least comparable to those of the Bank.[6]

The money-metric approach to global poverty estimation is inherently flawed. It lacks both coherence and meaningfulness. The approach lacks coherence because a concept of 'equivalent' purchasing power (needed to translate the IPL both spatially and temporally) cannot be defined without a conception of the *purpose* to which that purchasing power is intended to be put. However, by definition, the money-metric approach lacks such a conception. This was the focus of the critique of the money-metric approach in Reddy and Pogge[7] which emphasized that the purchasing power parity conversion factors used at present to translate the IPL spatially are inappropriate for the task of poverty assessment; since they are meant to capture 'equivalent purchasing power' over a broad range of commodities, rather than over the specific goods (in particular, foodstuffs) that must be commanded by the poor in order that they may escape absolute poverty. In particular, the conversion factors used, which encompass the cost of purchasing services (which are relatively inexpensive in poor countries) significantly overstate the purchasing power of currencies when they are applied to essential commodities such as food. The resulting poverty estimates are demonstrably too low in this particular sense – that they misrepresent the relative local currency costs of purchasing the same amounts of *necessities* in different countries.[8] The one dollar per day line is also demonstrably too low in another sense. It fails to correspond to the level of purchasing power required to attain basic human requirements in the base country in which the IPL is defined (the United States), where careful exercises show that the minimum cost of meeting basic nutritional requirements alone is likely to be several times higher than one dollar per day.[9] Perhaps unsurprisingly, nutritionally-based poverty estimates for Latin America lead to poverty estimates that are substantially higher than those produced by the Bank.[10]

The approach also lacks meaningfulness, because the IPL (again, as defined by the money-metric approach) is not specified in relation to an explicit conception of human well-being. As a result, whatever question is answered by the money-metric poverty assessment exercise, it is not especially relevant to determining the extent of the real human deprivations that arise as a result of income inadequacy (i.e., poverty as it is most widely understood). That task, which is the appropriate focus of poverty assessment, is ultimately and unavoidably a normative exercise, as it presupposes the specification of a space in which well-being is to be assessed and of a conception of minimal adequacy in this space. The normative character of the exercise is not, contrary to the view of some economists, an embarrassment. Rather, it is simply in its very nature. 'Telling the truth' regarding the extent of poverty in the world depends both on our having an appropriate concept of poverty and on our having the tools to assess its empirical extent.

Until now, global poverty estimates have also been based on a weak informational base. It is especially noteworthy that the International Comparison Program, which coordinates the price surveys that provide the basis for constructing PPPs, did not (prior to its most recent round) take any interest at all in collecting the prices of goods specifically relevant to poverty estimation. It appears to have begun to do this, as a direct result of the recent questioning of the poverty estimates of the World Bank, which now hosts the programme.[11] In addition, many countries – including some which are believed to contain large numbers of the world's poor (such as China and India) – simply do not participate in the surveys. For these and other reasons, the empirical basis of present global poverty estimates is extremely weak.

## THE ALTERNATIVE: A CAPABILITY-BASED APPROACH TO GLOBAL POVERTY ASSESSMENT

There is an alternative to the money-metric approach, astounding in its simplicity, which can bring about global poverty estimates that are both coherent and meaningful. The alternative is a capability-based approach, which seeks to identify whether individuals possess sufficient income to achieve the income-dependent 'elementary human capabilities' (as they have been defined by Amartya Sen: the 'beings and doings' that human beings generally need to possess if they are to live an adequate life). The ability to achieve income-dependent elementary human capabilities has long implicitly provided the standard of adequacy that has anchored poverty lines in well-designed poverty assessments within particular countries. For example, possession of income sufficient to enable an individual to consume a diet that contains enough calories and nutrients has long provided a means of specifying a poverty line. Famously, this is true of India's poverty assessments, which are grounded in norms of calorie adequacy. An approach of this type has the merit that the poverty line to which it gives rise has a meaningful interpretation.

Analogously, a capability-based approach to global poverty assessment would specify a uniform basis for constructing poverty lines, not only in one country but in all countries. By doing so, it would give rise to a common interpretation to the poverty lines thus arrived at in all countries. Moreover this interpretation would be meaningful by design. The approach would do away altogether with the need for PPP conversion factors which specify abstract rates of 'equivalence' between currencies, by specifying instead a common basis for defining poverty lines in all countries, related directly to the basic requirements of human beings. The alternative approach would require that a common conception of the relevant elementary capabilities be adopted in all countries. It would specify general guidelines for defining poverty lines in light of this conception, but permit poverty lines to be defined through a process otherwise specific to each country.

The specification of the elementary capabilities (for example, the ability to be adequately nourished) that must be possessed by an individual in order that he or she be deemed 'non-poor' should be undertaken at a global level, through a transparent and broadly consultative process. The manner in which this conception should be translated into detailed poverty lines in each country (for example, through requiring that poverty line incomes suffice to attain a certain level of calories and nutrients deemed adequate for individuals) might also be specified to a degree at the global level.[12] This approach offers a potential foundation for a 'people-centered' alternative to the current 'money-metric' approach to global poverty assessment.

Recent work has demonstrated that a capability-based approach to global poverty statistics *is* possible. It has been shown, using existing data from three countries in three continents (Nicaragua, Tanzania and Vietnam) that it is possible to undertake nutritionally-based assessments of poverty that are comparable across countries.[13] This work demonstrates that relative comparisons of the extent of poverty across countries can be significantly influenced by whether such comparisons are undertaken on the basis of a money-metric approach or the capability approach. For example, a comparison of the extent of poverty between Nicaragua and Vietnam was found in this preliminary exercise to be crucially dependent on the approach used. Such conclusions must be hesitant, however, since comparisons of this kind are undertaken on the basis of existing household surveys, which have not been designed to facilitate international comparisons.

It is interesting in this regard to note that the global private sector and international organizations have long produced estimates of the relative costs of living for executives and senior officials throughout the world, in order to inform salary scales.[14] These estimates are based on extraordinarily detailed assessments of the cost of living, which are implicitly 'capability-based'. It seems disingenuous, in this light, to argue that a parallel exercise for the world's poor is not feasible.

## A FAILURE OF ACCOUNTABILITY

The present money-metric approach to global poverty assessment under-standably emerged, under the imperative to produce poverty estimates for popular consumption and institutional use, as a 'rough and ready' means of estimating global poverty. However, that this approach has endured so long and has been as influential as it has been in the global policy environment is a testament both to the lack of accountability of those who produce these es-timates, and the failure to hold them to account. On the one hand, estimates of global poverty are produced in a non-transparent manner within inter-national institutions, and on the other hand those who use them, including activists, have lacked an adequate understanding of what they mean and how they are produced.

The Bank has shown little sign of undertaking a fundamental reassessment of its methodology of global poverty assessment. The modifications it has in-troduced in recent years, almost certainly due to the pressure from critics, are largely cosmetic. In particular its so-called PPPP project, which aims at con-structing PPPs more narrowly focused on necessities, offers such an example. Although this initiative will certainly help to diminish one of the distortions that are present in the Bank's approach, it cannot eliminate this distortion nor address other basic problems inherent in the approach. In particular, although the initiative can reduce the degree to which measures of purchasing power equivalence across countries depart from the true relative cost of purchasing basic necessities, it cannot do this coherently without identifying a relevant set of basic necessities and the relative weights to be attached to them. This exercise must in turn necessarily rely on specifying some conception of the ultimate *purpose* to which these necessities are meant to be put. However, the money-metric approach exactly avoids such a specification. More impor-tantly, the use of more appropriate PPPs will not help to address the lack of relation between the $1 and $2 per day money-metric international poverty lines and a meaningful conception of the elementary human requirements for which the level of income defined by the IPL should suffice. Once again, the money-metric approach precisely avoids explicitly anchoring the IPL in such a conception.

The apparent intransigence of the Bank in relation to its poverty esti-mates may be an instance of a broader phenomenon in the careers of institutions. Once institutional commitments are made to a specific way of doing things, there are strong pressures for its continuance, however 'suboptimal' the chosen way may come to be deemed, if only to protect the 'reputational capital' of the institution and the individuals who are attached to it.

In this particular instance, what is also at stake is the claim of economists, and of an institution largely shaped by them, to possess special technical expertise. Changes of leadership provide an important opportunity for institutional change, as individual 'reputational capital' can be separated from institutional 'reputational capital' on such occasions. However, the recent change of leadership at the World Bank, which has brought to its helm an individual who has shown contempt for the truth in his past public activities, offers little hope that such an opportunity will be grasped. The reasons for pessimism are compounded by the fact that there exist few organized constituencies which can be relied on to push the Bank to enhance the extent to which its statistics 'tell the truth' regarding the present world situation. Even those 'civil society' activists who otherwise watch the Bank carefully have shown little interest in the question, preferring to treat it as a matter for economic 'experts'.

The reluctance may be psychologically understandable. Who wishes to know how a sausage is made? In any case, the lack of interest in this debate, even on the part of many otherwise progressive economists, is notable. To a degree, this may be an instance of the general disregard for the conceptual and practical problems that arise in the collection of statistics, which are often viewed as 'mere data problems' that are unprestigious to study. However, it may also be an instance of the hold of dominant institutions and ideology over the discipline. The 'dollar a day' approach coheres well with the instinct of many economists to avoid explicit normative commitments and to favour money-metric assessment in other spheres. Less abstractly, the conclusion of both the Bank and its right-wing critics that the extent of world poverty is diminishing coheres well with the prior beliefs of most standard economists.[15] The close working relationship between practitioners of the discipline and the international financial institutions may also be consequential in explaining their approach to this and other issues.

It is perhaps unsurprising that right-wing critiques of the Bank's poverty statistics have received prominent publication and widespread journalistic coverage or acclaim, while other criticisms have received scant attention.[16] Journalists and even many activists appear to have too little tolerance for the complex and uncomfortable truth that 'we don't know'. It appears that many find comfort in a number, however inadequate its basis. The zeal for enumeration, perhaps fuelled by the false sense of security that a numerical estimate presents, can become an important obstacle to knowing and telling the truth, when the underlying basis of such estimation is weak.

## WHAT NEXT?

An important lesson of this debate is that activists cannot shy away from the details of data production. Economic statistics are too important to be left to the economists. It is necessary for activists to become familiar with the meaning and method of production of economic statistics in order to hold those who produced them appropriately accountable.

Activists should call for the United Nations to sponsor the equivalent, for global poverty statistics, of the construction of internationally comparable national income statistics, which was pioneered after the Second World War by the Nobel Prize-winning economist Richard Stone and the United Nations under the heading of the 'System of National Accounts'.[17] This effort received tremendous support from governments and international organizations, and due to efforts over several decades has been an enormous success. Countries have almost universally adopted methods of national accounting that facilitate both comparisons within nations over time, and comparisons between countries. This is an achievement that was barely dreamt of prior to the Second World War. The effort has been so successful that stock markets now tremble at the thought that the national income may dip by a small percentage, and vicissitudes in the national income become the subject of endless speculation and analysis by financiers, central bankers and economists.[18]

It is entirely possible similarly to invest in counting the number of the world's poor, by establishing appropriate international protocols for poverty line construction, survey design and analysis. If this has not been done so far, it is because this task has seemed to decision-makers to be less than urgent. This tells us a great deal about their priorities. It is interesting in this connection to note the following comment by Joseph Rowntree, who sponsored the first studies of the extent of poverty in England in the nineteenth century:

> I feel that much of the current philanthropic effort is directed to remedying the more superficial manifestations of weakness or evil, while little thought or effort is directed to search out their underlying causes. Obvious distress or evil generally evokes so much feeling that the necessary agencies for alleviating it are pretty adequately supported. For example, it is much easier to obtain funds for the famine-stricken people in India than to originate and carry through a searching enquiry into the causes and recurrence of these famines. The Soup Kitchen in York never has difficulty in obtaining adequate financial aid, but an enquiry into the extent and causes of poverty would enlist little support.[19]

# NOTES

1 See e.g. Robert Wade and Martin Wolf, 'Are Global Poverty and Inequality Getting Worse?', *Prospect,* March 2002.

2 See especially Surjit Bhalla, *Imagine There is No Country: Poverty, Inequality and Growth in the Era of Globalization,*Washington:Institute of International Economics, 2002, and Xavier Sala-i-Martin, 'The Disturbing "Rise" of World Income Inequality' (2002) and 'The World Distribution of Income (Estimated from Individual Country Distributions)' (2002) available on http://www.columbia.edu.

3 Statement to meeting of Central Bank Governors and Ministers of Finance in Ottawa, Canada on November 17th, 2001, previously available on www.worldbank.org. It is interesting to note that this speech is no longer on the website of the Bank, though the collection of speeches of Jim Wolfensohn presented there appears to be otherwise comprehensive. Moreover, the speech is only available on the website of the International Monetary Fund in an edited form from which this passage is absent.

4 These studies have been rightly criticized for extrapolating from limited data and for employing non-transparent and often inappropriate methods. See e.g. Branko Milanovic, 'The Ricardian Vice: Why Sala-i-Martin's Calculations of World Income Inequality are Wrong', 2002, available on http://papers.ssrn.com and Camelia Minoiu and Sanjay Reddy (forthcoming), 'The Use of Kernel Density Estimation in Poverty and Inequality Analysis' (provisional title).

5 See e.g. Shaohua Chen, S and Martin Ravallion, 'How Have the World's Poorest Fared Since the Early 1980s?', 2004, available on http://www.worldbank.org.

6 Xavier Sala-i-Martin, in the papers previously cited, adopts a poverty line of one dollar per day of *GDP per capita*, which automatically ensures that he arrives at lower poverty estimates than those of the Bank, which are based on a poverty line of $1 per day of private consumption. See e.g. Howard Nye, Sanjay G. Reddy, and Thomas Pogge, 'What is Poverty', letter to the *New York Review of Books*, 49(18), 2002, available on: http://www.nybooks.com.

7 Sandjay G. Reddy and Thomas W. Pogge. 'How *Not* to Count the Poor', Version 4.5, New York: Institute for Social Analysis, 26 May 2003, http://www.columbia.edu.

8 Perhaps to the extent of 30-40 per cent. See ibid.

9 See the 'Thrifty Food Plan' produced by the Center for Nutrition Policy and Promotion of the US Department of Agriculture, described at http://www.cnpp.usda.gov.

10   UN Economic Commission for Latin America, *Social Panorama of Latin America*, Santiago, Chile: ECLA, various years, and the comparison of poverty estimates from the two sources in Sanjay Reddy and Camelia Minoiu, 'Has World Poverty Really Fallen During the 1990s?', 2004, available on www.columbia.edu.

11   The Programme was previously hosted by the UN Dept. of Statistics, which gave up this role in the early 1990s due to lack of adequate financing.

12   This approach should of course make allowance for relevant sources of variation in these requirements, such as age.

13   See Sanjay Reddy, Sujata Visaria and Muhammad Asali, 'Inter-Country Comparisons of Poverty Based on a Capability Approach' available on www.columbia.edu.

14   See e.g. the 'post adjustments' produced by the International Civil Service Commission and the cost of living estimates produced by private consultancy firms such as Employment Conditions Abroad and Mercer Human Resources Consulting.

15   For a critical examination of this claim, see Sanjay Reddy and Camelia Minoiu, 'Has World Poverty Really Fallen During the 1990s?', available on www.columbia.edu.

16   Bhalla's work, *Imagine There is No Country*, was sponsored and published by the influential Institute for International Economics. Sala-i-Martin's work has been circulated by the prestigious National Bureau of Economic Research and is widely cited by leading economists. Sala-i-Martin obligingly provides a list of major world press outlets that have celebrated his results, on http://www.columbia.edu.

17   See e.g. http://nobelprize.org.

18   In which connection, see the interesting proposal for national income-based options derivative contracts in Robert Shiller, *Macro-Markets: Creating Institutions for Managing Society's Largest Economic Risks*, Oxford: Oxford University Press, 1993.

19   See the 'Founder's Memorandum' of 29 December 1904, available on http://www.jrf.org.uk.

# PLAYING WITH THE TRUTH: THE POLITICS OF THE THEATRE

## MICHAEL KUSTOW

In ancient Greek theatre, where drama was born, feelings could be expressed which were too dangerous to allow in society. Giving offence was, and remains, part of theatre's business. You can identify with a murderer through your imagination, but it doesn't mean you condone Macbeth. Through imagination, the feelings are exorcised. (Nicholas Hytner, Director, National Theatre of Great Britain[1])

… lies like truth. (William Shakespeare, *Macbeth,* Act Five, Scene 5)

On Saturday December 18 2004, a crowd of about 1,000 British Sikhs gathered outside Birmingham Repertory Theatre to protest about *Behzti* ('Dishonour' in Punjabi), a new play by Gurpreet Kaur Bhatti, a young woman playwright, a Sikh herself. People began chanting that her play was sacrilegious and an insult to their religion. The organized protest soon turned violent: bricks were thrown through windows, eggs hurled and when the crowds clashed with police, three officers were injured. Inside the theatre, two performances were taking place: *Behzti* and a play for children. As the protestors broke into the theatre, terrified children and their parents were trapped in the foyer along with the actors and theatre staff. On the Monday, the theatre 'very reluctantly' cancelled the remaining ten performances of *Behzti*. 'The Sikh community', said the theatre's executive director, 'was unable to guarantee that there would be no repeat of the violence. It is now clear that we cannot guarantee the safety of our audience… The theatre vigorously defends its right to produce *Behzti* and other similar high-quality plays that deal with contemporary issues in a multi-cultural society'.[2]

By now the play's author was in hiding, having received death threats. What the Sikh community spokesmen most objected to was a scene in which a mother brings her daughter to the local Sikh temple, the *gurdwara,* to find her a husband for an arranged marriage. The marriage broker, Mr

Sandhu, an apparently respectable local dignitary, is said to keep lists of suitable bridegrooms. But he is also notorious for rape and sexual abuse. The young woman is having her period, and stains show on her dress; two other women raped by Mr Sandhu, and now his accomplices, beat her up, getting her mother to join them. It turns out that Mr Sandhu has no list of suitable husbands; what he does instead is offer himself in marriage, and then rape the woman. One of his victims describes it:

> TEETEE: They stripped me first and covered my mouth. Then he bent me over and pulled my hair. He was young then so he had better control. Your Mr Sandhu went inside me and took what was human out of my body. My mother wept salty tears while she watched. Afterwards she beat me till I could not feel my arms or legs. Then she turned to me and said, now you are a woman, a lady. Now you are on your own, *behsharam*.[3]

Birmingham Repertory Theatre had been in negotiation with leaders of the Sikh community for weeks about the play. It agreed a statement with them, which was handed out to the audience. But the theatre refused their main demand – to alter the play by re-setting the offensive scene in a community centre, not in the sacred precincts of the temple. Theatres rallied to support the author and the theatre. Another Birmingham theatre, the tiny Birmingham Stage Company, offered to stage the play. The Royal Court, the Bush Theatre and Chichester Theatres called on all British subsidized theatre to join them in giving the play a rehearsed reading on the same day. Then a message came back from the playwright in hiding, asking them not to do so as it would put her and her family in even greater danger.

David Edgar, a leading British playwright who has lived and worked in Birmingham for most of his life, wrote:

> The Birmingham Rep has a superb record in giving voice to the culturally invisible communities that surround it. The theatre premiered Ayub Khan-Din's *East is East* and produced a ground-breaking mainstage dramatisation of the Hindu epic *Ramayana*. It is a bitter irony that this theatre, of all theatres, has been forced to pull Gurpreet Kaur Bhatti's second play, *Behzti*, one of a growing number of plays being written by young Asian women about the conflict between faith and institutional religion in culturally isolated communities. Its importance can be judged by the large number of young Asian women who have packed in to see it.[4]

On December 23, under the heading 'We must defend freedom of expression', the *Guardian* ran a letter signed by over 300 people, a cross-section of British theatre. Actors, dramatists, artists from all the ethnic minorities in the country, publishers, agents, professors, critics, artistic directors and technicians deplored the cancellation forced on the theatre by an angry mob, and reaffirmed that 'it is a legitimate function of art to provoke debate and sometimes to express controversial ideas. A genuinely free, pluralist society would celebrate this aspect of our culture. Those who use violent means to silence it must be vigorously opposed and challenged by all of us, whatever our faith, belief or opinions'.[5] Some of those most directly concerned with what the play was about also wrote to the *Guardian* letters page: 'As Asian women of Sikh, Muslim and Hindu backgrounds, we have been struggling for many years against attempts to silence our voices in relation to violence against women. The issues depicted in *Behzti* – rape, corruption and the abuse of power – are real and need exposure'.[6] For his part, Salman Rushdie attacked the government's failure 'to condemn the violence when they should be supporting freedom of expression … frankly, book shops and theatres are full of the things that would upset an interest group'.[7]

The right to provoke dialogue and generate debate has to be defended. But are there other considerations that should qualify this right, such as the risk of providing fodder for racism and prejudice? Does Gurpreet Kaur Bhatti's play go out of its way to use 'shock tactics' and offensiveness – placing its scene of sexual abuse in the Sikh temple itself, rather than in a community centre? Is there any justice in accusing her of 'letting down her community', of 'washing dirty linen' before an audience of non-believers? Who is to judge how far a playwright may go?

Doubtless the Sikhs who assailed the Birmingham Repertory Theatre, flooded it with e-mails from all over the world by people who had not seen the play, or even put themselves forward as rewriters of *Behzti*, believed they were defending Sikhism against a heretic, one of their own who had broken ranks. Doubtless there were calmer Sikh voices who would have been satisfied by the statement the theatre agreed with community representatives and handed out to audiences. In her foreword to *Behzti*, Gurpreet Kaur Bhatti does not write as an apostate: 'The heritage of the Sikh people is one of courage and victory over adversity. Our leaders were brave revolutionaries with the finest minds, warriors who propagated values of egalitarianism and selflessness'.[8] But has that legacy been propagated in the minds and words of the community leaders who condemn her play now? The community leaders and spokesmen who faced the media right after the riot talked as if the Sikh community were monolithic and homogeneous in its condemnation of *Behzti*.

'Community' is fast becoming a slithery term which closes down critical debate and rational argument. Little is gained by making it into a cosy
buzz-word, evoking ancestral bonds, placed in opposition to anything big,
centralized and threatening, like global corporations or the construction of
dams. At the other end of the spectrum, why should the tolerance of privileged liberals stop short at, for example, making time for Muslim prayers
at Stop The War rallies, as happens in England? If post-modern relativism
permits the cultivation of a portfolio of identities, like an actor adopting
roles, should it not go further, at least by arguing that fundamentalists and
their disruptions, e-mail blitzes and brick-throwing can be understood as
actions of the excluded, as a first step to forgiving them? Take this to its
conclusion and you get identity politics as the new feel-good public faith:
Let a multitude of identities bloom. Let faith schools thrive. Let books be
burned and theatres shut down, if they offend.

Nobody quite wishes to go that far, because such actions still seem to
cross a white line. Images of brown-shirts flinging books into the flames
come to mind. As does Heinrich Heine's warning that when you start by
burning books, burning people isn't very far away. The violent acting-out
of rage against perceived offensive performances or publications marks the
point where 'identity politics' or 'communitarianism' part company, not only
with democracy, and not only with the whole Enlightenment project: not
simply the project of Voltaire, Rousseau and Kant, but the universal values of
tolerance, rationality and an openness to learn – that can equally be found in
Sufism and Hinduism, and within Sikhism itself.

We need to place these skirmishes in a wider context. In his book *Jihad
versus McWorld*[9] Benjamin Barber suggests that we now live in a world in
which by and large there are only two human roles to be played: as members
of a tribe (*jihadists*, in a metaphorical sense) and as consumers in a globalized
economy. But man, as Aristotle famously wrote, is a political animal,[10] and
the third role which once distinguished human beings – being an involved
citizen in a *demos* – is still unachieved by most people. Neither globalism nor
tribalism has much use for democracy – or truth. Powerlessness breeds fanati-
cism. People seek refuge in religious or traditional beliefs, in strict forms of
faith, unchangingly handed down by their authoritarian forefathers, or else
in drugged obedience to the garish brand names, the wall-to-wall womb
of the super-mall or the world-wide products of the multiplex. Consumerism can be every bit as idolatrous as mass abasement before an evangelist
preacher. Francis Wheen speaks nothing less than the truth when he exco-
riates 'the *fortissimo* hosannas of those who regarded the global market as a
benign universal deity – immortal, invisible, omniscient, omnipotent'.[11]

In her introduction to the published text of her play, Gurpreet Kaur Bhatti affirms the exacting and elating possibilities of her art.

> I wrote *Behzti* because I passionately oppose injustice and hypocrisy. And because *writing drama allows me to create characters, stories, a world in which I, as an artist, can play and entertain and generate debate.* The writers I admire are courageous. They present their truths and dare to take risks whilst living with their fears. They tell us life is ferocious and terrifying, that we are imperfect and only when we embrace our imperfections honestly, can we have hope. Such writers sometimes cause offence. But perhaps those who are affronted by the menace of dialogue and discussion, need to be offended.[12]

## THEATRE'S DNA

There's a long history of 'going too far' planted in the genetic code of drama, and Gurpreet Kaur Bhatti is working within that tradition. Defenders of theatre's freedom of expression point to its origins in fifth century BC Greece. Transgression, unmasking and excess were planted in theatre's very nature from the start. From its invention in ancient Greece – or more specifically, the democratic city of Athens – it has been the job, indeed the vocation, of playwrights to probe difficult and dangerous feelings, to explore the outcast, the pariah and the Other, and to follow the actions of the protagonists to the furthest extreme. Outrageous actions are the bread and butter of theatre, leading to tears or to laughter.

Aeschylus' Agamemnon kills his daughter to enable a war to begin. Elsewhere he portrays the defeated Persians, Athens' enemy, in a way that inspires pity, not gloating. Sophocles' Medea, a foreign woman married to a Greek prince, murders their children to spite her unfaithful husband, in a kind of *kamikaze* act of despair. Greek comedy, though not so fundamentally outrageous in its form, laid about its targets with equal relish: famously, in Aristophanes' *Lysistrata*, a play in which the city's women refuse to have sex with their men until they stop making war, and the stage is soon filled with sex-starved men with painful erections.

Athenian drama – with its all-male, masked casts, infectious music and dancing – was a one-off performance for up to 20,000 people at a civic event that was also an occasion for the military and religious re-dedication of the city-state. In this many-layered situation, imagination was licensed to open up themes which divided society as well as values that united it. Athenians' sense of their citizenship was strong enough for them to face together some of the most rending moral and political situations the theatre has ever addressed.

The Greek tragedies were complemented by the satyr-plays, disrespectful aftermaths to the main event, performed by actors in half-human, half-goat forms, brandishing enormous penises. At the end of a long day, the audience followed these creatures into a topsy-turvy realm where all notions of duty, justice and propriety were overturned by the forerunners of medieval European carnivals' Lords of Misrule. Theatre's sensuous freedom of play has its roots in a polytheistic society where it was seen as something god-given, the god in question being the elusive Dionysus, the sexually-ambivalent, boundary-crossing deity of wine and theatre, who had come from as far away as India, dancing at the head of a train of aroused women.

This Dionysiac source gives theatre its exuberance, and its power to cast a spell. It also licenses it to play with and mock things that the world, its priests, censors, community leaders and legislators see as deadly serious.

From Dionysus comes theatre's drive to unmask and demystify, to reveal miscreants, hypocrites and killers. But its truth-telling is indirect – 'through indirections find directions out', says Polonius, though that may also be taken as Shakespeare's note to himself. Through disguise and deception, mistakes and misapprehensions, portents and oracles, the truth, in Shakespeare, will out. It is no accident that Hamlet turns to the travelling players to enact a drama which will reveal the usurper who has murdered his father. 'The play's the thing / In which I'll catch the conscience of the king'.

The pretence and make-believe of theatre may be its surest route to truth, as Kenneth Tynan grasped in his last years, gasping out truths into his diary (performed as a one-man show in 2005 by Corin Redgrave at the Arts Theatre in London): 'How much of theatre has to do with imposture! How much of world drama concerns people pretending to be what they aren't … Mistaken identity is not only what the craft of acting is all about, it is about what much of drama is all about. An actor is a man who pretends to be someone who is usually pretending to be someone else'.[13]

Offence is another weapon which theatre has never shirked in its thrust towards truth. In *The Merchant of Venice,* Shylock, the butt of a fiercely anti-semitic, mercantile Venice, gives as good as he gets, unforgettably destabilizing what would otherwise be a love-comedy. His come-uppance in a Venetian courtroom, through a quibble about a pound of flesh but not a drop of blood, leaves a bad taste in the mouth. Such is the *verismo* of Shakespeare's non-idealized, portrait that the institutional voices of Judaism continue to protest against what they see as Shakespeare's anti-semitism, but is better seen as his ruthlessly realistic imagination.

Theatre's transgressors and over-reachers have the power to seize the centre stage. Marlowe's Doctor Faustus goes way beyond the prevalent orthodoxy, and Molière's Tartuffe is an inspired religious con-man. Both commandeer the audience's imagination, force it to suspend its moral judgement. They are the bad guys you love to hate. As Hytner says, that doesn't mean you condone Macbeth the king-killer 'steeped in blood', the fore-runner of every blood-boltered Stalin, Pol Pot or Idi Amin. The force of the playwright allows you to enter into the world of another human creature before the shutters of judgement slam down and write him off.

Modern theatre's gaze on contemporary history began in the early years of the Russian Revolution, when agit-prop train plays and films combined the street theatre skills of an Eisenstein, the formal daring of a Meyerhold and the jagged urgency of film in the hands of Dziga Vertov newsreels.[14] In the 1920s the German director Erwin Piscator created a new form, 'epic theatre', which deeply influenced Brecht. Taking advantage of theatre's new technology – film projection, mechanized stages – Piscator brought not only the factual immediacy of contemporary events on stage but also a belief in the great Hegelian and Marxist tides of history.[15]

A member of the German Communist Party from 1918, Piscator insisted that the value of his theatre lay not only in 'multi-media', but in yoking new stage technology to revolutionary thinking. 'What would happen', he asked, 'if theatre were to introduce a wholly new architecture, making the stage a play-machine, a wonder-world, an arena for battling ideas, perhaps even setting the audience on a turntable, dynamically bursting the static illusion of the present stage? I do not say that new techniques will be the saviour of the theatre. I merely say that they can express new dramatic contents by liberating the creative forces of playwrights, directors and actors'.[16]

Piscator's work also called forth a new kind of acting, more like a witness in a court case than a romantically emotional leading player. In the work of Brecht, a great poet as well as a dramatist and director, these currents found their apotheosis in the productions at his Berliner Ensemble – *Galileo, The Threepenny Opera, Arturo Ui*. They were the poetic expressions of a dramatist, not 'fact-based theatre', but they bore in themselves the hallmarks of the epic theatre Piscator had invented; above all, a cool, conscious and aware performance style, always aware of the piece as a whole, not just the fate of the actor's character. 'Gestural' acting Brecht called it, seeking 'alienation', to give the spectator room to reflect, as opposed to 'identification', when the audience swoons in the presence of a star.

I was lucky enough to see the Berliner Ensemble in 1961, crossing over from West Berlin and staying afterwards in the theatre canteen to talk to the actors late into the night. It was a revelation at the time; but through the

1960s, with an even greater saturation of media reporting, theatre began more and more to turn away from Brecht's poetic and political drama to documentary evidence, with plays, often from Germany, about J. Robert Oppenheimer, the complicity of Pope Pius XII in the crimes of the Third Reich, and a massively edited version of the Frankfurt war-crime trials.

## THE FACES OF BRITISH THEATRE TODAY

Against this backdrop, it would be hard to overlook the basic conservatism of British theatre. In his now canonical book *The Empty Space* (1968), Peter Brook named four species of theatre in a famous taxonomy: The Deadly, The Holy, The Rough and The Immediate.[17] His categories have not been outdated, nearly forty years later. The Deadly Theatre persists, with some encouraging exceptions, in London's West End and Manhattan's Broadway; commercial theatre relies increasingly on revivals with casts headed by stars from movies and television, and on musicals (to be discussed a little later). High-culture Holy Theatre flourishes as ever in the world's opera houses, with their corporate entertainment parties and connoisseurs fondly recalling the great days of Maria Callas.

Defiantly non-cultural Rough Theatre still sprouts wherever the energies of the street, the carnival and the circus are summoned to create Dionysian theatre – in the lofts and cellars of the fringe locations, in site-specific venues and occasionally on the main stages of theatrical institutions. The Immediate theatre – for Brook the essential theatre, which packs more into 'each second and micro-second'[18] – may be rare, but it is unmistakable when you meet it. In 2004 I saw Shakespeare's *Othello* in London's Riverside Studios done by the itinerant English group Cheek by Jowl on a bare traverse stage. It was Meyerholdian in its swoops of energy, packs of actors sweeping across the stage, Shakespeare's text about jealousy and race borne along in a cat's cradle of movement and rhythm.

In recent years, there's been a marked revival of political theatre in Britain, still trying to find its own necessity, its way of truth-telling, in our news-drenched age. Fact-inspired productions in British theatre veer wildly between Brechtian epic construction (David Hare coined the phrase 'verbatim theatre' to describe his documentary account of the effects of the privatized railways, *The Permanent Way*), courtroom ritual, with its inherently dramatic progression of evidence and cross-examination, and the grotesque humour of Justin Butcher, whose new barbed comedy about WMD inspection in Iraq, *A Weapons Inspector Calls*, sending up J.B. Priestley's angry 1946 play *An Inspector Calls,* joined the National Theatre in 2005.

The Iraq war produced a flourish of new pieces, from Butcher's gleefully angry *The Madness of George Dubya* which used the plot of Kubrick's *Dr*

*Strangelove* to satirize Bush and Blair in Iraq, to Hare's *Stuff Happens* on the main stage at the National Theatre, an account of the events leading up to the attack on Iraq, with a cast as big as a West End musical playing Bush, Blair, Rumsfeld, Colin Powell, Condoleeza Rice and assorted diplomats, weapons inspectors, journalists, a Palestinian woman and an Iraqi exile. Directed with chilling calmness by Nicholas Hytner – the atmosphere sometimes recalled a wake – Hare's dispassionate chronicle had the quiet power of an artist speaking more in sorrow than in anger.

Even more sombre was *Guantanamo*, drawn from documents and interviews by Victoria Brittain and Gillian Slovo. Hyper-realist, with its iron cages and orange uniforms, *Guantanamo* brought home the emotional and physical reality of the detainees, even if it lacked the forensic drama shown by the earlier work of Nicolas Kent's Tricycle Theatre in north London, which has specialized in what it calls 'tribunal theatre'. Drawing on transcripts of official enquiries, these productions have laid bare, in a way that media cannot, the Nuremberg trials of 1945, police mishandling of the killing of black teenager Stephen Lawrence, Britain's export of arms to Saddam Hussein, the massacre at Srebrenica, and most recently, the events of 'Bloody Sunday' in Northern Ireland. Even when you know the words have been condensed, you become aware that the physical presence of the protagonists and theatre's charged present tense puts you into a different relationship with the material than when you're sitting back to watch reportage on a small screen. Because the curve of the action is uninterrupted, it's that much more telling, and there are no ad-breaks or new items, which sap the truth of what you see.

Another way British theatre in recent years has penetrated into the oppression and violence of the world has been to take a classic play and re-configure it for here and now. Sometimes this has involved a playwright's reinvention of a classic. At the Young Vic, playwright Martin Crimp took hold of Sophocles' tragedy of marriage and violence, *Trachiniae* and rewrote it as *Cruel and Tender*.[19] In a clinically precise production by Luc Bondy, it became a bloody nightmare, in which a mighty general who has massacred a village is reduced to a broken war-criminal pathetically yoked to a colostomy-bag, which is emptied on stage. 'I have purified the world for you', he growls. 'I have burnt terror out of the world for people like you. I am not the criminal, but the sacrifice'. Echoes of massacres and abuse from Sabra and Shatila to Abu Ghraib crisscross Crimp's taut re-visioning of Sophocles.

Other readings, especially of the Greek tragedies, were directors 're-writing' plays to bring out their contemporary relevance. Sometimes the result can be merely conceptual and schematic. But Nicholas Hytner kicked off his tenure at the National Theatre with a resonantly updated Shakespeare – *Henry V* in a Middle East war, with armoured personnel carriers scaling the Olivier Theatre stage, and the black actor Adrian Lester as King Henry. At the start of the play, he presided over a cabinet meeting eerily reminiscent of Blair and Bush scuttling around to find a *casus belli*, with everyone dressed in suits and touting smart document cases. It looked like a gathering in the White House or Downing Street now, and Shakespeare's text rang home across four hundred years:

> KING HENRY V
> My learned lord, we pray you to proceed
> And justly and religiously unfold
> Why the law Salique that they have in France
> Or should, or should not, bar us in our claim:
> And God forbid, my dear and faithful lord,
> That you should fashion, wrest, or bow your reading ...
> For God doth know how many now in health
> Shall drop their blood in approbation
> Of what your reverence shall incite us to.
> Therefore take heed how you impawn our person,
> How you awake our sleeping sword of war.

A flow of fresh public funding into the theatre, starting in 2002, helped theatre-makers in Britain to transcend parochialism. A new internationalism has been afoot, largely spearheaded by LIFT, the London International Festival of Theatre, run since 1984 by Rose Fenton and Lucy Neal. They have shown through their ten biennial festivals, importing plays and performers from as far as India and Russia, that the horizons of theatre can be limitless. LIFT also embarked in 2002 on a three-year inquiry into the nature of theatre, through performances, talks and installations, trying to connect the insights of ecology and the informality of anti-globalization politics with an extended practice of theatre.

This internationalism prods the imagination of home-grown talent and audiences, prompts bolder visual and physical metaphors, and pushes performances beyond the confines of British theatre traditions. New work and models from abroad meets the on-going practice of another enduring force of British theatre: the cluster of independent theatre groups, many of them still going strong after twenty years or more. Out Of Joint, Forced Entertainment, Improbable Theatre, The People Show, Theatre de Complicité – these are post-war British theatre's ensembles of creativity and continuity, and there is already another generation of experimenters at their heels.

One pioneering group, Theatre de Complicité, marked its twenty-first year in the business with a flurry of activity in 2004. *The Elephant Vanishes,* based on the stories of Haruki Murakami, was an evocation of alienated big-city life in Tokyo, performed by a Japanese cast, negotiating urban dreams and nightmares in a cats' cradle of video screens and replicated images, which recalled Fritz Lang's *Metropolis*. Simon McBurney, the company's founder, and his actors have learned from stand-up British comedy, the physical teachings of the great French mime Jacques Lecoq,[20] and the rigour of Japanese theatre. They also collaborate with John Berger, staging the story of Lucie Cabrol from Berger's book *Pig Earth* and devising with him *The Vertical Line*, a 'site-specific' performance about the people who made the first paintings on the walls of caves millennia ago. It took place in the lift-shaft and on the platforms of a disused Underground station at the Aldwych, three hundred feet below street level, and was an unforgettable work of theatre poetry.

In 2003 McBurney also did a chilling production of Shakespeare's *Measure for Measure* at the National Theatre. He revived *A Minute Too Late* there as well. This had been one of Complicité's earliest successes, a desperate clown show about dying and death. Three actors with a few poor props, handling a corpse which threatens to flop out of a hearse driven by a manic undertaker, create a piece about the awkwardness of dying, of trying and failing to imagine a beyond. This was theatre of fearless incongruity, crossing the boundaries of taste and the limitations of genres, grounded in the fluency and flexibility of the body. But how does this inventive piece – conjuring situations out of the air in an act of theatrical magical realism – relate to the bigger picture of what was really going on in most of the British theatre today?

## NO BUSINESS LIKE SHOW BUSINESS?

According to the West End theatre managers' association, a 1998 survey showed that only a fraction of the 11.5 million people who bought tickets for theatrical shows went to the National Theatre or the Arcola, to Riverside Studios in Hammersmith or the Tricycle in Kilburn.[21] Most of them went to the West End – the generic name for London's commercial theatre – and the greatest proportion of those went to see a musical, the hallmark genre of the West End (and, in New York, of Broadway). In doing so, they spent £433 million on restaurants, hotels, transport and merchandise – 'souvenir' programmes, CDs, DVDs and T-shirts – over and above the £250 million they paid for tickets. The theatre managers' report salutes the

> massive economic importance of 'Theatreland' – the other 'Square Mile' in London – on which depends the well-being of hundreds of British companies … London remains the Theatre Capital of the world with more shows and bigger audiences than anywhere else, including Broadway. World-wide earnings of the biggest British

shows dwarf those of Hollywood blockbuster films, e.g. *Titanic, Jurassic Park.*[22]

Show Business is serious business; 'tax revenues of more than £200 million were produced by West End theatre in 1997', says Wyndham, who estimates that 'as a net currency earner for the UK, West End theatre is similar in size to the entire UK Advertising, Accountancy and Management Consultancy industries – and hugely bigger than the UK Film and Television industry'.

The index of success for the commercial theatre, in 2004 as for the past four or five decades, comes not from the medium-size theatres (600 - 1,000 seats) where straight (i.e. spoken, not sung) plays can be presented, but from the performance of the big houses (up to 2,000 seats), which only a solid-gold, crowd-gathering, superlative-touting musical can fill: the Adelphi (*Chicago*), the Apollo Victoria (*Saturday Night Fever*), the Cambridge Theatre (*Jerry Springer The Opera*), the London Palladium (*Chitty Chitty Bang Bang*), the Prince Edward (*Mary Poppins*), the Theatre Royal Drury Lane (*The Producers*).

It is here that the drama of the West End is acted out: producers and backers scrutinizing box-office returns as anxiously as Hollywood checks the weekly numbers; the inflation of every backstage drama into a tabloid event, as in the departure of Richard Dreyfuss from the Mel Brooks musical *The Producers* four days before the start of previews. The producers said he left because of complications following back surgery. Dreyfuss said it was 'because I sing like a seal and dance like your Uncle Leo'. Would the show go on? For days the debate raged, until the miraculous resurrection of its New York star Nathan Lane ensured that it did.

It garnered a range of reviews which are, as New Yorkers might say, 'to die for'. 'To say that it unleashes an epidemic of bliss would be too mealy-mouthed'.[23] 'After three delirious hours one is left stunned by a combination of unstoppable laughter and sheer happiness'.[24] '[It] puts the comedy back into musical comedy. After years of quasi-operatic musicals that have turned poverty and oppression into a showbiz spectacle, we are at last allowed to laugh'.[25] *The Producers* is also a wry comment on the political economy of musicals, for its plot turns around the eponymous producer's scam of collecting a thousand investors for a musical which is bound to fail, and making off with their money. Trouble is, the musical within the musical, *Springtime for Hitler*, becomes as much of a smash hit as *the Producers* is. I made one big mistake when I went to see it; I did not take enough Kleenex tissues. By midway through act two I was holding my ribs and streaming tears of laughter. This is what show business should be like, and only rarely is.

It would be wrong to call all the musicals that blanket the West End business rather than art. There is theatrical art of the highest calibre in them: Susan Stroman's elegant direction and pulse-quickening choreography for *The Producers*; Julie Taymor's magical evocation of Kipling's jungle creatures through every species of puppetry in *The Lion King*; William Dudley's kaleidoscopic projected decors for *The Woman in White*.

But the price to be paid for these high-definition performances (apart from the £40 in London or $100 in New York that a decent seat will set you back) is an alteration of theatre's contract with its audience. These musicals establish a new paradigm for theatre – and indeed have altered the staging of classic drama, as directors from the public sector theatre direct musicals commercially and then import their techniques onto subsidized stages. With its aura of superlatives brandished on the front of theatres and in bold type in the classified ads, with its tourist-brochure offers of a combined ticket, dinner and overnight hotel, and with its ticket prices out of step with the cost of going to the cinema (or buying a CD or a paperback), West End and Broadway theatre has created a glittering market of its own. Because it shouts its wares so loudly, it persuades many people that it is the one thing they should sample if they are going to try theatre at all.

The National Theatre has risen to this economic challenge. A sponsorship of £1 million over three years by the travel services company Travelex enabled it to introduce a £10 ticket for a good seat in the major part of the year in the Olivier Theatre, with spectacular results. During Nicholas Hytner's opening season as director of the NT, 50,000 people watched a play for the first time, and the theatre posted an average attendance of 95 per cent. The audience on Travelex nights is younger, fresher, more informal, undaunted by having to book in advance, or feeling intimidated by the splendour of old buildings, or having to pay rip-off prices for an ice-cream or a drink.

A different kind of immediacy, a different place for truth has been created by Hytner's National Theatre, and other public theatres across the country. We have experienced, not the trumped up, over-the-top, inflated sense of occasion promised by the commercial theatre, emulating the 'event culture' of reality television and other voyeuristic aspects of our media, but something palpably communal and communicative, taking drama's wily and circuitous route to the truth, through tragedy, comedy or factual drama. Theatre, they implicitly say, is about learning to live together with strangers, with the Others. Not customers, not consumers as in the bright-lit playhouses of Broadway or the West End; but our compatriots for a two-hour, ephemeral togetherness in the land of theatre.

In 2004, at the Lyric Theatre in the heart of the West End, I saw an adaptation of *Festen*, originally a film by the Danish 'Dogme' film-makers that hit home like a sledge-hammer. It began once more on a bare stage, where family and friends gathered to mark the father's birthday. A hundred tiny oddities and discrepancies exposed a raw crime in his past, involving rape and suicide. The play was directed with a complex choreography by Rufus Norris, a young director whose career to date shows how boundary-breaking the British theatre can still be. Originally an actor, Norris directed fairy-tales for children and adults – *Grimm's Tales* and *Sleeping Beauty* at the Young Vic, where he also staged a Spanish Golden Age classic, Lope de Vega's *Peribanez*. Two years ago he went with playwright David Greig to Ramallah. They worked with a group of Palestinian actors and created a dark comedy about the everyday harassments and tragedies of the Palestinians under occupation. They brought a rehearsed reading of the play to the Royal Court Theatre. Norris played an Israeli sentinel at a road-block. All he did was shout 'no' in Hebrew.

Breaking the mould of a career is a long-standing tradition in the British theatre: Peter Brook, at eighty worshipped as perhaps the greatest theatre director in the world, started out doing French comedies and British farce in the West End, a musical on Broadway and American plays in Paris, as well as Richard Strauss at the Royal Opera House and Shakespeare at Stratford-upon-Avon. This creative promiscuity, this alliance of avant-garde experiment with red-blooded show-business, gives British theatre a zest and edge. It's not for nothing that at Christmas 2004 Ian McKellen, a fabled classical actor and mesmerising Gandalf in *Lord of the Rings*, played Widow Twankey in drag in the pantomime *Aladdin* at the Old Vic. This was the stage on which Laurence Olivier, Richard Burton and a galaxy of classical actors kept the plays of Shakespeare alive. As a teenager in the upper circle of the Old Vic I had an early immersion in Shakespeare, relishing the beauty of Claire Bloom and the alchemy of Shakespeare's language. Now the Old Vic is under the artistic direction of Kevin Spacey, the latest and most determined American émigré to London's theatre. Spacey's is a longer-term commitment than that of most American actors who come here for limited runs: he wants London to be his base, with occasional forays into Hollywood, not the other way around.

## CONCLUSION

The *Behzti* business, blowing up in a regional theatre but reverberating through the country, is one incident among many fluctuations in Britain's multicultural society. It is also a sign of new awareness of cultural clashes and cross-currents in those parts of British theatre that are not 'hermetically sealed' from the society it inhabits, as Arthur Miller once put it.

In 2002, after a thorough-going enquiry into the entire theatrical system, the Labour government made an unprecedented funding increase, putting

£25 million over three years into theatres across the country. Some of the positive effects of this, especially in terms of allowing theatres to transcend parochialism, were mentioned above, and it is important to recognize that the production of *Behzti* at Birmingham was one of the many imaginative new departures that theatres, no longer obliged to live from hand to mouth, were able to plan and schedule in recent years as a result of this infusion of cash. Research and development of experimental projects; exploration of new subject matter; new voices from different cultural traditions; collaborative co-productions between theatres; increased touring – these have been some of the results in the public-funded theatres across the country.

In spring 2005, however, there was a *peripeteia*, a total reversal of fortunes, as at the climax of a Greek tragedy. The government decreed a freeze on arts spending and made a skittish decision to devote more of the available funds to museums instead of theatres, presumably on the basis of 'You've had your turn, now give other arts forms a chance'. This means cutbacks, a return to hand-to-mouth or sudden death for many theatres, especially those outside London, who are now going to have to work on drastically tightened budgets.

This matters to theatre's ability to tell the truth. Telling the truth ought to be easier in live theatre than in other kinds of drama. It carries the weight and expectation of so much less financial pressure. Hollywood movies may reach global audiences of billions, but they have to, in the industry parlance, 'perform', in order at least to recoup their costs and if possible make a profit. Above a certain budget ceiling, movies conform to genres, conventions and to interference by 'the back office', stars, middle-men, agents and marketing executives. This lessens their capacity to tell the truth. The same applies, at a lower budget level, to television drama, with its formats, its narratives always anxious that viewers will switch channels, its season-after-season exploitation of formulaic series, its advertisers' requirements.

Theatre, by comparison, is a cottage industry. It is a labour-intensive, hand-crafted form, created by authors and actors, most of whom, defying the commercial logic of the age, perform in tiny auditoria and limited runs, living an insecure and often nomadic existence. In principle untrammelled by commercial and industrial pressures, theatre should have the potential, and sometimes achieves the reality, of telling the truth. The two-way contact between stage and audience shows up falsity and manipulation. But when truth is manifest on stage, you know it at once: witness, among many examples, the first night of Arthur Miller's *Death of a Salesman* in 1949, when the curtain fell and the audience was literally stunned silent by the truth of the play, held immobile in their seats while it sank in. Miller's play has played its part ever since in telling and showing the truth about the waste of human life in our system, and despite his death in 2005, it will continue to do so. As Willy Loman's wife says: 'Attention must be paid'.[26]

NOTES

1   In the *Daily Telegraph*, 21 December 2004.
2   Tania Branigan and Vikram Dodd, 'Writer In Hiding As Violence Closes Sikh Play', *The Guardian*, 21 December 2004.
3   From *Behzti* by Gurpreet Kaur Bhatti, London: Oberon Books, 2004, Scene 4.
4   *The Guardian*, 21 December 2004.
5   'We Must Defend Freedom of Expression', *The Guardian*, 23 December 2004.
6   Letter from Pragna Patel, on behalf of The Southall Black Sisters, *The Guardian*, 27 December 2004.
7   Rajeev Syal, 'I'm Disgusted Ministers did nothing as Sikhs Forced Play's Closure, says Rushdie', *Sunday Telegraph*, 26 December 2004.
8   Gurpreet Kaur Bashti, Foreword to Bhatti, *Behzti*, p. 10.
9   Benjamin Barber, *Jihad vs. McWorld,* New York: Ballantine, 1998.
10  Aristotle, *Politics,* I, 2.
11  Francis Wheen, *How Mumbo Jumbo Conquered The World*, London: Fourth Estate, 2004, p. 234.
12  Bashti, Foreword to *Behzti*, emphasis added, p. 12.
13  In *Tynan*, based on the book *The Diaries of Kenneth Tynan* edited by John Lahr, adapted by Richard Nelson with Colin Chambers, London: Faber and Faber, 2005, p. 40.
14  Camilla Gray, *The Great Experiment: Russian Art, 1863-1922*, London: Thames and Hudson, 1962.
15  John Willett, *The Theatre of Erwin Piscator: Half a Century of Politics in the Theatre*, London: Methuen, 1978.
16  Erwin Piscator, *The Political Theatre*, Trans. Hugh Rorrison, London: Methuen, 1980, p. 26.
17  Peter Brook, *The Empty Space,* London: MacGibbon & Kee, 1968.
18  In conversation with the author in 2003. See Mike Kustow, *Peter Brook: A Biography*, London: Bloomsbury, 2005.
19  Martin Crimp, *Cruel and Tender*, London: Faber, 2004.
20  Jacques Lecoq, *The Moving Body: Teaching Creative Theatre*, Oxford: Routledge, 2001.
21  *The Wyndham Report*, published by the Society of London Theatre, 15 July 1998.
22  Ibid., Introduction.

23   Paul Taylor, 'The Producers, Theatre Royal, Drury Lane, London', *Independent*, 12 November 2004.

24   Charles Spencer, 'Laughter all the way as Hitler's Troupers go Down a Storm', *Daily Telegraph*, 10 November 2004.

25   Michael Billington, 'The Producers', *The Guardian*, 10 November 2004.

26   Notably, in a 1996 essay on Mark Twain, Arthur Miller reflected on '…the artist's complicated disgust with his art, the disgust mixed with equal amounts of pride plus the feeling of control over the imaginations of other people and his guilt at having planted images in their minds which he knows are hot air molded to beautiful and sometimes meaningful forms. It is all a lie, a lie like truth'. Arthur Miller, *Echoes Down the Corridor: Collected Essays, 1944-2000*, Steven R. Centola, ed., New York: Viking: 2000, p. 262.

# POSTMODERNISM AND THE CORRUPTION OF THE ACADEMIC INTELLIGENTSIA

## JOHN SANBONMATSU

The destruction of truth is so advanced in capitalist culture that it should come as no surprise that even in the halls of Critical Theory, imagined *sanctum sanctorum* of independent consciousness and conscience, truth is now openly profaned and condescended to by some among those who, historically, have been charged with sheltering its sacred flame – the intellectuals. 'The truth never dies, but is made to live as a beggar', goes the Yiddish proverb, reminding us that truth has always suffered in this world. But no intellectual movement of recent memory has so beggared the truth as poststructuralism has.[1] With the postmodernist turn in theory, truth became a dirty word, and affirmation of truth came to be seen as a sign not of conviction but of one's pitiable naiveté.

The tide began to turn against truth, and in postmodernism's favour, in the late 1970s. It was then that French historian and philosopher Michel Foucault first boldly put truth in scare quotes. '"Truth"', he declared, 'is to be understood as a system of ordered procedures for the production, regulation, distribution, circulation and operation of statements .... "Truth" is linked in a circular relation with systems of power which produce and sustain it, and to effects of power which it induces and which extend it'.[2] No longer would 'the true' be understood, as it had for millennia, as that which is 'in accordance with fact or reality'. From now on, for a growing and influential sector of the intelligentsia, the true would be posed as *a problem to be solved*. The prerogative of truth was thus transformed from a right of the oppressed into an object of study for the technical or academic expert. Only the quali-fied 'specific intellectual' or 'genealogist' could speak meaningfully of truth – or rather, could investigate the conditions of the possibility of 'truth'. What discourses give rise to the appearance of truth? How does 'truth', as a form of power, a system of 'constraints', function and manifest itself? How does knowledge, as power, disguise itself as truth, in order to achieve its effects? These questions are not uninteresting. The trouble is that poststructuralism insists we are entitled to ask *only* such questions, and so conflates inquiry into the ways that discourse about truth produces particular effects with endorsing the claim that truth-telling as such is impossible.

This fateful move can be traced to Friedrich Nietzsche, the intellectual forefather of poststructuralism. The faith in truth of the Christian and Jewish traditions, Nietzsche held, was merely a distorted or intellectualized version of the frustrated will to power of the oppressed. It was for this reason that Nietzsche viewed truth with deep suspicion and hostility, seeing it as the origin of nihilism in European culture. 'There is no pre-established harmony between the furtherance of truth and the well-being of mankind', he wrote.[3] Rather, only the free, unapologetic exercise of power – power as power over – over the self, over others – could provide a ground for new human values. But the ancient prophets and theologians were not wrong to believe that the oppressed, lacking power, have only the truth to console them. Deny the oppressed even this – the right to bear witness to the way things really are – and they have nothing. Surrender the possibility of truth, and one surrenders too the possibility of comparing the way things are with the way things ought to be. Nietzsche's contempt for justice (which is at root always and only a claim of truth against *power*), was thus an attack on the very desirability of general or social liberation.

As brilliant, if one-sided, as Nietzsche's critique of religious asceticism and repression was, it succumbed at the tail end of the 20th century to the very nihilism Nietzsche hated and tried to vanquish. Postmodernism, misappropriating Nietzsche, embraces a nihilism without borders. And this nihilism has been institutionalized by the bureaucratic institutions and modern pedantic types that Nietzsche abhorred. Since Foucault's death in 1984, truth has been continuously put on trial, interrogated, and found guilty of being 'truth' – an epiphenomenon of power, an artifact of discourse – by countless postmodernist academics who have made theory a profitable career. The effect of this highly ritualized repetition compulsion by the erstwhile 'leading' wing of the intelligentsia has been to blunt the critical imagination and to erode our capacity for truth-telling, precisely at humanity's hour of greatest need.

This is not to say that no poststructuralist thinker has ever contributed to the history of ideas. Our thinking has been improved, for example, by Foucault's insights into disciplinary apparatuses, by Derrida's discussion of the *pharmakon* and the equivocal nature of signs, and by Jean-François Lyotard's far-sighted comprehension of the postmodern condition of knowledge and the waning of the intellectual. A fair accounting, however, would have to conclude that such contributions have on the whole been modest, and that they have come to us exclusively from 'first wave' poststructuralist thinkers, not from their subsequent innumerable (and mediocre) epigones.

Worse, such an accounting would also have to conclude that the many critics of postmodernism have been basically right: that postmodernism is explicit where it should be vague or open-ended – e.g., on the subject of the best means of praxis, which it offers in prescriptive form (dispersion, difference, anti-strategicism, etc.) – and exasperatingly vague or noncommittal where it ought to be most explicit – e.g., on the ethical values and strategic goals of social movements.[4] Such aporias and contradictions would be of little consequence but for the fact that many academics and some activists, who count themselves on the Left, turn first to postmodernism for theoretical guidance. As a result, the postmodernist sensibility has gravely damaged the critical instruments of not one but several classes of intellectuals.

## POSTMODERNISM IN THE ACADEMY

The very formlessness of postmodernism, its theoretical equivocations and lack of an explicit canon or defined method, has in fact been integral to its phenomenal success in the academy. A protean cultural identity as much as a theoretical canon, postmodernism has weathered decades of hostility from all sides and persuasions – radical feminist, Marxist, liberal, conservative – by constantly changing form, taking on new disguises, adapting itself to new conditions. Like a virus travelling through the body of critical thought, postmodernism has succeeded by commandeering the disciplinary apparatus nearest to hand and turning it to account – stamping out genetic replicas of itself for export to other fields, other sub-disciplines, other geographies. Once settled in its discursive host, the virus takes hold again, blooms, sends off new messengers. Incubated in the elite universities of the capitalist metropoles, the institutional centres dominating the global trade routes of intellectual production and exchange, the virus has exported itself to the periphery. In the early years of the 21st century, postmodernism calved a new generation of postcolonial theorists on the Indian subcontinent, provided solace to dispirited activists in Latin America, attracted leftist academics disenchanted with Marxism, and struck the fancy of Islamic fundamentalists in Iran. If it is true, as Mark Twain wrote, that a lie will travel half way around the world while the truth is still putting on its shoes, then let us begin by noting that no theory of recent vintage has travelled as fast, or as far, as postmodernism has.

But it is in the West, and above all in the United States, that postmodernism has left its greatest mark on the native intelligentsia. Just how great a mark is a subject of dispute. Barbara Epstein suggests that poststructuralism is so dominant in the humanities and social sciences that 'theory' is now essentially synonymous with the term 'postmodern'.[5] Poststructuralists themselves, however, tend to downplay their influence within the academy. Thus Dempsey and Rowe, replying to Epstein, write that poststructuralist approaches are popular only within 'marginalized theoretical subdisciplines of the marginalized divisions of the social sciences and humanities within US universities', as if they were members of an embattled minority or vanishing breed.[6] Such modesty, however, is difficult to credit. Far from being a small or insignificant movement, postmodernism is now *the primary field of knowledge for the education of the critical intelligentsia* in the United States. It is the leading theoretical tendency on the terrains of about two dozen different disciplines, subfields, and areas of study, including Cultural Studies, Postcolonial Studies, Rhetoric and Composition, English Literature, French Literature, American Studies, Film Studies, Women's Studies, Ethnic Studies (including Asian American Studies, African and African-American Studies, and Latin American Studies), Queer Theory, Media Studies, Communications, Music Theory, Science and Technology Studies, Theater and Performance Studies, Anthropology, Continental Philosophy, and Theology. Even in the social sciences – in Sociology, Economics, Geography, Psychology, and Political Science – among those academics who identify with the emancipatory or 'critical' tradition, postmodernism has begun to vie on at least equal ground with Marxism as the preferred theoretical 'tool kit'. In Critical Legal Studies, post-structuralism is triumphant – the lingua franca of left law scholars.

The shrewd critic will be tempted to point out that such achievements, impressive though they are, are materially irrelevant to civilization and life as we know them on planet earth. This would be a mistake. The academic humanities, where postmodernism has furnished a series of comfortable rooms for itself, are not as marginal either to the contemporary academy, or to the reproduction of knowledge in society at large, as critics such as Dempsey and Rowe imply. One has only to realize that the annual conference of the Modern Language Association dwarfs that of the American Sociological Association – in 2004, 8,900 scholars attended the MLA, a mere 5,600 the ASA – to appreciate the key role played by the humanities in the reproduction of the intelligentsia. Millions of undergraduates still enrol in courses in the humanities, many thousands of books still get published by humanities scholars each year, and over the last quarter century the number of humanities conferences, events, and journals has skyrocketed. It is certainly true that the humanities and arts have nowhere near the status of, say, the applied sciences or mathematics. Yet even in the rather dire context of today's neoliberalized university, the humanities remain of strategic importance, both within the overall political economy of academic knowledge and in the reproduction of the intelligentsia nationally and globally.[7]

To understand the role of postmodernism in the humanities, as well as the role of the humanities in the wider intellectual field, we first need to consider the problem of *mediation*. Intellectuals are so called not because they work solely with their heads or intellects (instead of their hands or bodies), but because of their distinctive role in what Gramsci termed the 'ensemble of social relations' in which intellectual activity takes place and produces certain effects. Because the work intellectuals do is connected not to the production of goods and services, but to the circulation of ideas and culture, their function is primarily ideological. This does not, however, mean that they produce ideas in a vacuum. Whereas other kinds of knowledge workers have a more or less direct role in the production process – e.g., managing insurance accounts, working in sales or service – intellectuals have a *mediated* relationship to production. Specifically, the intellectual's labour is mediated 'by two types of social organization' – the state and civil society ('the ensemble of private organizations in society').[8]

Intellectuals today are far more mediated than they were in Gramsci's time. We must first note that there are far fewer 'organic' intellectuals today (i.e., intellectuals who developed naturally out of particular classes and social groups), and many more 'traditional' ones (individuals tied to disciplinary regimes and professional associations). Not to put too fine a point on it, the sympathetic intellectual today is far more likely to enter a Ph.D. program than, say, to assume a leadership role in a political party or social movement, or to take up arms (the present author not excluded). Whereas the critical or revolutionary intellectual of the past would have emerged out of a particular class, a national or ethnic identity, or a church or religious network, today's intellectuals are ostensibly 'free-floating' – deracinated thinkers without close connections to specific movements or identities. Or rather, they would be free-floating, were it not for the chains binding them to a limb of the state apparatus: the accredited, degree-granting college or university. The destruction of the public sphere, the decline of social movements, and the virtual disappearance of an independent press has shunted much of the intelligentsia into the academic system. There, the 'state nobility' finds its mental labour mediated through the tenure process and the competition for scarce federal grants and fellowships (the National Science Foundation, the National Institutes of Health, the National Endowment for the Humanities, and so on).

The bureaucratization and professionalization of knowledge over the last century – particularly the last half century – has in turn shaped the content and form of knowledge itself. 'Universities', Russell Jacoby observes, 'hire by committees: one needs degrees, references, the proper deference, a pleasant demeanor'. As such, they 'encourage a definite intellectual form'. Serious authors today are obliged to precede their tomes with 'a dense list of colleagues, friends, institutions, and foundations', as if to suggest 'that the author or book passed the test, gaining the approval of a specific network, which filtered out the unkempt and unacceptable'. The result is cautious scholarship heavily cloaked in the armour of authority – 'a book inspected by scores of scholars, published by a major university, and supported by several foundations'.[9]

Over the last twenty years, institutional constraints and pressures on scholarly knowledge have increased greatly. By the early 1980s, competition among the leading capitalist powers had made necessary a complete overhaul of higher education. The result has been the most significant and far-reaching reorganization of education – hence of the means of knowledge production – in the history of the Western university.[10] 'The corporatisation of higher education', Diane Reay observes, 'has enabled the market to invade and reshape the practices, organisation and values of universities across the globe'.[11] In this context, the rise and consolidation of postmodernism, what I have elsewhere termed 'baroque theory' – lavishly designed, opaque discourses with no social use value – is to be comprehended against the background of resource scarcity, growing socio-economic inequality within the academic system, and the commodification of knowledge, including within the humanities and arts.[12]

Prior to about 1970, higher education in the West had been legitimated ideologically  in terms of the university's role in fulfilling traditional humanistic ideals – increasing the storehouse of human knowledge, shaping individual character, creating an informed national citizenry, and so on. The fact that this mission was largely a fiction, or that these lofty ideals worked hand in glove to promote the interests of capital and the state, is not the point. What is significant is that the legitimation mechanisms of the university have been transformed almost overnight. The fundamental purpose of higher education today is seen as providing a pool of educated workers capable of out-competing workers in other national economies (as well as other states within the USA).[13] As the professoriate is 'casualized', and programs and resources are reshuffled to highlight disciplines that generate income for the university (e.g., the biosciences and informatics), traditional humanities values and norms are being uprooted. Lindsey Waters, former editor in chief of one of the most prestigious university presses in the US, summed up the effects of these changes on humanities scholarship:

> If humanists do not keep firmly in mind what they are about, no one else will. Humanists study books and artifacts in order to find traces of our common humanity …. [T]here is a causal connection between the corporatist demand for increased productivity and the draining from all publications of any significance other than as a number. The humanities are in a crisis now because many of the presuppositions about what counts are absolutely inimical

to the humanities. When books cease being complex media and become objects to quantify, then it follows that all the media that the humanities study lose value. Money has restructured the U.S. academy in its own image, and money is a blunt instrument.[14]

However, the market pressures decried by Waters – which have increased the sheer volume of humanities scholarship, while diminishing its overall quality – have paradoxically tended to benefit scholars who are media-savvy or otherwise adept at marketing their academic commodities. On the one hand, the subordination of knowledge production directly to the interests of capital, rather than (during the Cold War period) chiefly to the national security state, has placed enormous personal, economic, and professional pressures on scholars in the humanities and social sciences. Some, however, have profited personally – and often handsomely – from the new conditions by adopting novel discursive and professional strategies. Six figure salaries are no longer unusual among rising academic stars. I recently learned of a talented young academic who was offered close to $190,000 to sign on with a top ethnic studies program in the US. In the new, intensely competitive environment of the humanities, only scholars who can package their works as 'cutting-edge' can maintain their cultural and academic capital.[15] In this context, the perceived sexiness of poststructuralist-inflected knowledge products has led directly to postmodernism's disproportionate intellectual sway over the humanities, as publishers flood their catalogues with works in cultural studies, postcolonial studies, etc. The rationalization of the university and the commodification of knowledge have generated the very conditions that have enabled poststructuralism to flourish.

The crisis in higher education and the fiscal disciplining of the professoriate has required scholars and academic administrators to develop new ways of justifying the mission of the humanities. One way has been to depict the humanities as a value-added source for technological innovation and entrepreneurialism. Postmodernism fits into this plan. At the University of California (the largest public university in the US), planners trumpet the importance of humanities research in boosting the University's prestige through national rankings systems like those of the National Research Council. But they also now emphasize the role of the humanities in achieving regional and national competitiveness. The most recent master budget of the UC system thus makes special mention of the 'systemwide Humanities Research Institute' at UC Irvine, which it credits with 'spearheading a transformative effort to bring technology to bear on cultural issues' and working 'closely with scientists and engineers to develop new approaches to interdisciplinary scholarship and collaborative research'.[16] In 2004, two key figures at the Institute, Cathy N. Davidson and David Theo Goldberg, published 'A Manifesto for the Humanities in a Technological Age' in *The Chronicle of Higher Education*, in which they made a passionate case for the role of the humanities in illuminating the social implications of technology and culture. It is telling that the authors felt compelled to justify the humanities in terms of their use value for capitalism: '… [I]ndustry, more than anyplace else, wants not only highly trained scientists; it wants scientists who can also understand applications, intellectual property, issues of equity, human awareness, perspective, and other forms of critical analysis and logical thinking …'.[17]

Significantly, of the twelve distinguished academics on the Board of the Humanities Research Institute at Irvine, six publish work in the area of poststructuralist cultural studies or postcolonialism.[18] And of the dozens of workshops, seminars, colloquia, and conferences sponsored by the Institute, most have been on recognizably poststructuralist themes, or have featured scholars with a poststructuralist flair. As a multi-campus research program reporting directly to the Office of the UC President, the Humanities Research Institute at Irvine thus plays an important role in training a new cadre of postmodernist academics. In the last 17 years, the Institute has sponsored some 45 project teams, involved over 600 national and international fellows and participants, and hosted in residence over '500 scholars and other specialists representing over 60 disciplines in the humanities, arts, social sciences, technological fields, and sciences'.[19]

The Humanities Research Institute at Irvine is a good example of the convergence of postmodernism with two signal processes in the production and circulation of academic knowledge in the humanities today. The first is the increased level of contacts between humanities scholars and commercial industry. Of the sixteen members on the Institute's Board of Governors, eight are professors of Literature or Film (including the current president of a top liberal arts college), two are professors of sociology and ethnic studies, one is Chairman of the National Endowment for the Humanities, one is CEO of a Holocaust foundation, one is director of the J. Paul Getty Trust, one is chairman of the Executive Committee of the Walt Disney Company, and one is director of an academic think-tank on technology issues whose corporate sponsors include IBM, Ericsson, Microsoft, Intel, Siemens, Applied Materials, and Texas Instruments. The fact that leading scholars now rub shoulders with Walt Disney World and the Getty Trust, while not ominous in itself, is indicative of a subtle but important shift in the institutional fortunes of critical thought. Critical knowledges, which in the 18th and 19th centuries were weapons deployed by organic revolutionaries against the state, are rapidly being transformed into value-added instruments of the state and capital. The integration of corporations, humanist intellectuals, private foundations, and public education is now almost seamless. Postmodernism, with its chame-leon-like ability to blend with its surroundings, has benefited from the new, corporate-enhanced environment. In what may be a sign of things to come, poststructuralist feminist theorist Lucy Suchman spent the mid-1990s working on the payroll of the Xerox research park in Palo Alto, applying postmodernist science studies discourse to developing new products for the Xerox Corporation.[20]

The Humanities Research Institute is in fact only one of a number of national and international humanities think-tanks that serve as nexus points for the reproduction and dissemination of postmodernist culture – institu-tions which have played a pivotal role in shoring up the market value of the humanities, chiefly by legitimating postmodernism within the academic field.[21] One key feature of this legitimation process, and the second mate-rial factor in the circulation of theoretical discourse today, is the rise of the academic star system. Rationalization and the competition for resources has combined with popular media culture to thrust a handful of academic schol-ars to the uppermost echelons of an increasingly inegalitarian and cutthroat humanities system. The rise of the academic star system in the humanities has not only greatly exacerbated inequalities within the university system and the humanities; it has also inflated the importance of poststructuralist approaches by setting up postmodernist theorists as exemplars for younger scholars to emulate. Typically, the curricula of the humanities institutes features the same 'A-list' of academic celebrities. At the School of Criticism and Theory, for example, a summer institute sponsored by the Society for the Humanities at Cornell University, the majority of the School's courses in 2005 were presided over by poststructuralist celebrities like Homi Bhabha, Joan Scott, Elizabeth Grosz, and Toril Moi.

The School of Criticism and Theory at Cornell also regularly takes out paid advertisements in academic journals, promising graduate students and young scholars the opportunity to 'study with leading figures in critical theory' and to 'explore recent developments in literary and humanistic studies'. As the ads unabashedly make clear: 'The program sets up levels of expectations of what it takes to be a top-flight academic and scholar, not only in the United States, but internationally'.[22] Clearly, no graduate student or young professor in the humanities today can afford to be uninterested in learning what today's expectations of being 'a top-flight academic and scholar' are. The intellectual is now forced, like any other consumer, to participate in what Zygmunt Bauman calls 'the endless chase for the appearances of use-value in which … commodities are wrapped'.[23] And of the available scholarly commodities in the humanities today, postmodernism still fetches the highest price. There still remain humanities and social science institutes that have managed to avoid celebrity worship and poststructuralist canards alike. To give but one example, the Women's Studies Department at Duke University (perhaps the best programme of its kind in the US) continues to sponsor institutes and conferences that are staunchly materialist, politically engaged, and historically grounded.[24] But most of the leading centres for the distribution of 'critical' theory in the United States, Canada, and Europe – in cities like Atlanta, Birmingham, San Francisco, New York, Dublin, and Cardiff – still place the poststructuralist star at the centre of their philosophical cosmos.

## POSTMODERNISM'S SCHOLARLY HABITUS

I have suggested that postmodernism has played a formative ideological role in the education of the contemporary intelligentsia, particularly its critical or radical wing. But one of the most striking aspects of postmodernism is that it functions less as a set of ideas or intellectual movement than as an *ethos* or 'habitus', a 'structuring structure' of practice that delimits the experiences of a particular culture.[25] Postmodernism is at once a milieu, an epistemological orthodoxy, and a shared common sense about the world. It is defined not by principles so much as practices: in Foucault's terms, regimes of 'truth' and ways of knowing the world, habits of bodily comportment and affect. This is why the most empirically satisfying accounts of life and thought in the academic humanities are to be found not in scholarly journals but in the satirical campus novels of writers like David Lodge, John L'Heureux, or James Hynes. Only vivid literary scenes, it seems, are able to convey fully the curious behaviour of the postmodern university intelligentsia.

One of the consequences of the rise of the academic star system (of which postmodernism has been the prime beneficiary and exemplar) is the reduction of the theorist to the status of a scarce commodity. The star system represents the penetration of the university system by mass popular culture and commodity fetishism. 'The individual who in the service of the spectacle is placed in stardom's spotlight', Guy Debord wrote, 'is in fact the opposite of an individual, and as clearly the enemy of the individual in himself as of the individual in others.... [He] renounces all autonomy in order to identify himself with the general law of obedience to the course of things'.[26] Indeed, the academic star is not so much a person as the fetish of a person: a charismatic body anointed by the market as a sign of academic capital.[27] Such a star or superstar not only commands attention, he or she distorts entire fields of knowledge, like a black hole warping academic time-space. Less prominent scholars in the system are interpellated as voyeurs or remote fans of the *spectacle* of theory. The leading stars' names themselves, cited repeatedly by other scholars, often serve as little more than 'markers of truth', ways of 'authorizing' scholarly procedure.[28] Sycophancy, as well as intellectual standardization, cannot help but result. The star's very proximity to power (academic capital) makes her or him coveted by graduate students, which in turn leads to corruption of the ethical relation between teacher and taught. Bourdieu observed of the fate of knowledge within highly competitive and hierarchical fields:

> The boldness or even rashness statutorily granted to some provides the best of justifications and the safest of alibis for the institutional prudence which is incumbent on the greater number. The cult of 'brilliance', through the facilities which it procures, the false boldness which it encourages, the humble and obscure labours which it discourages, is less opposed than it might seem to the prudence of *academica mediocritas*, to its epistemology of suspicion and resentment, to its hatred of intellectual liberty and risk.... [29]

At the end of his first year in graduate school at one of the 'flagship' humanities programs in the University of California system, a Persian Marxist friend of mine who, years before, had had to flee Iran after being sentenced to death there by the Islamic regime, angrily remarked that 'There is more intellectual orthodoxy [in his graduate program] than under the Ayatollah!' As this anecdote suggests, postmodernism, notwithstanding its veneer of radicalism and iconoclasm, in practice functions as a cultural force that stifles genuine critical inquiry and creative thought and penalizes those who dissent from its ideological frame.

Frederic Jameson has argued that a symptom of postmodernity is the waning of affect.[30] This is not quite correct, however. From the shallow depths of postmodern or commodity culture there erupt potent displays of aggression and hostility. The struggle for scarce university resources exacerbates the anxiety and insecurity; hence too, the aggressive instincts of a portion of the intelligentsia, which the postmodern subculture thrives on. If the personal is political, then in the highly competitive world of academia the personal is frequently also pathological. This is especially true of the contemporary, high-pressure humanities program, an autoclave where only pathogens of the stoutest genetic build can survive, thrive, and multiply. The liquidation of humanism in theory parallels and mirrors increasingly *inhuman* relations between and among graduate students, faculty, administrators, and university staff. In this regard, the received poststructuralist wisdom, that 'modern society cannot be saved',[31] perpetually leaves social practice vulnerable to scarcely concealed authoritarian impulses. It is telling that Michel Foucault's instinctive response to the paroxysm of the Iranian Revolution was initially not to sympathize with the leftists and feminists who participated in that upheaval, but to praise the extremist Islamist followers of the Ayatollah Khomeini. This was not simply an oversight on Foucault's part, but a stance that flowed organically out of his profound scepticism toward all modern institutions and norms, including those of representative democracy. As Janet Afary and Kevin Anderson remind us:

> ... [S]cholars often assume that Foucault's suspicion of utopianism ... hostility to grand narratives and universals ... and his stress on difference and singularity rather than totality would make him less likely than his predecessors on the Left to romanticize an authoritarian politics that promised radically to refashion from above the lives and thought of a people .... However, his Iran writings showed that Foucault was not immune to the [same] type of illusions that so many Western leftists had held with regard to [the USSR and China].[32]

Foucault's sympathy for the Islamic militants has its counterpart today in the offhanded contempt with which some young academics now treat the very idea of democracy – i.e., not merely 'really existing' democracy's imperfect or distorted practice.

Another striking aspect of the postmodernist habitus is the way that postmodern philosophy's casual indifference to truth as an ontological category – that is, as a means of ascribing signs or meaning to matters of fact, the Real – gets mirrored in the bad faith with which postmodernism's advocates engage in conversation and debate. I still recall, for example, a conversation I had with a fellow graduate student while attending a doctoral program in the humanities in the early 1990s. The student, who had apprenticed herself to a leading poststructuralist scholar, announced in seminar that truth did not exist, and that the assembled company had no business talking about it as though it did. At the break, I asked the student what she would say if I told her that, in the middle of our class, I had seen Abraham Lincoln open the door to our classroom, take a stroll around, and leave. Wouldn't she then have to assess whether such a thing really happened, or whether I had imagined it? 'Not at all', she confidently replied. 'I would be concerned for your safety and would try to protect you. Because we live in a disciplinary society that would try to interpellate you as "mad"'. The theorist-in-training here was not simply applying Foucault's critique of the discourse of madness; she was tacitly disavowing her participation in a shared or common *human condition* in which questions of truth are an inescapable and vital feature of our lives. An obscure Cartesianism lurks here: the poststructuralist's self-image is that of a disembodied mind hovering above the play of mere mortal events. Yet presumably the graduate student in this case did not doubt the existence of her TIAA-CREF benefits account, and was careful to check the accuracy – truthfulness – of its balance.

In my own graduate school experience, the students most insistent on the point that truth was nothing but a discourse also happened to be the ones most credulous toward occult systems like astrology. My postmodernist friends spent countless hours running horoscope programs on their comput-ers, and always swore to the accuracy and veracity of their astrological charts, even as they disputed all materialist and scientific descriptions of reality. Stendhal's ironic depiction of Fabrizio, the credulous young protagonist of *The Charterhouse of Parma*, a man who prides himself on being intellectually sophisticated but naively clings to his own brand of superstition, comes to mind: 'Fabrizio's reasoning could penetrate no further .... He was far from devoting his time to patient consideration of the real particularities of things in order to divine their true causes. Reality seemed to him flat and muddy ....'.[33]

In point of fact, poststructuralists exhort their followers *not* to inquire into causality – or politics. Thus Kirstie McClure:

> The task at hand is to rethink the political character of the desire for comprehensive causal theory as a reflection of the 'truth' of the social world – to examine, rather than yield to, the supposition that 'theory' is a guarantor of practical imperatives, a fund of justifica-tions for instrumental action, and an authoritative foundation.... Rather, in other words, than restricting attention to 'theories' as intellectual constructs bent on representing the truth of the world, we might attend to 'theorizing' as itself an activity ... a political practice always and inescapably implicated with power. 'Theoriz-ing' in this sense is always contestable, not simply or narrowly in terms of the 'truth' of its content or the 'accuracy' of its represen-tations, but more broadly in terms of its filiations, disaffiliations, and equivocations with the dominant understanding of 'the politi-cal'.[34]

The author goes on to suggest that 'what is at stake in these contests is a matter neither of explanatory adequacy nor of political efficacy ... but a matter of breathing room for the articulation of new knowledges, new agen-cies, and new practices ...'.[35] Needless to say, however, to suggest that theory should be purged of its traditional concern with 'practical imperatives', as well as a fundamental concern for truth and accuracy, is to rule out placing theoretical reflection in the service of *human beings*, rather than the preoccupations of the theorist. What comes to matter is professionalization, not liberation. Hence the otherwise incomprehensible advice of the senior post-colonial anthropologist who warns graduate students in Aboriginal Studies not to focus on oppression or injustice. Theory, he writes, should not be 'based on victimisation or oppression (symptomatic Recovery of Ideology – in other words, 'this is what's wrong'), but [on] a more affirmative [narrative] based on becoming, dissemination, and exchange'.[36]

## THE POSTMODERN WORLD
## OF THE LIBERAL ARTS STUDENT

Postmodernism has had an incalculable impact not only on the academic intelligentsia (doctoral students and faculty), but also on ordinary under-graduates. For an increasing number of students, postmodernism is their first – and in many cases last – exposure to critical thought. Such students typically have not had the benefit of prior training in heuristic disciplines or methods, and are not assigned texts critical of poststructuralist approaches. The conse-quence is that 'the best and the brightest' of the middle and upper classes are being educated into a mode of discourse that is relativistic and sceptical. As one postmodernist academic writes to another in David Lodge's novel, *Nice Work* (on the occasion of splitting up with her, and leaving academia altogether):

> Poststructuralist theory is a very intriguing philosophical game for very clever players. But the irony of teaching it to young people who have read almost nothing except their GCE set texts and *Adrian Mole*, who know almost nothing about the Bible or classical mythology, who cannot recognize an ill-formed sentence, or recite poetry with any sense of rhythm – the irony of teaching them about the arbitrariness of the signifier in week three of their first year becomes in the end too painful to bear ....[37]

Students exposed to postmodernism typically have one of two reactions. Either they are bewildered and appalled by it, or they come away mesmer-ized. For students who sense they are being sold a bill of goods but have no native intellectual or disciplinary ground from which to raise objections to the postmodernist project, the experience can be truly dispiriting and confusing. A returning undergraduate student I once knew told me of her demoralization when, on the first day of a women's studies class on sexuality, her 'sex positive' postmodernist cultural studies instructor proceeded to screen multiple clips from porn videos, including from a 'snuff' film purporting to show actual women being murdered. When one of the younger students in the class has raised her hand and asked why they were being shown women being killed, and in what way this could be considered erotic, the instructor replied, 'If you're not prepared to have fun, you shouldn't be in this class'. But many other students are attracted by postmodernism's self-referential playfulness, its apparent iconoclasm and lack of respect for tradition. For this group of students, postmodernist theory resonates with the nihilism of mass popular culture – the fast-moving, 'hip', faux alternative, cynical pose of MTV, Beavis and Butthead, *South Park*, and first-person shooter video games.[38] These students are rewarded by their instructors with the pleasure of the arcane – honorary membership in the priesthood of Theory.

More than this, they come to believe that they are involved in an important *political* project. For example, female undergraduates encountering women's studies or literature courses are taught that it is *political* to dismiss second wave (liberal and radical) feminism as outmoded, or to eschew the feminist pedagogy of consciousness-raising. Young 'post-feminists' are more comfortable discussing 'the lack' or 'the *differend*' than the material circumstances and experiences of being a woman in society today – e.g., fraternity violence and date rape, the feminization of poverty, the sexual objectification of women by the media, the pervasiveness of pornography. Actor Maggie Gyllenhall, who majored in English Literature at Columbia University in the late 1990s, has said in interviews that she was drawn to her role in the film *The Secretary*, in which she played a submissive office worker who becomes empowered through sado-masochist humiliation at the hands of her boss, by the film's 'political agenda' – the fact 'that it was intended to be transgressive and to push something forward'.[39] Gyllenhaal took the role in part, she says, 'to fight against all those old-school feminists' (i.e., those who used to think that it was bad politics for women to want to be dominated). 'I began to think that my entire college education was preparing me to defend the politics of this movie …'.[40]

But postmodernism now affects virtually all undergraduates, not just those majoring in literature, through the writing and composition programmes and centres that proliferated on college and university campuses in the 1980s and 1990s.[41] Many instructors and lecturers in such programmes, which now serve as the first point of contact between many undergraduate students and self-reflexive or theoretical bodies of knowledge, have adopted postmodernist theories as a way of addressing multicultural and pluralist themes in the classroom. Much of the critical literature in Composition, Education, Rhetoric, Writing, and Art Education now draws on poststructuralist figures like Derrida, Bakhtin, Cixous, Kristeva, and Lyotard.[42] The new writing critics champion approaches to literacy and writing that emphasize disjuncture, plurality, and a pedagogy carefully shorn of normative judgment or

standards. That is, rather than teach students to be able to discriminate analytically, or to notice the difference between the truth and a lie, educators stress
an 'expressivist' ideology that privileges individual expression over critical
thinking. Thus Alice Gillam, for example, in her influential essay, 'Writing
Center Ecology: A Bakhtinian Perspective', praised Bakhtin for celebrating
the 'centrifugal forces [of] ... *heteroglossia* [which] ... perpetually destabilize
language through multiple meanings, varying contexts, and the free play of
dialects'.[43] According to Gillam, a good writing tutor is not one who helps
students to realize a norm of academic or logical discourse, but rather to
achieve 'self-expression'. The enemy is univocality – anything which silences
or obscures the 'multiple voices' in the student's own text. For, she writes
(paraphrasing and quoting Bakhtin), 'the fact that we ... can never arrive at
certain answers nor establish a final, 'unitary identity' is 'not to be lamented',
but rather to be celebrated'.[44]

Similarly, the well-known education and writing theorist Kathleen Berry
declares that 'the democratic negotiation of, and resistance to injustice' leads
not to 'unity or totality as in authoritarianism and liberal humanism, but [to]
the complexity of author(ities) in postmodernism...'.[45]

> No longer is the teacher/textbook/society/institution the sole
> authority. Teaching/learning in the postmodern (con)text blurs
> dominant author(ity).... Teacher, teaching practices, assignments,
> testing, and evaluation will no longer be seen as authoritative
> distribution centers and measurements of knowledge ... Modern
> infrastructures of what and who counts as excellent in teaching and
> learning will be dismantled.[46]

While scholars like Berry and Gillam are undoubtedly well-meaning, it is
extremely disturbing just the same to see theorists conflating authoritarianism
with 'liberal humanism', or eschewing forms of undergraduate instruction
that might provide students with a cognitive handle on the confusion, nihilism, and alienated forms of culture and economy that envelop them. In fact,
cognitive confusion – the dropping of socio-economic and historical context
– has replaced the teaching of argument and of what, for want of a better
expression, we might term the sociological imagination. College composition and writing programmes have in this way become ground zero for the
postmodernists' fissioning of undergraduate student consciousness. When
enshrined as pedagogy or the philosophy of education, postmodernism leads
college instructors and educators to teach their students not about *power* – that
is, about the merest facts of our social existence – but about the impossibility
of knowing anything at all. 'I hope', writes yet another writing theorist, 'that

we postmodernists can hold our ground ... in the open field of a decentral-
ized community where there are no hierarchies, only *ad hoc* constructions,
no answers, only questions'.[47] Similarly, the editor of the online Deleuzean
journal *Rhizomes* praises 'creative and critical practices that encourage us to
unite ideas that seem most disparate or incompatible, thereby deliberately
*dislocating us from the known*' (emphasis added). Academic practices, she writes,
should 'be unpredictable, performative, and incomplete'.[48]

The postmodernist educator's avowed concern for radical democracy in
the classroom has one foot planted in poststructuralism and the other in the
pedagogy of Paolo Freire. But Freire, a socialist, never relinquished his hold
on reality, nor on his fervent belief that it was the responsibility of the educator to help the student develop a dialectical understanding of social structure.
Education, he wrote, should never be conceived as the transmission of an
ideological orthodoxy, but as the cultivation of the student's own 'critical
transitivity'. 'The critically transitive consciousness is characterized by depth
in the interpretation of problems; by the substitution of causal principles for
magical explanations; by the testing of one's "findings" and by openness to
revision; by the attempt to avoid distortion when perceiving problems and to
avoid preconceived notions when analyzing them ... by soundness of argumentation ... by accepting what is valid in both old and new'.[49] Thus, while
Freire emphasized equality between student and teacher, he never failed to
acknowledge the crucial role of the educator in coaxing the student toward
a more comprehensive awareness of power. Postmodernists, by contrast, seem
positively hostile to the notion that undergraduates should be taught how
to assess arguments analytically, or to perceive relations between particular
phenomena and the material and cultural totality in which they appear.

This obsession with incomplete knowledge, coupled with making a fetish
of 'democratic process', has been especially damaging to feminist pedagogy.
An obsessive poststructuralist feminist emphasis on *process* and method often
comes at the expense of normative instruction and dialectical inquiry. Meg
Woolbright, for example, relates the story of how she 'corrected' her feminist
student tutor's impulse to show her young charges how patriarchal values
were expressed in a particular work of fiction. By imposing her feminist
reading on the text, the tutor was 'reinforcing institutional norms of silence
and obedience' and 'the values of hierarchy and objectivity'.[50] Precisely *as*
feminist educators, Woolbright writes, we must 'admit ... that the dichot-
omization between feminist and patriarchal practices is a false one', and that
there is no 'right' way to write: the tutor errs when she reinforces 'the posi-
tivistic, patriarchal value that there is a "correct" reading ...'.[51] In other words,
rather than telling students that their interpretation of a text, or reality, might
be wrong, we should help students discover and express their own feelings

and experiences. Postmodernism thus leads to the intellectual's abdication of responsibility precisely for the *education* of consciousness. The student's own self-expression, rather than her understanding and politicization, becomes the *raison d'être* of pedagogy.

## FROM ACADEMIA TO ACTIVISM

Postmodernism has seriously compromised the ability of academic feminist thinkers to critique patriarchal violence and the objectification of women.[52] But if postmodernism has been damaging to feminist thought in the university, it has also had a palpable impact on activist feminist communities outside academia. Radical feminists like Irene Reti have pointed out that the rise of poststructuralist theories of sexuality has both legitimated sado-masochistic and pornographic practices within the gay and lesbian movement in ways that disturbingly mirror the violence of patriarchy at large, and has depoliticized feminism and the women's movement in the US.[53] Even feminist critiques of male violence against women have been blunted by the postmodernist sensibility.

On December 6, 1989, Marc Lépine, a frustrated would-be engineer, murdered fourteen young women students at the École Polytechnique in Montreal, after lining them up and shouting that they were 'all a bunch of feminists'. Reeling from the disaster, a group of Canadian feminists responded with *The Montreal Massacre*, a collection of feminist essays, poems, and letters published shortly after the event. Contributors to the book movingly recounted feelings of pain and outrage, or else offered material analyses of the sexual and political economy of Canadian patriarchy that gave rise to Lépine's violence. However, one essay struck a decidedly different note. Invoking the highly abstract, distanced language of Lacan's poststructuralist theories, a psychoanalyst named Monique Panaccio wrote:

> … Marc Lépine's insane act was directed at *jouissance*, which we are all supposed to say 'no' to, and that is why, beyond the tragedy for those who are personally affected by the loss of a dear one, this act is intolerable. While it is part of Marc Lépine's personal life story, it also touches each and every one of us in our own life story, causing us to *imagine* once again that there is a way to thumb our noses at castration and the Law, thus awakening… all that always remains of our grief over our separation from the Mother's body, and showing us both the mortal outcome of its failure and the mortal result of transgressing it …. Marc Lépine accomplished what is for all of us both desirable and taboo: incest and murder.[54]

According to Panaccio, Lépine's act was not, in the first instance, an enact-ment of misogynistic violence, but was a case of 'Madness ... running wild', a madness which 'has eluded social control and is attacking the very foun-dations of order'.[55] While admitting that the widespread feminist view of Lépine as representative of a 'kind of male thinking which threatens women with execution if they reject the place which keeps them socially inferior' was 'not entirely wrong', Panaccio suggested that 'the truth is surely not so simple'.[56] Lépine's attack was directed not against women or feminists (the simplistic, perhaps even simple-minded, view) but against *jouissance* – play outside the Law. To understand the 'truth' of Lépine's action, we must acknowledge it as an event unavailable to conventional means of descrip-tion. 'This is the point at which all discourse comes to a complete halt, whether psychiatric, feminist, psychological or other. This is the point where a limit is irreversibly, irreparably transgressed, where the Symbolic and the Imaginary topple over .... This is the point where love and hate merge in the site of what is unnameable'.[57] Having effectively declared Lépine's act to be *historically* unintelligible, Panaccio now implicates modern society as such in 'the unnameable' – i.e., in the facticity of the fourteen young corpses. 'Marc Lépine', she concludes, 'accomplished what is *for all of us* both desir-able and taboo: incest and murder'.[58] Lépine's atrocity, in other words, was a crypto-transgressive or subversive act that enacted our own collective fanta-sies (men's and women's alike).

What we see here is the osmosis of academic poststructuralism by the non-academic grassroots. Clinical psychotherapy has begun to be colonized by poststructuralist rhetoric.[59] The same dynamic can be observed elsewhere. Consider the following three passages. The first two are by academic theorists, Homi Bhabha and Hardt and Negri, while the third is by a self-described 'nineteen-year-old radical black feminist-student-activist-educator' (and fourth-year undergraduate at UC Berkeley), who is heavily involved in the 'abolitionist' anti-prison movement:

> [The] emphasis on the disjunctive present of utterance ... allows the articulation of subaltern agency as relocation and reinscription .... This is the historical movement of hybridity as camouflage, as a contesting, antagonistic agency functioning in the time-lag of sign/ symbol which is a space in-between the rules of engagement.[60]

> ... [We] might say that the sovereignty of Empire ... is realized at the margins, where borders are flexible and identities are hybrid and fluid .... In fact, center and margin seem continually to be shifting positions, fleeing any determinate locations. We could even

say that the process itself is virtual and that its power resides in the power of the virtual.[61]

... I wish to speak from the margins .... [I]t is necessary for us to locate and deconstruct the iterative space from which power flows, recognizing and continually addressing the fact that space (and, by extension, spatial metaphor) is in constant flux.[62]

What is significant is not only that the anti-prison activist now speaks in a Foucauldian idiom, but that she also affirms and reproduces the central tenets of the poststructuralist orthodoxy – a collapsed sense of temporality ('the now'), the spatial indeterminacy of power, and a prejudice against building alternative institutions. Postmodernist ways of knowing can in fact be found in a growing number of social movements. Many on-line activist communities and blogs now bandy about poststructuralist rhetoric or ideas without seeming to have any direct knowledge of, or connection to, the academic humanities. The Hacktivist website, for example, describes computer hacking as a 'rhizomic' form of political action, invoking a term popularized by Deleuze.

Postmodernism has even seeped into that most putatively universal of social movements – the movement for international human rights. When I recently engaged a friend of mine, a senior manager at one of the world's largest international human rights organizations, over questions of theory, he wrote: '... I don't find all of poststructuralism to be so negative. I think there is a liberatory potential in undermining Absolute Truth systems, including those of the Liberal Centre or the Authoritarian Left. I suspect a lot of these Truth systems take science as their archetype, and as an ex-quantum physicist I would certainly argue that the Truth claims of scientific ontology are untenable...'.[63] On the one hand, I agreed with my friend's further assertion (in the same email) that, 'In a post-Enlightenment spirit, I'm tempted to describe Human Rights, for example, as a myth – but in the positive sense of Sorel's 'Myth of the General Strike' (i.e. as an inspirational emblem rather than a concrete existent)'. On the other hand, I was struck by the fact that even members of the technical intelligentsia (my friend works in information technology) have come to think of scientific claims as mere narratives.

What is going on here? How do we account for the remarkable intrusion of an effete, complicated, and self-contradictory philosophical movement into the mainstream of grassroots activism? How has postmodernism succeeded in displacing what came before – namely, the entire Western Marxist tradition? A good part of the answer is that the historical crisis of socialism and left social movements in the 1980s and 1990s left a gaping hole in theories of praxis, a void which poststructuralism was able to fill. Confronted with the apparent waning of the socialist tradition and workers' movements, on the one hand, and the rise of the political right and fundamentalists on the other, activists at the grassroots have understandably been eager to embrace reassuring (if facile) narratives that seem both iconoclastic and faintly optimistic. The tales postmodernism tells – of the inevitability but also the virtue of movement fragmentation; of unending historical indeterminacy and flux; of the impossibility of knowledge of the totality; of the positive effects of globalization (border crossings, hybridity, and so on) – are appealing precisely because they seem to mirror the experience of postmodernity itself. Here lies the obscure truth of postmodernist theory – in both form and content postmodernism really does mimic the actual conditions of late capitalism. That this mimicry also faithfully reproduces the alienated social conditions, lies, and fragmented time-space of capitalism is less often acknowledged.

On the other side of the equation, many poststructuralist theorists themselves have undoubtedly craved connection. They too have wanted to 'make a difference' in a world where paths to effectual political and social struggle have been occluded or otherwise blocked. In historical psychoanalytic terms, we might speculate that postmodernism as an intellectual movement represents a form of collective psychic and affective flight from the despair and anxiety and denial generated by ecological destruction, mounting social chaos, and the loss of the dream of 1968. The legacy of the sixties movement has been ambiguous, as Isaac Balbus observes: 'Both the longing for (an idealized version of) what has been lost and the (seemingly) sober message that nothing valuable was ever really lost ward off the sorrow – and the guilt – that would inevitably accompany a fully embodied awareness of the magnitude of our loss. Both serve, in other words, to defend against the deeply difficult but absolutely indispensable task of mourning (what we used to call) the Movement'. According to Balbus, 'the atrophy of our imagination is a symptom of our *political depression*'.[64] Postmodernism, similarly, can be seen as an adaptive response by critical intellectuals to their own personal and political losses – even a form of what Marcuse termed 'repressive desublimation'.

While some academic postmodernists have warned of the 'contamination' of theory by practice, most have on the contrary taken pains to make themselves politically relevant.[65] There has in fact been growing fraternization between academics and activists in recent years, as postmodernist thinkers take on the role of *savants* to grassroots social movements. In recent years, for example, queer theorist Eve Kosofsky Sedgwick has participated in grassroots conferences on the 'Prison-Industrial Complex', while poststructuralist authors of such works as *Foucault, Cultural Studies, and Governmentality* and *The Transubstantiation of Queer Identity in Postmodern Capitalism* have appeared alongside veteran organizers at the 'Renewing the Anarchist Tradition' conference. In a similar vein, Michael D. Hardt, a Deleuzean theory maven at Duke University, has been fêted at meetings of the World Social Forum.

With the advent of new information technologies and the internet, academic postmodernism has also begun to seep into alternative popular youth culture. Numerous websites now actively promote postmodernism to young people and activists, creating a matrix of left politics, pop culture, and postmodernism. Often, such sites are maintained by intellectuals with formal schooling in poststructuralist theory. The manager of a website called 'The Postmodern Anarchist' has a Ph.D. in Cultural Studies in Education from Ohio State.[66] Another leading site is Voxygen, a popular youth- and women-oriented website with links to leading poststructuralist and cultural studies thinkers. Designed and maintained by Laura Sells, an Assistant Professor of Communications at Louisiana State University, the site describes itself as 'a compilation of interests in feminist cultural politics' with a special focus 'on issues relating to generations X and Y, popular culture, and virtual culture'. And its guiding premise? '... [T]hat power is everywhere and nowhere, that the codes that have defined our voices and identities can be identified and rewritten...'. The Voxygen site integrates links and paeans to poststructuralist feminist icons (one page is devoted to an 'Ode to Donna Haraway'), while forging purposive links with other sites featuring alternative female youth subcultures – S/M lesbian pornography, video gaming culture, and so on.[67] But the site also features links to traditional 'left' and liberal political organs like FAIR, the Southern Poverty Law Center, and even the AFL-CIO – further evidence, if any was needed, that the confusion or conflation of postmodernism with liberal and left values as such is now functionally complete.

## THE DEATH OF POSTMODERNISM?

In place of reason and argument – in short, dialectics – postmodernists celebrate cognitive confusion, 'paralogy', and an aesthetics of fragmentation.[68] Postmodernism obfuscates and muddies perceptual reality, rather than clarifying it.[69] Hence composition theorist Ruth Ray's assertion that theory should be understood as '"a lens, a philosophical perspective, a stance"', one that is 'narrative rather than paradigmatic' – 'an anti-foundationalist epistemology' rather than a 'method'.[70]

But theory is, on the contrary, precisely at its best when it serves as a paradigm of knowing, in Thomas Kuhn's specific sense of a perceptual framework providing the scientist or observer with a means for discerning patterns of meaning or order amidst an infinity of otherwise random and unintelligible phenomena. As Kuhn argued, 'neither scientists nor laymen learn to see the world piece-meal or item by item.... [Rather] both scientists and laymen sort out whole areas together from the flux of experience'.[71] What paradigmatic theories do, then, is to provide the engaged observer with a means for discriminating between useful and useless data. As Antonio Gramsci wrote in his prison notebooks:

> ...[R]eality is teeming with the most bizarre coincidences, and it is the theoretician's task to find in this bizarreness new evidence for his theory, to 'translate' the elements of historical life into theoretical language, but not vice versa, making reality conform to an abstract schema.... (Leonardo knew how to discover number in all the manifestations of cosmic life, even when the eyes of the ignorant saw only change and disorder.)[72]

In Gramsci's view, then, the role of the 'critical' intellectual – the revolutionary – is primarily to discern patterns of significance in history and culture, in order to identify more or less promising lines of action. Effective political knowledge is always rooted in a perception of the totality or gestalt of historical probabilities – in the complex interplay of economic and cultural factors, class interests, and human passion and will, over time. It is not a question of our being able to predict the future 'scientifically', but of understanding, as accurately and fully as we are able, the subtle combination of forces that structure the field of meaning and which therefore are likely to give rise to one or another phenomenon. This much radical or revolutionary theory has in common with other varieties of human political or strategic thought. What differentiates the critical theorist from other theorists or intellectuals is, first, her or his belief that society – the ensemble of social relations – can be changed, and second, the moral conviction that it ought to be changed. This may seem a trivial point, but it in fact places the critical intellectual 'in' the world in a qualitatively different way. The normative commitments of the critical intellectual – the subjective will to know the world in order to change it – enables a particular way of seeing and perceiving.

If we define critical theory in this way, as a means for making history and world intelligible *in order that we might act consciously to change history and world*, then the inadequacies of postmodernism become apparent. Postmodernism is a doctrine that systematically renders intelligibility impossible. That is its message, as well as its method. Knowing and not-knowing – the distinction is irrelevant to it. If Marxists in the nineteenth and twentieth centuries were overly confident about the power of thought to arrive at mastery of the totality – and they often were – today's generation of critical theorists commits the opposite mistake, stripping thought of the right and ability to

know the world at all. But without the ability to think clearly and critically about the nature of existing power (and about how to defeat it) we are
blind to historical possibility. It is therefore ironic that poststructuralism has
become conflated with 'theory' as such, because at root it is profoundly *anti*-
theoretical. Like the vulgar Marxism that it both arose out of and developed
in reaction against, postructuralism's doctrines have reduced complex social
and historical problems to a catechism of pre-digested formulas, mechanistic banalities, and unexamined and frequently tautological propositions
concerning the nature of society, power, and the subject. And its few modest
theoretical contributions can never begin to compensate us for the harm
done to critical thought by the destructive conceits that postmodernism has
spawned. I am speaking of the movement's naive spontaneism and amorality;
of the facile disavowal, by figures like Foucault and Lyotard, of the need for
political leadership on the Left; of the grand narcissism of the postcolonial
intellectuals (whose celebration of their own 'hybridity' and 'border crossings'
obscures the traumas of less privileged refugees and economic immigrants
made rootless by capital); of the deconstructionists' search-and-destroy
mission against empathy and imaginative identification in literary studies; of
the repellant defence of pornography and 'debasement' by poststructuralist
feminists; of the rococo Lacanian fetish of the dis-integrated subject; of the
refusal of the language of universals – now déclassé concepts like humanism,
liberation, revolution, and totality.

Postmodernist critics have ridiculed universal metanarratives and truth,
even while sombrely discussing such weightless metaphysical conceits as
*episteme*, phallologocentrism, *différance*, and 'the lack' – the contemporary
theorist's version of ectoplasm and ether. They have systematically privileged
local, particular movements over global and universal ones, without considering the exigencies or needs of actual practice. Unaware of or indifferent
to its own internal contradictions and elisions, postmodernism has preached
epistemological scepticism and radical historicism, all the while remaining
innocent of its own social determinations. But most damning of all, when it
comes to offering us something concrete, something really *useful* with which
to gain traction on the great intellectual, social, and political problems of
our day, postmodernism falls silent. Here, postmodernism truly distinguishes
itself: unlike virtually every other intellectual movement or ideology of the
past – anarchism, socialism, liberalism, libertarianism, conservatism, communism, fascism – postmodernism offers a theory neither of society nor of
politics and the state.

In the past, such obvious deficiencies in the doctrine have not affected its
fortunes. But reality may finally have begun to intrude upon the postmodern idyll. In the aftermath of the 9/11 terrorist attacks on the United States

postmodernists have been increasingly embarrassed by their inability to say anything of political or social substance.[73] There are even tantalizing signs that postmodernists themselves know or suspect that the party is over. The Society for the Humanities at Cornell, for example, has made its theme for 2006-07 'Historicizing the Global Postmodern'. In that program's description, a new defensiveness, a new ambivalence or anxiety seems to hover over the entire poststructuralist project, like a descending shroud:

> If we can speak of a post-modern moment that enabled humanists to engage critically the enlightenment logic of western modernity, then now is the time to historicize the logic attributed to the post-modern itself .... In a global context, has the post-modern de-centering of the humanistic subject, critique of enlightenment, and apparent embrace of fragmentation and hybridity acted as an emancipatory or conservative force? How has the postmodern challenging of the distinction between high and low culture, between the oppositional stance and the subversively ironic or parodic one, contributed to new modes of consuming and producing global commodity culture? And why, and in what political contexts, has blame for the shrinking of public space, the demise of public culture and, indeed, the perceived retreat from public engagement of the humanities themselves, been laid at the door of post-modernism? ... Arguably, the theoretical reach, seduction, and ambiguity marking the concept of the postmodern are symptoms of a certain privilege it has exercised .... Has the post-modern radically undermined, or rather revitalized and consolidated, Euro-centrism and new forms of cultural imperialism?[74]

Whether this self-agonizing project of reflection will lead to a genuine rethinking of the postmodernist project, or whether it will simply provide poststructuralists with new fodder for commodity innovation, remains to be seen: behind every narcissist's love of self is the repressed terror of having to face the true self. However, were postmodernism to gaze at its own reflection in the mirror of theory, it would be forced to acknowledge its *own* historical overdeterminations, its own ideologies, myths, and *episteme*. It would then certainly self-destruct. But then, what would be left to take its place? The trouble is that poststructuralism is now so institutionally and culturally entrenched, and the field of theory itself is now so hopelessly muddied by the proliferation and fragmentation of discourse that it has produced, that the implosion of the postmodernist project as such would not produce a sudden renaissance of praxis. Theory is useless, and prone to speculative distortions, without social movements to support and invigorate it, which explains why postmodernist theory has grown at the same rate that contemporary social movements have declined and lost momentum.

The crisis of the Left, of which postmodernism is both symptom and cause, will therefore not be dissolved simply by the collapse of the illusions of theory. What we need, and need urgently, is not merely a repudiation of the poststructuralist canon, but a bold new theoretical project – a paradigmatic theory of action that yokes materialist analysis to an unabashedly moral, utopian, ecological vision. Such a project, closely interwoven with practice, would both take up and go well beyond the lost thread of Marxist-humanist and socialist-feminist thought. The work of our combined intellects must be to map the totality of oppression and liberation – not by seeking the Holy Grail of a scientific theory of everything, but by establishing an ethical horizon for liberatory practice as such. Only by returning, in this way, to holism in theory and practice might we begin to undo the terrible damage inflicted by nihilism on our praxis, and on truth.

## NOTES

The author would like to thank Joel Brattin for his most helpful comments in preparing this manuscript.

1   Postmodernism began as a separate – initially aesthetic – current from poststructuralism, but the two did converge: the poststructuralist critique of humanism, subjectivity, and foundationalism became indistinguishable from a general rejection of modernity and modern institutions (hence 'post-modernism', a philosophical outlook). For the purposes of this essay the two are used interchangeably to denote a theoretical discourse and set of assumptions, rather than to describe a general social experience – i.e., a 'postmodern condition' (Lyotard) or 'condition of postmodernity' (David Harvey).

2   Michel Foucault, 'Truth and Power', *Power/Knowledge*, New York: Pantheon, 1980, p. 133.

3   Friedrich Nietzsche, §168, *Human, All Too Human*, in R.J. Hollingdale, ed., *A Nietzsche Reader*, New York: Penguin, 1977, p. 198.

4   See especially Terry Eagleton, *The Illusions of Postmodernism*, New York: Blackwell, 1997; Norman Geras, *Discourses of Extremity: Radical Ethics and Post-Marxist Extravgance*, London: Verso, 1990; Peter Dews, *The Logic of Disintegration*, London: Verso, 1987; and Teresa Ebert, *Ludic Feminism and After: Postmodernism, Desire, and Labor in Late Capitalism*, Ann Arbor: University of Michigan Press, 1996.

5    Barbara Epstein, 'Why Poststructuralism is a Dead End for Progressive Thought', *Socialist Review*, 25(2), 1995, p. 83.

6    Jessica Dempsey and James K. Rowe, 'Why Poststructuralism is a Live Wire for the Left', *Praxis (e)Press*, 2004 (www.praxis-epress.org).

7    In their defence of poststructuralism, Dempsey and Rowe essentially imply that Epstein's criticisms are alarmist, because that movement has little consequence politically. 'It is unclear how much institutional power poststructural [sic] theorizing, or theorizing in general, currently has to help or hinder progressive politics' (Ibid., p. 37).

8    Antonio Gramsci, §49, Fourth Notebook, in Joseph A. Buttigieg, ed., *Prison Notebooks*, Volume II, New York: Columbia University Press, 1996, p. 200.

9    Russell Jacoby, *The Last Intellectuals: American Culture in the Age of Academe*, New York: Farrar, Straus and Giroux, 1987, pp. 232-33.

10   On the corporatization of education, see especially Sheila Slaughter and Larry L. Leslie, *Academic Capitalism: Politics, Policies, and the Entrepreneurial University*, Baltimore: Johns Hopkins University Press, 1997; Derek Bok, *Universities in the Marketplace: The Commercialization of Higher Education*, Princeton: Princeton University Press, 2003; Ann Brooks and Alison MacKinnon, eds., *Gender and the Restructured University*, Buckingham: SRHE/Open University Press, 2001; Richard S. Ruch, *Higher Ed., Inc.: The Rise of the For-Profit University*, Baltimore: Johns Hopkins University Press, 2003.

11   Diane Reay, 'Cultural Capitalists and Academic Habitus: Classed and Gendered Labour in UK Higher Education', *Women's Studies International Forum*, 27, 2004, p. 33.

12   John Sanbonmatsu, *The Postmodern Prince: Critical Theory, Left Strategy, and the Making of a New Political Subject*, New York: Monthly Review Press, 2004.

13   As the 2005-06 budget for the University of California puts it: 'California's companies will be creating thousands of new professional and managerial jobs over the next ten years. The best way to keep these good jobs here in California is to have a workforce with the knowledge and skills to compete in the global marketplace. The CEOs of Intel, Hewlett-Packard, and Microsoft have all recently said that the best way to compete is to have a strong university system. Therefore, California must increase its investment in higher education and help ensure that enough highly-educated graduates are available to meet the workforce demands of a knowledge-based economy ...'. University of California 2005-06 Budget for Current Operations, Sacramento: University of California Board of Regents, 2005, p. 18.

14   Lindsay Waters, 'Bonfire of the Humanities', *The Village Voice*, 30 August 2004.

15   See Michelle Lamont, 'How To Become a Dominant French Philosopher', *American Journal of Sociology*, 93(3), November, 1987, pp. 584–622. Also, Niilo Kauppi, *French Intellectual Nobility: Institutional and Symbolic Transformation in the Post-Sartrian Era*, Albany: SUNY Press, 1996. Cf. Maria Ruegg, 'The End(s) of French Style: Structuralism and Post-Structuralism in the American Context', *Criticism*, 21(3), 1979.

16   University of California 2005–06 Budget, p. 161.

17   Cathy N. Davidson and David Theo Goldberg, 'A Manifesto for the Humanities in a Technological Age', *Chronicle of Higher Education*, 50(23), 13 February 2004, B7.

18   Recognizably postmodernist books and articles by Humanities Research Institute governors include: 'Heterogeneity, Hybridity, Multiplicity: Marking Asian American Differences'; 'Literary Nomadics in Francophone Allegories of Postcolonialism'; 'Cosmological Meditations on the In/Human: Lyotard and Beckett'; 'Post/Colonial Conditions: Exiles, Migrations, Nomadisms'; 'Crackers and Whackers: The White Trashing of Porn'; 'Ecce Homo, Ain't (Ar'n't) I a Woman, and Inappropriated Others: The Human in a Post-Humanist Landscape'; et cetera.

19   http://uchri.org/main.php?nav=sub

20   Sanbonmatsu, *The Postmodern Prince*, pp. 86–7.

21   There are other legitimation mechanisms as well. The issuing of 'definitive' anthologies, readers, and guides like the *Cultural Studies Reader* or *Queer Theory Reader* serves to legitimate new cottage industries in theory. The *Johns Hopkins Guide to Literary Theory and Criticism*, Second Edition, edited by Michael Groden, Martin Kreiswirth, and Imre Szeman (Baltimore: The Johns Hopkins University Press, 2005) subtly presents postmodernism as the logical and necessary fruition of the critical theoretical tradition. See Christopher Hitchens, 'Transgressing the Boundaries: Literary Scholars Embrace an Elite Language, Yet Imagine Themselves Subversives', *New York Times Book Review*, 22 May 2005, p. 18.

22   Advertisement in *Lingua Franca*, October 1997, p. 4.

23   Zygmunt Bauman, *Postmodernity and its Discontents*, New York: New York University Press, 1997, p. 190.

24   For example, a March 2005 symposium organized by the Department emphasized '[undoing] the theory/practice divide by reconciling the disproportionate victimization of women and children in ethnic conflict with a critical understanding of women's participation in and resistance to ethnic conflict itself'. *Duke Women's Studies Newsletter,* Spring 2005, p.

4. The program's director, the incomparable Jean Fox O'Barr, deserves credit for having kept feminist theory afloat in postmodernist times.

25   Pierre Bourdieu, *Outline of a Theory of Practice*, trans. by Richard Nice, Cambridge: Cambridge University Press, 1977.

26   Guy Debord, *The Society of the Spectacle*, trans. Donald Nicholson-Smith, New York: Zone Books, 1994, p. 39.

27   David Shumway, 'The Star System in Literary Studies', *PMLA*, 112(1), January 1997, pp. 85–100.

28   Ibid., p. 95.

29   Pierre Bourdieu, *Homo Academicus*, trans. by Peter Collier, New York: Cambridge University Press, 1988, p. 94.

30   Frederic Jameson, *Postmodernism, or the Cultural Logic of Late Capitalism*, Durham: Duke University Press, 1991.

31   Camille E.S.A. Acey, 'This is an Illogical Statement: Dangerous Trends in Anti-Prison Activism', *Social Justice*, 27(3), 2000, p. 209.

32   Janet Afary and Kevin B. Anderson, *Foucault and the Iranian Revolution*, Chicago: University of Chicago Press, 2005, p. 5. Foucault also expressed sympathy with extrajudicial and popular forms of justice (summary executions or mob killings by the people in revolutionary contexts). See Foucault, 'On Popular Justice: A Discussion with Maoists', in *Power/ Knowledge*, New York: Pantheon, 1980, pp. 1–36.

33   Stendhal, *The Charterhouse of Parma*, trans. by Richard Howard, New York: Modern Library, 1999, p. 152.

34   Kirstie McClure, 'The Issue of Foundations', in Judith Butler and Joan W. Scott, eds., *Feminists Theorize the Political*, New York: Routledge, 1992, pp. 364–5.

35   Ibid. Similarly, Homi Bhabha praises another postcolonial Indian critic for demanding 'a historiography of the subaltern that displaces the paradigm of social action as defined primarily by *rational action*, and seeks [instead] a form of discourse where affective writing develops its own language. History as a writing that constructs the moment of defiance...'. Homi K. Bhabha, 'Postcolonial Authority and Postmodern Guilt', in Lawrence Grossberg, Cary Nelson, and Paula Treichler, eds., *Cultural Studies*, New York: Routledge, 1991, p. 65 (emphasis added).

36   Stephen Muecke, 'Dialogue with a Post-Graduate Student Wanting to Study Aboriginal Culture', *Textual Spaces*, North Sydney: New South Wales University Press, Ltd., 1992, p. 204.

37   David Lodge, *Nice Work*, New York: Penguin, 1988, p. 314.

38   Thomas Frank has shown how the rise of a new business culture intersected both with the marketing of 'alternative' culture to youth and false populist narratives within academic cultural studies. Thomas

Frank, 'Alternative to What?', in Thomas Frank and Matt Weiland, eds., *Commodify Your Dissent: Salvos from The Baffler*, New York: W.W. Norton, 1997, pp. 153-4; see also Thomas Frank, *One Market Under God*, New York: Anchor, 2001.

39   Interviewed by Tom Dawson of the BBC for her role in *Secretary* (2003), www.bbc.co.uk.

40   'Maggie Gylenhaal's Secretary Challenge', 19 May 2003, www.contactmusic.com.

41   The spread of such programs is itself a symptom of the rationalization of higher education, the mass processing of students with an emphasis on providing them with skills, rather than with substantive knowledge.

42   See especially Arthur Efland, *A History of Art Education: Intellectual and Social Currents in Teaching the Visual Arts*, New York: Teachers College Press, 1990.

43   Alice M. Gillam, 'Writing Center Ecology: A Bakhtinian Perspective', in Christina Murphy and Joe Law, eds., *Landmark Essays on Writing Centers*, Davis: Hermagoras Press, 1995, pp. 128. For other theoretical texts on rhetoric and writing that celebrate cognitive fragmentation, see Nancy Welch's application of Julia Kristeva to writing tutor pedagogy in 'From Silence to Noise: The Writing Center as Critical Noise', *The Writing Center Journal*, 14.1, 1993, pp. 32-9. See also Nancy Maloney Grimm, *Good Intentions: Writing Center Work for Postmodern Times*, Portsmouth: Boynton/Cook, 1999; Lester Faigley, *Fragments of Rationality: Postmodernity and the Subject of Composition*, Pittsburgh: University of Pittsburgh, 1992.

44   Gillam, 'Writing Center Ecology', p. 134.

45   Kathleen S. Berry, 'Teaching as Postmodern (Con)Text', in *Teaching Voices*, University of New Brunswick Bulletin on University Teaching, 37, January 2004.

46   Ibid.

47   Jane Bowers, 'Plain Language from a Postmodernist Professor', *Writing on the Edge*, 2(2), 1991, p. 57.

48   Ellen E. Berry, 'Rhizomes, Newness, and the Condition of Our Postmodernity', *Rhizomes*, 1(Spring) 2000 (www.rhizomes.net).

49   Paolo Freire, *Education for Critical Consciousness*, New York: Continuum, 1973, p. 18.

50   Meg Woolbright, 'The Politics of Tutoring: Feminism within the Patriarchy', in Murphy and Law, *Landmark Essays*, pp. 238, 237.

51   Ibid., p. 238.

52   For example, as Kathy Miriam notes, the theory of poststructuralist feminist Judith Butler 'obscures the subject of feminist practice, which is

the liberation of women'. Kathy Miriam, 'Feminist Intellectualism and the "Pornographic Imagination": Deconstructing Butler', forthcoming in *Philosophy and Social Criticism*.

53  Irene Reti, *Unleashing Feminism: Critiquing Lesbian Sadomasochism in the Gay Nineties*, Santa Cruz: HerBooks Feminist Press, 1993.

54  Monique Panaccio, 'Lépine and the Roses: Beyond Eros', in Louise Malette and Marie Chalouh, eds., *The Montreal Massacre*, trans. by Marlene Wildeman, Charlottetown: Gynergy Books, 1991, p. 115.

55  Ibid., p. 111. But another contributor to the collection wrote: 'No he wasn't crazy. His aim was accurate, straight to the heart of the highest symbolic site, the university, and especially the Polytechnique where, day after day, women calmly make their way through the worst kind of prejudice'. Nathalie Petrowski, 'Red Riding Hood', in Malette and Chalouh, *Montreal Massacre*, p. 37.

56  Panaccio, 'Lépine', p. 111.

57  Loc. cit.

58  Ibid., p. 115 (emphasis added).

59  See, for example, the on-line journal, 'Postmodern Therapies', which promotes the use of Bakhtin, Derrida, and Wittgenstein in clinical therapeutic work, http://www.california.com.

60  Bhabha, 'Postcolonial Authority', p. 65.

61  Michael D. Hardt and Antonio Negri, *Empire*, Cambridge: Harvard University Press, 2000.

62  Acey, P. 208.

63  Personal communication, London, April 2005.

64  Isaac Balbus, *Mourning and Modernity: Essays in the Psychoanalysis of Contemporary Society*, New York: Other Press, 2005, pp. 80-90.

65  An example of the former is feminist political theorist Wendy Brown, who has called for the segregation of theory from topical social and political concerns: Wendy Brown, 'The Time of the Political', *Theory and Event*, 1(1), 1997.

66  On his site, Clay Richards describes himself as an 'anarchist blogger' who 'writes about politics, art, sexuality and emerging digital realities. More poststructuralist than postmodern ... the Postmodern Anarchist believes in anarchy without anarchists...', www.netweed.com/postmodernanarchist.

67  Website links on Sells' site include SusieBright.com, Gurl.com, Technodyke, Women Gamers, Grrl Gamer, Scarleteen, Geeks Girl Magazine, Chicklit, and Rockgrl Magazine (www.voxygen.net, 30 May 2005).

68  Thus Sue-Ellen Case, who writes in *The Domain-Matrix* that she has purposefully disorganized, and added several dense visual graphic layers

to, her text, in order to mimic the non-linear, disintegrative cognitive style of the internet: Sue-Ellen Case, *The Domain-Matrix: Performing Lesbian at the End of the Twentieth Century*, Bloomington: Indiana University Press, 1996, pp. 7–8.

69　Hence the significance of postmodernist critic Rey Chow's comment that, rather than seek to fill in the holes of history – i.e., augment existing Eurocentric narratives of history with narratives that highlight the historical experiences of ethnic minorities, women, and the oppressed – we 'need to detail history, in the sense of cutting it up'. Rey Chow, 'Postmodern Automatons', in Butler and Scott, *Feminists Theorize*, p. 115.

70　Ruth Ray, *The Practice of Theory: Teacher Research in Composition*, Urbana: NCTE, 1993, as paraphrased and quoted by Kristine Hansen in 'Face to Face with Part-Timers: Ethics and the Professionalization of Writing Faculties', in J. Janagelo and Kristine Hansen, eds., *Resituating Writing: Constructing and Administering Writing Programs*, Portsmouth: Boynton/ Cook, 1995, p. 34.

71　Thomas S. Kuhn, The Structure of Scientific Revolutions, Second Edition, Chicago: University of Chicago Press, 1970, p. 28.

72　Antonio Gramsci, §48, Third Notebook, in Buttigieg, *Prison Notebooks*, p. 52.

73　In 2002, Anouar Majid wrote an article entitled 'The Failure of Postcolonial Theory After 9/11' (in *The Chronicle of Higher Education*, 1 November 2002), in which he pointedly observed that the postcolonial emperor has no clothes. 'Enthralled by the triumphant creed of hybridity – premised on the notion that people, as well as nations, are made up of incommensurable, mobile, unstable parts – many postcolonial theorists sought the signs that confirmed this faith, not the ones that complicated it', Majid wrote. 'That people everywhere were serious about their gods and still yearned for a sense of place didn't matter to scholars busy showing how the worldwide movement of people, with its resulting instabilities, was destabilizing power relations among nations by undermining the claim to national and cultural purity'.

74　Focal Theme 2006/2007, 'Historicizing the Global Postmodern', Society for the Humanities at Cornell University (www.arts.cornell.edu), 1 June 2005.

# TELLING THE TRUTH ABOUT CLASS

## G. M. TAMÁS

One of the central questions of social theory has been the relationship between class and knowledge, and this has also been a crucial question in the history of socialism. Differences between people – acting and knowing subjects – may influence our view of the chances of valid cognition. If there are irreconcilable discrepancies between people's positions, going perhaps as far as incommensurability, then unified and rational knowledge resulting from a reasoned dialogue among persons is patently impossible. The Humean notion of 'passions', the Nietzschean notions of 'resentment' and 'genealogy', allude to the possible influence of such an incommensurability upon our ability to discover truth.

Class may be regarded as a problem either in epistemology or in the philosophy of history, but I think that this separation is unwarranted, since if we separate epistemology and the philosophy of history (which is parallel to other such separations characteristic of bourgeois society itself) we cannot possibly avoid the rigidly-posed conundrum known as relativism. In speaking about class (and truth, *and* class and truth) we are the heirs of two socialist intellectual traditions, profoundly at variance with one another, although often intertwined politically and emotionally. I hope to show that, up to a point, such fusion and confusion is inevitable.

All versions of socialist endeavour can and should be classified into two principal kinds, one inaugurated by Rousseau, the other by Marx. The two have opposite visions of the social subject in need of liberation, and these visions have determined everything from rarefied epistemological positions concerning language and consciousness to social and political attitudes concerning wealth, culture, equality, sexuality and much else. It must be said at the outset that many, perhaps most socialists who have sincerely believed they were Marxists, have in fact been Rousseauists. Freud has eloquently described resistances to psychoanalysis; intuitive resistance to Marxism is no less widespread, even among socialists. It is emotionally and intellectually difficult to be a Marxist since it goes against the grain of moral indignation which is, of course, the main reason people become socialists.

One of the greatest historians of the Left, E.P. Thompson, has synthesized what can be best said of class in the tradition of Rousseauian socialism which believes itself to be Marxian.[1] *The Making of the English Working Class* is universally – and rightly – recognized to be a masterpiece. Its beauty, moral force and conceptual elegance originate in a few strikingly unusual articles of faith: (1) that the working class is a worthy cultural competitor of the ruling class; (2) that the *Lebenswelt* of the working class is socially and morally superior to that of its exploiters; (3) that regardless of the outcome of the class struggle, the autonomy and separateness of the working class is an intrinsic social value; (4) that the class itself is constituted by the *autopoiesis* of its rebellious political culture, including its re-interpretation of various traditions, as well as by technology, wage labour, commodity production and the rest. Whereas Karl Marx and Marxism aim at the *abolition* of the proletariat, Thompson aims at the *apotheosis* and triumphant survival of the proletariat.

Thompson's Rousseauian brand of Marxism triggered a sustained critique by Perry Anderson, one that is now half-forgotten but still extremely important. Although his terms are quite different from mine, Anderson sought to show that Thompson's conviction that he was a Marxist was erroneous.[2] Thompson had participated in a number of movements and intellectual adventures inspired by Marxism, and his fidelity to radical socialism – under twentieth-century circumstances – meant loyalty to Marxism's revolutionary legacy. But Thompson had to ignore the Faustian-demonic encomium of capitalism inherent in Marx, and so he had to oppose 'critical theory', and then theory *tout court*.[3] Anderson later described this decomposition of 'Western Marxism' – away from class to 'the people' – in conceptual terms,[4] a diagnosis that has been proved right by events since.

## ROUSSEAU VERSUS MARX

The main difference between Rousseau and Marx is that Rousseau seeks to replace (stratified, hierarchical, dominated) society with *the people* (a purely egalitarian and culturally self-sustaining, closed community), while Marx does not want to 'replace' society by annihilating 'rule' and the ruling class *as such*, but believes that capitalism (one specific kind of society) might end in a way in which one of its fundamental classes, the proletariat, would *abolish itself* and thereby abolish capitalism itself. It is implied (it is *sous-entendu*) that the moral motive for such a self-abolition is the intolerable, abject condition of the proletariat. Far from its excellence – extolled by the Rousseauians – it is, on the contrary, its wretchedness, its total alienation, that makes it see that it has 'nothing to lose but its chains', and that it has 'a world to win'. In the

Marxist view it is not the people's excellence, superiority or merit that makes socialism – the movement to supersede, to transcend capitalism – worthwhile, but, on the contrary, its being robbed of its very humanity. Moreover, there is no 'people', there are only classes. Like the bourgeoisie itself, the working class is the result of the destruction of a previous social order. Marx does not believe in the self-creation or the self-invention of the working class, parallel to or alongside capitalism, through the edification of an independent set of social values, habits and techniques of resistance.

Thus there is an *angelic* view of the exploited (that of Rousseau, Karl Polányi, E.P. Thompson) and there is a *demonic*, Marxian view. For Marx, the road to the end of capitalism (and beyond) leads through the completion of capitalism, a system of economic and intellectual growth, imagination, waste, anarchy, destruction, destitution. It is an *apocalypse* in the original Greek sense of the word, a 'falling away of the veils' which reveals all the social mechanisms in their stark nakedness; capitalism helps us to *know* because it is unable to sustain illusions, especially naturalistic and religious illusions. It liberated subjects from their traditional rootedness (which was presented to them by the *ancien régime* as 'natural') only to hurl them onto the labour market where their productive-creative essence reveals itself to be disposable, replaceable, dependent on demand – in other words, wholly alien to self-perception or 'inner worth'. In capitalism, what human beings *are*, is contingent or stochastic; there is no way in which they *are as such, in themselves*. Their identity is limited by the permanent re-evaluation of the market and by the transient historicity of everything, determined by – among other contingent factors – random developments in science and technology. What makes the whole thing demonic indeed is that in contradistinction to the external character, the incomprehensibility, of 'fate', 'the stars', participants in the capitalist economy are not born to that condition; they are placed in their respective positions by a series of choices and compulsions that are obviously man-made. To be born noble and ignoble is nobody's fault, has no moral dimensions; but alienation appears self-inflicted.

Marx is the poet of that Faustian demonism: only capitalism reveals the social, and the final unmasking, the final *apocalypse*, the final revelation can be reached by wading through the murk of estrangement which, seen historically, is unique in its energy, in its diabolical force.[5] Marx does not 'oppose' capitalism ideologically; but Rousseau does. For Marx, it is history; for Rousseau, it is evil.

It was Karl Polányi who best described the foundations of Rousseauian socialism, of which he himself was an archetypal representative.[6] According to Polányi, the great discovery of Rousseau was the discovery of 'the people'. This is not as trivial as it may seem. The common assumption of all philosophy – in contradistinction to Christianity – is that raw, untutored humanity is worthless. Ancient Greek philosophy, to which all subsequent lovers of wisdom were supposed to have supplied nought but footnotes, held that virtue was knowledge. But knowledge (science, philosophy, even *litterae humaniores*) is a social institution, possible only in certain situations of high complexity, sometimes called 'civilization', which would allow the growth and betterment of that knowledge. Thus, augmenting science presupposes a necessary or at least plausible perfectibility of civilization and the general salutary character of social institutions useful or indispensable for the advance of cognition.

Rousseau reversed the philosophical trend of more than two millennia when he said that arts, letters, sciences, 'culture' and 'civilization' did not contribute to the moral progress of humankind – on the contrary. The basic intuitions of persons living in circumstances which would not be conducive to the advance of knowledge and the ever-growing refinement of arts, mores and manners were, he thought, superior to whatever complex, unequal and sophisticated societies could boast of. Superior in what sense?

These intuitions were deemed to be superior because the development of civilization required an ever-growing separation between humans – high culture, according to Nietzsche, presupposes slavery that can sustain a leisured aristocracy dedicated to war and play and beauty – to the extent that all 'virtues' are necessarily confined to a few. Even in societies where essential communication still takes place among people personally acquainted with each other (affection and sympathy are possible only among such persons) the main 'civilizational' transactions are dispatched by abstract mediation such as script. In order to maintain a modicum of fairness and uniformity in society, it is necessary to codify law and religion. People will believe and revere the same prescriptions ('values') by reading or being read to (by officials), instead of coming to agree as a result of shared experience and feeling. Script and code (uniform law, scriptural religion, formal education, high art) will change from tools of mediation in society, aiding contact and co-operation, into a social goal, a motivational source of future action – in other words: authority. But this is an authority based on the familiar transformation of a tool into an end or a goal. It is a 'fetish'.

Rousseau thought that we would have remained both more virtuous and much happier were we bereft or at least rid of mediation. He knew it was too late, and his recipes for a solution are famously desperate; they take essentially the shape of a *purge*, 'cleansing', *épuration*. All Rousseauian socialist solutions (for this reason extremely popular in peasant societies, that is, in societies with a still strong cultural recollection of peasant experience and ideals) aim at simplification. Simplification towards a more natural (or, with luck, a completely natural) way of life. It is, after all, Karl Polányi's famous thesis that market societies are not natural, that they are the exception rather than the rule in history.[7] On the one hand, he resists the idea that capitalism is a natural order, whose emergence was only prevented in the past by scientific and technological backwardness and blind superstition; and he resists the idea that competitiveness and acquisitiveness are 'instincts' characteristic of all societies, only repressed in the past by chivalric and religious 'false consciousness' (and here he is of one mind with Marxists in 'historicizing' competition and the market.) On the other hand, Polányi regards non-market societies as 'natural' for being in the historical majority. He believed that we should orient our social action towards a re-establishment of what modern capitalism has falsified.

The other great Rousseauian socialist, Marcel Mauss, has shown that most acts of exchange in the history of humankind were motivated not by a desire for gain, but for ostentatious display and the satisfaction of pride.[8] Yet another Rousseauian socialist, Georges Bataille, one of the few truly prophetic geniuses, has generalized Mauss's point in drawing attention to society's *need* for unproductive losses, waste and destruction, which contradicts any notion of utility.[9] Sacrifice, he reminds us, etymologically means 'the production of the sacred'. The sacred is the result of *unnecessary* bloodshed. Non-genital and non-reproductive sexuality has long been considered 'a waste'. All these elements have been classified under the rubric of 'the irrational', since only equitable exchange conforms to the official idea of rationality which cannot, ever, account for a surplus which appears as 'savage' or 'illusory'. But then bourgeois society, in the guise of 'representative government', has always equated 'the people' with the 'irrational'. The apposite clichés (savage 'crowds', 'masses') have been inherited from the late Roman republic.

Rousseau's innovation was the unheard-of provocation of declaring the people – the servants of passion – morally and culturally superior to reasoned and cultured discourse and its *Träger*, the civilized elite of Court and University, and even the counter-elite of *belles-lettres*, experimental science, and the Enlightenment pamphleteering and journalistic culture to which Rousseau himself, of course, belonged. Against that discourse, again in terms of Roman republican controversies, Rousseau championed the martial, athletic, bucolic and folk-art virtues of nature-bound, egalitarian communities.

In the famous Second and Third Maxims of Book IV of his treatise on education, Rousseau says: '*One pities in others only those ills from which one does not feel oneself exempt*'. And: '*The pity one has for another's misfortune is measured not by the quantity of that misfortune but by the sentiment which one attributes to those who suffer it*'.[10] These maxims are the kernel of a manifesto for solidarity. Pray consider: Rousseau does not presuppose anything else but bare humanity in any individual. This presupposition is purely personal, subjective, psychological – available through introspection. It is based, as is well known, on fear: fear of suffering, which we can understand in others as well. There is no external or 'objective' measure for suffering, nor is there any need for it; it is sufficient for us to have a feeling for the perils lurking around us in order to have a feeling for the probable predicament of others. We pity others to the extent of our understanding and sympathy for a situation we can imagine ourselves to have been in, and to the extent of our picturing *their* feelings at such a juncture. On this small foundation stone – a pebble, really – is the edifice of a solidary community built.

To wish to put an end to imaginable and avoidable suffering is enough for the construction of social justice, since fear and imagination are natural givens in the human animal, but there is another hidden idea here, an idea even more revolutionary. This we could call the rejection of any and all theodicy. The church explains suffering by sin. How could a benevolent and omnipotent God cause suffering and death? Only as a retribution for something inherent in all humans but at the same time willed by all humans: the original sin of disobedience. (Reductionist theories of human nature play the same role in modern agnostic societies.) If we do not think that original sin is indeed inherent in human nature, suffering is unnecessary; and vice versa, if suffering is felt and understood in others, if then it can be counterbalanced by the succour of those who may not be good but who have an instinctive distaste for the ominous threat of visible misfortune in their environment – well, then the plausibility of original sin seems remote.

Moreover, if suffering is avoidable, there is nothing to prevent us from assuming that the alleviation of human suffering is a duty. We are bound by duty only in cases that appear feasible. If suffering is not natural, in the sense that it is not a necessary consequence of our natures, then it must be social and historical, subject to change – and why should we not hasten that change? If, say, inequality is caused by natural selection, revolutions are meaningless; if it is not, making revolutions is meritorious.

Rousseauian socialism is anti-theodicy; it opposes the tragic and conservative view of original sin or natural *fatum* with the splendid philosophical fiction of free-born men and women who are everywhere in chains. If the free-born are reduced to a servile condition, the culprit cannot but be society, the wrong kind of society. If human nature does not need to be moulded to be receptive to freedom, since we are free by definition, it is social organization that wants changing.

Human nature being tantamount to liberty, our true nature is the source of the liberty that is falsified and denied to us; hence the assumption that those enslaved are morally superior to the slavers. Rousseau's theory suggests that there is a separate culture and a separate morality inherent in the people; a culture and a morality that attracts the sympathy and the solidarity of all persons of good faith.

This brings us back to E.P.Thompson's Rousseauian socialism. He formulated the matter with classical simplicity when he described eighteenth century radicalism's

> ... profound distrust of the 'reasons' of the genteel and comfortable, and of ecclesiastical and academic institutions, not so much because they produced false knowledges but because they offered specious apologetics ('serpent reasonings') for a rotten social order based, in the last resort, on violence and material self-interest .... And to this we must add a ...cultural or intellectual definition of 'class'. Everything in the age of 'reason' and 'elegance' served to emphasise the sharp distinctions between a polite and a demotic culture. Dress, style, gesture, proprieties of speech, grammar and even punctuation were resonant with the signs of class; the polite culture was an elaborated code of social inclusion and exclusion. Classical learning and an accomplishment in the law stood as difficult gates-of-entry into this culture .... These accomplishments both legitimated and masked the actualities of brute property and power, interest and patronage. A grammatical or mythological solecism marked the intruder down as an outsider.[11]

Thompson is quite right: since Parmenides, 'reason' has always or nearly always been a symbolic mark of ideological mastery, opposed to 'the people' as the repository of unreason.[12] But the trouble with Rousseauian socialism is not that it unmasks the high-falutin pretensions of ruling-class doctrine, but that in doing so it treats the 'demotic' as 'natural'. Whatever seems to be beyond the ken of demotic culture, (in our case, working-class culture but in Rousseau's case, peasant folklore), Rousseauian socialism holds to be unnecessary or artificial. This would be true only if the proletariat were pristinely self-created and not the complicated product of capitalist society.

The main idea of Rousseauian socialism is, obviously, equality. Equality is a many-sided notion, but within this tradition it means the renunciation of the superfluous, from luxury to the cultivation of the self, from agonistic competition (resulting in *excellence*) to the enjoyment of high art divorced from the needs of the community. The Greek word for equality, *homonoia*, also means etymologically 'being of one mind'. The Rousseauian community is frugal, musical and martial. It is hostile to individuation and text.[13] It is also hostile to *opinion*. Opinion is an aspect of sociability in bourgeois society, while being the traditional enemy of philosophy, the counterpart of the quest for truth. The empty variety of individual opinions is reducible to a mind bent to the service of powerful interests, an expression of the self which is neither a result of an unbiased, dispassionate contemplation of reality (nature) nor an authentic outward sign of inner feeling. The competition of diverse opinions is not even a competition of egos for their own sake, merely a competition for quick adaptation to the demands of power with the aim of advancement: an adaptation without a true belief in the excellence of the opinion assumed.[14] Bourgeois sociability is false; the people – restored to its natural status – is (or was) authentic. 'True feeling' as the criterion of adequate elementary morality is reminiscent of the Calvinistic idea of 'justifying faith' in Rousseau's Geneva.[15]

Equality, thus, is opposed not only to hierarchy, but to variety or diversity as well. The expression 'chattering classes' was invented much later by Don Juan Donoso Cortés, but Rousseau was certainly opposed to *Öffentlichkeit* qua 'talking shop'. Opinion as instrument is a travesty of any honourable intellectual endeavour. The same would go, I am afraid, for any 'freedom of expression' conducive to a frivolous parataxis of competing egotisms. Rousseauian socialism is moralistic, not historicist. Lukács said that nature becomes landscape when one looks at it as it were from outside, when one is separated from it. For Rousseau and the Rousseauians, 'the people' is nature not landscape; it is not considered from afar. Solidarity, pity, sympathy have ordained closeness. Propinquity enjoins a modesty of political aims. The emancipation of the people does not mean the abolition of the people (as in Marx the emancipation of the proletariat means – decisively – the self-abolition of the proletariat). It means the abolition of *aristocracy and clergy*; basically, it is not the abolition of 'class' but the abolition of 'caste' or 'estate', whereby the Third Estate – the commoners – become The Nation.

## THE REALLY-EXISTING
## WORKING CLASS (AND BOURGEOISIE)

Why (and how) could modern socialists mistake the abolition of caste for the abolition of class? There are several reasons.

One is the oldest conundrum of the workers' movement, to wit, the fact that wherever successful proletarian movements or revolutions have taken place, they triumphed not against capitalism, but against quasi-feudal remnants of the old regime that, naturally, went against their self-understanding and their self-image. All the endlessly complicated debates about class consciousness are influenced by this primordial fact. This is also why Arno Mayer's theory concerning 'the persistence of the old regime' is so crucial to Marxist debates.[16]

Class struggle, as prosecuted by the workers' movement, instead of extolling the paradoxical, demonic 'virtues' of capitalism, was forced not only to attack it, but also to defend itself. It defended itself by insisting on the excellence of the 'Grand Old Cause', the moral superiority of those who fought for working-class autonomy, supposing they were an exception to the general rule of bourgeois society. This resulted in an enduring achievement which lasted about a century, from the 1870s to the 1970s: the creation of a counter-power of working-class trade unions and parties, with their own savings banks, health and pension funds, newspapers, extramural popular academies, workingmen's clubs, libraries, choirs, brass bands, *engagé* intellectuals, songs, novels, philosophical treatises, learned journals, pamphlets, well-entrenched local governments, temperance societies – all with their own mores, manners and style. A Hungarian sociological survey from 1906 shows that a working-class housing estate in Transylvania has one portrait of Marx and one of Lassalle per flat, workers are teetotal in a heavily drinking society, and open atheists and anticlericalists in a polity dominated by the church militant; church weddings are frowned upon, there are attempts at a healthy diet, non-competitive sports (not shared with outsiders) are encouraged (in Central Europe there were special socialist workers' athletic championships and mass musical choir contests until 1945); non-socialist charities are rejected, parties are held only in daylight to avoid immorality, and at least the men are trying – in a country of barefoot illiterates one generation away from the village primeval – to read social science and serious history. Admirable as this is, it must have been, for all intents and purposes, a *sect*.

This counter-power developed its own political superstructure and ideology, from 'reformist' social democracy to revolutionary anarcho-syndicalism, a whole separate world where the bourgeoisie's writ did not run.[17] The amalgamation of Rousseauian and Marxian socialism resulted from the special interests of this established counter-power or adversary power: the workers' movement was often Rousseauist in regard to itself and Marxist in regard to the bourgeois enemy.

What did this mean in terms of its struggle? In the nineteenth century there had to be struggles against throne and altar, for universal suffrage, for the right to organize and to strike; then national unity was re-forged in the Great War as if the class struggle could be switched off at will; after that war the proletariat liberated the miserable Eastern peasantry that had been kept in a servile condition (this was the most massive historical achievement of the communist regimes)[18]; later it had to create Popular Fronts and Résistance alliances against the fascist peril – there was always something that prevented proletarian politics (in Marx's sense), apart from heroic episodes by revolutionary minorities.

The reasons for this in post-1914 socialism seem self-evident: the need for self-legitimation of the workers' movement in view of its defeat but persisting power, and its repeated contribution to bourgeois revolutions liquidating the semi-feudal remnants of the old regime. A dispensation oriented to transcending capitalism remained – and still remains – utopian, while the 'secular' triumph of social democracy in the West and the transformation of the old regime into a tyrannical state capitalism under Bolshevik rule in the East offered a vindication for the movement, justified mainly by a puritanical and egalitarian system closer to Calvin's and Rousseau's Geneva than to Marx's classical Walpurgis night.[19] 'Welfarism' was not limited to the West: the Soviet bloc's idea of legitimacy was also a steady growth of income, leisure and accessible social and health services. 'Planning' was a common idea of Mao's Red China and de Gaulle's bourgeois and *patriotarde* and *pompiériste* France. Jacobinism was common to both. The *staatstragende* community, the addressee of welfare statism and egalitarianism, had to be defined somehow: it was the people, offered equal dignity by 'citizenship'.

To help us understand this properly, it is useful to return to what Thompson was complaining about in his debate with Perry Anderson and Tom Nairn. In a celebrated series of essays,[20] the latter tried to demonstrate that the weaknesses of the British workers' movement were caused by a peculiarity of British capitalism: it was the economic preponderance of efficient and market-friendly farming on the great estates and the disproportionate political influence of the landed aristocracy, both richer and more powerful than the incipient bourgeoisie – if there is such a thing (culturally) at all in England – that limited the breadth of vision, the vigour and the scope of any proletarian socialism in the British Isles. This was also, according to Anderson, the reason for England's subsequent decline in all the respects that are crucial to the criteria of European 'modernity', including an astonishingly large number of blind spots in British 'high culture', especially in the so-called social and human sciences.[21]

The great emotional force of 'class' as a special English *socio-cultural* problem – defined in the common usage as an intricate system of almost tribal markers such as diction, dress, speech habits, even posture, forms (and ritualistic denials) of courtesy, diet and the like – has its roots in this. These caste-like, sometimes quasi-ethnic differences of 'class' gave a special *cachet* to the class struggle in England, denying the possibility of a bourgeois-Jacobin ideology of 'community' or 'national unity'. Conservatives on the Continent would vehemently deny the mere existence of the class struggle, but High Tory ranters and satirists like, say, Peregrine Worsthorne or Auberon Waugh (indeed, both Waughs, *père et fils*), would declare their enjoyment in doing down the widow and the orphan, and were constantly waging a gallant fight against the vulgarian with his 'job', 'holiday', 'telly' and 'pop "music"'. In England, the class enemy was highly visible, but he or she was never or almost never 'the bourgeois', but 'the toff', 'the terrific swell' opposed to those who were common as muck. Even today the supposedly yuppified, classless 'estuary English' has a 'posh' version.

All this has pre-modern accents. It seems obvious that for the creation of 'a people' the annihilation of the upper classes would be necessary, as in eighteenth-century France, where *only* the Third Estate became *the nation* and where class relations had been ethnicized (the aristocracy: Nordic; the people: Celtic, Gallic; cf. Norman blood in England, Varangians in Russia, etc.). Class identity of this kind is definitely pre-socialist. Socialist movements had used it in the past, creating enormous difficulties for themselves later. Its use succeeded only where they could combine the specific demands of the usually small and culturally (and sometimes ethnically) 'different' proletariat, with the general (or 'bourgeois') democratic enthusiasms of the usually peasant, provincial majority led by the middle classes and journalistic opinion: for republic instead of monarchy, universal suffrage, anti-clericalism (or *laïcité*), agrarian reform (i.e., redistribution of land), reduction of birth privileges, a citizen army, ethnic minority rights, votes for women, and the like.

This was a fundamental dilemma of Austro-Hungarian and Russian social democracy and, later, of East and South Asian communism (in India and Nepal, to this very day). During the *belle époque*, socialism in the East was faced with either the prospect of victory at the helm of a bourgeois democratic revolution against an aristocratic old regime with elements of modernizing militarism (*die Soldateska*), or certain defeat and annihilation while preserving the purity of the 'Western' proletarian idea. When Gramsci called the October revolution in Russia a 'revolution against *Das Kapital*', he was apposite and to the point in this sense (not that Lenin and Trotsky knew exactly what they were doing). But even earlier, it was clear that universal suffrage, socio-cultural egalitarianism, democratic parliamentarism and a more secular and tolerant, less militaristic society would be realized east of the Rhine, south of the Alps and west of the Pyrénées, *only* by the socialist movement, not by the feeble liberal bourgeoisie, in predominantly farming societies.

On the whole, socialists decided to assume the leadership of non-socialist, democratic revolutions. The result was *nationalism*, both in the debacle of August 1914 and in the unavoidable transformation of Leninism into Stalinism. The truth is that modern capitalist societies as we know them today would have been entirely impossible without movements whose 'false consciousness' was precisely socialism. Socialism as a political movement was a tool of capitalist modernization not only in the East, but also in Central and Western Europe; the bourgeoisie itself did, historically speaking, very little by way of creating, or even fighting for, modern capitalist society.[22] Let us recall that the allegedly bourgeois revolutions of the nineteenth century were invariably led by the landed gentry; these revolutions had been completed in Central and Eastern Europe in 1918-19 by the socialist workers' movement – this latter case being one of the most important and most neglected aspects of the vexed problem of the origins of fascism and national socialism, directed both against the bourgeoisie and the proletariat. This may sound strange to Western ears, but is thoroughly comprehensible for a German, an Italian, an Austrian or a Hungarian of a certain age and/or *Bildung*.[23]

The bourgeoisie wrought gigantic changes in the texture of the world – economic, social, technological, scientific, artistic and ideological – but almost nowhere did it play a leading political role.[24] Bourgeois power (even social and cultural hegemony) proved impossible in the absence of a *modern* (in practice, a Lassallean-Marxist) socialist movement. This seems to be the unspoken, never openly stated conclusion of the debate between Anderson and Nairn and their adversaries. The decline of England, the unchanging *personnel* of British politics and public administration and the other elements of decadence so poignantly and pugnaciously described by Anderson and Nairn must be – at least partially – caused by the lack of a modernizing revolution led by the proletariat. It is, I believe, rather significant that the most 'contemporary' ideological campaign in favour of a modern capitalism in Britain was conceived not by mainstream liberal or social democratic ('labourite') tendencies, but by a *côterie* of former communists (the 'New Times' crowd around *Marxism Today*, a once-Communist monthly). When English Marxists like Anderson and Nairn were discussing the lack of a revolutionary bourgeoisie in Britain, they must have been painfully aware of the even more glaring lack of a revolutionary *workers'* movement, which seems to have been the only effective weapon against any kind of aristocratic rule, wherever such a rule existed and persisted. But they were more or less hobbled by their desire for an authentic *proletarian* revolution, which has never occurred in its anti-capitalist purity anywhere – yet.

This perhaps explains why the origin of capitalism, especially English capitalism, is such an important political question or *Kampffrage*. The 'Brenner Debate' was and remains decisive in this respect. But it is in the work of Ellen Meiksins Wood that all the threads come together, and the theoretical and political consequences are most clearly stated.[25] Answering Anderson's harsh questions about 'the "absent centre" of English social thought', Wood insisted: 'The individualism and ahistoricism of English social thought, its fragmentation, have more to do, then, with the advance of capitalism than with its inhibition'.[26] She characterizes the parallel and contrast with continental Europe thus:

While in France Bodin was describing the state as a unity of 'families, colleges or corporate bodies', Sir Thomas Smith defined the commonwealth as a 'multitude' of free individuals. While the French state continued to serve as a lucrative resource for the propertied classes, the English were increasingly preoccupied with individual appropriation by purely 'economic' means…. The replacement of corporate entities by individuals as the constituent units of society, the separation of the state and civil society, the autonomization of the 'economy' – all these factors associated with the evolution of English capitalism conduced to the atomization of the social world into discrete and separate theoretical spheres. And with it came a detachment of the social sciences from *history*, as social relations and processes came to be conceived as *natural*, answering to the universal laws of the economy ….[27]

This seems to be the very opposite of Perry Anderson's view. But it is, at the same time, another Marxian correction of E.P. Thompson's Rousseauism. The emphasis in Wood's work on the separateness or autonomy of the 'economy' and 'the economic' points, rather promisingly I think, towards a much-needed Marxian political science. This autonomy of the economy may account for peculiarities in English political culture that would, according to Perry Anderson, explain the lack of a radical socialism in Britain, the substitution of 'class culture' for 'class' and the notorious (and idealized) absence of great, salvific social theorems in the national culture. But the sudden modernization of Britain under Thatcher and Blair yields surprising results, as Anderson himself recognizes in another of his breathtaking surveys:

By the [nineteen-]eighties, the net effect of these changes was a marked disjuncture between high culture and politics in Britain. In most European cultures, such a pattern has historically been quite frequent. In many, indeed, the normal stance of intellectuals has tended to be oppositional, swinging against the pendulum of regimes rather than with it. In England, this has not been so. Here, the larger portion of the intelligentsia has generally sung in harmony, if not unison, with the established power of the day, from the time of Coleridge's first scoring of its part after the Napoleonic wars. The present position is an anomaly in this record ….[28]

Nevertheless, the problem remains: part of the Left will see 'class' in cultural and political terms, and this is indeed an effective aid to sustaining an oppositional stance against 'a rotten regime' in the name and on behalf of a people judged capable of achieving for itself a cultural and moral autonomy vouchsafed by a working-class politics.[29] The case of England is crucial for several reasons: it is traditionally 'the distant mirror' of capitalism.[30] It cannot possibly be denied that the shift to culture in class theory was and is caused by the fate of socialism (i.e., of the workers' movement): to succeed only in the sense of making capitalism more modern, democratic, secular and (perhaps) egalitarian via cross-class alliances forces the workers' movement to abandon the specific proletarian calling envisaged by Marx. Western and Northern social democrats, Eastern and Southern communists alike have replaced emancipation with equality, Marx with Rousseau. Marxian socialism has never been attempted politically, especially not by Marxists.[31] Egalitarianism and statism (in democratic and tyrannical versions) were the hallmarks of the main official versions of socialism, everywhere.

These are also the key elements of the contemporary popular image of socialism, and the key elements of the colourful pop ideology of the 'new social movements' as well, aiming at righting injustice by enlarging and radicalizing the idea of equality and trying to impose this idea on the bourgeois states and international financial organizations they despise (they themselves do not wish to take power; theirs is an *étatisme* by proxy). The 'statism by proxy' of the new social movements (we won't vote for you, we won't smash your power through revolution, but we want you to draft bills and pass acts of parliament and UN and EU resolutions that we deem useful and edifying), in spite of their many beauties and quite a few successes, is still statism, experimenting with a radical idea of equality of all living beings, hesitating between straight reformism and utopian self-sufficiency and exodus.

The retreat to egalitarianism, statism and 'culture' thus appears to be a quasi-permanent feature of socialist movements. In almost every case, this can only be explained by the fact that they must engage with an adversary, bourgeois society, which is replete with historical imperfections derived from the caste societies out of which they emerged.

## FROM CASTE TO CLASS TO PEOPLE

That the retreat from Marx to Rousseau is a also tendency *among Marxists,* as in the most important case of E.P. Thompson, is of particular importance. Technically, this is sometimes a reaction against an alleged rigid determinism in Marxian class theory (an allegation effectively refuted by G.A. Cohen)[32], but more frequently (again, also in E.P. Thompson's case) it happens owing to a fatal misunderstanding concerning the conflation of 'class' and 'caste' (*Stände, états,* or in Hungarian, *rendek*). Caste society, the remnants of which are still with us, even today, is based on a view of human nature radically different from the Enlightenment view, so ingrained in modern thinking as to be almost invisible and implicit, scarcely in need of being articulated.

For most of history, humanity was not thought to have been co-extensive with humankind. Women, slaves, foreigners, children were almost invariably excluded everywhere, but so were people who had to work for a living (*banausoi*), people who had become retainers in a chieftain's retinue, persons exercising trades that were ideologically considered repellent or religiously taboo, people with physical deficiencies, whole nations subjugated in war, persons belonging to another religion or denomination, persons without property, enemies of the state, members of 'inferior' races, and so on. These and many others were not supposed to share with the rest the prerogatives of full-fledged human beings. There was resistance to this state of affairs among some Stoics, Cynics and Epicureans, the early Christians and some medieval heretics, some Buddhists and other assorted riff-raff. But on the whole the title of 'man' (let alone of 'citizen', which is still limited by nation-states)[33] was a prerogative circumscribed by criteria of excellence, hence the absence of an idea of equal and universal rights and obligations.

Caste or 'estate' is a whole life, with dimensions capitalism has since nullified. Let me quote a few words from the greatest authority on the caste system:

> ...the lot of the Shudras is to serve, and...the Vaishyas are the grazers of cattle and the farmers, the 'purveyors' of sacrifice...who have been given dominion over the animals, whereas the Brahmans-Kshatryas have been given dominion over 'all creatures'.... [T]he Kshatrya may order a sacrifice as may the Vaishya, but only the Brahman may perform it. The king is thus deprived of any sacerdotal function.... The Brahman naturally has privileges.... He is inviolable (the murder of a Brahman is, with the murder of a cow, the cardinal sin), and a number of punishments do not apply to him: he cannot be beaten, put in irons, fined, or expelled....[34]

The contrast with modern capitalist society could not be more obvious: each caste (or estate) is a complete way of life, embodying a cosmological principle. Caste is a differential system of privileges, endowments and 'gifts' which represent a model of the social world, based on a philosophical doctrine concerning human functions, and a scale of values, embodied by various closed groups whose commerce with one another is a function of their respective rungs on the ladder of human values, religiously determined. All this is strengthened by a well-entrenched system of prejudices. The English word *villain*, French *vilain,* has its origin in the late Latin *villa-*

*nus*, villager, peasant. 'Ignoble' originally means a person devoid of noble rank. The Hungarian *paraszt*, 'peasant', originates in the Slav stem \*prost, 'simpleton', etc., all signs that contempt and deference did not need excuses. Medieval ditties made fun of hunchbacks, beggars, cripples, fat people and, simply, the poor. Explanations for the ill-fate of some were, apart from social theodicy, racial and warlike. The upper castes were (in the whole Indo-European area) supposed to be *fair*, the servants, the aborigines, the slaves, the foreigners, *swarthy*.[35]

The tripartite scheme of social hierarchy (*oratores, bellatores, laboratores*) does indeed identify social groups with human functions, but in ascribing function to person and group and vice versa, if these persons and groups remain within their prescribed or pre-ordained confines, it absolves them from responsibility: *responsibility is conceivable only in transgression, not by the fact of differential human condition*, such as membership in a social class. Choice (and the 'quality' of the individual) does not enter into it at all, and therefore misery does not need the intricate theodicy which is the bad luck of Christendom.

The target of egalitarian rebellion was always this ascription and adjudication, i.e., doubt concerning just deserts, and the ambiguity of the idea of 'God's children' and the radical distinctions regarding dignity (and the sheer scope of human life) inherent in caste society. The complaint that kings and barons are not chivalrous and gallant, that monks and nuns are not sagacious and chaste, is perennial. For the rebels, the world is turned upside down, merit trampled underfoot, while crime is rewarded with honours and plenty. Virtue, unlike moral goodness or intelligence, adheres to caste, not to persons or to humanity as such. What is virtue for one caste, is not for another. Pride is good in one, humility in another. Achilles, the greatest warrior, is incomprehensible apart from his semi-divine, princely heroism which coexists with extreme prickliness, sulkiness and sensitivity and a morbid preoccupation with slights and with the insufficient deference shown to him by equals whom he was bound to consider inferiors – a universal type encountered in ancient epics. Heroism is very much a matter of bodily integrity and beauty, athleticism, elegance, sexual glamour and a pronounced distaste for being 'dissed'. Heroism is play and display; all this is allowed under the disquieting but glorious threat of death on the battlefield, the untimely deaths of rich young men.[36]

In sharp contrast with caste, class is an abstraction (I do not mean only a scientific idealization, but a *lived* abstraction as well) in a society where freedom of contract exists. In such a society subordination, hierarchy, domination, rank, dignity, etc., are not only random, totally unconnected to the quality of the individual, but also *seen as such*. Fate is no longer, as in Greek tragedy or Corneille (and as late as Kleist), an accident of birth, but an accident of the social division of labour and other similar historical kinds of serendipity.

If it is true, and I think it is, that Marx's theory does not purport to be a theory of human nature as such, but a theory of capitalism, then the immortal words of *The Communist Manifesto*, according to which '[t]he history of all hitherto existing society is the history of class struggles', must be false. Class is unique to capitalist society. Class is, first of all, a structural feature of the system; belonging to a class is a condition legally and, quite often, socially, open to anybody. This openness of class as a contingent social position is what makes capitalism great and gives it the aura of Mephistophelian liberation through ever 'more extensive and more destructive crises', as the *Manifesto* also puts it. In order to achieve this gigantic 'creative destruction' (an expression of Schumpeter's inspired by Bakunin) there was a need to unleash the forces of individual freedom – a freedom, that is, from a legally and coercively enforced classification of human beings into groups of birth and status.

Addressing class as such is, intuitively, very difficult.

> Within the production process, the separation of labour from its objective moments of existence – instruments and material – is *suspended. The existence of capital and of wage labour rests on this separation. Capital does not pay for the suspension of this separation which proceeds in the real production process* – for otherwise work could not go on at all.... But as use value, labour belongs to the capitalist; it belongs to the worker merely as exchange value. Its living quality of preserving objectified labour time by using it as the objective condition of living labour in the production process is none of the worker's business. *This appropriation, by means of which living labour makes instrument and material in the production process* into the body of its soul and thereby resurrects them from the dead, does indeed stand in antithesis to the fact that labour itself is objectless, is a reality only in the immediate vitality of the worker – and that the instrument and material, in capital, exist as being-for-themselves.... But to the extent that labour steps into this relation [with its moments of material being], this relation exists not for itself, but for capital; labour itself has become a moment of capital'.[37]

The distinction between castes could not be farther away from this portrait of the worker who may be alienated and exploited, but certainly is no stranger to capital; on the contrary, he is one of its 'moments', one of its structural features. This is clearly not something anybody could abolish by decree or by law. If the worker is a feature of capital, the worker can change capitalism into something else only if he or she changes himself or herself, in an extra-moral sense.

Looked at from the ulterior vantage-point of the revolutionary, we may rather confidently say that *the abolition of caste leads to equality; but the abolition of class leads to socialism.* Yet as we have seen, the retreat from socialism to egalitarianism, from Marx to Rousseau, the retreat from critical theory to ahistorical moral critique, from Hegel and Marx to Kant, has been the rule, rather than the exception, in the history of the Left. It is therefore in need of some explanation.

First, one has to take into account the psychological needs of opposition to any system one was brought up in. All social systems – through mythologies, patriotic chronicles, traditions and the like – pretend and, indeed, must pretend that they are natural, and that their failings are due to inherent clashes within human nature, and that unhappiness all too obviously caused by impersonal factors is somehow retribution, either visited upon people because of their imperfections, or because of some fatal breakdown in the system itself caused by ingratitude, impiety or the inscrutable decree of a higher force of some sort. Blaming the system will always appear as an easy pretext for failing to blame oneself, dissatisfaction being always regarded as a weakness of the unsuccessful, of the insufficiently noble or the insufficiently insightful – in short, of the Thersites of this world. People have to be on a solid moral footing if they are to dare to say 'no'. Thus, it seems necessary to establish that there is an innate excellence residing in those who have been held by the ruling order to be inferior, and that the inversion of the established moral order or moral hierarchy happens to be both the superior truth and a satisfactory motivation for its reversal. The oldest rhetorical tricks can be employed here:

> Blessed be ye poor: for yours is the kingdom of God. Blessed are ye that hunger now: for ye shall be filled. Blessed are ye that weep now: for ye shall laugh. Blessed are ye, when men shall hate you, and when they shall separate you from their company, and shall reproach you, and cast out your name as evil, for the Son of man's sake.... But woe unto you that are rich! For ye have received your consolation. Woe unto you that are full! For ye shall hunger. Woe unto you that laugh now! For ye shall mourn and weep. Woe unto you, when all men shall speak well of you! For so did their fathers to the false prophets. But I say unto you which hear, Love your

enemies, do good to them, which hate you, Bless them that curse you, and pray for them which despitefully use you.[38]

The moral order is reversed, but even the threat of that reversal is turned upside down, for those who would suddenly find themselves at the bottom of the moral heap will be forgiven and saved. This sums up nearly all revolutionary manifestoes we can think of. The scary flip of the moral coin is made unthreatening – even the frightening curse, 'ye shall mourn and weep' is made good – by the invocation of universality: 'love your enemies'. But the right to forgive will be conferred upon those who did not have the power to forgive, and thus to condemn, before. Power is being taken away and given anew; this is why the Son of Man is also called the Lord.

A second reason why the retreat from socialism to egalitarianism has been the rule is the need for a trans-social or meta-social foundation for the possibility of a change which might reduce or even obliterate injustice and domination. This is (intuitively) the suppleness, the plasticity, the flexibility, the malleability of human nature and the randomness of intellectual, aesthetic or physical endowment, distributed capriciously among all ranks, races, creeds and provinces. In other words: a belief in the possibility of equality without upsetting too much the shape of society which – even if equality of income, opportunity, status and access to political power were achieved – would still contain elements of domination, either by government (tempered by law), or by various social hierarchies of command and control in the workplace, education and family, as well as a continuing social division of labour.

But domination married to equality would not contradict the possibility of equality only if the perpetual re-creation of inequalities is constantly upset by new forces 'from below' which constantly re-establish equality.[39] Redistribution (the only way to perpetually impose and re-impose equality if the other customary aspects of society remain essentially the same) can be implemented only by an extremely strong state able to defeat the resistance of those from whom something shall be taken away. But the strength of the state is apt to reinforce domination concentrated in the hands of the few, which will, then, further reinforce domination, naturally unfavourable to an equality of condition or of social positions, and so on without end. All this is likely, though, only if the malleability of human nature is allowed free rein by the dominant or 'hegemonic' culture; hence the permanent *Kulturkampf* concerning the pre-social or 'natural' equality of persons *before* redistribution, from 'blue blood' to natural selection to the Bell curve.[40]

Third, egalitarianism was (and up to a point, still is) an expression of a dynamic of individuals uprooted from 'caste'. As well as fighting against the market system, socialists found themselves still fighting against the remnants of a feudal order, i.e., *for* a system where surplus value would be extracted on the market (from people legally free and assenting to obligations arising from contract), not through coercion and social-cum-religious conditioning. Put more simply, they had to execute successful bourgeois *and* proletarian revolutions at the same time. Hence the endless wrangling of nineteenth-century social democrats about the problem of the peasantry, when they sometimes had to advocate the creation of competitive small farm businesses in order to win the rural allies they needed to enable them to smash the landed aristocracy and gentry, the political ruling stratum of most countries until quite recently.[41] Central European socialists (especially in Germany and Austria-Hungary) worried a great deal about *their* capitalism not being created by an autochthonous bourgeoisie, but in fact this was much more generally true.[42] The problem of Kautsky and Lenin (and Luxemburg and Szabó and Dobrogeanu-Gherea and Mariátegui) may actually be a universal problem.

Fourth, *et nunc venio ad fortissimum*, there is a deep moral and psychological difficulty with Marxism, intertwined with the historical problematic. Marxism, after all, proposes the abolition of the proletariat, not its apotheosis. Because of reification and alienation, it holds with Simone Weil that *la condition ouvrière*, being a worker, is the worst condition a human being can find herself or himself in. (And Simone Weil is quite right in believing that perfect solidarity with the working class means the assumption of, and acquiescence in, servitude and squalor. But this is, of course, the opposite of the sense of solidarity in the tradition of non-Marxian socialism.) The meaning of Rousseauian socialism is the re-establishment of the purity of the people through the forcible destitution of the upper castes and the exclusion of extraneous economic elements such as commerce; the people is held to be capable of discovering its virtue, which has been obliterated or corrupted by oppression and inequality, servitude and deference. This presupposes an Essence of Man to be found through philosophical means, an essence whose vacuity historical materialism was created to demonstrate. The 'enlargement' of Marxism in the normative sense (with, usually, some kind of Kantian moral philosophy) nearly always means a retreat towards equality and Rousseau.[43]

On the other hand, this ever-recurring retreat makes good psychological sense. It is well-nigh impossible to wage a battle to the death (which revolution, however slow and gradual, necessarily is) if there is no sense that it is fought on behalf of people who deserve sacrifice, whose cause is morally superior because *they* are superior to the foe. The anti-luxury ideas of Rousseau and his countless ideological forebears declare 'the great and the good' to be superfluous. This notion may be plausible (although still unpleasant) in the case of caste society, but in the case of class society, Marx is adamant that

... in my presentation, capital profit is *not* 'merely a *deduction* or "robbery" on the labourer'. On the contrary, I present the capitalist as the necessary functionary of capitalist production and show very extensively that he does not only 'deduct' or 'rob', but forces the *production of surplus value*, therefore the deducting only helps to produce; furthermore, I show in detail that even if in the exchange of commodities *only equivalents* were exchanged, the capitalist – as soon as he pays the labourer the real value of his labour-power – would secure with full rights, i.e. the rights corresponding to that mode of production, *surplus value*.[44]

This is not consonant with the millenary voice of rebellion. That voice, on the contrary, tells us that 'we was robbed', the thrifty by the thriftless. That honest toil was not paid in full, owing to the superior coercive power of the mighty. That ascribing a necessary 'productive' role to the ruling classes is pernicious 'ideological' mendacity. All value is created by the workers – this is Lassalle's view, and not Marx's.[45] All official and triumphant 'socialist' art from Soviet social realism to Latin American muralists glorifies proletarian might, sinews, purity, work and victorious confrontation with the puny and unclean enemy – unlike the few works of art truly inspired by a Marxian vision, from George Grosz and Gyula Derkovits to the more extreme avant-garde. These latter creations are almost invariably dark and pessimistic. Their problem was succinctly summarized by Georg Lukács thus: '[T]he objective reality of social existence is *in its immediacy* "the same" for both proletariat and bourgeoisie'.[46]

The working class is not situated outside capitalism. It embodies capitalism as much as the bourgeoisie does. In a way perhaps even more: reification touches it in a radical manner. Nevertheless, Lukács emphasizes the inextricable interrelatedness of 'rationalization' and irrationality brought about by capitalist crises.[47] The redemption of 'social evil' is possible only if 'evil' is separated from the redeeming feature; but this is not feasible. Since it is not only classes, i.e., human groups, that are divided from one another, but whole social spheres and, especially and crucially, 'the economy', which is separated from the other realms of social life by capitalism, the economy is *quasi*-liberated from the yoke of bloodline (birth) and the ancient fusion of politics, religion and custom.[48] But the separation of the economy from the rest, owing to the specifically capitalist method of extracting surpluses on the market, as it were 'peacefully', instead of through direct coercion, as before, creates a commonality between the fundamental classes in capitalism where the mere conquest of power by the lower classes may not overcome the separation and therefore will fail to establish a classless society – as has indeed happened.

The pressures which resulted in one of the characteristic abandonments of the Marxian class view are impeccably described in another of Ellen Meiksins Wood's excellent books.[49] In a series of sharpish attacks on a number of post–Marxist semi–converts, she selected authors (whose subsequent careers she on the whole accurately predicted) who tried – in view of the repeated defeats of socialist movements and the even then perfectly clear *cul-de-sac* of communist parties in or out of power – to find, at first, a substitute for the working class as the vanguard of revolution; but unlike the New Left, not in the 'person' of Third World peasants, inner–city blacks or young intellectuals, but in a new cross–class coalition of rebellious 'people' desirous of a new kind of democracy. *The Retreat from Class* shows how the transformed concept of 'democracy' (from the ancient Greek understanding of it as the rule of the free–born poor, to the idea of pluralism and the division of power, acceptable to the ruling class, so much so that the original democratic idea came to be seen as 'anti-democratic') contributed to the change of the socialist *telos* from an end to exploitation and domination (*ergo*, classless society) into a mere hope for cultural 'hegemony'. A hegemony, that is, of egalitarian forces bent on abolishing discrimination, privilege, social exclusion: but even within egalitarian discourse these authors (Wood's 'new true socialists') stressed recognition rather than redistribution (to use Nancy Fraser's subsequent phrase), and pluralism rather than socialism.[50] The problem here is basically the same as during the 'revisionism' debate around Eduard Bernstein's book, or the ongoing quarrel on 'reformism'.[51]

This weighty heritage inspires Rousseauian socialism. It is the rearguard battle of 'the people' which is and isn't identical with bourgeois society. This was certainly what made Marat, Robespierre, Saint-Just, Desmoulins, Hébert and Gracchus Babeuf so lofty and unforgiving: humiliation, not alienation. In semi–feudal peasant societies, such as the countries of Eastern and Southern Europe in the first half of the twentieth century, it was this, the spirit of *jacquerie* combined with an intimation of a *sansculotte* revolution, which gave a special vigour and savagery to the idea of 'class' and 'socialism', since both were combined with strong remnants of 'caste' and 'equality'. Neither Marat and Saint-Just, nor the English Levellers and their successors about whom E.P. Thompson, Raymond Williams, Christopher Hill, Raphael Samuel and their confederates wrote, dreamed of a kind of egalitarian change that would be conducive to a society of market, contract and money. But while overturning caste changes countless things – hierarchy (status, if you wish), moral nomenclature, relations of obedience and deference, prescribed biographies, connubiality and commensality, spatiality and religion – it cannot touch the economy, which has just come into its own right as an autonomous sphere of the human condition. Above all, it does not replace hierarchy with equality, only caste (or estate) with class.

This is what happened to West European social democracy and 'euro-communism'[52] (and British radicalism from Lloyd George and Keir Hardie to Attlee, Bevan, Laski and Beveridge), and to East European, Chinese and Vietnamese 'communism': they have unwittingly and unwillingly either created or reinforced and modernized capitalist society in their countries. It is not certain that the anti-globalization movements of today, with their sincere calls for planetary (the word 'international' is avoided nowadays, for some reason) equality will not contribute to yet another rebirth of a more attractive, slimmed-down, fairer and smarter capitalism, after destroying the superannuated global financial institutions and the more shameless neo-conservative governments − even though the anti-globalists, too, obviously want much, much more.

## EPILOGUE

Our argument has established that revolutionary mobilization in the past was almost invariably aimed at the economic, social, cultural, racial, legal, religious, racial, sexual and intellectual humiliation inherent in 'caste'; it was an egalitarian mobilization against aristocratic orders of variegated kinds. It is true that 'democracy' in practice never meant the effective rule of the lower orders, albeit their influence has increased from time to time (never for long, though), but it alleviated a burden we neglect too easily. Equality of dignity, the principle of civic rights and liberties (even if most often honoured in the breach), shifted the struggle for emancipation to new levels, both more profound and more intractable.

Let's not forget that bourgeois liberty, i.e., modern (liberal) capitalist class society, was not quite safe until very recently. It should not be forgotten, either, that this element played an important role in the anti-fascist struggle (not understood by purely and uncompromisingly proletarian radicals like Amadeo Bordiga and some, by no means all, left communists). An explanation is here in order. Fascism and National Socialism are constantly interpreted, not without justification, as instances of 'reactionary modernism', as a sub-species of twentieth-century revolutionism, etc., initially in order to stress their not negligible parallels and similarities with 'communism', especially Stalinism, often under the aegis of the (untenable) 'totalitarianism' dogma. However justified and novel these approaches were, they contributed to the (all too frequent) neglect of the obvious. Southern and Catholic fascism wanted to introduce the *Ständestaat* (always translated as 'corporate state' but literally meaning 'the state of estates', a sort of new caste society), based on the theories of Othmar Spann, Salazar and others, all inherited from Count Joseph de Maistre, the Marquis de Bonald and Don Juan Donoso Cortés, with a mix of the 'elite' theories of Vilfredo Pareto and others. There were variants of the same neo-feudalism in Nazism, too, with racist and sexist elements of 'arischer Männerbund' (Aryan male fraternity) and similar pseudo-historical nonsense, very much in vogue then among fashionable people like Carl Schmitt and others of his ilk.

What all this verbiage amounted to was a quite serious attempt to re-introduce caste society, that is, human groups with radically different entitlements and duties (against uniformizing and levelling, 'mechanistic' conceptions of egalitarian liberalism and socialism *and* bourgeois individualism): the *Führerprinzip* in all occupations (witness Heidegger's infamous 'Rektoratsrede', i.e., commencement address); vocational groups dissolving classes (e.g., steelworkers would have meant, in the future, Krupp and Thyssen *as well as* the steel-workers proper); untouchables (Jews and other condemned races), and so on. The fascists were quite serious in wanting to go back to before 1789, as they (or at least their predecessors) had been announcing loudly since the 1880s. Since pre-modern and aristocratic memories were still alive in Central and Southern Europe, the modernist-egalitarian impulse against fascism was quite strong, and since this impulse was carried by the Left, and since the murderous attack of fascism and Nazism was directed against them *and* the liberal bourgeoisie and intelligentsia, small wonder that Popular Fronts were born and were quite sincere in their fight *against the revival of an oppressive past*, and against an anti-egalitarian and anti-Enlightenment obscurantism. This fight was pre-socialist in its historical and ideological character, but unavoidable (and one has to admire the gall of Horkheimer and Adorno in disregarding this aspect altogether).

So, egalitarian, anti-aristocratic and anti-caste – thus 'Rousseauian' – struggles were fully justified as late as the Second World War. We forget the backward-looking character of fascism and Nazism at our own peril. Serious attempts to create a new nobility were launched, beginning with the *vitéz* or warrior 'estate' in the first, radical phase of Vice-Admiral von Horthy's counter-revolution in Hungary and ending in Himmler's SS mystique; the *vitéz* (former First World War soldiers, commissioned and non-commissioned, of impeccably Gentile ancestry) were offered land and a small stipend and were organized in quite an effective knights' order from 1920; their Supreme Captain was the Regent, von Horthy, himself. The *vitéz* order was revived in Hungary after 1989, albeit only as a nostalgic association of the extreme right. But 'corporatist' ideology is still alive in contemporary Hungary; from time to time there are proposals to revive an unelected upper chamber consisting of delegates of all 'respectable professions', all the bishops, etc. Most recently such a proposal was advanced by a 'socialist' prime minister, a former Communist central committee member.

But since the rather recent global triumph of capitalism, egalitarian mobilizations against caste, although still the dominant form (*viz*. battles against poverty, for jobs, against local and global discrimination, for gender and racial equality, for fairness for the indigenous or 'first' peoples, and so on) appear insufficient, because inequality (if still a pertinent term at all) has different causes from those it had in the past. When, in the vast literature of the disillusioned Left, we read about the irrelevance of class, the vanishing proletariat, we can still see the unconscious amalgamation of caste and class. Since the *immanent*, intra-capitalist fight for equality led by socialists possessed by the 'false consciousness' of fighting against alienation and exploitation, has ended; since the historically forced synthesis of these two aspirations has been dissolved through the final evanescence of the remains of aristocratic order, deference and birth privilege; since the 'socialist' states have reverted to capitalist type, as a result of the successful conquest of agrarian aristocratism by 'communist' parties;[53] it is for the first time that pure capitalism makes an appearance.

One should be careful here. The historically-forced synthesis of egalitarianism and socialism is obviously not over in the 'developing' world where egalitarian movements based on the petty merchants of the bazaar, the peasantry and the lower clergy ('Islamic radicalism') are attacking the Westernized elites and military states with an islamicized Khmer Rouge rhetoric or, in Latin America, with an 'indigenous' millenarism. It is a telling fact that 'revolutionary openings' are on offer again on capitalism's periphery, where new strategies of the 'weakest link' and of 'combined and uneven development' are reformulated for the benefit of a new generation of 'vicarious revolutionary' dupes.

That said, on a global plane capitalism appears in the stark, unforgiving light of its final triumph. It is completely, utterly, absolutely itself. It is like Rome being perfectly realized in Byzantium. We reconstruct Roman society from the legal documents written later and elsewhere, in which Roman law was generalized and synthesized by people culturally remote from Latium but who nevertheless understood, and what is more, lived and experienced 'Rome' in its unadulterated Roman 'haecceity' as *Romaioi*. Balzac and Dickens might not be able to understand the completed ultra-capitalism of today, but we see that we are the accomplished heirs of their characters.

There has never been an experiment in Marxian socialism. It is an open question if there can ever be one, *if* indeed Marx was right in his fundamental assumptions. The stumbling block was and remains the paradox of class, that is, of the exploited as a collective revolutionary agent. In the battle for equality before the law, defining the task of the revolutionary agent was quite easy, as we can see from the Putney Debates (1647) where Rainborough is arguing against Ireton and Cromwell: since nobody is responsible for their mothers and fathers, what can birthright then possibly mean? The claimants are outside, the lords within; the former are clamouring to get in, the latter protesting against people with no property, i.e., with no interest in the common weal, getting in; but nobody doubts that it is worthwhile to be inside.[54]

In modern capitalism, there is no inside, as there is no upwards direction. There is no route by which you can leave and there is no place that is fundamentally unlike yours and there is no one who is not, in some way, *yourself*. The primary quality of labour – that which ought to be liberated by socialist action – is not injustice. It is a general and irremediable divorce of persons' inner forces, desires and capacities, from the aims at the service of which they must develop and exercise these forces. The best characterization I know of this is by Moishe Postone:

> Alienated labor ... constitutes a social structure of abstract domination, but such labour should not necessarily be equated with toil, oppression or exploitation. The labour of a serf, a portion of which 'belongs to' the feudal lord, is, in and of itself, not alienated: the domination and exploitation of that labour is not intrinsic to the labour itself. It is precisely for this reason that expropriation in such a situation *was and had to be* based upon direct compulsion. Non-alienated labour in societies in which a surplus exists and is expropriated by non-labouring classes ['castes' in my sense, GMT] necessarily is bound to direct social domination. By contrast, exploitation and domination are integral moments of commodity-determined labour.[55]

As far as we are aware, only direct (coercive) social domination was ever overturned by popular revolt. As the experience of so-called 'real socialism' shows only too clearly, a change in legal ownership (of the means of production) from that of private citizens or their associations to that of the state or government means as little (for the workers) as the passage of a company from ownership by a family into that of a pension fund. The 'expropriation of the expropriators' did not end alienation. The illusion that capitalism was ever defeated is linked to the non-Marxist idea of an anthropological turn away from 'artificial' society (the anarchy, wastefulness and inefficiency of the market, self-destructive individualism, greed and assorted social pathologies, etc.) to true human nature where people will act (not work) creatively after their hearts' desire. This is, again, Rousseau, not Marx – or at least not the mature Marx – the analyst of bourgeois society.[56] Marx's historicism is thorough and radical. He did not describe the human condition when describing capitalism; indeed, his description is meant as a refutation of any such idea, and this refutation is pursued throughout his *oeuvre*. As Postone puts it: 'The "essence" grasped by Marx's analysis is not that of human society but that of capitalism; it is to be abolished, not realized, in overcoming that society'.[57]

Neither value nor labour are perennial qualities of human existence, nor is class. Class, in contradistinction to 'caste', is not a framework for a whole life or a *Lebenswelt*. This is why the disappearance of the cultural identity of the old working class does not change the fundamental character of capitalism one whit. Class, not being a human group with common interests and common moral and cultural values such as, say, solidarity and contrariness, but a structural feature of society, is not an actor. *Contra* E.P. Thompson, it *is* a 'thing'.[58]

Class is that feature of capitalist society which divides it along the lines of people's respective positions in relation to reification/alienation, i.e., their degree of autonomy vis-à-vis subordination to commodities and value. The concomitant differences in wealth, access, etc., could, in principle, be remedied by redistribution and mutual 'recognition'. But greater equality of this kind (which may appear as a utopia right now, but there are very strong forces pushing towards that utopia which is well within the realm of possibilities) can achieve better consumption, but not better 'production' – that is, not unalienated labour. Equality, arrived at through redistribution, does not and cannot preclude domination and hierarchy – a hierarchy moreover that, unlike in aristocratic systems, does not build upon a cosmology and a metaphysics that could effect a reconciliation with reality (and what else is reality than servitude and dependence?).

No doubt the cruelty, craftiness, low cunning and high logistics used in the expropriation of surpluses go on as always, but the enemy is less and less a culturally circumscribed bourgeoisie as described in Benjamin's *Arcades Project*,[59] but a capitalism without a proletariat – and without a bourgeoisie – at least, without a proletariat and a bourgeoisie as we know them historically, as two distinct cultural, ideological and status groups not only embodying, but *representing* 'socialism' and 'capitalism'.[60] It is this representation which happens to be obsolete, and perhaps it was secondary to begin with, in spite of its mobilizing force which makes the blood flow faster when listening to the *Marseillaise* or the *Internationale* (curiously, *both* were played at East European demonstrations at the beginning of the twentieth century).

The truth about class is not a proud self-representation through a legitimizing ethic: this belongs to an era of conflict between rebellious universalism (read: egalitarianism) and particularism (read: aristocratism and the *esprit de corps* of haughty elites from dukes to abbots). The dominant ideology of the new, purified capitalism is, naturally, freedom. Freedom, as conservatives have been pointing out since the late eighteenth century, means the uprooting of corporate, *standesgemäß* identities and replacing them with mobility, flexibility, elasticity, ease, a propensity to, and a preference for, change. It is, in appearance, 'classless'. But it isn't. It does not 'prefer' the bourgeoisie as a closed, culturally identifiable, status group ('estate'); instead it underpins capitalism as a system.

Some people mistake the absence of identifiable cultural and status groups on either side of the class divide for *an absence of class rule*. But this is false. The capitalist class rules, but it is anonymous and open, and therefore impossible to hate, to storm, to chase away. So is the proletariat. Legal, political and cultural equality (equality here only means a random distribution of – very real – advantages and privileges) has made class conflict into what *Capital* makes it out to be. Class conflict is dependent on the extraction of surplus; it is not a battle between two camps for superior recognition and a better position in the scheme of (re)distribution. That battle goes on still, to be sure, but it is essentially the battle of yesteryear. The bourgeoisie is by now incapable of autonomous self-representation; the representation of its interests is taken over more and more by the state. Since the state represents, and looks after, capitalism, the old-style self-representation of the working class is moribund, too, but the state is *not* supplanted – as was the case, at least symbolically, in the past – by political institutions of counter-power. Thus revolutionary proletarian movements, although they now barely exist, are cast into outer darkness.

The truth about class is, therefore, that the proletariat had, historically, two contradictory objectives: one, to preserve itself as *an estate* with its own institutions (trade unions, working-class parties, a socialist press, instruments of self-help, etc.); and another one, to defeat its antagonist and to abolish itself as a class. We can now see that the abolition of the working class *as an 'estate', as a 'guild'*, has been effected by capitalism; capitalism has finally transformed the proletariat (*and* the bourgeoisie) into a veritable class, putting an end to their capacity for hegemony. Class hegemony of any kind (still quite vivacious and vigorous in Gramsci's time) was exactly what was annihilated. Class as an economic reality exists, and it is as fundamental as ever, although it is culturally and politically almost extinct. This is a triumph of capitalism.[61]

But this makes the historical work of destroying capitalism less parochial; it makes it indeed as universal, as abstract and as powerful as capitalism itself. What political form this may take, we don't know.[62] Nevertheless, it is now truly the cause of humanity. There is no particular, local, vocational, 'guild' bias to this cause, nor is any possible. The truth of class is of its own transcendence. The proletariat of the *Manifesto* could stand outside because it could lose nothing but its chains. No one is outside now – although not in the sense of Antonio Negri: nation-states and classes continue to exist, and they do determine our lives.[63]

The question is, could there be a motivation for a class that exists in deprivation – and is now even deprived of a corporate cultural identity – to change a situation which is dehumanizing and dangerous, but not humiliating to the point of moral provocation?

We don't know.

What is certain is that the last flowers have fallen off the chains. The working-class culture which inspired so much heroism and self-abnegation is dead. That culture was modernist in the sense of taking aim at hierarchy and trying to achieve a secular, egalitarian and rights-based society. This the working class mistook for socialism. It is not. It is capitalism. Capitalism could be itself only if and when aided by socialist delusion.[64] We are now free of this delusion. We see the task more clearly. But all the rest is utter defeat.

NOTES

This is an edited and abridged version of a longer manuscript.

1    *The Making of the English Working Class*, London: Penguin, 1963.
2    A first-rate specimen of the decaying art of polemic, worthy of its target, is Perry Anderson's *Arguments Within English Marxism*, London: NLB/ Verso, 1980. He says in an important passage: 'Today, too, Thompson is entirely justified in summoning historical materialism again to take full and self-critical measure of [William] Morris's greatness. However, his ulterior theorization of the reasons why Marxism as a whole long failed to take up the legacy of Morris cannot be so easily accepted. The former, he maintains, pertains – or at least pretends – to "knowledge", the latter to "desire". These are "two different operative principles of culture" which may not be assimilated to each other. Spelling out the distinction, he writes: "The motions of desire may be legible in the text of necessity, and may then become subject to rational explanation and criticism. But such criticism can scarcely touch these motions at their source." What is wrong with this account? Essentially that it substitutes an *ontological* for a *historical* explanation of the record of relations between Morris and Marxism'. (p. 160). Bingo. Rousseauian socialism can be (and is) empiricist, utopian and moralistic (and, occasionally, *passéiste*) but never, ever, historicist (in the sense of *Historismus*, not the Popperian nonsense;

cf. Friedrich Meinecke, *Die Entstehung des Historismus,* I–II, Berlin: R. Oldenbourg, 1936; see also Meinecke's *Machiavellism* [a translation of his *Die Idee der Staatsräson in der neueren Geschichte,* 1925], ed. by Werner Stark, New Brunswick: Transaction, 1998, esp. the chapter on Ranke, pp. 377–391).

3    E.P. Thompson, *The Poverty of Theory,* London: Merlin, 1978.

4    Perry Anderson, *In the Tracks of Historical Materialism,* Chicago: The University of Chicago Press, 1984. The book also contains instructive political analyses. The term 'Western Marxism' originated with Karl Korsch (q. v.), was made popular first by Maurice Merleau-Ponty in his epochal *Adventures of the Dialectic* [1955] Evanston: Northwestern University Press, 1986, pp. 30-58 (and reinvented by Anderson himself in his famous *Considerations on Western Marxism*) London: NLB, 1976, where he notes rather presciently the shift of Marxist theory away from economics and politics to culture and art, another telling sign of decline for a revolutionary doctrine: see pp. 49-74.

5    To quote the perhaps most famous words in the modern history of ideas: 'All fixed, fast-frozen relations, with their train of ancient and venerable prejudices and opinions, are swept away, all new-formed ones become antiquated before they can ossify. All that is solid melts into air, all that is holy is profaned, and man is at last compelled to face with sober senses his real conditions of life, and his relations with his kind'. Karl Marx and Friedrich Engels, *The Communist Manifesto* [1847], ed. by Gareth Stedman Jones, London: Penguin, 2002, pp. 222-3.

6    In an essay written but never published in English, and available only in Hungarian translation: 'Jean-Jacques Rousseau' [1953], in K. Polányi, *Fasizmus, demokrácia, ipari társadalom,* Budapest: Gondolat, 1986, pp. 244-258.

7    Karl Polányi, *The Great Transformation* [1944], Boston: Beacon Press, 1957.

8    *The Gift,* London: Routledge, 1970. Cf. the chapters 'Don, contrat, échange' and 'Sources, matériaux, textes à l'appui de "l'Essai sur le don"', in Marcel Mauss, *Oeuvres* 3, présentation de Victor Karady, Paris: Les Éditions de Minuit, 1969, pp. 29-103. Paul Veyne has also demonstrated how in the ancient Greek city-states, this kind of display became a system, *euergetismos,* the system of 'good works' whereby the richest aristocrats were forced by the community to sacrifice large chunks of their wealth for public purposes (military, naval, religious and athletic) in exchange for honours, but on pain of confiscation and exile, *in lieu* of taxation. Honour was equated with giving up, not amassing, wealth. *Civisme* meant sacrifice. See his *Bread and Circuses,* London: Penguin

Books, 1990, an abridged version of *Le Pain et le cirque*, Paris: Les Éditions du Seuil, 1976.

9    See his *The Accursed Share*, New York: Zone Books, 1991. Cf. Georges Bataille, 'The Notion of Expenditure', in Bataille, *Visions of Excess*, ed. by Allan Stoekl, Minneapolis: University of Minnesota Press, 1993, pp. 116-129; for background see his 'The Moral Meaning of Sociology', in Bataille, *The Absence of Myth*, ed. by Michael Richardson, London:Verso, 1994, pp. 103-112. On war as play, he spoke in a radio interview (on Nietzsche) with Georges Charbonnier on 14 January 1959, see Bataille, *Une liberté souveraine*, ed. by Michel Surya, Paris: Farrago, 2000, p. 130.

10    *Emile, or On Education*, ed. by Allan Bloom, New York: Basic Books, 1979, pp. 224, 225.

11    E.P. Thompson, *Witness Against the Beast: William Blake and the Moral Law*, New York:The New Press, 1993, pp. 109-110. Rousseauian socialism was often attracted to counter-cultural *intermundia*, far away from official 'polite' culture. Bataille, the alleged 'crazed pornographer' is a case in point; see his texts from the 1930s anti-Stalinist left subculture, *L'Apprenti sorcier*, ed. by Marina Galletti, Paris: Éditions de la Différence, 1999; cf. *Laure: Une rupture*, ed. by Anne Roche and Jérôme Peignot, Paris:Éditions des Cendres, 1999 (letters of Laure, Bataille, Boris Souvarine, Pierre Pascal, Simone Weil).The subversive potential of demotic or popular culture was shown to great effect by Robert Darnton; see his *The Great Cat Massacre*, New York:Vintage, 1985, and particularly *The Literary Underground of the Old Regime*, Cambridge: Harvard University Press, 1982. It is small wonder that it was he who pointed out the parallels between the clandestine literature of pre-revolutionary France and the underground *samizdat* literature in Eastern Europe (of which the present writer was a modest practitioner); see R. Darnton, *Berlin Journal 1989-1990*, New York: W.W. Norton, 1991. It is pretty characteristic that defeated Marxian socialists would retreat to the 'antinomian' stance and discover the 'authentic' proletarian culture, like Jacques Rancière in his *The Nights of Labor*, Philadelphia:Temple University Press, 1989. It is significant that Rancière was Louis Althusser's comrade-in-arms and ends up as an ally of E.P.Thompson.

12    This does not mean, of course, that Rousseauian socialists are averse to faux-naïf appeals to reason. See, for instance, P.-J. Proudhon, *Les Confessions d'un révolutionnaire, 1849*, ed. by Daniel Halévy and HervéTrinquier, Paris: Éditions Tops, 1997, p. 141.

13    At the same time, Rousseau would extol the merits of a music rooted in a parochial community, necessarily based on the cadences of an ethnic language. As in Rousseau, 'Lettre à d'Alembert' [1758], in Jean-Jacques

Rousseau, *Oeuvres complètes*, V, Pléiade edition, Paris: Gallimard, 1995, p. 15.

14  '… the Savage lives in himself; sociable man, always outside himself, is capable of living only in the opinion of others and, so to speak, derives the sentiment of his own existence solely from their judgment'. Jean-Jacques Rousseau, *The First and Second Discourses*, ed. by Victor Gourevitch, New York: Harper Torchbooks, 1990, pp. 198-9.

15  For a neo-Weberian analysis of puritan elements in Rousseau's views on inwardness and moral economy see Alessandro Ferrara, *Modernity and Authenticity: A Study of the Social and Ethical Thought of Jean-Jacques Rousseau*, Albany: State University of New York Press, 1993, pp. 111-151.

16  Arno Mayer, *The Persistence of the Old Regime*, New York: Pantheon, 1981.

17  See the classical statement about the oligarchical tendency in (mainly socialist) political organizations: Robert Michels, *Political Parties* [1915], London: Macmillan, 1968; cf. Carl E. Schorske, *German Social Democracy 1905-1917*, New York: Harper Torchbooks, 1972, esp. pp. 88-145.

18  See G.M. Tamás, 'Un capitalisme pur et simple', *La Nouvelle Alternative*, 60-61, March-June 2004, pp. 13-40.

19  'Meta'-capitalist transcendence had to stay utopian in order to be able to fall back on moral rather than historical criticism. This amounted to a transition from Hegel to Kant, which, as Lukács well demonstrated, is a certain sign of defeat. The philosophical manifesto of the 1918 German revolution shows this clearly in its theologizing metaphysical rhapsody: see Ernst Bloch, *The Spirit of Utopia*, Stanford: Stanford University Press, 2000, pp. 237-8.

20  See Thompson's famous essay 'The Peculiarities of the English', *Socialist Register 1965*, written against Anderson's 'Origins of the Present Crisis', *New Left Review*, I/23, January/February 1964, and Tom Nairn's 'The English Working Class', *New Left Review*, I/24, March/April 1964.

21  See the series of superb and gloomy reports in Perry Anderson, *English Questions*, London: Verso, 1992, pp. 48-104, 121-192, 193-301. This *réquisitoire* of English decadence and philistinism has many parallels in Matthew Arnold, *Culture and Anarchy* [1869], ed. by Samuel Lipman, New Haven: Yale University Press, 1994.

22  This, perhaps necessary, tactic of the socialist movements was criticized very early on. See the important essay of the greatest Hungarian Marxist before Lukács, Ervin Szabó (an anarcho-syndicalist), 'Politique et syndicats', *Le Mouvement Socialiste*, 1909, t. 1, pp. 57-67; cf. Ervin Szabó, *Socialism and Social Science*, ed. by J.M. Bak and G. Litván, London: Routledge, 1982. The clearest statement of the problem as regards

Bolshevism is to be found in Herman Gorter, *Open Letter to Comrade Lenin* [1920], London: Wildcat, n.d. [1989]; cf. Herman Gorter, 'Die Ursachen des Nationalismus im Proletariat' [1915] and 'Offener Brief an den Genossen Lenin' [1920], in A. Pannekoek and H. Gorter, *Organisation und Taktik der proletarischen Revolution*, ed. by Hans Manfred Bock, Frankfurt/Main:Verlag Neue Kritik, 1969, pp. 73-87, 168-227.

23 Ervin Szabó attributes the 1848 revolution in Hungary to a class conflict between landed gentry and landed aristocracy; see his 'Aus den Parteien und Klassenkämpfen in der ungarischen Revolution von 1848', *Archiv für die Geschichte des Sozialismus und der Arbeiterbewegung*, 1919, pp. 258-307 (fragment from a larger work in Hungarian, this latter considered a classic).

24 See Perry Anderson, 'The Notion of Bourgeois Revolution' in *English Questions*, pp. 105-118. The whole concept of 'bourgeois revolution' seems to disintegrate as a result of late twentieth-century Marxist research.

25 She was even able to appropriate the dividends of the most blatantly conservative work of historiography which, during the Thatcher decade, declared the bankruptcy of the plebeian school in history initiated by the CPGB Historians' Group in the 1950s: see J.C.D. Clark, *English Society 1688-1832*, Cambridge: Cambridge University Press, 1988. Clark proves himself to be the scourge especially of E.P. Thompson, in 'a tract for the times' quite enjoyable in its acidity and its fashionably anti-snobbish return to those supremely unfashionable writers, Sir Lewis Namier and Sir Herbert Butterfield; see esp. pp. 141-161, 258-276.

26 Ellen Meiksins Wood, *The Pristine Culture of Capitalism*, London:Verso, 1991, pp. 91-2.

27 Ibid.

28 'A Culture in Contraflow', in Anderson, *English Questions*, p. 300. See also his essays in *A Zone of Engagement*, London:Verso, 1992.

29 This is a problematic best illuminated in a few wonderful books by T.J. Clark such as *Image of the People: Gustave Courbet and the 1848 Revolution* [1973], London: Thames and Hudson, 1999. See his masterpiece, *Farewell to an Idea: Fragments from a History of Modernism*, New Haven: Yale University Press, 1999, the best summation in existence of the intricate and profound *identity* of modernism and political radicalism (my favourites are the chapters on Pissarro and on 'Freud's Cézanne', pp. 55-167); summations though, disturbingly, are of *the past*, are they not?

30 There is a book, sadly overlooked, in spite of its many merits, which analyses the political aspect of Marx's picture of England: David MacGregor, *Hegel, Marx, and the English State*, Toronto: University of Toronto

Press, 1996, especially strong on contracts and the Factory Acts; cf. David MacGregor, *The Communist Ideal in Hegel and Marx*, Toronto: University of Toronto Press, 1990.

31  The only exceptions are the failed revolts of Left Communists, Council Communists, anarchists and anarcho-syndicalists. It is only they who ever tried to elaborate a Marxian political project. See [Philippe Bourrinet], *The Dutch and German Communist Left*, London: ICC, 2001 and the numerous and voluminous works of Hans Manfred Bock. There is a recent re-edition of Anton Pannekoek's *Workers' Councils* [1948], ed. by Robert Barsky, London & Oakland: AK Press, 2003.

32  'A compressed statement of [Thompson's] argument: Production relations do not mechanically determine class consciousness (*p*), therefore: Class may not be defined purely in terms of production relations (*q*). *P* is true, but *q* does not follow from it. We are at liberty to define class, with more or less … precision, by reference to production relations, without inferring, as Thompson says we are the bound to do, that the culture and consciousness of a class may be readily deduced from its objective position within production relations. The opponent Thompson envisages commits the same fallacy as his critic. He too supposes that if *p* is true, then *q* is true. That is why he bases a denial of *p* on a denial of *q*, and erects a mechanical Marxism which ignores the open drama of historical process. The difficulty is not the opponent's premiss, whose innocence Thompson fails to disprove, but the hasty reasoning with which he follows it. Thompson's motive is to insist on *p*, with which we have no quarrel. But he mistakenly supposes that one who accepts a structural definition of class, and so rejects *q*, is thereby committed against p. There is no good reason to think that'. G.A. Cohen, *Karl Marx's Theory of History: A Defence* [1978], expanded edition, Oxford: Oxford University Press, 2001, pp. 74-5. The antiquated, 'period' feel of Cohen's analytical style, quite extraneous to the book's main argument, not to speak of its historical and philosophical sensibility, does not detract from its value, notwithstanding its untenable theory of 'theory' and such. Moreover, what G.A. Cohen has to add on class is even more important: '"The separation of the free worker from his means of production" – the phrase encapsulates the structured characterization of the proletarian …: his "freedom" is his ownership of his labour power, his "separation" is his non-ownership of his means of production. The text thus recommends individuation of social forms (and thereby "economic epochs of the structure of society") in production relational terms … [T]he production relation binding immediate producers will be broadly invariant across a single social formation: there will be no unordered *mélange* of

262    SOCIALIST REGISTER 2006

262    SOCIALIST REGISTER 2006

262    SOCIALIST REGISTER 2006

slaves, serfs, and proletarians ... [We] say that there are as many types of economic structure as there are kinds of relation of immediate producers to productive forces. From the Marxian viewpoint, social forms are distinguished and unified by their types of economic structure, as individuated by the production relations dominant within them' (pp. 78-9). It is an open question, though, whether this is valid also for non-capitalist societies, where the separation of the economy from the rest of society and *la chose commune* has not happened.

33  See my 'On Post-Fascism', *Boston Review*, Summer 2000, pp. 42-6, reprinted in A. Sajó, ed., *Out and Into Authoritarian Law*, Amsterdam: Kluwer International Law, 2002, pp. 203-219. Cf. G.M. Tamás, 'Restoration Romanticism', *Public Affairs Quarterly*, 7/4, October 1993, pp. 379-401.

34  Louis Dumont, *Homo hierarchicus* [1966], complete revised English edition, Chicago: The University of Chicago Press, 1980, p. 66.

35  See Georges Dumézil, *La Courtisane et les seigneurs colorés*, Paris: Gallimard, 1983, pp. 17-36.

36  A splendid book on this theme: Georges Dumézil, *Heur et malheur du guerrier*, Paris: Flammarion, 1992, influenced, alas, by the waffle on 'der arische Männerbund' and 'die kultische Geheimbünde der Germanen' (Stig Wikander, 1938 and Otto Höfler, 1935, respectively), but no matter: I recommend the superb chapters on the Tarquinii, Indra the sinner, and the comparison of the Horatii and the Aptya. See also the incomparable treatise of the great Émile Benveniste, *Le vocabulaire des institutions indoeuropéennes*, Paris: Les Éditions de Minuit, 1993, esp. vol. 1, book 3, ch.1 on 'La tripartition des fonctions', and ch. 2, on 'Les quatre cercles de l'appartenance sociale', pp. 279-319, and vol. 2, book 2, 'Le droit', pp. 97-175.

37  Karl Marx, *Grundrisse* [1857-1858], London: Penguin, 1993, p. 364.

38  Luke 6, 20-2, 24-8.

39  I tried to demonstrate, long ago, that this is an illusion: G.M. Tamás, *L'Oeil et la main*, Geneva: Éditions Noir, 1985 (original Hungarian *samizdat* edition: 1983).

40  A compendium of anti-egalitarian prejudices, very much a predecessor of neo-conservative views of our own day, but funnier, is Max Nordau's *Degeneration* [a translation of *Entartung*, 1892], with an introduction by George L. Mosse, Lincoln: University of Nebraska Press, 1993, with amusing rants against Ibsen, Tolstoy, Baudelaire, Wagner, Nietzsche, Huysmans and others. It was enormously popular when it appeared precisely because it pointed to the impotence of egalitarianism, especially of Christian and Jacobin origin, against bourgeois society.

41  It is quite astonishing to see the power of the old landed interest until the Second World War in the westernmost state of Europe; see David Cannadine, *The Decline and Fall of the British Aristocracy*, New Haven: Yale University Press, 1990, with highly instructive appendices. The data first collected by W.D. Rubinstein are inventively and entertainingly interpreted. The book bolsters some of the Anderson–Nairn claims, albeit belatedly. The peasant question was raised by Karl Kautsky; the debate raged in Germany, Austria–Hungary and Russia; there was also an interesting contribution from Rumania, by Constantin Dobrogeanu-Gherea on 'the new serfdom'; later, the criticism of Lenin, Trotsky and the October Revolution *from the Left* was frequently based on the need of the 'socialist revolution' to distribute land to the peasants, creating thereby petty entrepreneurial capitalism in agriculture, that had to be 'liquidated' subsequently by the centralizing re-distributive state in a violent self-repression of the revolution or, according to the Stalinists, the liquidation of phase I of revolution by phase II ('collectivization' through massacre and famine).

42  Cf. Perry Anderson, 'The Notion of Bourgeois Revolution'. The historical points are discussed in Ellen Meiksins Wood's illuminating book, *The Origin of Capitalism: A Longer View*, London: Verso, 2002, esp. pp. 95-146. Apart from its striking originality, it contains an excellent survey of recent controversies, around Perry Anderson's *Passages from Antiquity to Feudalism* [1974], London: Verso, 1992 and *Lineages of the Absolutist State* [1974], London: Verso, 1979, and the Brenner Debate (see *The Brenner Debate: Agrarian Class Structure and Economic Development in Pre-Industrial Europe* [1976], ed. by T.H. Aston and C.H.E. Philpin, Cambridge: Cambridge University Press, 1988). There is a sharp attack on Ellen Meiksins Wood and Robert Brenner by Ricardo Duchesne in 'On the Origins of Capitalism', *Rethinking Marxism*, 14(3), Fall 2002, pp. 129-137, which for lack of specialist expertise I cannot appraise, but as an outsider, I am not wholly convinced. Central and East (including Russian) experience seems to me to bear out Meiksins Wood's contentions, as far as I can judge.

43  This is what Andrew Levine fails to see in his interesting book, *A Future for Marxism? Althusser, the Analytical Turn and the Revival of Socialist Theory*, London: Pluto, 2003. It is quite ironical that the two authors who in the nineteen-seventies tried to recreate a pristine left theory, Louis Althusser and G.A. Cohen, should be Mr Levine's heroes in a book which accepts egalitarianism (in John Roemer and others) and 'normative' political philosophy (in the later G.A. Cohen) as an egress for wayward Marxism without any further ado. Andrew Levine's contention that

G.A. Cohen and others have brought Marxism into the 'mainstream' is rather extraordinary. Imagine a system of beliefs that has influenced the lives of hundreds of millions of people on four continents, taught around nocturnal camp-fires in dozens of civil wars and hundreds of trade union institutions, debated by dozens of revolutionary or reforming govern- ments, brought into the 'mainstream' of a tiny and transient chapter in the history of thought, analytically styled political philosophy. Academic myopia often beggars belief. Whatever analytical remains from analyti- cal Marxism is rather the 'period piece' feel, a combination of Oxford flippancy and Cambridge philistinism, besides a commendable striving for clarity. Being 'no-nonsense' and 'tough-minded' and 'anti-bullshit' is more a question of style than anything else. Just as nobody takes seriously Spinoza's Euclidean pretensions or Hobbes's aspirations to be 'scientific', and just as this does not prevent us from appreciating their work, the 'analytical' style of a certain Marxian writing, however secondary, does not preclude its insights from being illuminating or useful. But it is strange, passing strange, that an eccentric manner should be considered 'mainstream', while the grand tradition of post-Renaissance European social philosophy – of which Marxism is, of course, a part – should be seen as marginal. Andrew Levine also speaks about the 'insularity' of French academic philosophy, which reminds one of the famous English headline, 'Fog over Channel, Continent cut off'. Marxists used to be internationalist revolutionaries, didn't they?

44    'Notes on Adolph Wagner' [1879-80], in Marx, *Later Political Writings*, ed. by Terrell Carver, Cambridge: Cambridge University Press, 2002, p. 232.

45    In the draft programme of German social democracy you could find the sentence: 'Labour is the source of all wealth and all culture'. To which, Marx responds: 'Labour is *not the source* of all wealth. *Nature* is just as much the source of use-values (and what else is material wealth?) as labour, which is itself only the expression of a natural power, human labour power. This line can be found in any children's primer and is correct in so far as the *implication* is that labour requires certain means and materials. However a socialist programme cannot allow a bourgeois phrase like this to conceal the very *circumstances* that give it some sense'. 'Critique of the Gotha Programme', in Marx, *Later Political Writings*, pp. 208-9.

46    'Reification and the Consciousness of the Proletariat', in Lukács, *History and Class Consciousness: Studies in Marxist Dialectics* [1923], Cambridge: The MIT Press, 2000, p. 150.

47  'The transformation of the commodity relation into a thing of "ghostly objectivity" cannot... content itself with the reduction of all objects for the gratification of human needs to commodities. It stamps its imprint upon the whole consciousness of man; his qualities and abilities are no longer an organic part of his personality, they are things which he can "own" or "dispose of" like the various objects of the external world. And there is no natural form in which human relations can be cast, no way in which man can bring his physical and psychic "qualities" into play without their being subjected increasingly to this reifying process .... This rationalization of the world appears to be complete, it seems to penetrate the very depths of man's physical and psychic nature. It is limited, however, by its own formalism .... On closer examination the structure of a crisis is seen to be no more than a heightening of the degree and intensity of the daily life of bourgeois society. In its unthinking, mundane reality *that* life seems firmly held together by "natural laws"; yet it can experience a sudden dislocation because the bonds uniting its various elements and partial systems are a chance affair even at their most normal. So that the pretence that society is regulated by "eternal, iron" laws which branch off into the different special laws applying to particular areas is finally revealed for what it is: a pretence. The true structure of society appears rather in the independent, rationalized and formal partial laws whose links with each other are of necessity purely formal (i.e. their formal interdependence can be formally systematized), while as far as concrete realities are concerned they can only establish fortuitous connections' (Ibid., p. 101). It appears that contingency is the outcome of the extreme rationalization (described by Max Weber) of society's technological, administrative, legal, logistical, military, etc. sub-systems in a framework of outlandish randomness. No truly rational control is conceivable over such a collection of disparate 'facts'.

48  I spoke about this problem *à propos* Fichte (the Rousseauian and Kantian revolutionary genius) in 'Fichte's "Die Bestimmung des Gelehrten"': A Sketch', *Collegium Budapest Workshop Series 12*, Budapest: Institute of Advanced Study, 1997, passim, and in 'From Subjectivity to Privacy and Back Again', *Social Research*, 69(1), Spring 2002, pp. 201–221.

49  *The Retreat from Class* [1986], London: Verso, 1998.

50  'In order to place ourselves firmly within the field of articulation, we must begin by renouncing the conception of "society" as founding totality of its partial processes. We must, therefore, consider the open-ness of the social as the constitutive ground or "negative essence" of the existing, and the diverse "social orders" as precarious and ultimately failed attempts to domesticate the field of differences'. So write Chantal

Mouffe and Ernesto Laclau in their *Hegemony and Socialist Strategy* [1985], London: Verso, 2001, pp. 95-6. Wood's response is rather cruel: 'After much theoretical huffing and puffing, has not the mountain laboured and brought forth – pluralism? The alternative – which always lurks menacingly in the background – is a doctrine according to which some external agency, somehow uniquely and autonomously capable of generating a hegemonic discourse out of its own inner resources, will impose it from above, giving the indeterminate mass a collective identity and creating a "people" or "nation" where none existed before. The sinister possibilities inherent in such a view are obvious'. *The Retreat from Class*, p. 63. (Two remarks here: I think more highly of Mouffe's and Laclau's talents than Meiksins Wood does; and I think the 'sinister possibilities' are already quite obvious in Gramsci's Machiavellianism. The end result, though, is indeed pluralism and the egalitarianism of 'recognition' of the contemporary NGO variety.)

51    An extremely interesting anthology of texts from the *Socialist Register*, centred around a few seminal articles by Ralph Miliband, discusses the case of Britain while considering the general problem of whether the construction of a cross-class alliance led by labour could ever achieve socialism: David Coates, ed., *Paving the Third Way: The Critique of Parliamentary Socialism*, London: Merlin, 2003, with contributions by Ralph Miliband, John Saville, Leo Panitch, Colin Leys, Hilary Wainwright and David Coates.

52    See Ernest Mandel's prescient *From Stalinism to Eurocommunism*, London: NLB, 1978. The PCI's overall political role was not all that different from that of Labour or the SPD or SPÖ.

53    See G.M. Tamás, 'Un capitalisme pur et simple'. There is an earlier, non-socialist essay by the same author, with some realization of this problem; See G.M. Tamás, 'Socialism, Capitalism and Modernity', in Larry Diamond and Marc F. Plattner, eds., *Capitalism, Socialism and Democracy Revisited*, Baltimore: The Johns Hopkins University Press, 1993, pp. 54-68; see also my 'Victory Defeated', in Larry Diamond and Marc F. Plattner, eds., *Democracy After Communism*, Baltimore: The Johns Hopkins University Press, 2002, pp. 126-131.

54    David Wootton, ed., *Divine Right and Democracy: An Anthology of Political Writing in Stuart England*, Harmondsworth: Penguin, 1986, pp. 285-316. Gerrard Winstanley said, 'This is your inward principle, O ye present powers of England. You do not study how to advance universal love. If you did, it would appear in action'. (*Ibid.*, p. 321). This is the authentic voice of revolution.

55  Moishe Postone, *Time, Labor and Social Domination: A Reinterpretation of Marx's Critical Theory* [1993], Cambridge: Cambridge University Press, 2003, p. 160.

56  The philosophical doctrine of a reconstructed people – reconstructed through the abolition of commerce and the market proper – is Fichte's, in *Der geschloßne Handelsstaat* [1800], ed. by Fritz Medicus and Hans Hirsch, Philosophische Bibliothek #316, Hamburg: Felix Meiner Verlag, 1979, esp. pp. 89-126; cf. Johann Gottlieb Fichte, *Grundlage des Natur-rechts* [1796], ed. by Manfred Zahn, Phil. Bibl. #256, Hamburg: Felix Meiner, 1991, pp. 156-184; Johann Gottlieb Fichte, *Die Staatslehre, oder über das Verhältniss des Urstaates zum Vernunftreiche...* [1813, posthumous], in I.H. Fichte, ed., *Fichtes Werke* IV, Berlin: Walter de Gruyter & Co., 1971, pp. 497 *ad fin*.

57  Postone, *Time, Labor and Social Domination*, pp. 62-3.

58  See Thompson's famous preface to *The Making* (p. 11): '...class is a relationship, and not a thing...'.

59  Walter Benjamin, *The Arcades Project*, Cambridge: Harvard University Press, 2002. It is quite instructive to compare the grand portraitists of the late bourgeoisie, Henry James, Thomas Mann, Marcel Proust, André Gide, Roger Martin du Gard, Robert Musil, Italo Svevo, Alberto Moravia, Tibor Déry – with Walter Benjamin. The last generations of the old bourgeoisie are distinguished by a certain weakness and tenderness towards small things; it is the first non-labouring class that has no discernible social or political function. Politics is still made by the *grands seigneurs* or the new professionals (lawyers and apparatchiki); glory, elegance and courtliness are still preserves of the nobility together with sports, duels, military prowess and sexual licence. Arts are the only terrain where neither professionalism nor 'caste' plays an important role. Inwardness (*Innerlichkeit*), plush comfort, solitude, *consumption of culture* (from newspapers to operas) are the world of the *flâneur* which he escapes by *flâner*. It is only Mann and Déry among those listed above who could be said to have been conscious of an apocalyptic dimension to all this (think of the function of toothache in *The Buddenbrooks*). These authors all believed that it should be proletarian socialism, however barbaric it may turn out to be, which takes the place of the ailing, self-indulgent, morbidly eroticized microcosm of the cultivated bourgeoisie with its Mahler and Debussy and Klimt and Schiele. They never thought of corporate management, tabloid television and pop music.

60  About this the best Marxian (or any kind of) analysis is by Robert Kurz in his largely untranslated books and his periodicals (*Krisis*, its lighter Austrian counterpart, *Streifzüge*, and now *Exit*). He is the thinker closest

to Moishe Postone I know of. I believe he is the most original thinker on the German, and perhaps European, Left nowadays. He deserves to be more generally known.

61  The intellectual history of the highly interesting and important discussions (chiefly among Marxists) on class as a problem of political philosophy is summarized (and an original solution thereof is attempted) on a very high theoretical level by Stephen A. Resnick and Richard D. Wolff, *Knowledge and Class: A Marxian Critique of Political Economy*, Chicago: The University of Chicago Press, 1987. It is a thousand pities that I cannot argue with it here.

62  A starting point in envisaging the future function of the class-in-itself would surely be the imposing work of Erik Olin Wright, the greatest authority on class today. There are continuing sociological investigations about this: see the innovative work of Stanley Aronowitz and Michael Zweig. None of the above makes their kind of valuable work superfluous, quite the contrary.

63  On the debate concerning the new imperialism, see G.M. Tamás, 'Isten hozta, Mr. Bush', *Élet és Irodalom* (Supplement), 22 April 2005.

64  'Revolutionary theory is now the sworn enemy of revolutionary ideology – *and it knows it*': Guy Debord, *The Society of the Spectacle* [1967], §124, New York: Zone Books, 1995, p. 90.

# ON TELLING THE TRUTH

## TERRY EAGLETON

A brief history of truth might go something like this. In pre-modern times, truth was by and large a phenomenon set apart from the lowly material world. It was loftier than everyday realities, dwelling in some Olympian sphere of its own; or alternatively it could be thought of as deeper than them, lurking elusively at the heart of things. Getting at the truth thus meant discarding the empirical shells of phenomena in order to pluck out their vital essences. This view of truth survives well into modernity, as Hegel among others would attest; but it is only with modernity proper that truth descends to earth on a dramatic scale, as the mind turns from religious or Platonic ideals and buckles itself in Baconian style to the actually existent.

Something similar occurs in literature. It is not until the celebrated rise of the novel in early-modern times that the ordinary workaday world is considered to be fit matter for literary treatment. Common-life characters had of course staged their appearance in earlier writing, but almost always as servants, foot soldiers, spear-carriers or buffoons. The idea that common-or-garden social experience might be worthy of investigation as precious in itself, rather than as exemplary of some higher truth, is a revolutionary one. As Charles Taylor has pointed out, it has its roots in Christianity;[1] but it takes a long time for this demotic agenda to infiltrate the charmed domain of artistic culture. What is comic about the first great novelistic hero, Don Quixote, is just his nostalgic patrician refusal to embrace this brave new world of bourgeois realism.

It is impossible for us now to recreate the excitement and bemusement of the first readers of, say, Daniel Defoe, reared as many of them would have been on a diet of epic, pastoral, elegy and tragedy, at encountering a narrative which seemed to find everyday existence extraordinarily enthralling. What helped to make it so was the fact that it was early *capitalist* existence, in which frenetic change, sickening instability and the thrills and spills of survival in a predatory world were the name of the game. It also helped that, as a great deal of literature from Balzac to Brecht attests, the capitalist and the criminal are terrible twins, requiring much the same sorts of skills and aptitudes. Thanks to the emergence of the capitalist market, it was now possible to write a fable of everyday life which had all the virtues of a gripping thriller.

Yet if the mind had buckled itself to the actual, it was only to soar above it. In the aesthetic sphere, this becomes known as the transcendence of art, the way it dips into the gutter only to elevate what it finds there to the stars. Art is an alchemical process, which takes the dross of daily experience and transmutes it into the gold of aesthetic form. It trades in the empirical; but in order to be art, rather than some mere documentary record, it must do so in a way which lays bare its ideality or typicality. As such, this aggressive new mode, known as realism, is still in line with the old idealising genres of pastoral, heroic, epic and the like, as the twentieth-century avant garde artists protest. Balzac's ideality may be a more fleshly kind than Dante's, but art's relationship with the real is still an ambiguous one, embracing and refusing it in the same gesture.

There is a similar ambiguity in philosophy. Empiricism may conceive of a mind empty and inert enough to take the vivid impress of actual things; but this humility before the real is ultimately in the name of rising above it in order to master it, harnessing knowledge to the ends of political and technological dominion. If we examine the shape and texture of things with self-forgetful attentiveness, it is in order to uncover the underlying laws that govern their behaviour; and this, in turn, is with a view to intervening in them so as to turn them to our own benefit. The human subject who appears to John Locke and David Hume as little more than a welter of discrete sensations is also politically speaking the active, unified, sovereign self. In this sense, the epistemology of the Enlightenment, on the surface at least, is intriguingly at odds with its politics.

However snugly the mind presses up to the world, then, a gap must be maintained between them, one which allows us space to manipulate whatever it is we have in our cognitive sights. To this extent, the whole Enlightenment project contains the seeds of its own later postmodern subversion. For the more this gap allows the material world to be worked upon by human technologies, the more densely mediated that world becomes, until it becomes hard to catch a glimpse of the thing itself through the thick mesh of concepts and instrumental procedures which intrude between ourselves and it. Immanuel Kant's 'noumenal' sphere is one name for this problem in high modernity. By the time of late modernity, we catch ourselves asking whether there is really anything out there at all, or whether the real is no more than a transient effect of our own ways of doing business. We have now subjugated our surroundings so thoroughly that we are left with nothing but our own technologies of domination to gaze anxiously or admiringly upon, the real world having meanwhile dwindled to nothing beneath their remorseless operations. Power is meant to elicit truth, and so indeed it does: he with the largest research grant is most likely to stumble upon it. But it also occludes it, as the providers of the research grant discreetly hint that they would rather not have a result which discredits their commercial product. As our top-heavy technologies of truth come to shut out the world they mediate, the pre-modern gulf between truth and empirical reality returns in postmodern guise. It now takes the form of a social order cut off from the world by the very discourses which are supposed to open it up. The difference is that for the Platonists as for the *X-Files*, the truth is out there, beyond the realm of common experience, whereas for postmodernism the truth is in here.

Truth in these conditions is whatever we need in order to do what we want to do. In pragmatist fashion, you can resolve the contest between truth and power by more or less conflating the two. Truth becomes a matter of what we actually get up to – an alluringly practical, material hypothesis for radicals, though one at odds with their suspicion that truth generally turns out to be the opposite of what we get up to. Yet the realist conception of truth as whatever is the case is notoriously hard to banish. For one thing, if truth is about our needs, then we need to know what it is we need, which would appear to usher some realist notion in the back door again just as it has been unceremoniously booted on to the front porch. Much the same is true of the prescriptivist or Nietzschean claim that truth is what we legis-late into being, a view which suffers from the defect that we must already know something of how it is with the world to avoid the embarrassment of positing situations which are plainly impossible. If truth is simply a function of power and interest, how do we know this? And does this claim describe what is the case, or is it itself a function of power and interest? A coherentist theory of truth, for which those propositions are true which rub shoulders amicably with the rest of our propositions, is dogged by something like the same inexorable return of realism: how can we *know* that one proposition fits in with others? Truth, which began as an exalted affair way out of our sublu-nary reach, has ended up in the present as altogether too close for comfort. It is a symptom of the fact that we late moderns are apparently incapable of getting outside our own heads.

The discerning reader may have noted that this history of truth has been a mite selective. Yet it serves to highlight a certain paradox of modernity, namely that the only way of finally mastering reality is to abolish it, in which case there is nothing left to master. You are left high and dry with your own lonely sovereignty, as the world itself slips through your fingers and leaves you grasping at thin air. Unless the material world offers some resistance to your designs upon it, it is impossible to know it at all, since it is a thing's recalcitrance which signals that there is something there to be grasped. But this resistance is also intolerable, since it signifies that your power is incomplete. What you must do is purge reality of its inherent meanings so as to reduce it to clay in your hands; but what virtue is there in manipulating a meaningless world? If truth is something you impose upon things, only to pull it out again in the process known as knowledge, is not this as pointlessly circular an action as that of the man in Wittgenstein's *Philosophical Investigations* who passes money from one of his hands to the other in the belief that he is making a financial transaction?

You are left, then, with a Hobson's choice between a real but intractable universe, and a docile but unknowable one. The more dominion you exert, the less you understand anything but your own project – a myopia which at present is known as United States foreign policy. It is those whose satellites can map every inch of the planet who tend to produce schoolchildren for whom Malawi is a Disney character. Those most ignorant of geography are those with their military bases in every quarter of the globe. In this scheme of things, power and truth cannot easily co-exist. The more you have of the former, the scarcer the latter commodity becomes.

Moreover, if there is nothing out there to rebuff your rule, the whole of reality having been long since battered into submission by the imperious will, there is nothing out there either to legitimate your own authority. You become, in Kierkegaardian phrase, a monarch without a country, with no curb on your whimsical fantasies. It is, so to speak, the Michael Jackson syndrome on a global scale. The only legitimation becomes self-legitimation; but how can the self be a source of validation if it has not itself been validated? There is no threat to your power only because there is nobody and nothing left to challenge it – in which case, since power lives only in the response it provokes, it begins gradually to implode. You cannot consolidate your identity by rolling over the rest of humanity, since identity, even in Washington DC, is a differential affair which requires the irrefragable existence of others. The ideal solution to this dilemma was the Marquis de Sade's, who dreamed of a victim who would be submissive yet responsive, because he could be tortured indefinitely but never quite killed. As long as there is someone left to scream, you can rest assured that your sovereignty is not turning in a void.

At the very acme of his control, then, Enlightenment Man is plunged into a certain tragic impotence. There is no merit in bestriding a world which you have knocked the stuffing out of. Who esteems the recognition of slaves? Voluntarism, or the cult of the imperial will, is the other face of nihilism. Unless the Iraqis and their fellow victims of Western imperialism assent to your rule, your own sovereignty will simply be discredited, however much of their oil you may conveniently snatch in the meantime. Yet such hegem-

ON TELLING THE TRUTH    273

ony implies accurate knowledge, which is exactly what the psychotic fantasy known as absolute power undermines. If such power acknowledges the truth of its adversary, it ceases to be absolute; if it does not, it ceases to be effective.

A form of reason which can take in the whole world at a glance, rather like some super-surveillance device of the future, must be abstract enough to find particularity a problem. The Enlightenment threatens to deliver us the kind of knowledge which is so general that it is unable to penetrate the particular. There can be no science of an individual daisy or tadpole, as there can be a science of the species as a whole. We are faced with the absurdity of a form of truth-production so powerful that it is brought to its knees by the sensuously specific. Reason is accordingly in need of a prosthesis, a kind of sub- or pseudo-science which will grant it access to the uniquely particular; and this is known as the aesthetic, which was invented in 1750 at the heart of Enlightenment Europe.[2] There could now be a science of the concrete, which would later re-emerge as phenomenology and *Lebensphiloso-phie*. Indeed, if there could not be such a science we would be in serious political trouble, since how can reason hold sway over a citizenry of which it has no inside knowledge? If coercion is to give way to hegemony, a sovereign rationality must know the truth of the subject; and this is one function (there are other, more subversive ones) of the novel in modern times, which as a kind of dramatized sociology represents a knowledge more 'lived' and inward than anything political science can provide.

This contest between truth and power comes to a head in modern times, but it has pre-modern origins in the medieval theological debates between realists and nominalists. Theological realists like Thomas Aquinas tend to hold that the world is a particular way, and that even God must respect this fact. It was he, after all, who decided to make it that way, and like the rest of us he must live with his mistakes. For nominalists like Duns Scotus, by contrast, God cannot be restricted by his own Creation, so that the way things are must be purely arbitrary. God must surely be able to make $2 + 2 = 5$, or turn Dick Cheney into a drag queen, if he is to be omnipotent. For the nominalists power trumps truth; and postmodern relativists, for whom the way the world is, is either no way at all or entirely arbitrary, are their latter-day inheritors. They are, so to speak, the modern dunces.

In this sense, that most fashionable of all postmodern doctrines – anti-essentialism – has a spectacularly dubious political history. It is only because postmodern theorists do not read such uncool authors as Scotus or Aquinas that this fact has not come to light. For the medieval anti-realists, there was no essential truth to things, since such essences would simply obstruct the infinite power of the Almighty. For the postmodernists, rather similarly, the world must be random, protean, diffuse and fuzzy at the edges if subjectivity (or, for the more cynical of the postmodern brigade, consumerism) is to be unfettered. But for 'God' in medieval debates one can always read the 'United States' in contemporary ones. Indeed, since America is such an egregiously godly nation, no parallel could be more appropriate. The more you strike essences from the world, the more you leave it clay in the hands of the all-mighty. There is no more devout anti-essentialist than absolute power. Truths must be constructed rather than inherent if they are not to act as a brake upon one's projects. If a thing has no identity of its own, it will all the more compliantly take the impress of yours.

The latest postmodern assault on truth is known in the White House as faith-based politics. This is not quite, as it first appears, a matter of ignoring facts which do not chime with your political views, but of ignoring facts which do not fit in with certain other facts. As far as theories of truth go, then, it has a smack of coherentism about it, but also of constructivism. In fact, so-called faith-based politics simply presses some common-or-garden postmodern doctrine to a parodic extreme. It is a commonplace of the work of critics like Stanley Fish, for example, that facts are simply whatever our interpretative frameworks constrain us to define as such.[3] Truth, in a word, is institutional. It is not that facts give rise to interpretations, but that insti-tutionalized interpretations give birth to facts. What you count as a factual truth will be defined by your interests, beliefs, commitments and desires.

As for some Kuhnian philosophy of science, then, there cannot be argument over the facts, since conflicting interpretative communities will formulate the issues at stake in ways which leave no common ground of agreed facts for them to scrap over. There are no conflicts, simply incom-mensurabilities. What you adduce as evidence for your conservative view of the world will not constitute evidence for a radical like myself, since what counts as evidence is determined by our prior commitments and beliefs. It is always possible to say 'But that's not what I call a fact!', in a kind of Nelson's-eye epistemology. We can know the world is there because it resists us, but on this theory what counts as such resistance varies from one conceptual frame-work to another. The fact that a number of people in Washington as I write seem not to have noticed that there is widespread native resistance to their authority in Iraq, perceiving instead only a small handful of crazed foreign infiltrators, is a political version of this point.

Where, then, do those interests and beliefs hail from? The critique of ideology has traditionally had something to say on this question, but a post-ideological history is bound to be reduced to silence on this question. It will not do to suggest, as classical thinkers from Aristotle to Marx have claimed, that one's interests, beliefs and desires arise from a reflection upon how it is with the world. On the contrary, for this post-classical theory, this is to stand the matter on its head, since one's view of how it is with the world arises from one's interests, beliefs and desires. The traditional ethico-political question was always: what is to be done, given the facts of the matter? And this involved trying to steer a troublesome passage from fact to value, theory to practice. You could, it was supposed, work your way up from how it was to how it should be – from how things stood to how you should go to work on them. Truth in the empirical sense could generate true action in the moral or political sense.

Postmodernism decisively severs this bond, but in a novel kind of way. Now, no amount of investigation of the way things are will tell you how to act – not, however, as some previous thinkers considered, because it is hard to see how you can move from the one domain to the other, but because 'the way things are' is in any case constructed by your values and desires. There are not really two distinct spheres here at all, which is why the question of how to negotiate a passage from one to the other becomes irrelevant.

Postmodernism dissolves the so-called naturalistic fallacy, however, only at an immense price. For interests, beliefs and desires are now left hanging in the air, bereft of any foundation in factual truth. They are the primordial bedrock which one cannot dig beneath, since what you found there if you did would itself be determined by them. And this conveniently seals such beliefs from critical inquiry. One is lumbered with one's beliefs rather as one might be afflicted by typhoid. Reason is no court of appeal here, since your interests and beliefs will determine what counts as reasonable in the first place. Whereas truth was once an absolute perched sublimely above empirical history, now it is desires and interests which are absolute. You cannot get behind them, any more than you can get behind the Almighty. A pragmatic age has landed itself with a new kind of transcendentalism.

In fact, if you are to have a candidate for the absolute at all, truth is a far more plausible one than interests, beliefs and desires. These latter are self-evidently empirical and historical, whereas truth is historical in a rather more ambiguous kind of way. There are, to be sure, all kinds of different truths in different situations; but it would be hard to imagine a human culture which lacked the concept of something being the case, and still lived to tell the tale. Perhaps this is what makes the difference between a historical and a historicist view of truth. We should not imagine that all timeless truths are exalted: some truths are unchanging because they are sub-historical rather than supra-historical, pertinent to the kind of material animals that we are. In the end, it is our bodies which give us an objective world. There is objectivity for a tiger, one which overlaps with our own version of it; but it is not entirely our sort of objectivity, since our bodies, and thus our material forms of life, are so different. Perhaps this is what Wittgenstein had in mind when he remarked in the *Philosophical Investigations* that if a lion could speak, we would not be able to understand what it said.

Besides, if modes of truth-production are undeniably historical, the product itself is less obviously so. This, perhaps, is the kernel of truth to be rescued from rationalism. States of affairs are historically shifting, but true statements about them are not. If it is true today that capitalism is an unjust form of life, then the claim will still be valid long after the system has passed away. It has not ceased to be true that Ireland entered into a union with Britain in 1800 simply because it is no longer 1800. One can contrast this with aesthetic judgements. It may well be that the judgement that Shakespeare is an inferior writer was true for some critics in 1750 but was not true in 1950. What is beautiful in Tonga is probably not what is beautiful in Toronto. Claims about truth and falsehood, however, outlive their historical moments, a fact which historicist theories of truth generally fail to take account of. Whether moral claims are more like factual or aesthetic ones in this respect is a matter of ferocious contention. If slavery is wrong in 2005, was it therefore wrong in 50 BC?

There is a sense, then, in which faith-based politics is postmodern theory in action, however distasteful both parties might find the affinity. Paul Wolfowitz might be surprised to hear that he is in some sense in the same camp as a bunch of long-haired moral relativists who delight in Robert Mapplethorpe. But the fact that postmodernism is largely irreligious should not obscure the parallel between the two positions. Faith-based politics, like the Bush White House in general, is a curious mixture of mean-minded pragmatism and visionary idealism, since if you treat truth as purely instrumental it can play no cognitive role in restraining your vainglorious fantasies. For both creeds, there is something called belief which goes all the way down, and with which there is finally no arguing. Foundational truths go out of the window, then, but only to leave you with a different kind of dogmatism.

Taken together, these beliefs and commitments, along with their associated practices, make up what we call a culture. What is now absolute, in the sense of immune from fundamental rational inquiry, is not some Platonic Idea, Christian God or Spinozist Substance but, ironically enough, the everyday, variable stuff of a specific way of life. It is here, as Wittgenstein would say, that one's theoretical spade hits rock bottom, and one is forced to bring argument to a close with the wry acknowledgement: 'This is just the kind of thing we do'. Truth is a product of cultural convention. Of course there are still true or false judgements to be passed on this or that question; but what falls outside their scope is the deep cultural grammar which allows us to identify such issues and pass such judgements in the first place. This grammar cannot itself be spoken of as true or false, any more than one could claim that Hindi is grammatically superior to Hungarian. This cultural logic is now as much immune to critique as the most lofty forms of classical Reason. Culture becomes the transcendental condition of truth.

Culture is a popular idea with postmodernism for all kinds of reasons, but one of them is that it seems to conflate the realms of fact and value, a move which, as we have seen already, is typical of postmodern thought. It is both a descriptive term and a normative one, a distinctive way of doing things and an implicit commendation of this condition. It is not only a fact that particular groups of people do things in their own unique way, but somehow commendable that they do so. The very fact of diverse cultures is also a value. Plurality is always preferable to homogeneity – so that a range of politically diverse societies, a few of them with neo-fascist leanings, would on this reasoning be preferable to a dreary continuum of socialist-feminist ones. As with most liberals and some adolescents, what is valuable is not so much what I do as the fact that *I* choose to do it, in my uniquely self-expressive way.

Noam Chomsky remarks somewhere that the conception of an intellectual as one who speaks truth to power is mistaken on two counts. For one thing, power knows the truth already; and for another thing, it is not power, but its victims, who need the truth most urgently. It comes as no surprise that most of those who are cavalier about the idea of truth these days have no pressing political need for it. It is not an insistent political imperative for Stanford professors, as it might be for Malaysian sweatshop workers. But one might amplify Chomsky's point by adding that power does not need to be told the truth because it is in some ways irrelevant to it. Not, to be sure, in every way: Western capitalism holds sincerely to such moral truths as the beneficial nature of free markets or the ennobling character of liberal democracy. In practice, however, such large moral truths are supposed to interfere with the system's operations as little as possible. If postmodernism tends to collapse facts and values, the capitalist system itself continues to hold them as rigorously apart as any dedicated Kantian. Moral truths are like alcohol: it is when they start interfering with your everyday life that it is time to give them up.

Take, for example, George Bush's talk of freedom, or – as he sometimes calls it to prove that he is not semantically impoverished – liberty. Freedom is a wonderfully convenient concept for Western politicians, because it has both a high-minded spiritual and a low-minded material sense, and one can seem to be meaning the former while in fact intending the latter. Freedom is what the lost souls of Guatanamo Bay thirst for, and what piles Iraqi hospitals high with mutilated bodies. It is what inspires Saudi dissidents and bankrupts small farmers. It is one of the few languages in which archbishops and chief executives, oilmen and Oxford philosophers, are equally fluent. One can point, naturally, to the contradictions between Bush's talk of freedom and his squalid support for right-wing autocracies. But this is not quite the point. For this is to assume that such high-pitched rhetorical talk is actually intended to hook directly on to practical affairs; and this would be a kind of category mistake, rather as if one were to take the sob-choked platitudes of an Oscar winner as some incisively analytic discourse, to be scribbled down and assiduously checked for its scientific veracity.

Ideology is indeed intended to legitimate your behaviour, but in a way which is no more intended to withstand too literal or intent a scrutiny than one's perfunctory inquiry after the health of a colleague's cousin. High moral truths and low empirical facts belong to different genres, so to speak, which move at different levels and are governed by different protocols. Bush's talk of freedom is certainly in earnest, but so is a fine performance of *Macbeth*. High-pitched moral truths are constructed to accommodate a fair amount of ambiguity and inconsistency. It belongs to our values to regret that we that we do not always live up to our values. 'Let freedom light a million fires in the hearts of men!', or some such inanity, is not meant to be sheer humbug, but neither is it meant to have the same status as 'I could just fancy a Melton Mowbray pork pie'. One should not, in the technical jargon of linguistic theory, take the performative language of ideology in too constative a spirit.

This is one reason why the postmodern idea that an assault on truth is somehow radical is so mistaken. The fact is that those who run the present system are not much interested in truth at all; but the postmodernists fail to see this because they take them at their word when they spout about eternal verities. They imagine that advanced capitalism still needs essences, absolutes and unchanging ideals, and that to deconstruct these things is therefore to undermine the system. It is true that the United States is at present touting a virulently metaphysical version of the free market, which could certainly do with a spot of deconstruction. But this is untypical of capitalist states, most of which are secular, pragmatic and disenchanted, and which are forced to be so by virtue of their own material operations. Ideology usually has a more high-pitched, hand-on-heart, metaphysical ring to it in the USA, given the nation's peculiar religious background. But it is not beyond question that capitalism in general could easily survive the death of metaphysics, even if it is true that God, in Johnsonian phrase, has been an unconscionable time a-dying ever since Nietzsche issued his somewhat premature obituary notice for him. What will help to keep God and metaphysics alive for the present, no doubt, is the fact that the West is fighting a full-bloodedly metaphysical adversary. The fact that they speak of Allah and Mohammed means that you must counter them with you own native gods, Freedom and Democracy.

Most pre-modern civilizations would no doubt have found extraordinary the idea that one could conduct one's political or economic affairs other than in the context of moral and cultural norms. Socialism is an attempt to revive this notion for the modern age. If the truth in its ethico-political sense is largely irrelevant to late capitalism, it is among other reasons because there is something embarrassingly amateur about it in a thoroughly technologized world. There are no technical qualifications in moral indignation. In a tightly stratified, professionalized society, anything that anyone can do, such as tying a child's shoelaces or objecting to the destruction of the planet, is bound to be devalued. The humanities, which specialize in moral truth, are thus bound to seem rather quaint in this context. Confronted with such hard-nosed professionalism, they must decide whether to beat it or join it – whether to launch a humanistic critique of its soulless procedures, or whether to imitate those procedures by going positivist or scientistic themselves. Marxism has been viewed at different times in both lights, as both a moral critique of scientism and a scientistic critique of morality.

The problem with trying to beat your adversary is irrelevance. Since late capitalism, as we have seen, does not in practice lose much sleep over moral truth, your critique is bound to move at a different level from its target. The problem with seeking to join the system, of which behaviourist psychology or high structuralism are examples, is that you win accreditation only at the risk of losing your identity. Along with beating and joining there is also trumping, of which post-structuralism, hermeneutics and the later philosophy of Wittgenstein may serve as examples. The point here is to claim that scientific and technological truth are simply specialized versions of everyday knowledge, much more like moral or artistic discourse than is commonly recognized. This tends to work splendidly in universities, but not so splendidly in government ministries or corporation boardrooms. It also tends to land you with some rather embarrassing right-wing allies.

Caught in this dilemma, the humanities can always make a meta-move, taking as their object of critique the very fact that the prevailing system is largely impervious to moral critique. But this does not resolve the conflict between an 'amateur' ethical humanism and the technical or professional system it seeks to criticize. What is needed is a discourse which is both technical and humane, ethical and analytical, and it is this which characterizes all the most interesting moments of literary criticism. By far the most ancient form of such criticism, rhetoric, concerns itself with both the rigorous analysis of language and the practice of moral or political persuasion. Each dimension, moreover, is viewed in terms of the other. In the twentieth century, the so-called Cambridge school of criticism (the Leavises, Empson, I.A. Richards, L.C. Knights and their colleagues) saw an internal relation between rigorous verbal discrimination and the spiritual health of an entire civilization.

George Orwell lent this view a more radical inflection, while the Russian Formalists, the European avant gardes and (with a different political colour) the American New Criticism were likewise alert to the bonds between technical linguistic analysis and political critique. The most distinguished of all British twentieth-century cultural critics, Raymond Williams, was bred in this 'Cambridge' lineage, while the great European philologists from Bakhtin and Auerbach to Curtius and Spitzer yoked the most formidable professional erudition to a generously humanistic vision. What the literary work shares in common with the culture around it is language, which provides the vital link between the two; and this is also a link between the delicately particularized and the ambitiously abstract. At its worst, literary criticism has been a parody of both, linking a vacuous moral universalism to a myopic cult of the particular.

Such universalism, however, has been increasingly on the defensive in a period of militant particularism. There are no longer universal truths, simply claims about the world which cannot be abstracted from their political origins and effects. This is a misleading opposition, since in the militant epoch of the middle class, the doctrine of universal truth was itself closely bound up with a revolutionary politics. Once that revolution was accomplished, however, and the bourgeoisie no longer needed to pitch their struggle in such grandly totalising terms, postmodern particularism becomes the order of the day. Universalism and internationalism give way to those rather different animals, globalization and cosmopolitanism.

In the writing of neo-Nietzscheans like Michel Foucault, a suspicion of truth is part of a well-nigh pathological aversion to the whole notion of subjectivity.[4] For there clearly can be no truths without human subjects; and human subjects are simply those bodies in which power has scooped out a hollow known as personal inwardness or psychological interiority, so that it might subjugate them all the more effectively. Creatures without truth are creatures without chains, and the whole notion of emancipatory knowledge comes to seem like a contradiction in terms. Self-reflection is not the first step towards freedom, but a thickening and refining of the very subjective stuff in whose folds power secretes itself, while craftily fostering in us the illusion that our inwardness is a value rather than a form of bondage. There is an echo of the Schopenhaurian Will in this gloomy scenario — indeed, Schopenhauer stands to Hegel rather as Foucault stands to Marx. Both of them give a pessimistic twist to Enlightenment thought, regarding the human autonomy it values so highly as the ruse of a power or Reason which has turned malevolent.

Foucault's aversion to subjectivity is in part a structuralist hostility to consciousness as such, one he inherits from his mentor Louis Althusser. He is not even prepared to speak of ideology, a term with too subject-centred a resonance, and prefers to discuss 'technologies' instead. Althusser does not himself censor the term as 'humanistic'; but his celebrated essay on the topic sails close to a kind of social behaviourism, one for which ideology is more or less identical to the performance of certain practices.[5] There is a touch of the renegade Roman Catholic in this: the Catholic church has always insisted in its quasi-materialist way on faith as a matter of ritual and codified conduct, not of some jealously preserved Protestant inwardness. Grab them by their behaviour and their minds and hearts will follow is a venerable papist precept. For Althusser, it is ideology which opens up that illusory inner sanctum known as autonomous subjectivity, in order to build itself a home there. It is, so to speak, a parasite which creates its own host. Once again, then, subjectivity is contaminated from the outset, and truth along with it. This is why Althusser must split off truth from subjectivity, in that knowledge-without-a-subject which is science or theory.

Theory for Althusser can provide a critique of society because, like Spinoz-ist Reason, it can inspect it as though from the outside, sealed off from the vicissitudes of history in some windless enclosure of its own. Ideology, by contrast, cannot provide a basis for such critique, since it is not really a matter of consciousness at all but of unreflective everyday practice. In this sense, the opposite ends of our brief history of truth come together in Althusser's work: ideas are both elevated above history *and* too bound up with the world to gain a critical purchase upon it. Foucault, for his part, certainly wants such a critical perspective; but it is one which can only be implicit in his historical researches, since he rejects Althusser's Theory and presents a reworked version of his notion of ideology. Ideas are so bound up with historical formations, so pre-eminently practical and material, that they would seem unable to establish the kind of distance from their contexts which might allow them to reflect critically upon them. And this must logically apply to Foucault himself. It is here that his adroitly affect-less literary style rides to the rescue, insinuating in its dispassionate *hauteur* a kind of critical distance from the materials he presents which cannot, in fact, be theoretically justified.

What would appear to be missing here, crushed out of existence between truths which are too ideal and truths which are too pragmatic, is the fact that critical reflection is part of the way we inhabit our history, not a way of standing disinterestedly apart from it. Getting some critical distance from our contexts is part of the peculiar way we are bound up with them. As self-transcending (which is to say, historical) beings, we are never either wholly inside or wholly outside a situation, but cusped perpetually between the two. It is this which allows us to act and simultaneously to reflect on our action. The pragmatists and neo-Nietzscheans, by contrast, draw from the fact that ideas are always materially 'situated' the false conclusion that overall critique is thereby impossible. In a move which is astonishing to those for whom critique and materialism are intimately allied, the critical function of knowledge is sacrificed to its material character.

These thinkers are so eager to combat idealist notions of truth, by insisting (quite properly) on the historical, institutional, socially interested nature of knowledge, that they fail to notice that they have just deprived themselves of all critical vantage-point on the status quo. In their view, to stand back from ourselves that far means falling over the epistemological edge. To subject our way of life to such full-blooded criticism, we would need to leap out of our own skins, gazing upon ourselves with the estranging eyes of a Venusian. They do not see that situatedness and radical critique belong together. One must be, as they say, in a position to know – which is why, say, women or poor peasants or the victims of Western imperialism know more of the truth of their condition than their masters. If they were standing nowhere at all, which is what some mistakenly take objectivity to mean, they would know nothing whatsoever. Nothing is as blind as a God's eye view. Not everyone is so situated as to be capable of objective judgements. One can usually tell those who are not from the way they place the term objectivity in scare quotes.

Nietzsche taught us to see truth in quasi-biological terms, as bound up with the struggle of the species for mastery over its natural environment. Our faculty of cognition has itself evolved; and one precious development of it, ironically enough, is that refusal to grant too grandiose a role to consciousness which Nietzsche himself shares with Marx and Freud. For the most fertile currents of modern philosophy, there is always something prior to thought – something which puts it in place but partially evades its grasp, whether one calls it labour or being-in-the-world, difference or the Other, power, the unconscious or the pre-reflective. Yet though Nietzsche seeks to dethrone consciousness in this materialist way, he is strikingly unconcerned with the social or institutional basis of truth, a project which is taken up by some of his successors.

Once this happens, however, there is always a danger of conflating the two kinds of inquiry. For what does it mean to claim that ideas are driven by interests? It can mean, for example, that we have the kind of conceptual world we do because of an arduous evolutionary struggle, in which our senses evolve in ways necessary for certain species-specific kinds of activity.

This, if you like, is a sort of pragmatism; but it is a 'deep', quasi-anthropological variety, pitched in flagrantly unRortyan fashion at the level of the material species itself. But it can then be easily run together with a less ontological, more ideological sense of the interest-driven nature of knowledge, such as the drug companies' suborning of medical research. Since both are instances of 'interested' knowledge, a certain kind of postmodern cynic can argue that the latter sort of thing is really quite as inevitable as the former. Those who object to the suborning of medical research or the denial of global warming can thus be mocked as pathetically old-fashioned champions of the myth of disinterestedness.

In a similar way, the Wittgensteinian appeal to 'forms of life' hovers ambiguously between the anthropological and the political. When we say 'this is just the kind of thing we do', do we mean such things as imagining time moving forwards, counting in a certain style or distinguishing between the animate and inanimate, or do we mean failing to donate mosquito nets to Africa because we are too stingy? How far down do forms of life go? The fact that what counts as disinterested inquiry is determined by criteria deeply embedded in our culture is not to say that there is no such thing. What else could it possibly be? Wittgenstein himself did not believe in some idea of truth quite independent of our species-being or deep cultural grammar; but this did not mean that he endorsed the politics of his own culture. It did not stop him from referring scornfully to the British Cabinet as a lot of wealthy old men, or running off to Moscow in the depth of the Stalinist terror in the hope of being trained as a doctor there.

One way of distinguishing between radicals and others is that radicals suspect that the truth is usually unpleasant. In this sense, it resembles the inevitable. Leftists tend to practise a hermeneutic of suspicion: the truth, they believe, is usually uglier and more discreditable than the general consensus imagines. The truth may be precious, but it is not on the whole congenial. This is not cynicism: on the contrary, it arises from radicals' lack of trust in the present political system, which arises in turn from their faith in the human capacities which it stifles. Even so, it is difficult to distrust a great deal of what is said around you without becoming sardonic and hardboiled, qualities which are at odds with the political faith which leads you to such distrust in the first place. It is true that scepticism and faith are not in the end at loggerheads, since a realist ethics maintains that only in confronting the worst can you hope to overcome it. In this sense, it has much in common with the tragic vision. In anything less than the long term, however, it is hard to be sceptical of much that passes for truth without turning into the kind of person you least want in any decent civilization of the future. 'I wouldn't want to be part of a society that included the likes of me' is the socialist version of Groucho's joke. Those who fight hard and bitterly for justice are often compelled to be least exemplary of the social order they prefigure.

There is, however, a rather less downbeat perspective as well. The truth, like diamonds, is valuable partly because it is hard to get at. Marx thought that if the truth was spontaneously available on the surface of things, there would be no need for science. It is because there is a gap between how things are and how they appear that science is necessary. It looks as though the sun is coming up, but actually the earth is going down. The truth for Marx is what goes on behind our backs. It belongs to the truth, as Martin Heidegger argued, that it withdraws or conceals itself; and this concealment is built into it, not just some regrettable accident. That phenomena do not spontaneously divulge the truth of themselves is part of that truth.

This, in turn, means that knowledge and virtue are closely allied. For if the truth is not self-evident, then establishing it involves such moral qualities as patience, humility, tenacity, selflessness, self-discipline, self-criticism, clear-sightedness, a nose for humbug and the like. And since the truth, as we have suggested, is generally rebarbative, it also involves honesty, courage and a readiness to break ranks. The Platonists may be mistaken to see a link between truth and beauty, though mathematicians and astrophysicists may beg to differ; but they are surely not wrong to see a connection between truth and goodness. So though truth and virtue may be in conflict when it comes to the hermeneutic of suspicion, this is one sense in which they are on intimate terms with one another.

Freud is only one of a mighty lineage of thinkers to have taught us that the mind's capacity for self-deception is well-nigh bottomless; but he is unduly reticent when it comes to the other story that must be told – that the human longing for truth, even quite useless truth, has the ferocious persistence of a biological drive, and like hunger or sexual desire is not easily suppressed. Even so, though we need the truth in order to thrive, it is not what we live for. Nietzsche thought that to love truth at all costs was a kind of madness. If truth is indispensable to justice and compassion, it is not as important as they are. Those who find themselves living for the truth – who spend their time, for example, fighting some gross deception on the part of the state – are admirable, but they are not a model of how to live, as they themselves might be the first to acknowledge. In a decent society, they would not need to campaign in this way. If postmodernism generally undervalues truth, it is partly because some of its modernistic predecessors made a fetish out of it. Perhaps it is when we come to need the truth less urgently that we will realize that our political emancipation is complete.

## NOTES

1   See Charles Taylor, *The Sources of the Self*, Cambridge: Harvard University Press, 1989, Part 3. The classic account of the emergence of realism is Eric Auerbach, *Mimesis*, Princeton: Princeton University Press, 1953.

2   See my *The Ideology of the Aesthetic* (Oxford: Basil Blackwell, 1990), ch. 1.

3   See, for example, Stanley Fish, *Doing What Comes Naturally*, Oxford: Oxford University Press, 1989.

4   See, for example, Michel Foucault, *The Order of Things*, London: Tavistock, 1970, and *The Archaeology of Knowledge*, London: Tavistock, 1972.

5   See Louis Althusser, 'On Ideology and Ideological State Apparatuses', in *Lenin and Philosophy*, London: Verso, 1971.

# Socialist Register – Published Annually Since 1964

Leo Panitch and Colin Leys – Editors
**2005: THE EMPIRE RELOADED**

How does the new American empire work? Who runs it? How stable is it?
What is the new American Empire's impact throughout the world?
What is its influence on gender relations? On the media? On popular culture?

Contents: Stephen Gill: The Contradictions of American Supremacy; Varda Burstyn: The New Imperial Order Foretold; Leo Panitch & Sam Gindin: Finance and American Empire
Chris Rude: The Role of Financial Discipline in Imperial Strategy; Scott Forsyth: Hollywood Reloaded: The Film as Imperial Commodity; Harriet Friedman: Feeding the Empire: Agriculture, Livelihood and the Crisis of the Global Food Regime; Vivek Chibber: Reviving the Developmental State? The Myth of the 'National Bourgeoisie'; Gerard Greenfield: Bandung redux: Imperialism and Anti-Globalization Nationalisms in Southeast Asia; Yuezhi Zhao: China and Global Capitalism: the Cultural Dimension; Patrick Bond: US Empire and South African Subimperialism; Doug Stokes: US Counterinsurgency in Colombia; Paul Cammack: 'Signs of the Times': Capitalism, Competitiveness, and the New Faces of Empire in Latin America; Boris Kagarlitsky: The Russian State in the Age of American Empire; John Grahl: The European Union and American Power; Dorothee Bohle: The EU and Eastern Europe: Failing the Test as a Better World Power; Frank Deppe: Habermas' Manifesto for a European Renaissance: A Critique; Tony Benn & Colin Leys: Bush and Blair: Iraq and the American Viceroy

343 pp. 234 x 156 mm.

**0850365465 hbk £35.00**                                          **0850365473 pbk £14.95**
*Canada: Fernwood Publishing; USA: Monthly Review Press; UK and Rest of World: Merlin Press*

Leo Panitch and Colin Leys – Editors
**2004: THE NEW IMPERIAL CHALLENGE**

"As Rosa Luxemburg observed, it is 'often hard to determine, within the tangle of violence and contests for power, the stern laws of economic process.' This is what Panitch, Gindin, Harvey, Gowan, and their colleagues on the Marxist left are trying to do …. For this, whatevever our other differences, the rest of us owe them much gratitude" George Scialabba, *Dissent*, Spring 2004

What does imperialism mean in the new century?
Do we need new concepts to understand it?
Who benefits, who suffers? Where? Why?

Contents: Leo Panitch & Sam Gindin: Global Capitalism and American Empire; Aijaz Ahmad: Imperialism of Our Time; David Harvey: The 'New' Imperialism - Accumulation by Dispossession; Greg Albo: The Old and New Economics of Imperialism; Noam Chomsky: Truths and Myths about the Invasion of Iraq; Amy Bartholomew & Jennifer Breakspear: Human Rights as Swords of Empire; Paul Rogers: The US Military Posture - 'A Uniquely Benign Imperialism'?; Michael T. Klare: Blood for Oil - The Bush-Cheney Energy Strategy; John Bellamy Foster & Brett Clark: Ecological Imperialism - The Curse of Capitalism; Tina Wallace: NGO Dilemmas - Trojan Horses for Global Neoliberalism?; John Saul: Globalization, Imperialism, Development - False Binaries and Radical Resolutions; Emad Aysha: The Limits and Contradictions of 'Americanization'; Bob Sutcliffe: Crossing Borders in the New Imperialism.

290 pp. 234 x 156 mm.

0850365341 hbk £30.00                                            085036535X pbk £14.95
*Canada: Fernwood Publishing; USA: Monthly Review Press; UK and Rest of World: Merlin Press*

Leo Panitch and Colin Leys – Editors
**2003: FIGHTING IDENTITIES – Race, Religion And Ethno-Nationalism**

"these contributions... show a left able to avoid both economic reductionism and post-modern identity-fetishism in confronting and understanding a world of mounting anxiety, instability and violence." Stephen Marks, *Tribune*.

Contents: Peter Gowan: The American Campaign for Global Sovereignty; Aziz Al-Azmeh: Postmodern Obscurantism and 'the Muslim Question'; Avishai Ehrlich: Palestine, Global Politics and Israeli Judaism; Susan Woodward: The Political Economy of Ethno-Nationalism in Yugoslavia; Georgi Derluguian: How Soviet Bureaucracy Produced Nationalism and what came of it in Azerbaijan; Pratyush Chandra: Linguistic-Communal Politics and Class Conflict in India; Mahmood Mamdani: Making Sense of Political Violence in Postcolonial Africa; Hugh Roberts: The Algerian Catastrophe: Lessons for the Left; Stephen Castles: The International Politics of Forced Migration; Hans-Georg Betz: Xenophobia, Identity Politics and Exclusionary Populism in Western Europe; Jörg Flecker: The European Right and Working Life- From ordinary miseries to political disasters; Huw Beynon & Lou Kushnick: Cool Britannia or Cruel Britannia? Racism and New Labour; Bill Fletcher Jr. & Fernando Gapasin: The Politics of Labour and Race in the USA; Amory Starr: Is the North American Anti-Globalization Movement Racist? Critical reflections; Stephanie Ross: Is This What Democracy Looks Like? -The politics of the anti-globalization movement in North America; Sergio Baierle: The Porto Alegre Thermidor: Brazil's 'Participatory Budget' at the crossroads; Nancy Leys Stepan: Science and Race: Before and after the Genome Project; John S. Saul: Identifying Class, Classifying Difference

396 pp, 234 x 156 mm.

0850365074 hbk £29.95                                            0850365082 pbk £16.95
*Canada: Fernwood Publishing; USA: Monthly Review Press; UK and Rest of World: Merlin Press*

Leo Panitch and Colin Leys – Editors
**2002: A WORLD OF CONTRADICTIONS**

Timely and critical analysis of what big businesses and their governments want, and of the problems they create.

**Contents:** Naomi Klein: Farewell To 'The End Of History': Organization And Vision In Anti-Corporate Movements; André Drainville: Québec City 2001 and The Making Of Transnational Subjects; Gérard Duménil & Dominique Lévy: The Nature and Contradictions of Neoliberalism; Elmar Altvater: The Growth Obsession; David Harvey The Art Of Rent: Globalization, Monopoly and The Commodification of Culture; Graham Murdock & Peter Golding: Digital Possibilities, Market Realities: The Contradictions of Communications Convergence; Reg Whitaker: The Dark Side of Life: Globalization and International Crime; Guglielmo Carchedi: Imperialism, Dollarization and The Euro; Susanne Soederberg: The New International Financial Architecture: Imposed Leadership and 'Emerging Markets'; Paul Cammack: Making Poverty Work; Marta Russell & Ravi Malhotra: Capitalism and Disability; Michael Kidron: The Injured Self; David Miller: Media Power and Class Power: Overplaying Ideology; Pablo Gonzalez Casanova: Negotiated Contradictions; Ellen Wood: Contradictions: Only in Capitalism?

293 pp, 234 x 156 mm.

0850365023 hbk £30.00                                           0850365015 pbk £16.95
*Canada: Fernwood Publishing; USA: Monthly Review Press; UK and Rest of World: Merlin Press*

**Previous volumes:**

Leo Panitch and Colin Leys – Editors
**2001: WORKING CLASSES, GLOBAL REALITIES**

Socialist Register 2001 examines the concept and the reality of class as it effects workers at the beginning of the 21st Century.

"an excellent collection". Bill Fletcher, *Against The Current*

**Contents:** Leo Panitch & Colin Leys with Greg Albo & David Coates: Preface; Ursula Huws: The Making of a Cybertariat? Virtual Work in a Real World ; Henry Bernstein: 'The Peasantry' in Global Capitalism: Who, Where and Why?; Beverly J. Silver and Giovanni Arrighi: Workers North and South; Andrew Ross: No-Collar Labour in America's 'New Economy'; Barbara Harriss-White & Nandini Gooptu: Mapping India's World of Unorganized Labour; Patrick Bond, Darlene Miller & Greg Ruiters: The Southern African Working Class: Production, Reproduction and Politics; Steve Jefferys: Western European Trade Unionism at 2000; David Mandel: 'Why is there no revolt?' The Russian Working Class and Labour Movement; Haideh Moghissi & Saeed Rahnema: The Working Class and the Islamic State in Iran ; Huw Beynon & Jorge Ramalho: Democracy and the Organization of Class Struggle in Brazil; Gerard Greenfield: Organizing, Protest and Working Class Self-Activity: Reflections on East Asia; Rohini Hensman: Organizing Against the Odds: Women in India's Informal Sector; Eric Mann: 'A race struggle, a class struggle, a women's struggle all at once': Organizing on the Buses of L.A.; Justin Paulson: Peasant Struggles and International Solidarity: the Case of Chiapas; Judith Adler Hellman: Virtual Chiapas: A Reply to Paulson ; Peter Kwong: The Politics of Labour Migration: Chinese Workers in New York; Brigitte Young: The 'Mistress' and the Maid' in the Globalized Economy; Rosemary Warskett: Feminism's Challenge to Unions in the North: Possibilities and Contradictions; Sam Gindin: Turning Points and Starting Points: Brenner, Left Turbulence and Class Politics; Leo Panitch: Reflections on Strategy for Labour.

403 pp. 232 x 155 mm.

0 85036 491 4 hbk £30.00                                    0 85036 490 6 pbk £16.95

*Canada: Fernwood Publishing; USA: Monthly Review Press; UK and Rest of World: Merlin Press*

Leo Panitch and Colin Leys – Editors
**2000: NECESSARY AND UNNECESSARY UTOPIAS**

What is Utopia? An economy that provides everyone's needs? A society which empowers all people? A healthy, peaceful and supportive environment ? Better worlds are both necessary and possible. "This excursion to utopia is full of surprise, inspiration and challenge". Peter Waterman

**Contents:** Preface; Transcending Pessimism: Rekindling Socialist Imagination: Leo Panitch & Sam Gindin; Minimum Utopia: Ten Theses: Norman Geras; Utopia and its Opposites: Terry Eagleton; On the Necessity of Conceiving the Utopian in a Feminist Fashion: Frigga Haug; Socialized Markets; not Market Socialism: Diane Elson; The Chimera of the Third Way: Alan Zuege; Other Pleasures: The Attractions of Post-consumerism: Kate Soper; Utopian Families: Johanna Brenner; Outbreaks of Democracy: Ricardo Blaug; Real and Virtual Chiapas: Magic Realism and the Left: Judith Adler Hellman; The Centrality of Agriculture: History; Ecology And Feasible Socialism: Colin Duncan; Democratise or Perish: The Health Sciences as a Path for Social Change: Julian Tudor Hart; The Dystopia of our Times: Genetic Technology and Other Afflictions: Varda Burstyn; Warrior Nightmares: Reactionary Populism at the Millennium: Carl Boggs; The Real Meaning of the War Over Kosovo: Peter Gowan.

301 pp. 232 x 155 mm.

0 85036 488 4 hbk £30.00                                    0 85036 487 6 pbk £14.95

*Canada: Fernwood Publishing; USA: Monthly Review Press; UK and Rest of World: Merlin Press*

Leo Panitch and Colin Leys – Editors
**1999: GLOBAL CAPITALISM VS. DEMOCRACY**

The essays here not only examine the contradictions of both neo-liberalism and 'progressive competitiveness', but demonstrate that no democracy worth the name can any longer be conceived except in terms of a fundamental break with it.

**Contents:** Preface; Taking Globalisation Seriously: Hugo Radice; Material World: The Myth of the Weightless Economy: Ursula Huws; Globalisation and the Executive Committee: Reflections on the Contemporary Capitalist State: Konstantinos Tsoukalas; Contradictions of Shareholder Capitalism: Downsizing Jobs; Enlisting Savings; Destabilizing Families: Wally Seccombe; Labour Power and International Competitiveness: A Critique of Ruling Orthodoxies: David Coates; Between the Devil and the Deep Blue Sea: The German Model Under the Pressure of Globalisation: Birgit Mahnkopf; East Asia's Tumbling Dominoes: Financial Crises and the Myth of the Regional Model: Mitchell Bernard; State Decay and Democratic Decadence in Latin America: Atilio Boron; Comrades and Investors: The Uncertain Transition in Cuba: Haroldo Dilla; Unstable Futures: Controlling and Creating Risks in International Money: Adam Tickell; Globalisation; Class and the Question of Democracy: Joachim Hirsch; The Challenge for the Left: Reclaiming the State: Boris Kagarlitsky; The Public Sphere and the Media: Market Supremacy versus Democracy: Colin Leys; The Tale that Never Ends: Sheila Rowbotham

364pp. 232 x 155 mm.

0 85036 481 7 hbk £30.00                                    0 85036 480 9 pbk £14.95

*Canada: Fernwood Publishing; USA: Monthly Review Press; UK and Rest of World: Merlin Press*

## All Merlin Press titles can be ordered via our web site: www.merlinpress.co.uk

In case of difficulty obtaining Merlin Press titles outside the UK, please contact the following:

**Australia:**
Merlin Press Agent and stockholder:
Eleanor Brash: PO Box 586, Artamon: NSW 2064 Email: ebe@enternet.com.au

**Canada:**
Co-Publisher and stockholder:
Fernwood Books, 8422 St. Margaret's Bay Rd, Site 2a, Box 5, Black Point, Nova Scotia, B0J 1B0
Tel: +1 902 857 1388: Fax: +1 902 422 3179 Email: errol@fernwoodbooks.ca

**South Africa:**
Merlin Press Agent:
Blue Weaver Marketing
PO Box 30370, Tokai, Cape Town 7966, South Africa
Tel. and Fax: +27 21 701 7302  Email: blueweav@mweb.co.za

**USA:**
Merlin Press Agent and stockholder: Independent Publishers Group, 814 North Franklin Street, Chicago, IL 60610.
Tel: +1 312 337 0747  Fax: +1 312 337 5985 frontdesk@ipgbook.com

Publisher: Monthly Review Press:
Monthly Review Press, 122 West 27th Street, New York, NY 10001
Tel: +1 212 691 2555 promo@monthlyreview.org